The Shadow of Loma Prieta

THE SECRET HISTORY OF SANTA CRUZ COUNTY SERIES
Edited by Derek R. Whaley

This series brings to light long out-of-print books, dusty manuscripts, and other lost material documenting the history of the county from pre-colonial times to the present.

The History of Rancho Soquel Augmentation
The Tragedy of Martina Castro by Ronald G. Powell
The Reign of the Lumber Barons by Ronald G. Powell
The Shadow of Loma Prieta by Ronald G. Powell

Ronald G. Powell

The Shadow of Loma Prieta

Part Three of the History of
Rancho Soquel Augmentation

Edited by Derek R. Whaley
With an afterword by Jeff Thomson

First published in 2022 by
ZAYANTE PUBLISHING
Santa Cruz, California, USA

www.zayantepublishing.com

© 2022 Zayante Publishing

First edition, October 2022

Designed by Derek R. Whaley
Cover and layout: Derek R. Whaley

The moral right of the authors has been asserted.

Material from this book courtesy the Ronald G. Powell Collection, Special Collections, McHenry Library, University of California, Santa Cruz.

Front: Portrait of Nesine Marks

Back: Maple Falls, 1981, from the Ronald G. Powell Collection, courtesy Sandy Lydon, Aptos History Museum; Carolyn Hansen and Christina Johnston near Camp 5, ca 1919, from the Paul Johnston Collection, courtesy Woods Mattingley, Aptos History Museum.

All rights reserved. Without limiting the rights under copyright reserved above, no part of this publication may be reproduced, stored or introduced into a retrieval system, or transmitted, in any form or by any means (electronic, mechanical, photocopying, recording or otherwise), without the prior written permission of the copyright owner.

ISBN 978-1-953609-44-1 (printed book)
ISBN 978-1-953609-45-8 (ebook)

To Nessin "Nisene" Marks (1859–1955),
for teaching her children the beauty of nature . . .

. . . and to Agnes (1883–1976),
Herman (1885–1982), and
Andrew Marks (1889–1976),
for turning their mother's passion
into a legacy we can all experience.

Contents

Introduction by Derek R. Whaley ix

The Shadow of Loma Prieta
    Chapter 1: Into the Dark Hinckley 3
    Chapter 2: A Great Calamity 57
    Chapter 3: Along the Ridgetop Rails 109
    Chapter 4: The Residue of Success 155
    Chapter 5: The Feller's Last Felling 221
    Chapter 6: From Exploitation to
        Preservation 283
    Chapter 7: Marked for Posterity 323

Afterword by Jeff Thomson 385
Notes 395
Select Bibliography 407
Index 415

INTRODUCTION
by Derek R. Whaley

I never knew of The Forest of Nisene Marks State Park growing up. Aptos was just too far removed from me. It was the place where my mom worked as a professor at Cabrillo College, and where my family occasionally attended church services at Twin Lakes Church. I remember damaged buildings falling into Aptos Creek after the Loma Prieta Earthquake in 1989. And I have a strangely specific memory of watching *A Kid in King Arthur's Court* at the Aptos Twin Cinema in the summer of 1995. But being raised in Felton, California, Henry Cowell Redwoods State Park was *my* state park. So, there is an irony that it is I who have edited this trilogy of books concerned with the history of the former Rancho Soquel Augmentation.

The first hints of the deep history of the Aptos and Soquel Creek watersheds came to me during my research for *Santa Cruz Trains: Railroads of the Santa Cruz Mountains*, as well as for various blog posts over the years at SantaCruzTrains.com. It was during these late nights of reading, researching, and writing that I began to understand just how important this section of the Santa Cruz Mountains was to local industry. The South Pacific Coast Railroad first reached the headwaters of the West Branch of

Introduction

Soquel Creek in 1879, where lumber crews found timber for railroad ties, bridge bents and posts, and tunnel framing. Later, this area would become the hamlet of Laurel, founded by the well-respected lumber and property baron, Frederick A. Hihn. But it was only one of many communities that emerged within the Augmentation. Others arose on the Summit and on all three major watersheds—Soquel, Aptos, and Valencia Creeks. Many of these communities are now long gone, while only some of those that survived have retained an independent identity.

The reason so few communities remain is that their livelihoods were based on the lumber industry, and the inevitable result of deforestation is a loss of jobs. In a period of less than forty years, the ancient redwoods along the banks of Aptos Creek within Martina Castro's former Shoquel Augmentation land grant were clear-cut, their millions of years of uninterrupted growth punctuated by the desperate need to build the cities of the Central Coast of California. Small-scale water-powered lumber mills were replaced with industrialized steam mills, while crude mountain roads made way for railroads. By the end of the nineteenth century, only remote sections of unharvested timberland remained, mostly within Hinckley Gulch, along Bridge Creek, and across the ridge to the headwaters of Soquel Creek. Unlike in earlier eras, functional worker villages never developed in the mountains after 1902—logging crews lived in crude camps that moved according to the needs of the company. And when the operations were done, the workers moved on, leaving only desolation in their wake.

The history of the Shoquel Augmentation land grant and the earlier lumber operations in the property have been told in Ronald G. Powell's first two volumes in this series, *The Tragedy of Martina Castro* and *The Reign of the Lumber Barons*. *The Shadow of Loma Prieta* marks the last of Powell's writings on the subject and takes the story to the present. In many ways, this book is a direct sequel to *The Reign of the Lumber Barons* since many key figures and companies from that book continue their stories here. However, it also is a very different story. Whereas Powell's second book tells of the golden age of logging in the Augmentation, this book explores what happened afterwards. How small-scale logging continued for decades. How the Southern Pacific Railroad's Loma Prieta Branch continued to be used in increasingly innovative ways. How various parties tried to use the former timberland for other projects, including for housing and oil drilling. Lastly, it shows how the Augmentation emerged from a century of exploitation to provide the state with two important protected reserves: The Forest of Nisene Marks State Park and the Soquel Demonstration State Forest.

Powell never wrote a proper foreword, preface, or afterword for this work. However, he did write one for a derivative book, *The Castros of Soquel*, which summarized many of the important moments otherwise recorded in *The Tragedy of Martina Castro*. I include part of his preface here since it remains relevant:

> *TO THE READER:*
>
> *This book is the culmination of over sixteen years of frustrat¬ions, researching, and writing. What began as a simple hike into The Forest of Nisene Marks State Park to enjoy the serenity provided there soon evolved into researching the story of the Loma Prieta Lumber Company, Grover & Company, the ever-complicated early day pioneer Frederick A. Hihn, and an assortment of additional personalities, each with their own story to tell.*
>
> *After several frustrating years, I realized that to truly understand the history of the area I was hiking and exploring, the story of the entire area—not just a small portion—was necessary. After realizing this and expanding my research effort, understanding finally began....*
>
> *The format of this book is not to the liking of a publisher interested in profit, but in truth, profit from a book with the subject covered here will never be achieved using any format. Because the story presented in this book is extremely complicated and dispels so much accepted history of the Soquel/Capitola and Soquel Augmentation areas, a different approach was decided upon. It was decided not to attempt a narrative style format, but instead present the story in a "date sequence style."... It is hoped that this simplified style of presentation will be of more assistance to future historians.*
>
> *As a sidenote here, I decided to publish this book on a limited scale myself for several reasons: First, only minimal profit,*

Introduction

if any, is possible from a book of this type and size. Second, because the story presented corrects so much of the covered area's written history, no organization or person would accept it at face value (in other words, much time would be spent in answering questions and in education). And third, editing and rewriting would only add an additional delay to an already frustrating and excessively long period.

Sincerely, Ronald Powell

 This preface demonstrates Powell's penchant for understatement and underselling his abilities and discoveries. He dismisses the salability of his "date sequence style," underestimating his audience's love and respect for chronology. This style is time-honored dating back to Antiquity and endures to the present in many mediums, such as annotated timelines and blogs. More vitally, his research has certainly been of assistance to many future historians. Even before the publication of The History of Rancho Soquel Augmentation, his works in their unedited format have been frequently cited by local historians, and his discoveries and arguments have and will continue to shape historians' understanding of the history of the Augmentation.

 Powell also demonstrates his humility in this preface. This work is massive! Were it to include all of the photographs he captured in the 1970s and 1980s, as well as the historical photographs he kept in his private collection, the second and third volumes would be at least twice their present sizes. It is a shame that he decided against editing and rewriting them, although the delays and frustrations are understandable. Since the time that Stan Stevens first made me aware of Powell's work in May 2019, three and a half years have passed editing and rewriting. The task has not always been easy, as Powell well knew. What is clear, though, is that his research is based on some of the best sources available to him in his day. His heavy reliance on primary sources, including land transfer records, newspaper articles, and oral histories, combined with his personal explorations within the Augmentation, grounds this work in strong supporting evidence. And while historians may disagree with or correct his findings, it is not his sole responsibility to answer for his conclusions. The work speaks for itself and it sets a challenge for future historians to find the answers to those questions themselves.

Editing Powell's magnum opus for publication has naturally placed me in a prime position to make corrections and addendums, where necessary. Indeed, it would be irresponsible of me to allow known errors to remain in this book. My first task, however, was to fix this volume's citations. Powell decided, possibly out of a desire for expediency, to skip adding citations in the final three volumes of his original seven-volume manuscript. He provided a bibliography, but it is missing key sources used in compiling information for the period after 1900. Over his two decades of research, Powell had conversations with many veterans of the lumber trade, park rangers, and others knowledgeable in local affairs, and many of these sources were mentioned neither in the bibliography nor in the body of the work itself. As a result, I have tried to give citations wherever possible, or at least allude to the probable sources of information. But unless an endnote includes a page number or other precise notation, it should be considered an educated guess at best and, even if accurate, may not include all of the sources Powell used when writing a section.

Generally speaking, the material comprising *The Shadow of Loma Prieta* was the best-written and best-organized in Powell's original manuscript. As a result, it required less editing and consolidating than prior volumes. However, the work did include one notable chronological mistake beginning in Chapter 3 that continued through Chapter 4. Namely, Powell accidentally skipped the year 1912 in his history of the Molino Timber Company. This had a knockdown effect for all Molino-related entries from 1913 to 1918, with most events occurring a year late in the narrative. In isolation, this issue could have been overlooked, but when mixed with entries relating to other operations in the Augmentation, the entire chronology became confused and illogical for this period. To remedy this, I checked carefully through Powell's own writing as well as his sources to determine the actual progression of events. Certain independently-verified waypoints helped provide a framework while cues within the history were used to correct the chronology. The result, I think, is a much more plausible and logical timeline of events.

As with the previous two books in this trilogy, this final volume in The History of Rancho Soquel Augmentation would not have been possible without the help of local researchers, friends, and readers. My deepest

Introduction

thanks to Dr. Kara Kennedy for providing thorough editorial advice and continuous support and encouragement to publish this important work. Thanks also to Kanda Whaley and Dr. Lindsay Breach for providing edits and feedback. A special thanks to Jeff Thomson of the Advocates for Nisene Marks State Park, who provided the afterword to this volume. And lastly, a thank you to Stan Stevens, for making me aware of Powell's work to begin with and providing me with the original manuscript and documents used to compile and edit the books in this trilogy.

Editing and revising Ronald Powell's manuscript into these three published books has been difficult at times, but well worth the cost. The history of Rancho Soquel Augmentation is not just the tale of a tract of land's evolution from a Mexican ranch to two state parks and dozens of private properties. It is the story of Santa Cruz County itself, from its days as an outpost on the distant fringe of a globe-spanning empire, through its years as a Mexican territory, to its height as an industrial powerhouse, to its present as a community trying to balance urbanization and environmentalism. The Augmentation has been touched by each era of the county's history, and now that large parts of it are protected for conservation, it will continue to serve the county for many decades to come.

Derek R. Whaley
October 23, 2022

The Shadow of Loma Prieta

Chapter 1

~

Into the Dark Hinckley

The Hinckley:
Primitive, Mysterious, Foreboding, and Isolated

Few over the years have attempted to discuss Hinckley Gulch. Those who have written about it describe it as "primitive," "mysterious," "foreboding," or "isolated," each of which adequately describes the gulch in important ways. Until recently, there was no formal access to the gulch. Visitors could view it from the Hinckley Fire Road along Hinckley Ridge or the Aptos Creek Fire Road along China Ridge, but both were far, far above Hinckley Creek. In the late 1980s, a trail was completed by the California Department of Forestry and Fire Protection (CAL FIRE), the overseer of the Soquel Demonstration State Forest, along the top of Santa Rosalia Ridge. But like the fire roads, it too provides only limited access to the gulch and the creek beyond.

When I first began my explorations in The Forest of Nisene Marks State Park in late 1978, I came across an interview held by Special Collections at the University of California, Santa Cruz. It was a recording of an old-timer and was made shortly after the formation of the park in 1965. In it, the interviewee said:

> FACT or FANCIES? Valley with giant redwoods that lumbermen couldn't get out...but lumber[men] peeled bark to preserve it...hunters said they have seen it...to ring-a-tree is to kill it...so it must have been felled.

This confusing statement intrigued me for years. Because I was unable to understand all of its meaning, I decided to concentrate on the part concerning the trees. I wanted to find the big redwoods left behind, those that the lumbermen could not get out and had been seen by hunters.

I began my search along Aptos Creek, in the surrounding areas outside the state park, in the Arden Forest (Tract 7 of Shoquel Augmentation), along Bates Creek, and then along the north side of Santa Rosalia Ridge above the East Branch of Soquel Creek, all to no avail. Finally, I entered Hinckley Gulch, spending many an hour searching its 2,500 acres. Before I entered the deep depths of the gulch, I found many large old-growth redwoods growing along the top of Santa Rosalia Ridge, but these trees were not left behind because the lumbermen could not get them out—they were left standing because their tops had been broken off by strong winds. Without their tops, they had lost too much of their potential lumber to make the effort of getting them to the mill worthwhile.

Finally, after several years had passed, I came across an area along the gulch's north side that contained many old-growth redwood trees as well as stumps and abandoned felled trees. While those standing were not the size of the trees in the Rockefeller Grove in Humboldt Redwoods State Park, or even the trees in the Big Tree Grove in Felton, still they were impressive enough to bring me back many times in order to better understand the reason they were left standing.

As I continued exploring Hinckley Gulch, I came to depend on the memoirs of Albretto "Bert" Stoodley. Stoodley had several attributes that today we can be thankful for: he was curious, alert, well educated, and—of most importance—an avid photographer. Through his pictures he has provided a pictorial history of the Molino Timber Company's activities

Into the Dark Hinckley

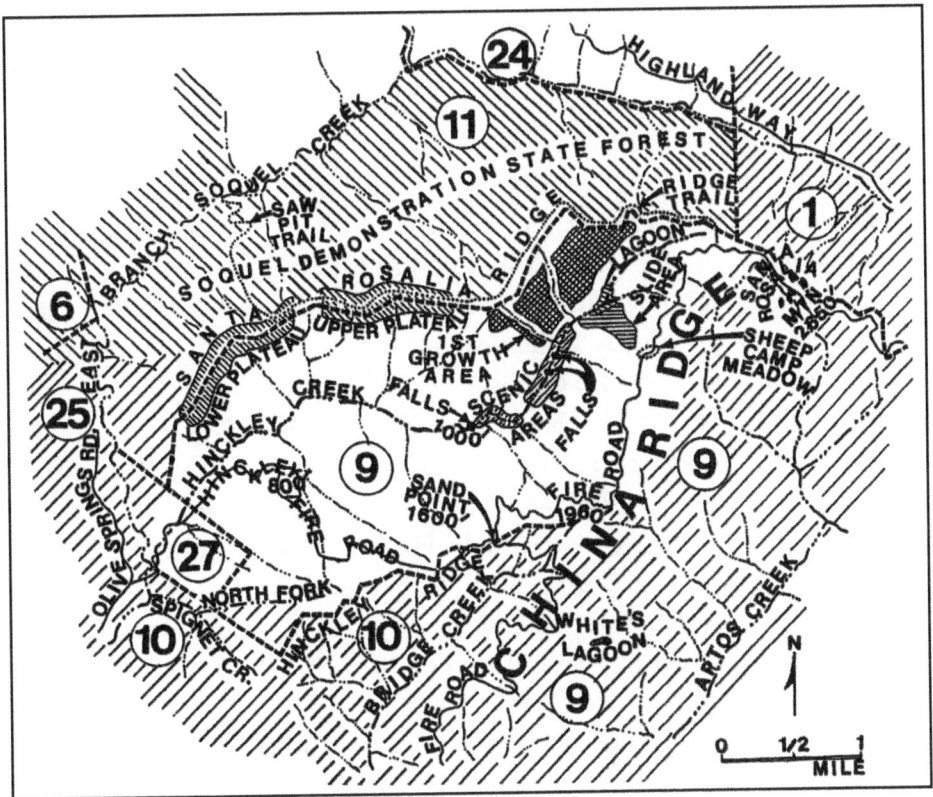

FIGURE 1.1 HINCKLEY GULCH SHOWING MAJOR GEOGRAPHICAL FEATURES

in the 1910s as well as the Loma Prieta Lumber Company's operations to 1940. In his later years, Stoodley recorded his memories of many important events, beginning with his arrival in the county in 1902 and continuing into the 1940s. He referred to Hinckley Gulch simply as "The Hinckley." I do not know if he used the term out of frustration, disgust, or respect. I like to believe that it was because of all three feelings, feelings that I had many times during my exploratory years in the gulch.

There are no developed roads or trails that head down into the depths of the Hinckley, but this does not mean that there are no paths to follow that will allow the curious to enter and enjoy selected areas. The gulch is honeycombed with old trails made for both people and pack mules. There is also the narrow-gauge railroad bed that can be followed from the fire road at the back of Sand Point for a little over two miles. While there are many old trails to follow, due to vegetation growth and changes to the terrain since logging ended in 1918, one can expect to encounter a number of obstacles. Many of these were created or made worse by the storm of 1955–1956, the storm of January 4, 1982, the two that followed in February and March 1982, the storm of February 1986, and the Loma Prieta Earthquake of 1989. It was during this last storm that the third and largest body of water in The Forest of Nisene Marks State Park was created at 1,640-foot elevation on Hinckley Creek. Before the storms of 1982, it was possible to hike in one day along a well-defined trail staying for the most part within sight of Hinckley Creek from its headwaters to the East Branch of Soquel Creek. Today, this is not possible. It is highly doubtful that the gulch can be hiked in one day from the creek's headwaters to Soquel Creek while keeping Hinckley Creek within close proximity. Entire sections have fallen away to be carried downstream by Hinckley Creek, interrupting trails that can only be circumvented via long and arduous detours. And one final difficulty is the lagoon on Hinckley Creek, which does not allow passage from any direction without long detours.

The Plateaus: Santa Rosalia Ridge

Two nearly level plateaus occupy a portion of the divide between Hinckley Creek and the East Branch of Soquel Creek. Both are narrow and almost equal in length, about 3,000 feet long, and can be reached by the Soquel Demonstration State Forest's Ridge and Saw Pit trails. The elevation of the upper plateau varies from 1,800 feet at its eastern end to 1,600 feet, while the lower of the two averages about 1,300 feet. Growing on the two plateaus are the largest old-growth redwoods south of the Big Trees Grove in Henry Cowell Redwoods State Park in Felton. A hike through these magnificent, isolated trees gives evidence of their struggle to survive against Mother Nature's natural elements—fire and wind—and against the most destructive force of all: humans. Many of the largest trees measure between 10 to 14 feet in diameter with several approaching 16 feet. While Mother Nature has made several attempts to destroy these trees, she has for the most part been responsible for their survival. Years before the Loma Prieta Lumber Company's loggers reached these trees, wind had broken off the tops of many of them, rendering them far less valuable than other trees to the company. And there they stand today for the few to enjoy who care to venture along the Ridge and Saw Pit trails.

First Growth Area: Santa Rosalia Ridge

Growing along the north side of Hinckley Creek on Santa Rosalia Ridge within a 240-acre area from creek to ridgetop are many abandoned old-growth redwoods. While the majority of the remaining trees are hidden in difficult-to-reach areas, many may be viewed via a system of unmarked trails. This area was first logged by the Loma Prieta Lumber Company beginning around 1904. Because the sawmill was located far downstream and the journey that the logs had to travel was so difficult, loggers only cut down the best trees and then took only the choicest sections, leaving the remaining parts to rot away.

When the Molino Timber Company reached this general vicinity in 1916, it logged the trees on the ridge and then those adjacent to Hinckley Creek along the north side, turning them all into splitstuff, such as grape stakes, fence posts, railroad crossties, shingle and shake bolts, and cordwood. When the time came to finish harvesting the remaining timber, it experienced problems with the cable that carried the splitstuff from the north side of Hinckley Creek over to the railroad grade. Rather than repair the cable, Molino decided to abandon the area, thus leaving it in its present condition.

The Grinding Rock and the Native American Trail

The earliest evidence found to date of Native American activity within The Forest of Nisene Marks State Park was discovered in Hinckley Gulch. At the 1,900-foot elevation on Santa Rosalia Ridge is a large rock on which Awaswas-speaking people of the Ohlone Native Americans ground one of their staple food ingredients: acorn meal. They would use the stone as a mortar to pulverize tanoak acorn into a mush using a stone pestle. The use of these tools created indentations in the rock that tell an archaeologist that there was early human activity in the area. How did the Ohlone arrive at the rock and why? Was the route they traveled the same path that old-timers say couriers used when they carried messages between Mission Carmel and Mission Santa Clara before Mission Santa Cruz was built in 1792? Possibly.

Santa Rosalia Ridge extends six miles from the confluence of Hinckley Creek and the East Branch of Soquel Creek eastward to the headwaters of Corralitos Creek. If the old timers are correct, the runners would surely have travelled to the west of Santa Rosalia Mountain. This assumption is based on the near impassible low growing vegetation east of the mountain. This likely route would take them through Hinckley Gulch along a trail that has clearly been lost to time. However, until the 1982 storms, the trail from China Ridge to the rock was very much in evidence and hikeable. Many times, I used the well-worn path to get down to Hinckley Creek from the Fire Road on China Ridge, and then explore along the creek's north side. When I first found the trail, I assumed it was made by loggers because it was the only practical route to reach Hinckley Creek in the area. It wasn't until I discovered the rock about 1988 and then read the findings of Brian D. Dillon made in 1992 that I realized the importance of the trail and rock.

Dillon was hired by the California Department of Forestry and Fire Protection to conduct an archaeological and historical survey and inventory of the newly purchased Soquel Demonstration State Forest. To quote from his report, *The Archaeological and Historical Survey of Soquel Demonstration State Forest*: "Despite the outstanding work of recent students, Santa Cruz County archaeology has lagged behind that of neighboring areas. If Santa Cruz County archaeology can be said to be in its infancy, within the county the least studied and most poorly understood region is that of its mountainous interior."

When it was originally proposed that the lands that comprise today's Soquel Demonstration State Forest be added to The Forest of Nisene Marks State Park, the park management plan concluded: "There are no known significant cultural resources on the subject lands which, in themselves would help justify and support the acquisition of this property as an addition to the state park." Before Dillon's study, there had never been a concerted effort towards locating cultural resources in the area; therefore, it is not surprising that none had ever been recorded. He stated in the introduction of his work that "there are no known Native American sites in the study area; however, Native American sites do exist in adjacent areas." Yet after conducting his research, he found that

> *our 1991 field research revealed six previously unrecorded sites: two are prehistoric (500 to 1600 AD); three are historic (this period begins in 1769); and one contains both prehistoric and historic components. Far from the area being devoid of history and archaeology, it now appears that the East Branch of Soquel Creek in prehistoric times was an important resource or provisioning area for the Native Americans. The comparative abundance of bedrock mortar sites indicated that the tanoaks so numerous in the area were considered an important prehistoric source of acorns; more speculative is the likelihood that the fish resources, either trout or steelhead, of Soquel Creek may have been the original attraction to the area, perhaps even before the invention of bedrock mortar technology relatively late in prehistory....*
>
> *The prehistoric sites found contain surface artifacts, permanent features in the form of both bedrock mortars and rock art, and probably also subsurface deposits, plus a bedrock boulder with multiple mortars.*

Although Dillon's explorations were restricted to the north side of Santa Rosalia Ridge, his findings help explain the presence of the rock in Hinckley Gulch. It indicates a well-worn route that Native Americans used to reach the East Branch of Soquel Creek within the vicinity of Hihn's Sulphur Springs. It is too bad that a similar study has not been conducted in The Forest of Nisene Marks State Park. During my many exploratory hikes, I came across many large rocks similar to the one found over in Hinckley Gulch, but not being an archaeologist and unfamiliar with the ways of the Ohlone, I never stopped to examine them for mortar indentations.

Portions of the trail the Native Americans followed on China Ridge can be traced on a map and easily followed for the most part. Beginning at the headwaters of Bridge Creek at the 1,960-foot elevation where Hinckley Ridge ends on China Ridge, Native Americans would have gone northeast along the top of China Ridge until reaching Sheep Camp Meadow. The meadow is located at the 2,208-foot elevation along the Aptos Creek Fire Road about two-thirds of the distance between Sand Point Overlook (elevation 1,600 feet) and the Soquel Demonstration State Forest's Ridge Trail's head (elevation 2,480 feet). It is easily identified: there is a large, unused metal water storage tank partially hidden among the trees at its upper end.

After the fire road was completed in about 1939, land was leased within the vicinity of the meadow to a sheep herder. The bank holding the land in trust for the Loma Prieta Lumber Company built a cabin for the shepherd to live in the grove of trees at the meadow's south end. After the shepherd reached the meadow with his sheep and he settled in, it did not take long for him to realize that there were better places to graze his sheep. After a short stay, both shepherd and sheep departed the area. The cabin remained standing well into the 1940s and was used by hunters until it eventually collapsed.

When Native Americans reached the area, they would have turned to the northwest to head down the narrow ridge along the north side of today's slide area. When they reached Hinckley Creek, they would have climbed a short, steep hillside and found a large, peaceful area covered with fern and grasses interspersed among giant redwoods. At the back end of this area is the bottom of the steep climb to the top of Santa Rosalia Ridge. About halfway between these two areas is the wide, level, redwood-covered place on which the grinding rock is located. A short journey across the top of the divide and then down towards the East Branch of Soquel Creek are the grinding rocks found by Dillon, all located within the Soquel Demonstration State Forest.

Once the top of the divide between Hinckley and the East Branch Soquel Creek was crossed, Native Americans were faced with many routes to follow to reach Los Gatos Creek and the Santa Clara Valley. Only further archaeological studies will find the paths used through the state park and forest, especially the route used to reach the headwaters of Bridge Creek at the 1,960-foot elevation on China Ridge.

The Lagoon and the Falls: Hinckley Creek

Surely The Forest of Nisene Marks State Park's most unique new feature is the lagoon formed in Hinckley Gulch during the February 1986 storm, the park's third such year-round body of water. It lies at the 1,640-foot elevation and is a little over 500 feet long and 50 feet wide at its widest point. Because of the surrounding terrain, the lagoon cannot be viewed in its entirety from any one point. A difficult hike down from Sheep Camp Meadow on the fire road is required to view its southern half. To see the northern end, you must hike about halfway back up the hillside and then journey down again slightly to the north.

At the southeastern end of the lagoon and continuing downstream for about eight-tenths of a mile is an area with many scenic waterfalls. These falls run along smooth bedrock with most falling a distance of one to ten feet. However, the highest is thirty-five feet with another around twenty feet. Since Hinckley Creek is seasonal, these waterfalls are not always active. The best time to visit them is during the rainy season in late spring.

1,000-Foot Elevation: Hinckley Creek

At 1,000-foot elevation lies the area planned by the Loma Prieta Lumber Company to serve as the western end of a 1.75-mile-long tunnel that would have extended the Southern Pacific Railroad's Loma Prieta Branch an additional two miles from Bassett Gulch. In this area, timber would have been loaded onto cars for the journey to the mill near the village of Loma Prieta. Today, this level, 200-foot-wide, 800-foot-long valley-like area provides the adventurous hiker with a serene, intriguing, and isolated area to enjoy. It can be reached by the creek from either direction or from the Ridge Trail along the top of Santa Rosalia Ridge. While these routes are practical, they are also difficult to navigate; therefore, it is recommended that the area be approached from the Aptos Creek Fire Road one mile north of the Sand Point Overlook. From here, there are only unmarked trails to follow with several combining into a single route down a narrow ridge heading directly toward Hinckley Creek. After a half mile journey, the trail ends 200 feet directly above the creek. However, nearby there is a narrow trail cut into the rock that allows an adventurous hiker down to the creek.

When Hinckley Creek is finally reached, there are several features worth seeking out. At the upper end, there is a large redwood tree resting on its stump untouched except by the original fellers. At the lower end, in two side gulches, lie additional fallen redwood trees. Meanwhile, across the entire lower end are several twenty- to thirty-foot-long logs. Also, there are several four-foot-long, eight-to-ten-foot diameter logs sitting on end ready to be turned into either splitstuff or cordwood. It is obvious that the activity here on this shelf was unexpectedly interrupted.

Slide Area: China Ridge

During my years exploring the Augmentation, I always studied my U. S. Geological Survey map before each hike. When I reached the end of the Molino Timber Company's railroad line at the 1,800-foot elevation on China Ridge in 1979, my map told me that just beyond the line's end I should drop down into a gulch. The map also indicated that along the gulch's upstream east side there was a ridge that was at least 200, possibly 300 feet higher than the ridge the railroad ended on. When I took the few necessary steps from the end of the line expecting to drop down into a gulch, what I found shocked me!

Instead of looking down into a gulch whose headwaters should have begun just below Sheep Camp Meadow on the Aptos Creek Fire Road to my right, I was looking across what appeared to be a level, near barren area that sloped down toward Hinckley Creek with a few living and dead standing trees scattered about, interspersed with patches of low-growing vegetation. At the time I discovered the area, I estimated that it would measure about 900 feet from Hinckley Creek southward toward Sheep Camp Meadow and the Fire Road and 800 feet across. After closer examination of the area, my first impression was incorrect: it was actually irregular, covered with small- to medium-sized rocks and many small rivulets. When did the area begin to slide down towards Hinckley Creek? Because the gulch is shown intact on the first USGS maps made in 1919, and also on the 1954 revised version, the sliding probably began during the heavy storms of 1955/1956.

Along Hinckley Creek, the south side of the slide consisted of a high collection of mud, dead vegetation, and trees. This was why, when earlier I had hiked along the creek, I failed to notice the sliding of the area—I couldn't see over the piled-up debris, which appeared as just a normal side of the gulch without closer inspection. After a closer investigation of the area, it was obvious that it had been sliding for years. As new debris moved down towards the creek, the old was pushed into the creek to be washed away during the rainy season.

This area changed more dramatically with the storms of 1982 and 1986.

Afterwards, all of the remaining standing trees, whether dead or alive, and most of the vegetation were now at the bottom of the gulch waiting to be washed away by the creek. Another noticeable change was on the north ridge, especially the lower sections, which were beginning to slip away and were no longer possible to hike. As each winter came and went, more of the area and ridge continued to slide into Hinckley Creek. Eventually, in the February 1986 storm, almost the entire lower half of the north ridge fell into the creek, forming the dam that created the lagoon. At the upper end of the lagoon, the creek now flows directly into the body of water, while below the lagoon's surface, the creek bed is buried under tons of mud and debris.

The 1989 Loma Prieta Earthquake further changed the landscape on China Ridge. The temblor caused the upper section of the north ridge, which had remained somewhat intact when the lower section fell into the creek, to begin its own accelerated descent into Hinckley Gulch. As the ridge has shifted and eroded, the old Native American route from the top of China Ridge down to the creek and up to the grinding rock on Santa Rosalia Ridge has vanished.

* * *

These are not the only areas of interest in Hinckley Gulch. At the lower end of the gulch are the remains of the road to the Loma Prieta Lumber Company's mill on which large wagons carried supplies and lumber. There is also the site of the mill itself as well as that of Allen Rispin's former Hinckley Basin housing development. From the failed development, the path of the wooden flume Rispin built to provide water to firefighters can be followed with remnants of it still surviving in sections. Also from the development is a former mule trail that follows the creek northeast for nearly 1.5 miles along the sharp twists and turns of Hinckley Creek.

I feel fortunate that while I was physically able, I explored many areas of interest throughout the Augmentation and surrounding land and that on many of these trips, my camera was my companion. I also consider myself lucky that many of my explorations took me into the beautiful and interesting Hinckley Gulch before the destructive storms of the 1980s.[1]

The F. A. Hihn Company begins constructing mill at Laurel

After harvesting timber along Gold Gulch south of Felton for several years, the F. A. Hihn Company decided in January 1900 to relocate its primary lumber mill to Tract 16 in the Augmentation near the headwaters of the West Branch of Soquel Creek. Light timber harvesting operations had occurred along Burns and Burrell (Laurel) Creeks for decades, but they were never extensive and were always through contractors. That left much of the surrounding land unharvested. The Hihn Company also felt it was an ideal location because the Southern Pacific Railroad had a nearby station and tracks close enough to not require an extensive spur or branch line. T. D. Sargent was placed in charge of erecting the facility.

The *San Jose Herald* was critical of the move and said as much on February 21, 1900:

NEW SAW MILL.

Big Forest Destroyer to be Erected at Laurel.

> *Laurel, a post office on the summit of the Santa Cruz mountains, presided over by a gentleman named Crichton, who is at once, postmaster, storekeeper, majordomo, mayor, political boss, reformer and pound-keeper, is as neat a little mountain home as can be found anywhere. The chief occupation of the people is to avoid falling out of the town and into Santa Cruz.*
>
> *There is a boast ahead for this elevated paradise. F. A. Hihn of Santa Cruz proposes to erect a big saw mill there which will give employment to 75 or 100 men. Then Laurel will see her beautiful forests disappear, while she holds the "kitty" on the operation.*

The fact that this announcement was made in a San José newspaper did not escape the notice of the *Evening Sentinel*, which commented: "The time must have arrived when the people hereabouts will go to the Garden City for Santa Cruz news." Nonetheless, a few months later, during a tour of the

Summit area in July 1900, one of the *Sentinel*'s reporters noted less critically that the "mill is approaching completion, and judging from the dimensions of the frame work and size of the timbers it will be a very substantial mill. The machinery is on the ground ready to be placed in position."[2]

The Loma Prieta Lumber Company begins grading a road into Hinckley Gulch

Following five years of surveys and planning, the Loma Prieta Lumber Company concluded in 1899 that it would have to abandon its milling operations on Aptos Creek, which had been running since 1884. To replace it, the company decided to build a new mill facility at a site near the confluence of Hinckley Creek and the East Branch of Soquel Creek within Tract 9 of the Augmentation. Originally, the lumber company's directors had hoped to convince the Southern Pacific Railroad to extend its Loma Prieta Branch beyond Bassett Gulch to the headwaters of Hinckley Creek via a tunnel. However, after several surveys and timber yield assessments, the railroad rejected the option as too costly, especially considering the high annual price of maintaining the existing right-of-way. An alternative plan to extend a railroad spur along Bridge Creek into the F. A. Hihn Company's Tract 10 and transport logs over Hinckley Ridge to the spur was also deemed infeasible when the Hihn Company announced its intention to harvest timber in that tract.

The Loma Prieta Lumber Company was out of options. It would be a tedious task to operate a mill on Hinckley Creek since the company would not be able to directly use the railroad to transport logs and lumber. There were also management problems to overcome. Whereas the company had once been run by knowledgeable individuals, by the time that it needed to relocate its mill to Hinckley Creek, this was no longer the case. The new management had several shortcomings, the most problematic being that it was now run by two men not sufficiently experienced in logging. Almeron C. Bassett was the former superintendent of the Coast Division of the Southern Pacific Railroad and had a lifetime of experience working for railroads and investing in various projects, but he had never handled the day-to-day responsibilities of running a lumber mill. Meanwhile, Timothy

Hopkins, adopted heir of the Central Pacific and Southern Pacific railroad magnate Mark Hopkins, was more at home among San Francisco high society than in the mountains above Aptos.

The company's first step toward relocating to Hinckley Gulch was removing its corporate offices and lumberyard from Loma Prieta. In April 1899, the Southern Pacific Railroad recorded on its employee timetables a new station on the Santa Cruz Branch—Opal—located 4.1 miles from Santa Cruz high above the west bank of Soquel Creek. Today, its location is occupied by Jade Street Park near the end of 47th Avenue in Capitola. The Loma Prieta Lumber Company leased the land from the F. A. Hihn Company and paid the railroad for a switch into the property. Within the lumberyard, several short spurs branched off from the main track and ran along tall piles of lumber awaiting export. Several buildings were also erected in the yard, one of which served as the local company offices. The corporate offices, meanwhile, were moved to San Francisco. Of the various other buildings at Opal, one was a mercantile store and another was a grain, hay, and feed store. The lumber company also drilled a well on the property which fed a 20,000-gallon water tank. Mill workers relied on supplies brought to the Hinckley from Opal, and they sent all of their lumber and splitstuff by wagon to the yard for distribution. The company owned several other yards in the area, too, including in Watsonville, Santa Cruz, Gilroy, Hollister, Salinas, Monterey, Pacific Grove, and San Juan Bautista.

Although the station was established in April 1899, it was not until April 1901 that most of the local Loma Prieta Lumber Company staff relocated to Opal. Other obstacles had to be surmounted first, most importantly access to the mill site. Hinckley Gulch could only be entered from the southwest corner near Hinckley Creek's confluence with the East Branch of Soquel Creek. In June 1900, Adi W. Wyman was given the contract to build a twenty-foot-wide road from the Soquel San Jose Road through Olive Springs Resort and to the mill site. However, George Olive resisted. He was not enthusiastic at the prospect of daily logging traffic passing through the resort he had spent the past five years developing and promoting. The facility featured mineral springs, campsites, summer cabins, and year-round homes, and Olive was still expanding. By 1900, it even had an occasional society column in local newspapers. As such, Olive feared what would become of it if logging wagons were constantly kicking up dust and disturbing guests. He attempted to sue the lumber company to deny it access to the gulch, but the judge dismissed the case, citing Judge Samuel McKee's ruling in the Shoquel Augmentation Partitioning Suit of August 8, 1864, where he stated: "there be and is hereby reserved to each and every party to such partition [of the Augmentation] a right-of-way over the nearest convenient route from the lands set off and assigned to him or her by this decree across the lands of the others to a public highway." The company had a legal right to a right-of-way and the only way out of Hinckley Gulch was through Olive's resort. Olive would have to live with it.

The distance from Soquel Drive in Soquel to the turnoff onto Olive Springs Road is 4.5 miles. Today it is a paved road, but then it was dirt and could not be used by heavy lumber-laden wagons during the rainy months. From the turnoff on today's Soquel San Jose Road, it is another mile to reach the dirt road that heads to the confluence of the creeks. Today called Hinckley Basin Road, this gated dirt road begins on Olive Springs Road opposite the Olive Springs Quarry Company's way-in station. The difference in elevation between this intersection and the confluence of the two creeks is about 86 feet, which was too steep for loaded wagons. As a result, the road builders created a gentler grade from the road to the creek bed. This bypass survives today about 0.4 miles to the south, although it is on private property. Marked by a mossy stone entry gate to the right of Olive Springs Road, the road descends gently around a modern artificial pond called Millpond Lake and then continues north until crossing the East Branch of Soquel Creek over a bridge just south of Hinckley Basin Road. Permission is required from the owners to follow this former accessway into the Hinckley.

When workers were sent into the Hinckley by the Loma Prieta Lumber Company to begin constructing the road to reach the mill, they encountered continuously difficult terrain. Because of its steep sides, no highline would ever reach from creek to ridge top, while due to the gulch's steepness and the narrow, twisting bed of Hinckley Creek, the creek was never considered as a means to bring logs to the sawmill nor was a railroad considered to carry lumber out of the gulch. Concerning the gulch's steepness,

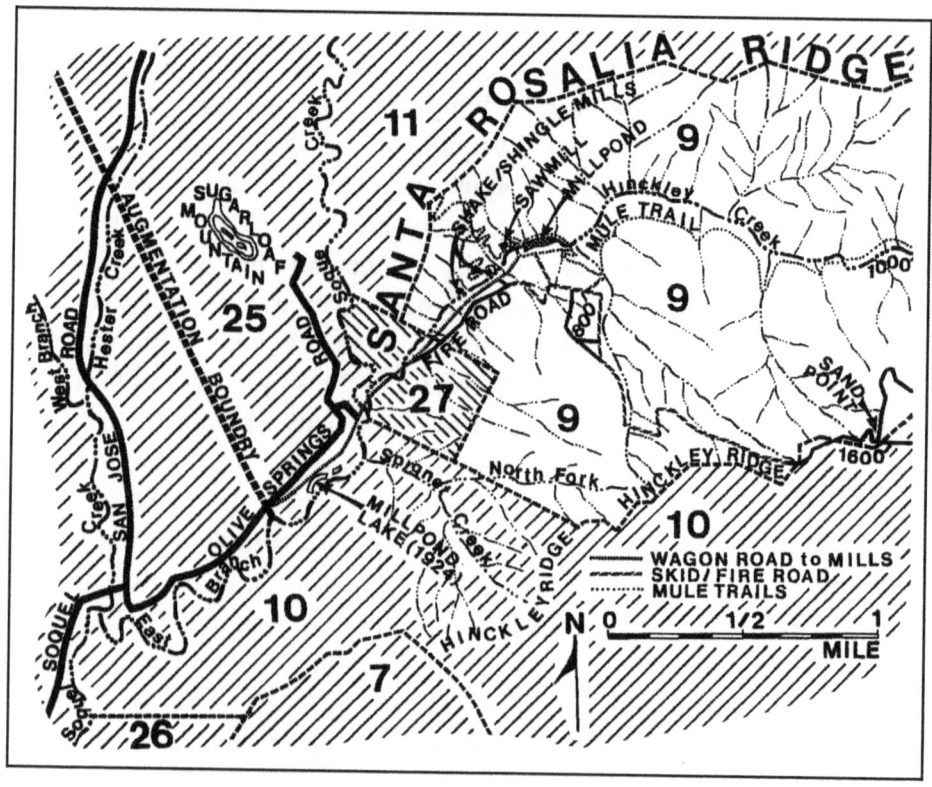

FIGURE 1.2 ROADS AND TRAILS TO THE HINCKLEY GULCH MILL

from the 280-foot elevation at the East Branch of Soquel Creek, Hinckley Creek's headwaters lie at the 2,600-foot elevation, just four and a half miles away to the northwest, which is a ten percent average rise. The gulch is extremely narrow with near vertical sides that fall from distances varying between 50 to 200 feet.

It is difficult to determine the exact route that the wagons travelled from the East Branch of Soquel Creek to the mill because storms over the years have altered the channels of Soquel and Hinckley Creeks more than once. Originally, for its entire length from Soquel San Jose Road to the mill—1,000 feet through Olive Springs Resort and 2,600 feet through Tract 9—only one bridge was required. Now, five fords across the creeks are needed. The wagon road split from today's Hinckley Basin Fire Road about 300 feet beyond the third ford, just before the fire road begins its steep ascent to Hinckley Ridge, with the wagon road turning toward the

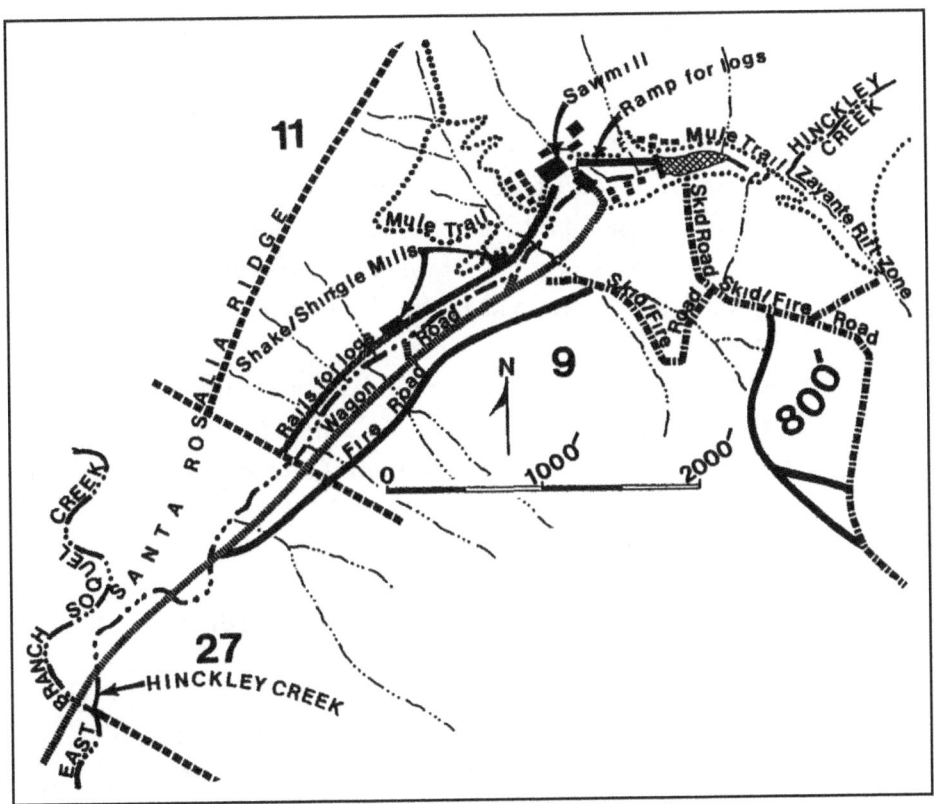

FIGURE 1.3 THE LOMA PRIETA LUMBER COMPANY MILL AT HINCKLEY CREEK
SHOWING THE MAIN COMPLEX AND NEARBY SKIDROADS AND MULE TRAILS

creek and crossing it a final time.

On the northwest bank of Hinckley Creek, the wagon road continued north slowly climbing up the canyon's northern wall atop three shelves of increasing elevation. The first two were relatively small and hosted the Loma Prieta Lumber Company's shingle and shake mills. The third and largest shelf, where the road ends, was the site of the lumber mill. Because Hinckley Gulch is so narrow, the company could not build its millpond directly adjacent to the mill, as was common practice. Instead, it was located about 1,500 feet upstream, a fact that was confirmed after the storms of early 1982, which allowed the cement foundation of the millpond's dam to be found.

When I discovered remnants of the road to the mill in 1979, it was still easy to follow. A simple climb down to the creek on an old trail, a few steps over a four-foot diameter iron wheel, and then a hop across the creek on rocks, and I reached the end of the road and sites of the three mills. After the storm of 1986, though, this road has become extremely difficult to navigate and the mill sites have seemingly vanished. Numerous sections have slid into Hinckley Creek while fallen trees and thick vegetation block parts of the former road. Instead of hiking atop the 2,600-foot-long right-of-way, you must climb down to the creek or scramble up the steep side of the gulch in numerous places. While the road and mill sites remain accessible, it is a difficult journey to reach them.

Tragically, the construction of the road had one unlikely victim. On February 2, 1901, Herbert Houghton and his wife, Harriet, were walking along the road when tragedy struck. The *Santa Cruz Surf* reported:

TERRIBLE ACCIDENT.

A Soquel Couple Meet With a Serious Mishap.

A terrible accident occurred Saturday at noon near Olive's Sulphur Springs. Mr. and Mrs. Herbert Houghton left their home at Soquel for the neighborhood of Olive's Springs. Mr. Houghton had his gun with him and was hunting wild pigeons which are so very plentiful in that vicinity.

A new road is being built in that region for the Loma Prieta Company to lead to their new mill and it was along this road that Mr. and Mrs. Houghton were walking.

The men at work on the road were blasting and two charges had been placed in stumps. As is their custom they gave an alarm so as to let any person near by know what was to happen and then ran over the hill to a place of safety.

Mr. and Mrs. Houghton heard the signal. The first blast went off and not knowing another they proceeded on their way. After going a short distance, and when within several feet of a stump the second blast occurred and the explosion did its awful work.

Mrs. Houghton was thrown forty feet and her arm was broken in four places. Her husband met a worse fate. He was

> *blown some distance and a redwood sliver two and a half inches in length lodged in his head, penetrating the skull, and when pulled out the brain oozed from the wound.*
>
> *Mrs. Houghton, with her broken arm and bruised body, showed much pluck and walked in much pain, a half mile to the cook house, where she notified the men of what had happened. The men immediately went to the scene of the accident, and all they could do was done to relieve the sufferings of the unfortunate people. They were placed in a wagon and brought to their home at Soquel.*
>
> *It is believed impossible for Mr. Houghton to recover. They are being attended to by Dr. Davis of Soquel and Dr. Congdon of this city.*

Herbert Houghton's death shortly afterwards prompted a lawsuit between Harriet and the Loma Prieta Lumber Company in an attempt to recoup $14,000 in damages for the loss of her spouse and the father of their children. A jury ruled in her favor on August 20, 1902, setting the record at the time for the largest sum ever awarded for damages in Santa Cruz County. Upon appeal, Loma Prieta was also charged legal fees for Harriet on August 19, 1903. A further appeal fell on deaf ears and Harriet's award was upheld on September 6, 1904. However, on December 6, 1907, the California Supreme Court ruled that the lumber company was not liable for injuries caused by one of its contractors and the ruling was overturned.[3]

The F. A. Hihn Company mill at Laurel opens

In the first week of November 1900, the F. A. Hihn Company completed construction of its new mill at Laurel and fired up its saws for the first time. The *Evening Sentinel* reported on October 30:

> *The new Hihn saw-mill, located just below Laurel Station, on one of the branches of the Soquel creek, is to be started up this week. Mill builders are crowding its completion. Its average capacity is given at 25,000 feet of lumber per day, and the cost*

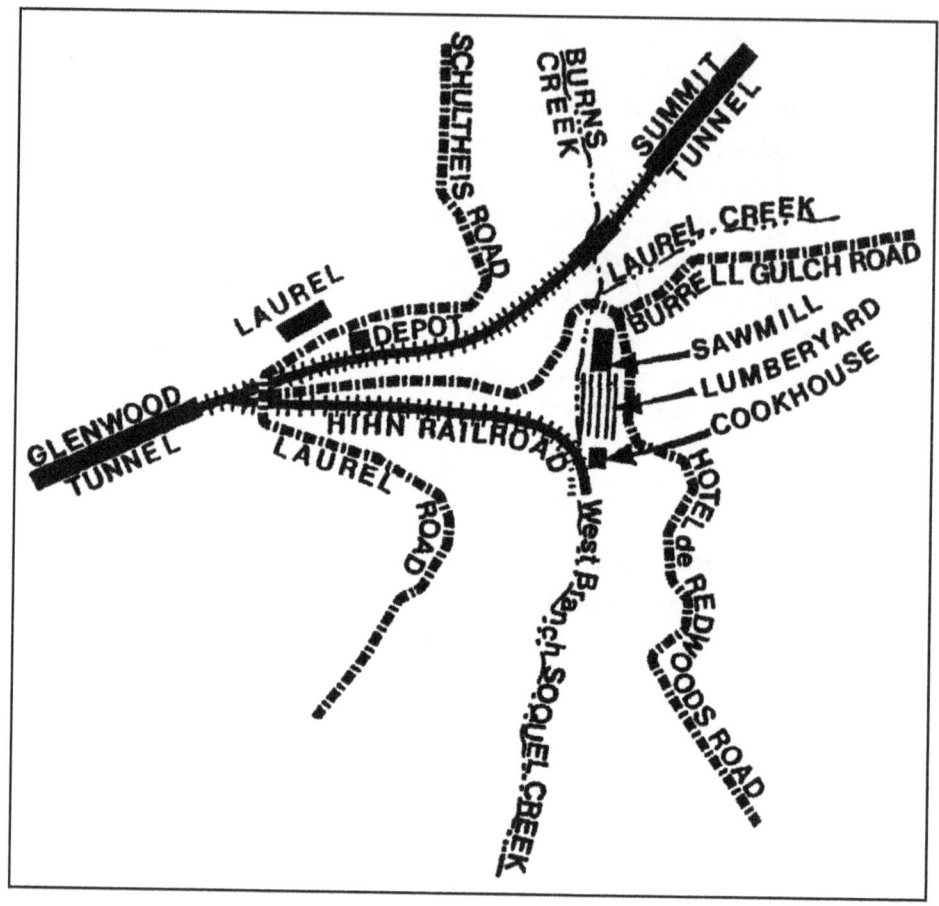

Figure 1.4 The F. A. Hihn Company's mill at Laurel with nearby roads

of this mill will be somewhere between $25,000 and $35,000. Its construction was commenced on the 15th of last May. Its advantages over the other saw-mills of this county are said to be varied. It employs a band-saw 54 1/2 feet in length, and is prepared to handle logs fifty feet in length. Capt. Falk, under whose supervision this mill has been erected, says the band-saws to be used will save 1,000,000 in every 7,000,000 feet of lumber sawed, and that it is estimated 20,000,000 feet of lumber will be cut before the mill is moved, part of it coming down the creek, but the larger part being hauled up the stream. From the mill the lumber is to be hauled to the rail-

road station over a steep incline by a cable attached to the mill. Work on this road has not yet been commenced.

Ultimately, the mill cost $65,000 including the incline but had a larg-

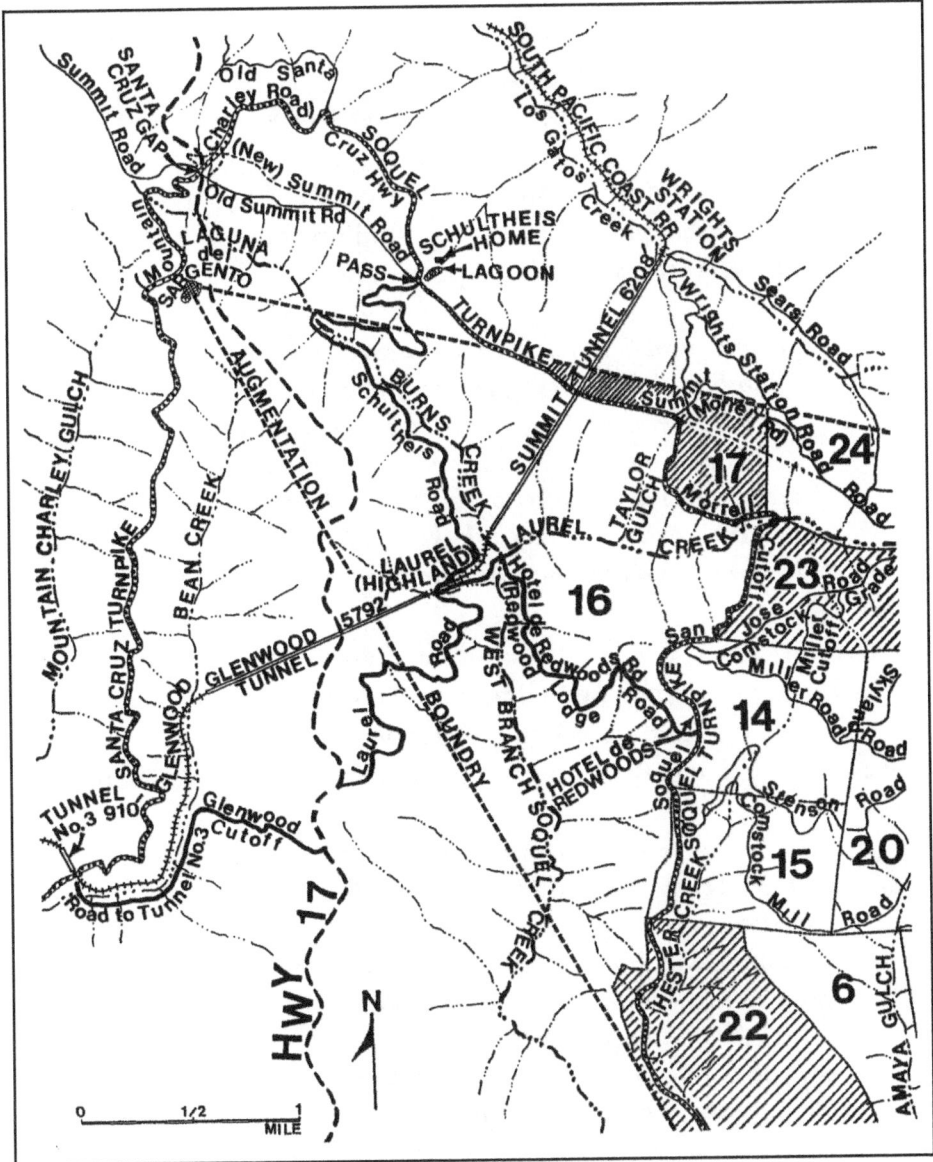

Figure 1.5 The northwestern corner of the Augmentation

er capacity of 45,000 board feet of lumber per day. The Hihn Company also built a box mill with a capacity of 1,000 boxes per day, a shingle mill able to turn out 30,000 shingles per day, and a planing mill. At its peak, the Laurel mill employed about 100 workers. Frederick Hihn planned to run it throughout the winter of 1900–1901, though this went against common practice.[4]

Hinckley Creek mill opens

The Loma Prieta Lumber Company facility on Hinckley Creek opened in early May 1901, although the precise day is unknown. In an interview with A. C. Bassett on April 13, the *Surf* reported that

> *the Company will be ready to commence transferring timber into lumber on the Hinckley tract in about three weeks. A saw mill, shingle mill and a shake mill are going in to this body of 2500 acres of virgin timber, and will make things hum. A shake mill is a new feature of the lumber business in this section. Mr. Bassett says sawed shakes are being manufactured in the north and meeting with much favor from consumers.*

The *Sentinel* stated that the large mill had an average output of 30,000 board feet of lumber per day, a dramatic decrease from the 72,000 board feet output of the Aptos Creek mill. A reporter, John Morrow, visited the mill as it was still under construction in March to report on developments:

> *Last Friday being good Santa Cruz weather I went on a trip up Soquel creek. I found the road good, being neither muddy nor dusty, and the grain crops looked fine.*
>
> *Four miles above Soquel at the long bridge, I left the main road and turned to the right, up a steep hill, past Mr. Littlejohn's place. All along here, for the distance of half a mile, the Supervisors are widening, straightening and grading the road. One and a quarter mile above the Littlejohn place the Loma Prieta Co. have a gang of men and teams building a bridge across the Soquel creek at, or near the mouth*

> *of Hinkle creek. For a mile or more up the last named creek a good broad road has been made to the flat where the Loma Prieta Mill will soon be located. All along this piece of road many teams are at work cleaning out the numerous landslides, caused by the winter rains.*
>
> *A new road has lately been made, starting at a point between the new bridge and J. B. Brown's cottage. Turning off to the right it winds back and forth in a zig-zag way, always up hill, for the distance of about one mile. It is a good road, but quite steep. I guess the grade is about 18 inches to the rod. At present it ends on top of a high hill, where there is plenty of timber. Here a large gang of men are building a boarding-house, cook-house and many smaller houses for the accommodation of the employes. Messrs. Chace & Peterson are the owners, and are building a shingle mill here, and they expect to have timber enough to keep the mill running for five years or more.*
>
> *The Soquel creek is quite flush and goes rippling and bubbling, and looks very tempting to trout fishers, but I never fish any. No. I always buy mine. They come cheaper. Game warden, please take notice.*

Some of the staff housing and the cookhouse were built by crews as early as January. Because there would be over 100 men working at the site, a number of one-man and two-men cabins, additional bunkhouses, outhouses, and other facilities were built throughout the area. Many of these facilities were located on a higher shelf along the north side of the creek and just beyond the north end of the wagon road. There were also a number of buildings located upstream opposite the millpond. The boilers from the Aptos Creek mill arrived in April, shortly before the mill opened, but much of the machinery from the old mill remained behind to allow the facility to run at a reduced capacity to process remaining logs.

The narrowness of Hinckley Gulch meant that the mill's layout was novel. Based on explorations of the mill site and study of the only known photograph showing this arrangement, the shelf that the mill occupied was about 20 feet below the wagon road. The space the main mill occupied was

75 feet across from ridge to ridge and somewhere between 250 to 300 feet long. The lumber mill was at the lower end while the cookhouse and the largest of several bunkhouses were located directly opposite and slightly above the entrance on the steep side of Santa Rosalia Ridge. It is obvious after studying the picture that they moved Hinckley Creek's channel closer to China Ridge in order to provide more room on the shelf.

The millpond was connected to the lumber mill via a tramway. A donkey engine dragged a waterlogged piece of timber onto a waiting tramcar that was then pulled by cable 1,500 feet to a ramp that brought the log into the mill. Cut lumber would then be set out to dry on the southwest side of the mill. Any timber that was needed for the shingle and shake mills would first pass through the lumber mill, although it is unclear if the larger mill would process the timber in any way before passing it on to the smaller mills. More rails were installed from the lumber mill south to the boundary of Tract 27, providing direct access to the smaller mills and plenty of opportunities for wagons to be loaded along the road. However, space was still at a premium. Because of the steep grade, wagons had to be led by at least eight horses, which made turning around very difficult. The only space wide enough was directly in front of the lumber mill, where a loop was made so that wagons could be relieved of supplies and loaded with lumber or splitstuff. Traffic to and from the mill was controlled since the road was only wide enough for one wagon at a time.

Once the mill opened, operations followed a set schedule. All workers lived on site and, unlike with the mill on Aptos Creek, they did not have their families with them. They could live in a bunkhouse or a cabin, the latter usually with another person. Monday through Saturday, breakfast was served at 5:30 a.m. and work began at 6:00. It continued with only a 50-minute catered lunch break as an interruption until 6:00 p.m., or 5:00 p.m. on Saturdays. Dinner was served shortly after work ended. On Saturday evenings, most of the workers would head to Soquel to socialize, eat and drink, or return to their families. For eleven hours and ten minutes of work, men were paid $1.50 daily. This rate was increased in 1904 to $2.00 daily.

Besides the actual milling activity, contractors were engaged in hauling the lumber and splitstuff to Opal each day. The Loma Prieta Lumber

Company did not own their own wagons but rather hired teamsters, who were paid $2.00 per thousand pounds of cargo. In 1903, the teamsters struck for a higher rate and negotiated $2.50 per half ton. The company used five wagons daily, with a sixth on call for special deliveries. Each vehicle consisted of a large main wagon and a trailer. At maximum capacity, a wagon and trailer could haul 8,000 board feet of lumber, which weighed around twenty tons. A team of eight or more horses pulled each wagon from the mill to the Opal lumber yard. The sixth wagon, when hired, usually carried green slabs (the exterior part of a log that has one flat side and one curved side) to the O'Neill Brothers & Callahan Paper Mill in Soquel, where they were processed into dark-colored paper to be used by local butchers for meat wrapping.

The minimum ten-times daily travel of heavy industrial wagons through George Olive's resort did leave the impression that Olive feared when he filed his lawsuit in 1900. The *Sentinel* on September 21 reported that:

> *The road to and through Olive Sulphur Springs has been so changed as almost to obliterate the Springs. They do not now look like a summer resort, the terminus of a road. On the other hand the cottages look like they were partially occupied by mill employees, and all day long large teams, unloaded going up the gulch and heavy loaded coming down, are constantly passing. The loads are lumber, wood, bark and split lumber. The slabs all go to the Soquel paper mill. The Loma Prieta saw-mill has a five years' run without changing location.*

The same day, news also broke that there was a fire raging in Hinckley Gulch. The *San Francisco Call* asserted that the "fire can be seen from here and during the day Loma Prieta Mountain was hidden from view by the clouds of smoke." A timely rainfall helped quell the fire, allowing lumber crews to resume their first year of activity in the Hinckley.[5]

Schillings' Camp established on the Loma Prieta Branch

Timothy Hopkins' Tract 8 in the Augmentation, between Love Gulch to the boundary of the Augmentation, still had a number of standing and usable fallen redwood trees within it in early 1901. This was the same area that had hosted the Molino shingle mill between 1883 and 1897, but the area alongside the Loma Prieta Branch and on the west side of the tracks had remained untouched due to the wishes of the Pacific Improvement Company to preserve this part of the forest to encourage tourism. With the abandonment of the village of Loma Prieta and the dwindling of milling activity in the area, though, Hopkins felt he could finally cut the remaining timber. He contracted the job to John and Lawrence Schilling, who decided to cut it into splitstuff. The brothers were the owners of several mules, which were the means by which they planned to remove the timber from the forest. The two had recently completed a similar contract for the F. A. Hihn Company in either Gold Gulch near Felton or Valencia Creek in Aptos.

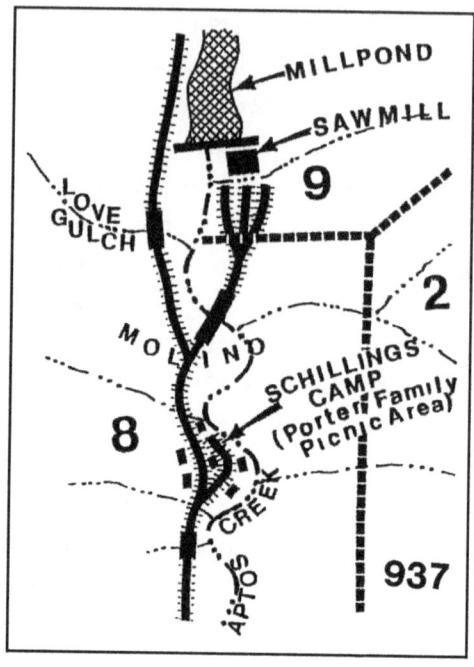

FIGURE 1.6 LOCATION OF SCHILLINGS' CAMP ON THE LOMA PRIETA BRANCH

The most convenient area that would provide access to the Loma Prieta Branch was at the parking lot for today's Porter Family Picnic Area. Here, the Schillings built a mid-sized camp to support the local timber-processing operation. The camp hosted a barn for mules, a small blacksmith shop, a large shed, and a hay store for feed. There were also several cabins for the workers who went into the forest each day to build trails for the mules and load the material onto the animals. Pieceworkers, who turned the felled logs into splitstuff, lived in the forest and rarely appeared at the camp. Across the tracks from the camp, two homes were built for the Schilling brothers, one for each of them, where they lived throughout the four years that the camp operated.

Schillings' Camp was supplied with water via a pipeline that was extended from the Loma Prieta mill and, ultimately, from Spring Creek two miles to the north. The pipe ran under the railroad bridge over Aptos Creek at Molino Junction and continued running parallel to the tracks underground until reaching the camp. The camp hosted at least one railroad spur on the east side of the branch line. The camp continued operating through the fall of 1904, at which point there were insufficient trees to justify its continued operation.[6]

The John Thomas Porter Company is established by Warren Porter

In June 1901, Warren Porter resigned his position as secretary of the Loma Prieta Lumber Company, a title he had held since 1884. He was replaced by Alfred L. Williams, who retained the position until his death on May 16, 1914. Williams was born in Rio Vista, California in 1861 and arrived in Santa Cruz County in 1890. He began his local lumbering career with Grover & Company but eventually moved with his wife and two daughters to Loma Prieta to work for the mill there, where he quickly became one of the most well-respected workers.

Porter, meanwhile, furthered his burgeoning political career while also inheriting the local political and economic position of his father, John T. Porter, who had died in 1900. In September 1901, Warren and his siblings incorporated the John T. Porter Company to handle all of the properties and material interests of their late father. Meanwhile, Warren continued to sit on the board of directors of the Loma Prieta Lumber Company and the Pajaro Valley Savings Bank and also joined the board of the state prison system in 1901.[7]

Incline cable tramway at the F. A. Hihn Company mill at Laurel is completed

When construction first began on the F. A. Hihn Company mill at Laurel, crews knew that scaling the hillside would be necessary to bring the lumber to the railroad grade. The mill site was about 25 feet below the station, and there was not enough room to build a proper railroad spur down to the mill. For the first year, workers set up a highline rig and lifted pallets of lumber up to the grade, where they were directly loaded onto waiting flatcars. But this was only ever a temporary solution.

On August 26, 1901, crews finally completed construction of an incline tramway. This was a narrow-gauge track that descended 1,600 feet from a siding at the Southern Pacific Railroad station down to the mill. It only had one sharp turn, which brought it to the broad, flat lumber yard to the south of the mill. A large steam donkey was brought in to run the cable. Railroad flatcars would be slowly led down the steep railroad grade via gravity, and then fully-loaded cars would be brought back up via the cable. Because of the tight confines of the small Laurel freight yard, cars were sometimes pushed into the Glenwood–Laurel Tunnel (Tunnel No. 3) before being arranged on one of the sidings for later pickup by a passing train.

Around the same time that the incline was completed, the company also petitioned Southern Pacific to install a new spur beside the mainline just southwest of the Summit Tunnel and across the Burns Creek bridge. The railroad company agreed and designated the location Edric, after Frederick Hihn. Since two bridges—a railroad bridge over Burns Creek and the Hotel de Redwood vehicular bridge—blocked access to the headwaters of Burns Creek and the top of the Hihn Company's property, the spur was probably installed to allow logging crews to drag logs to the railroad grade, where they could then be taken to Laurel and lowered down the incline to the mill or highlined over the road to the millpond. The station first appeared on Southern Pacific records in January 1902 and remained on the books until October 24, 1909, by which point most of the usable timber at the top of the property was likely logged.[8]

Hinckley Creek mill shuts down for the winter

The Loma Prieta Lumber Company ended its first season at Hinckley Creek in November 1901. At the time, 5.5 million board feet of lumber had been processed at the main mill, while another 3 to 4 million board feet of timber had been processed at the shingle and shake mills.

As with the previous winter, there is no evidence that the F. A. Hihn Company mill at Laurel shut down for the winter.[9]

Hinckley Creek mill opens for the season

As the rains slackened and the ground began to dry, the mill of the Loma Prieta Lumber Company roared to life in the spring of 1902. For much of the winter and early spring, timber cutting crews and peelers had been working in the forests preparing logs for transport to the mills. Unfortunately, as logging crews worked their way up Hinckley Gulch and its tributaries, it became increasingly difficult to haul logs down to the millpond. Indeed, the grades became so steep that even oxen trains could not be safely used and were retired. Instead, donkey engines were brought in and intricate rigs were installed to either drag or highline logs to the millpond. Mule teams were able to continue hauling splitstuff, but the difficult terrain prematurely tired the animals. In response, relay stations were placed between the headwaters of Hinckley Creek and the mill where splitstuff loads could be transferred to fresh mules.

During my trips into the Hinckley, I found terrain that is impossible to describe satisfactorily—the gulch must be visited to be appreciated. The hillsides along Hinckley Creek are steep and difficult to hike, beautiful as well as intriguing. I found many old-growth redwood trees, good sized second-growth trees, many fallen trees, some intact and untouched, others missing their choicest sections. And, as expected, throughout the gulch I found stumps—stumps everywhere!—many that ranged from 2 to 16 feet in diameter, with most averaging 6 to 10 feet.

There were also many trails for both people and mules that provided access, not always readily, to every nook and cranny in the gulch, from the headwaters of Hinckley Creek to the East Branch of Soquel Creek. They are those that I used to explore the gulch and that I repaired and marked when necessary. However, many of these trails have since disappeared due to the storms of the 1980s. It was once possible to follow with little effort the main route followed by the mules from Hinckley Creek's headwaters to the mill site, enjoying along the way the many delights available to the eye. But this is no longer possible. Many parts of the trails have disappeared under landslides or eroded away. Today, it would tax even the most experienced hiker to complete this journey in a day, while the hike in the opposite direction would be even more difficult.[10]

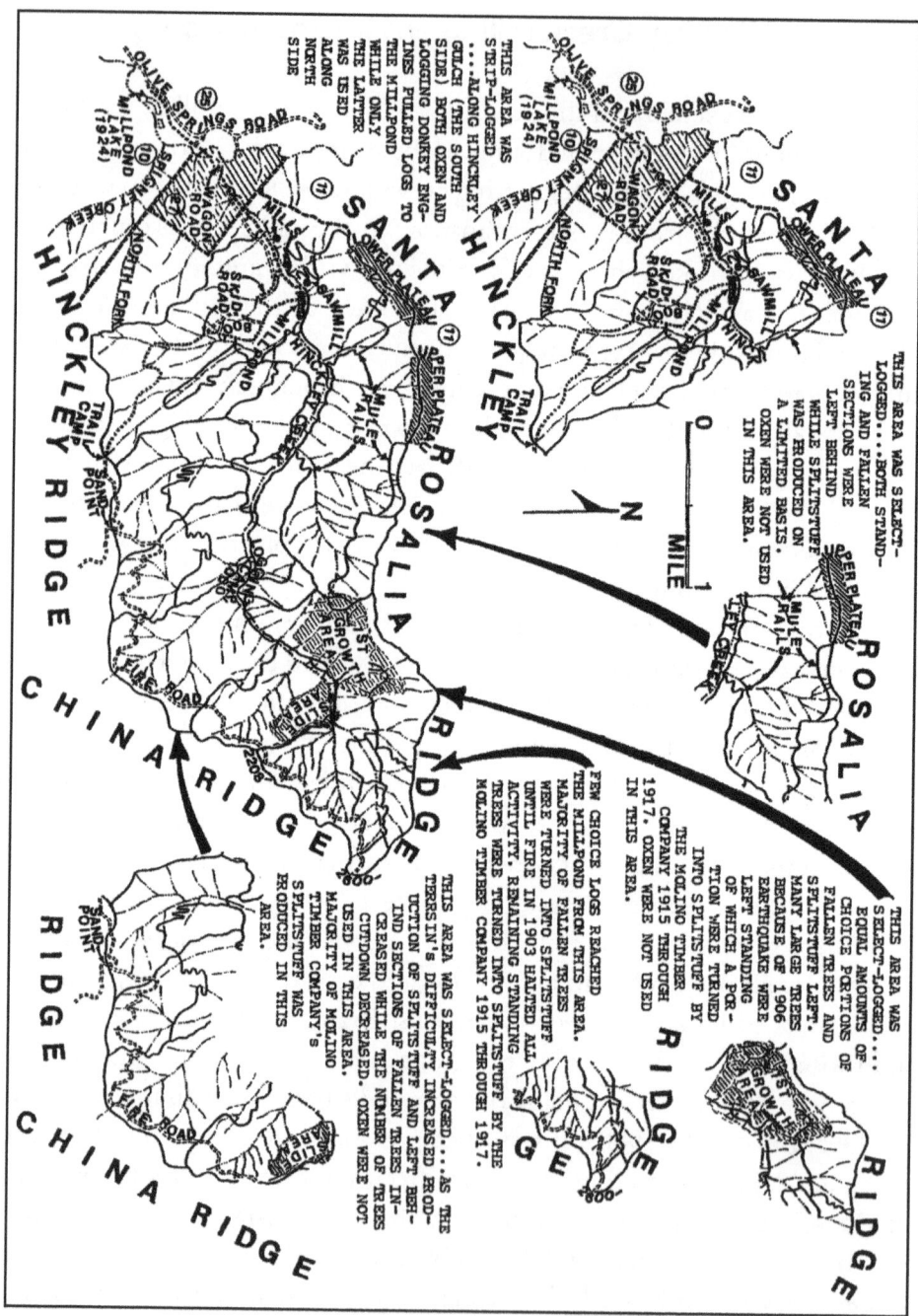

Figure 1.7 Descriptions of various logging methods used by the Loma Prieta Lumber Company while harvesting timber in Hinckley Gulch

Bert Stoodley is hired by the Loma Prieta Lumber Company

Albretto "Bert" Stoodley was born in Hamden, Delaware County, New York in the Catskill Mountains on March 23, 1873 to Willis and Eluna Stoodley. As a teenager and into adulthood, he worked in the local lumber industry. In early 1902, he decided to move to California and arrived in Soquel around June 1902. Within two weeks of his arrival, he was hired by the Loma Prieta Lumber Company as a bookkeeper. Soon afterwards, he was promoted to clerk and continued in that position until 1914. He and his young family moved into a home in Camp Capitola in October 1902 and remained there for many years.

Stoodley had several talents, one of which was his excellent record-keeping skills, which is why we know so much about the later years of the Loma Prieta Lumber Company and the Molino Timber Company today. Despite starting work at a young age, he was remarkably well-educated and curious. He also was an avid photographer and documented many of the activities in the Augmentation in the 1910s and 1920s.[11]

The F. A. Hihn Company mill at Laurel burns down

All factors considered, the first two years of operation at the F. A. Hihn Company mill at Laurel went well. The *Sentinel* reported in late August 1902 that 197 carloads of lumber were shipped from Laurel amounting to just over 1 million board feet. The company was optimistic that it would increase that number substantially by the end of the year. However, fate was not on its side.

Just before midnight on September 1, 1902, a fire broke out at the mill, possibly due to arson. The engineer of the mill, J. O. Dunham, provided the specifics to the *Sentinel*, which reported:

> ... *the fire was discovered in the shingle mill. An alarm was given. When the men were aroused the entire mill was in flames. At 3 A. M., F. A. Hihn was notified. With D. W. Johnston he reached the scene at 5:45 A. M. Mr. Hihn immediately assumed charge, directing the movements of the men.*

> *Although he realized that the Hihn Co. had sustained a heavy loss, he was calm and cool. Such a loss would have staggered the majority of the citizens of the county, but to the capitalist it was a financial incident, something that had to be taken chances with. Not a dollar of insurance was on the property.*
>
> *When Mr. Hihn arrived the mill was a total loss. It gained such headway that it was impossible to save it. The fire spread to the adjoining timber, illuminating the country for miles around. A trail was dug out, and the fire was brought under control. By hard work the dwellings occupied by the employes were saved. Mr. Dunham lost all of his tools, valued at $300.*
>
> *The fire spread to the yard, which contained 3,500,000 feet of lumber, of which 2,000,000 were saved.... It is estimated that the total loss exceeds $100,000.*

Shortly afterwards, Frederick Hihn announced that he would commence rebuilding the mill immediately. The new mill would be larger and more efficient.[12]

Hinckley Creek mill opens for the season

While the F. A. Hihn Company's mill at Laurel was still under construction, the Loma Prieta Lumber Company's mill in Hinckley Gulch was preparing for another season. Logging crews had reached the 1,000-foot elevation near the halfway point in the gulch, which was where the company had hoped to extend the railroad several years earlier. Crews set up a long-term camp here with plans to harvest the surrounding timberland over the next three seasons. The makeshift facilities could house around twenty-nine men.

The terrain uphill from the camp proved problematic to the workers and as they climbed ever higher, what they sent downstream to the lumber mill was smaller and smaller. At the same time, the amount of splitstuff they produced increased substantially, since that could be transported more easily. Yet the distance to travel from the headwaters of Hinckley Creek to the mill was overburdening the pack mules and tiring the workers. Many of the pieceworkers, who cut the splitstuff, chose to live in the forest during the harvest season just to save their energy.

The year 1903 also brought other changes to the Loma Prieta Lumber Company's operations in the county. The company convinced the nearly-completed Santa Cruz, Capitola and Watsonville Railway, an electric streetcar line, to establish a stop at the Opal lumber yard. This allowed Bert Stoodley to travel directly from Santa Cruz to work without interruption. The company also obtained a liquor license from the county, which allowed them to sell alcohol both at their Opal mercantile store and to employees working in the Hinckley.

The most important development, though, was the erection of a barley mill at Opal. The mill was intended to provide feed for the mules operating in the Hinckley, presumably because the cost of importing refined barley was proving needlessly expensive. The mill was erected at the west end of the lumber yard and a new well was dug to provide it with its own source of water. It consisted of a large building with a boiler, an engine, a large tank for steaming the grain, and rollers to flatten and partly grind the grain. After a charge of barley was put in the tank, steam from the boiler entered the tank for a short period of time. Then, by a conveyor, the barley was carried to the rollers. After the rollers had flattened and partly ground the grain, it was sacked and sent to the mule barn for storage or sent by wagon to the Hinckley.

According to Stoodley, the company's general manager would usually go to the Salinas Valley to buy hay and barley for the mules and horses, being very careful to get a good grade. He would often mention a weed that he called *tetolote* that he preferred not be mixed with the hay. The barley had to be plump with no shriveled grains mixed in. It usually was purchased from the Salinas Valley Milling Company, which was run by Timothy Hopkins at the time.[13]

The F. A. Hihn Company mill at Laurel reopens

After many months of reconstruction, the F. A. Hihn Company mill in Laurel reopened at some point in May 1903. However, not all was well in Laurel. On July 20, mill workers called for a general strike due to long hours and Frederick Hihn firing a superintendent who had struck a worker.

Fifteen friends of the superintendent had quit in response while the others went on strike, the first such action ever taken against the company. Rather than deal with the strikers, the company decided to close the mill early for the season. This decision quickly brought the workers to the negotiating table and the strike was called off after only two days. Hihn refused to budge on the issue of hours, noting that he worked longer hours than any of them, and he also defended his firing of the superintendent, proclaiming that "he will never employ a quarrelsome man."[14]

The F. A. Hihn Company expands operations to Watsonville

The *Surf* reported on July 30, 1903:

> *To further complicate matters for the Loma Prieta people, it is said that the F. A. Hihn Co. of Santa Cruz, controlling large holdings of redwood at Laurel, in the Santa Cruz mountains, have decided to invade their territory about Monterey bay, commencing the campaign at Watsonville, where a big drop in the price of redwood is already reported to have taken place. It is said that the Hihn company have decided to operate all through this section, and that, although not so powerful as the Loma Prieta, they are prepared to put up a stiff fight for the business. People in a position to know claim that this rivalry is likely to affect the prices on mill work also.*[15]

Large forest fire within the Augmentation

September 1903 was a terrible month for the Augmentation. From the last days of August, the northern boundary along Los Gatos Creek in Santa Clara County was barraged by a slow-moving deadly forest fire that killed Louis Matty near Wrights and severely damaged many of the homes along the Summit that had survived the similarly disastrous fire of October 1899. By September 8, a second fire had been detected in the vicinity of the Loma Prieta and was adding to the thick blanket of smoke that shrouded Santa Cruz County.

Into the Dark Hinckley 1903

On September 17, the *Surf* reported in a well-circulated article,

> *The fire up Valencia Creek is still raging and for eight days it has been sweeping over the country. It has traveled twenty miles over valuable timber land most of it belonging to the F. A. Hihn Company.*
>
> *It started in back of the Loma Prieta Mill country, went up through Hinkley Gulch and has wrought the worst devastation and waste up through the Valencia Gulch which has been made bare for many miles. Thousands of feet of fine timber have been destroyed and a couple of cabins belonging to the Hihn Company. The fire sweeps from the gulch to the ridge and sweeps at a great rate. A home belonging to a Mr. Remey, near Valencia, was burned to the ground and the fire surrounded the Hihn vineyard.*
>
> *For over a week a force of men have been trailing and back firing but have not yet been able to gain control of the fire. Reinforcements were sent from town today. The fire is also burning on the Ryder timber claims in the Corralitos direction.*

On September 18, the freight crew of the Santa Cruz Branch of the Southern Pacific Railroad responded to a request to salvage timber material from the Loma Prieta Lumber Company mill on Aptos Creek. The company arrived at the scene with a locomotive and caboose and hauled out several flatcars filled with lumber. Yet the company still lost 1,600 cords of redwood and 600 cords of oak from its Hinckley Gulch land. The Hihn Company, meanwhile, had lost a large amount of tan oak bark from its property on Bridge Creek. By September 22, the fire had moved north toward Hihn's Sulphur Springs, but it must have been contained shortly after since it disappears from newspapers after this point.

Because the loss of over 2,000 cords of redwood and oak is meaningless if not compared to the amount of timber it required to produce it, it is useful to convert this amount into something meaningful. A cord measures 4 x 4 x 8 feet, which would require an 8-foot-long log, which means at least 2,000 logs were burned in this fire. Two thousand logs of this size total about 1.6 million board feet of lumber, enough to build 152 five-room houses. It would take 48 mules, each carrying the equivalent of 150 board feet of lumber weighing 700 pounds each, 221 round trips of up to five miles from the timber field to the mill. Another 150 large wagon loads would subsequently be needed to transport these cords to Opal.[16]

Olive Springs Resort

Although George Olive's Olive Springs Resort faced the unenviable fact that its main road now doubled as a thoroughfare for the Loma Prieta Lumber Company's large wagons, it survived and even thrived in the years that followed. A long article in the *Surf* published on September 28, 1903, explains:

OLIVE'S SPRINGS.

A Resort That Holds Popularity Against Great Odds.

Curative Properties of the Waters, and the Sylvan Scenery are Permanent Attractions.

When George Olive bought a cutover timber tract on Hinckley creek a dozen years ago, he little thought that his name would thereby become perpetuated.

But the sulphur, iron and soda springs which were developed, more by accident than intent, drew people out there first from curiosity. Then came campers and cottages, and the evolution of a to-be-famous resort is now well under way.

The milling operations of the Loma Prieta Lumber company in the gulch beyond the springs, and the lumber hauling past the springs has marred the beauty of the original settlement, near the springs, but it also brought compensation in a better road and regular mail facilities.

The road from Santa Cruz to the springs is now a delight every inch of the way, and on Sundays, when lumber teams are not to be encountered, is a regular speedway. The springs is very proud of the growing importance which has entitled it to the formation of a school district.

The F. A. Hihn Company donated about an acre of land for the school site, and the Loma Prieta company donated the lumber. Volunteers erected the building, and the young idea is now being taught "to shoot" under direction of Miss Anna Bias.

The school-grounds offer object-lessons in botany, forestry, and geology without dependence upon text books. And this reminds us to observe that it is worth a ride out to the springs to see the collection of canes and curios Mr. Olive has gathered. It includes many rare petrified specimens of bones and tusks of animals long since extinct. Oysters in stone, preserved when oysters grew as large as a man's cap; of turtles, etc.; blocks of oak and pine wood in which the grain and growth are as plainly visible as in a stick fresh from the ax.

The double cabin, constructed entirely (except doors and windows) of hewn and split stuff, with an ornamental "bead" of sapwood on the edge of the clapboards, has been previously described in the Surf. *It is Mr. Olive's intention to add more buildings of this character.*

When this tract was cut-over forty years ago, the woodsmen were not as ruthless as at the present time, and there are many fine redwoods still remaining on his land, each of which has the makings of a cabin in it, and from which eight to ten-foot boards can readily be split.

The timber in the Spignet Gulch did not prove as valuable as expected and instead of a five years' run at the shingle mill it has been abandoned after a year and a half's cutting.

The mill-site has admirable possibilities as a camp ground. Water in abundance is here, brought half a mile in a V flume. The abandoned barns would furnish stable accommodations, and there is fuel ready for the cookstove or the camp-fire to hand for several seasons. This point is 150 feet in altitude above the springs, but the grade is not steep, and compensating views of San Francisco mountain in the foreground, and the Vine Hill region, and Ben Lomond beyond, are to be had on the way up.

San Francisco mountain is so called, it is said, because the bay of San Francisco can be seen from its summit. It is a nearly perfect cone, rising naked 2,000 feet, and surmounted by a Druidical grove, or group of trees, at the apex. One wonders why and how they are growing there.

There are many gallant climbs to be had in the vicinity of the springs, if one is willing to invest the muscle, and no athletic exercises are comparable in value for physical well-being with mountain climbing. Fishing, up or down Soquel Creek, is a pastime every day available, and it is worth while, without regard to the number of trout taken.

Visitors to the springs all go through the abandoned tunnel and look out on the cornfield and the creek on the other side, but it pays to go on up to Smith's place and see the orchard and watermelon patch. In this orchard is the original Summer Queen apple-tree. Many believe this will be proven to be the best August apple grown in California.

Wildcats grow up here also. Mr. Olive has one in a cage—not tame, but in captivity—and the morning of our visit Mr. Smith had caught, in a trap, a twenty-pounder. Wildcats have as keen a relish for yellow-legged chickens as a Methodist minister, and they get more of them in this section.

Despite these diversions, it is upon the springs themselves that Olives must depend for popularity. Conductor Sam Davis, of the narrow-gauge, tried for twenty years to find something to settle his stomach, and struck it up here last summer. He bought a cottage and brought many friends hither. There is water of the right sort for everybody—sulphur, iron, and soda—atmosphere of the purest, scenery and seclusiveness for those who seek it.

With sanitary cleanliness preserved, and accommodations increased, the future of Olive's Springs will grow bigger and brighter.

San Francisco Mountain is today known as Sugarloaf Mountain, and is partially quarried by the Olive Springs Quarry Company. As a result, it no longer retains its conical shape. Although it had a relatively high peak, though significantly less than 2,000 feet, a person could not see as far as San Francisco from it. The name instead likely has a Spanish or Mexican origin that has since been forgotten. The tunnel mentioned in the article was through Santa Rosalia Ridge just above Soquel Creek, which Roger Hinckley and John Shelby bore for their water-powered sawmill around 1858. The mill was later sold to Richard Savage in 1859, who owned it at the time of the Shoquel Augmentation Partitioning Suit. Meanwhile, William Smith owned 26 acres in the Augmentation on the north side of Santa Rosalia Ridge on part of the property that had been Hinckley and Shelby's mill.[17]

Mills open for the season

In Spring 1904, the mills of the Loma Prieta Lumber Company on Hinckley Creek and the F. A. Hihn Company at Laurel reopened for the season. While it was business as usual for the latter company, the former had decided to return to Santa Cruz for the first time since the collapse of the Santa Cruz Lumber Company five years earlier. In March, the Loma Prieta Lumber Company began erecting a new planing mill on the Blackburn property across from the Santa Cruz Union Depot. The facility sprawled across the southern ends of Washington and Center Streets with a yard capable of holding over 1,500,000 board feet of lumber. The small planing mill, measuring 60 x 40 feet, sat along Pacific Avenue beside the Union Traction Company's car barn. The property also hosted a 16 x 20 foot branch office for retail sales.[18]

Land transfer from the Santa Cruz Bank of Savings & Loan to J. W. Forgues concerning Tract 7 in the Augmentation

On March 15, 1904, the Santa Cruz Bank of Savings & Loan sold a total of 794 acres of land in Tract 7 of the Augmentation to J. W. Forgues, one of the former directors of Grover & Company. Prior to this transaction, the bank had sold a total of 304 acres in the tract's south end.[19]

The F. A. Hihn Company plans a wagon road from the Laurel mill to the East Branch of Soquel Creek

In April 1904, Frederick Hihn approached the Santa Cruz County Board of Supervisors with a proposal that they appoint surveyors to plan a road from his mill at Laurel in Tract 16 of the Augmentation to the East Branch of Soquel Creek in Tract 11. The purpose of the road was to allow the F. A. Hihn Company to haul logs from its properties along the creek (Tracts 1, 6, 10, 11 and 25) to its mill. Even though there was an existing road between Laurel and Soquel San Jose Road—Hotel de Redwoods Road (today's Redwood Lodge Road)—this route was narrow, twisting, and too difficult for large wagons. Hihn wanted a road that was more capable of supporting log-laden wagons. The supervisors agreed to the request and hired D. D. Emery, A. S. Seayrs, and C. O. B. Lewis to survey the route.[20]

The Loma Prieta Lumber Company's workers go on strike

On August 16, 1904, an article appeared in the *Surf* revealing that workers at the Hinckley Creek mill of the Loma Prieta Lumber Company had gone on strike. It reads:

MILL MEN STRIKE.

NINE AT LOMA PRIETA LUMBER MILLS QUIT WORK.

Dissatisfied With Wages, They Ask or a Twenty-Five per Cent Increase.

For some tine past there has been dissatisfaction among the employees of the Loma Prieta Lumber Company's hands at the new sawmill near Olive Springs over the inequality of wages. Some were working 11 hours for $2 per day, while others working less hours were receiving from $2.50 upward. Today a long contemplated strike materialized. Nine *men went out, asking for a raise of 25 per cent. One man, Geo. Rosse, went back to work in another man's place, at the same wages.*

This fact and others convince the dissatisfied men that the company wants to displace some men by choosing from among the strikers, but remaining ones propose to hold together for what they believe to be just demands.[21]

Land transfer from J. W. Forgues to the Capitola Park Company concerning Tract 7 in the Augmentation

Only nine months after acquiring Tract 7 in the Augmentation, J. W. Forgues sold 732 of his 794 acres to the Capitola Park Company on December 9, 1904. Indeed, Forgues was actually acting as an agent for the company

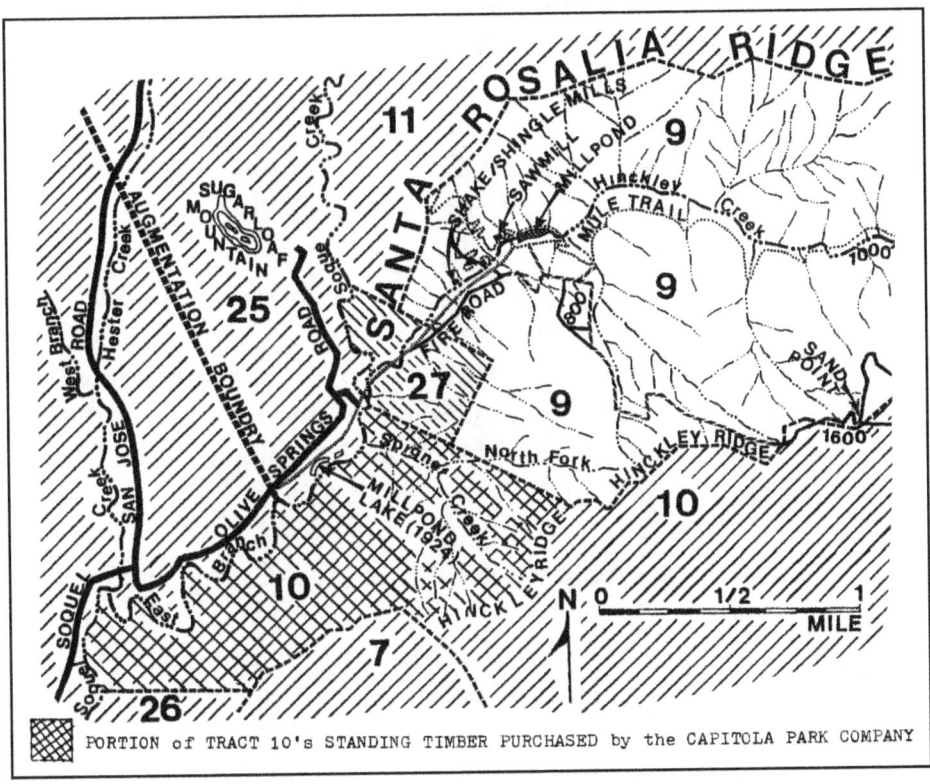

FIGURE 1.8 THE PART OF TRACT 10 PURCHASED BY THE CAPITOLA PARK COMPANY

when he made the initial purchase, although he did not reveal this fact at the time. The company, despite its use of Capitola in its name, was not local but rather headquartered in San Francisco.[22]

Frederick Hihn leases 453 acres in Tract 10 to the Capitola Park Company

Around the same time that J. W. Forgues sold part of his tract in the Augmentation to the Capitola Park Company, the F. A. Hihn Company did the same. It either sold stumpage rights or leased 453 acres within the western portion of Tract 10 to the company. A later analysis of the property shows that this land could produce approximately 24 million board feet of lumber, which made it the most valuable land of the Hihn company's yet to be harvested. The Hihn Company leased or sold rights to this tract because it was isolated and difficult to harvest at its Laurel mill. It thus became the problem of the Capitola Park Company to profitably harvest this valuable timber area.[23]

The F. A. Hihn Company builds a fence along Santa Rosalia Ridge

Loma Prieta Lumber Company's logging crews in Hinckley Gulch began to reach the top of Santa Rosalia Ridge, which marked the boundary of Tracts 9 and 11 in the Augmentation, in early 1905. In response, the F. A. Hihn Company hired E. D. Perry to resurvey the border between the two tracts. As soon as the line was established, the company sent in workers to install a fence, portions of which survive to this day.[24]

Olive Springs Resort advertises Ideal Camp Sites

Starting on June 17, 1905, George Olive began promoting his Olive Springs resort daily in the *Surf* with the following advertisement:

> *Ideal camp grounds, Sulphur, Soda, Iron and Magnesia Springs. Two streams of running water; feed for horses at*

> *reasonable rates to campers."*
>
> GEO. OLIVE, *Proprietor*

Olive Springs continued to operate for several more years. In 1943, the 39th Report of the State Mineralogist summarized:

> *This picturesque property, which still remains practically in its natural state, comprises 100 acres, located on Hinckley Creek near its junction with Soquel Creek, and extending to the top of the ridge between the two streams....*
>
> *Hinckley Creek flows through a deep canyon here, the walls of which stand nearly vertical. Seepages and springs occur at numerous points in the creek bed and in the sandstone formation which forms the canyon wall. The rock is very soft in places and is in the process of decomposition.*
>
> *Of probably a dozen springs on the property, five have been some what improved by constructing small concrete basins around them. These five are known as the White Sulphur, Sulphur, Sulphur and Iron, Magnesium, and Magnesium and Iron Springs, but the names mean little. All are cold.*[25]

Survey for wagon road between Laurel and the East Branch of Soquel Creek is completed

In the summer of 1905, the three surveyors hired by the Santa Cruz County Board of Supervisors submitted their plan for the F. A. Hihn Company's wagon road from Laurel to the East Branch of Soquel Creek. The map that the surveyors prepared does not indicate how wide the road was to be or whether it was intended for wagons or a railroad line. But based on elevations notated at several locations along the proposed route and several curves that would be exceptionally sharp, even for a narrow-gauge railroad, it can be assumed that it was intended for wagons.

Within Tract 16 alone were 1,400 acres of untapped redwood forest, which an estimate in 1891 found could produce up to 50 million board feet of lumber. In addition, the completed road would expand access to another 163 million board feet, which combined would allow the Laurel

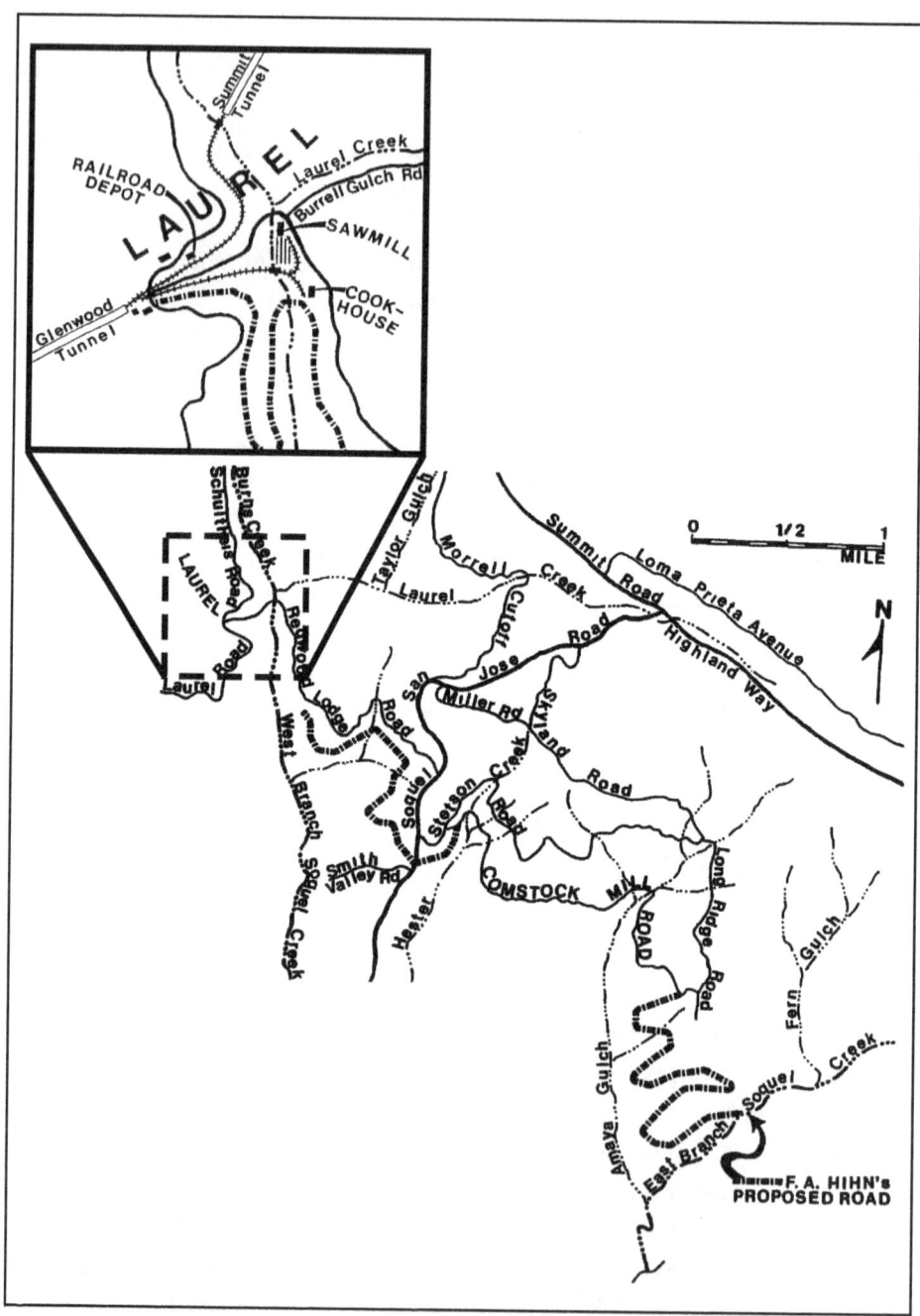

FIGURE 1.9 SURVEYED ROUTE OF ROAD BETWEEN
LAUREL AND THE EAST BRANCH OF SOQUEL CREEK

mill to operate six days a week, eight weeks per year, for 20 to 25 years at its current capacity.

The final route of the proposed road began in Laurel at the mouth of the Glenwood Tunnel, elevation 900 feet, and then twisted its way eastward, keeping well below the existing Redwood Lodge Road. It reached Soquel San Jose Road just to the south of Stetson Road at 1,220-foot elevation. From Soquel San Jose Road, the proposed road followed the original route graded by the Comstock brothers to reach the Soquel Turnpike, which today is a private road called Comstock Mill Road that ends on Long Ridge Road at 1,320-foot elevation. Just before Comstock Mill Road reaches Long Ridge Road, a twisting path carries the road to the point where it reaches the East Branch of Soquel Creek, where the elevation is 640 feet. This is today's Long Ridge Trail within the Soquel Demonstration State Forest and marks the original route of Hihn's earlier Spanish Ranch Road.[26]

The Loma Prieta Lumber Company opens a new lumberyard in Santa Cruz

The milling season ended early in 1905 due to heavy rains disrupting daily operations. Nonetheless, the Loma Prieta Lumber Company was also expanding its local profile in the hope of out-competing the F. A. Hihn Company. On December 1, it opened a new lumber yard at the corner of Soquel and Branciforte Avenues. It was the fourth such yard in the county, the others being at Opal (Capitola), Watsonville, and the Santa Cruz Union Depot.[27]

Winter rains damage the Hinckley Creek mill

As winter arrived and the year 1906 began, rain continued to fall unceasingly, saturating the ground while keeping the creeks at or near flood levels. On the evening of January 18, a large storm hit mid-county accompanied by an unseasonal thunderstorm, which passed over the headwaters of Hinckley Creek. It was a disaster for both the Loma Prieta Lumber Company's operations and Olive Springs Resort.

Several articles appeared in the *Surf* concerning the storm and the damage that resulted, the first two appearing side-by-side on January 19:

Soquel Creek Booms.

The Water the Highest in Twelve Years.

Much Damage in Loss of Poultry, Wood and a Retaining Wall.

Soquel Creek was the highest last night for twelve years, and considerable damage was done by the raging torrent.

The water was within a few feet of the Park House, and backed up from the creek until it was opposite Angell's grocery store.

One of the heaviest losers was Robert Canham, who had 200 cords of fine pine wood ready for the market which was cut and was carried away from the Himmelmann place.

About two hundred dollars damage was done to the Ben Holsey place, about half of his lot being carried away.

The retaining stone wall on the C. J. Holmes place was carried away, and the water came into the South Coast paper mills, and some of the machinery was under water.

In the Sam Alkire home the water was six inches deep on the floor, and Mrs. Alkire had to be carried out by boat.

Billy, the barber, lost four dozen chickens.

In the same issue, a smaller notice advised:

Loma Prieta Mill Washed Out.

The report reaches the SURF office this afternoon that the Loma Prieta mill, on Hinckley creek, has been entirely washed out during the storm last night. Further particulars could not be obtained this afternoon.

The next day, a more thorough article described the destruction at the mill, as well as some of the damage to Olive Springs Resort:

Hinckley Creek

Went on the Rampage Thursday Night.

Taking the Loma Prieta Mill

And Its Belongings and Appurtenances Far Down the Stream. Much Damage in Vicinity of Olive Springs.

Further particulars in regard to the destruction of the Loma Prieta mill have been received. The ribbon of a stream, Hinckley creek, which flows through the gulch where the mill is situated, had enlarged to a torrent that came rushing through the narrow gorge, carrying with it the collected drift for years.

Above the dam which is just ahead of the mill, a jam of logs was formed, and further up the creek was another of logs. The upper jam gave way and came down with the swift current, striking the jam just above the dam and in short time the dam gave way and the double jam and dam went crashing into the big mill, lifting it from its foundations, breaking the timbers that supported the corrugated iron roof as if they were pipe stems, and landing it above the machinery, and then the whole outfit was carried down to Soquel creek, and machinery and timbers all scattered from the site of the mill to the sands of the beach near Capitola, where they have been washed by the waves.

The whereabouts of the two immense boilers in the mill are not known, but are somewhere in Soquel Creek between Olive Springs and the beach.

The office of the mill was also carried down in the torrent, and also a number of cabins.

Luckily, the mill was closed down and all the lumber had been removed from the yard. The course of Hinckley creek has been changed, and the stream now runs through the center of what was once the big lumber yard.

The mill is a total loss, and among the pieces of machin-

ery destroyed was the circular saw, gang edger, trimmer, slab saw, etc., and the company estimate the loss at $30,000.

The entire road from Olive Springs to the mill is washed out, and the county bridge, seventy-five feet in length, which crosses the Soquel creek, went out to sea.

The barn belonging to George Olive, with its contents of several tons of hay, is a complete loss.

Mr. Olive's horse was drowned, and has been picked up on the Seabright beach.

The kitchen and the contents of the Van Winkle house were also swept entirely away.

J. W. Walker and a crew of men at the mill watched the destructive work as long as possible, and then they had to run to the side of the mountain to escape.

A couple of Portuguese remained in their cabin, and fearing danger, ran to a friend's cabin, but had only left their cabin when it was upturned and went as the rest of the buildings did.

Two more men escaped a horrible fate in a similar manner, just fleeing from their cabin in time.

This mill was built about two years ago, and was one of the very best and largest in the county.

The debris at the mill site is forty feet in height.

One unexpected survivor of the disaster was Olive's horse, who in fact did not drown but was found several days later. The shake and shingle mills were not so lucky, though—both were also destroyed in the onslaught, according to Bert Stoodley. Stoodley commented in his memoirs that, "normally tranquil Hinckley Creek became a raging torrent" during that storm. The damage caused by the collapse of the millpond was made worse by the number of cut but uncollected trees that were littered along the hillsides north of the pond. As the rain saturated the ground, these began to roll down into Hinckley Creek and then float to the pond, which swelled with the stormwaters and influx of timber. The flood became increasingly more dangerous, too, since every structure it destroyed added to the amount of debris it took downstream to Soquel

Creek and, ultimately, the Monterey Bay.

A short article in the *Mountain Echo* published on January 20 listed the rainfall totals for the previous ten days. They were:

- January 11: 0.73 inches
- January 12: 2.14 inches
- January 13: 5.93 inches
- January 14: 5.14 inches
- January 15: 0.58 inches
- January 16: 1.01 inches
- January 17: 3.51 inches
- January 18: 3.83 inches

Thus, over the eight days, 22.87 inches of rain dropped in the Santa Cruz Mountains. In comparison, the total for the first ten days of the month was only 3.81 inches.

A final retrospective on the flood was published by the *Surf* on January 22 and emphasized the damage to Olive Springs:

At Olive Springs

The Course of Soquel Creek Changed.

George Olive, a Heavy Loser by Land Being Washed Away.

George Hodgdon has returned from a trip to Olive Springs, where he is owner of a cottage in conjunction with John Bias, and after the receding of the waters, reports much damage, and also that the course of Hinckley and Soquel creeks is changed.

Of the nine summer cottages at the resort, he reports only four as intact—the Lukens, Patterson and Effey cottages being almost a complete loss. The boarding house, Bias-Hodgson, Lathrop and Litchfield remain.

He estimates the loss to the cottage owned by his daughter,

Miss Dora Hodgson, as about $250. The kitchen was taken away, and the rest of the house stood on one piece of underpinning, as all the others were washed out, but on each side of the house were trees that held it in place, and on one side ten cords of wood were caught and piled up.

He reports the creek running within several feet of the front of his house at present.

Mr. Van Winkle, who lived in one of the cottages, the night of the freshet, had placed lanterns up through the trees, so as to watch the approach of the water. When the jam broke, he heard the noise of the oncoming water, and had just time to grab his child and make for an old cabin high and dry, where he built a fire on the ground floor and remained with his family for the night.

Mr. Hodgdon believes Mr. Olive's loss about three thousand dollars caused by the creek washing away much of his camp ground.

The Soquel creek is now within four feet of the old Olive house, and within 2 1-2 feet of the cabin which had been occupied by Miss Helen Byrne, the school teacher, there being a high bank between the house and the river.

Near the saloon, the debris for a great distance lies fifteen feet in height.

Across the creek where Frank Smith had reclaimed about two acres of land, his hard labor was all carried away in a short time, and only rocks remain. The loss is about $1,000.

The Loma Prieta Lumber Company assessed the damage and decided to rebuild the mill and millpond at their original sites. After Hinckley Creek dropped to a reasonable level and the ground began to dry, a crew of workmen were sent to the gulch to begin rebuilding the mill and supporting structures. The first structure they rebuilt was the cookhouse, followed by several bunkhouses. These were built further upstream and higher along the hillside to avoid liquefaction that was occurring closer to the creek. Next came the millpond and the ramp that allowed logs to be pulled to the sawmill.

The skeleton crew of workmen, several occupying the rebuilt structures, worked feverishly through the winter to clear the logjam and reconstruct the lumber mill, but their efforts were constantly interrupted by renewed bouts of heavy rain. The *Evening Sentinel* on March 26 reported:

DAMAGE AT SOQUEL BY STORM.

Ed. "Sentinel":—The big storm that has been predicted by the weather prophets has at last come and is doing much damage in the vicinity of Soquel. About 2:30 P. M. Friday the rain came down in torrents, and it looked like Soquel would be all flooded. It rained so hard and the water rushed down the hills so fast, that the culverts would not carry off the water, and consequently the street from the Congregational Church down to Ellis' corner was flooded. The water got on the sidewalk in front of Ellis' store and came within an ace of getting inside of the building.

There were three big landslides on the Parrish hill, and quite a strip of good pasture land was damaged by it. The Soquel creek is booming and is reported to be higher than it has been for years. Wood and lumber and all kinds of trash is coming down the creek. The creek is steadily rising and it is feared that it will be much higher before long.

The Bates creek bridge has been washed away. Several of the residents have their lots full of water and the water in the old livery stable is knee deep.

E. C. Webb nearly lost all of his chickens during the high water, and his wife and daughter got wet through while trying to save their poultry.

About two dozen men and boys have been having sport all the afternoon spearing wood, and quite a big pile has been accumulated.

It is feared that several bridges will be washed out before the storm is over.

Soquel, March 23.

Despite the challenges, progress toward repairing the damage from the January storm was being made by mid-April, with the ramp to the mill nearing completion. Construction on the mill itself had not yet begun, although all of the boilers, headrigs, and other machinery had been recovered and were sitting on a high shelf above the creek awaiting installation.

The F. A. Hihn Company mill at Laurel was likewise delayed in its opening with crews waiting for the ground to dry before damming Burns Creek and starting up the boilers. Fellers were active throughout the winter preparing trees to be dragged to the mill, but that activity had likely been interrupted frequently due to the rains and may have ceased altogether to avoid potential logjams downstream. At the same time, the Hihn Company was eagerly awaiting the standard-gauging of the Southern Pacific Railroad's track through Laurel, which was set to commence in late April. The narrow-gauge track between Wright's Station and Los Gatos was scheduled to be removed on April 18, after which all railroad traffic from Laurel would have to go south until the tunnel to Wrights was enlarged to support the broader gauge. Once completed, this wider track would be able to move substantially larger loads of lumber and splitstuff from the Laurel mill to the Hihn Company's regional yards. In anticipation, the company may have planned to delay the opening of its mill until after the standard-gauge trackage to Los Gatos was completed later in the year.[28]

CHAPTER 2

~

A Great Calamity

5:02 a.m., April 18, 1906

AN EARTHQUAKE

The Most Severe and Extensive That Ever Visited California

A calamity, the measure of which it is impossible to compass at this hour, has befallen Santa Cruz, and probably extended throughout Central California.

All preceding earthquakes in history and tradition in this region become insignificant temblors in comparison with the present visitation.

Shortly after 5 o'clock the earth commenced to rock and roar, brick walls burst asunder, chimneys toppled to the ground or came crushing through roofs. Movable things on shelves and tables and hanging on walls sought the floor, and consternation reigned in strong hearts, while many weak ones nearly collapsed under the shock.

The fact that it was daylight relieved the terror that the timid ones felt, although but few people were up. Those who were, witnessed a scene that will never fade from memory. In brick buildings the creaking sounds caused by an earthquake, even the slightest to which California is accustomed, is one of the most gruesome sounds, but this morning it amounted to a crushing which startled sleepers like the knell of impending doom! The panic of fear soon passed, however, as the worst was over. In a few minutes the streets were filled with a dazed and bewildered people, thankful for an escape from a more appalling catastrophe, but aghast with the wreck and ruin before their eyes....

The worst disaster reported in this region occurred at the Loma Prieta mill site, on the Hinckley gulch.

Here both sides of the canyon walls appeared to crush together and a mass of earth estimated at a hundred feet in depth filled the canyon, crushing in and burying the workmen who were living in cabins at work on the new mill.

Mill, buildings and road were all submerged. Mr. Williams, the resident representative of the company, sent doctors to the scene, and dispatched laborers by the wagonload as fast as they could be obtained, but on arrival at the scene, it was found impossible to reach the men or to make much progress in rescue work. The stream is completely choked by the debris, and the impounded water will form a menace to all the valley below. The entombed men, as far as known, are believed to be Foreman Walker, J. O. Dunham (the engineer), H. E. Estrada, Alex Morrison, Gus Vollandt, Frank Jones, Fred Peaslee, A. Buckley and Charley June (the Chinese cook).

Messrs. Walker, Buckley and Peaslee are married men, the others are single....

A representative of the SURF made the trip to Hinckley's Gulch this afternoon in an automobile. The road was blocked by a slide about a mile and a half this side, and the trip had to be completed on foot.

> *About 200 men are engaged in rescue work. Other relays are preparing food and coffee. The hill slid down from one side and literally scooped up the mill and two cabins, landing many of the timbers and logs a hundred feet high on the opposite bank. There were about 100 men employed in the gulch altogether, in three camps, but they are all accounted for except for those mentioned....*
>
> *Unable to reach the outside world by train or wire, several parties started for San Jose in automobiles, but slides on the road near Olive Springs prevented progress.*
>
> *Reports state that the Sears House and the Hotel de Redwood, in the Highland region, suffered severely.*
>
> *What news has been received from other cities indicate that they all suffered more than Santa Cruz. If reports be true, San Jose has met with a terrible disaster and heavy loss of life, and the fact that San Francisco could not be reached by telephone or telegraph, indicates nothing less than a catastrophe.*

The above article appeared in the *Surf* on the day that the San Francisco Earthquake struck. In many ways, it was a fortunate twist of fate that the Loma Prieta mill was still under repair at the time. Although James Walker and his crew of carpenters, laborers, and support staff perished in the horrific landslide that destroyed the mill for the second time in four months, dozens more would have been killed had the mill been operating at the time. The other workers—about 90 in total—were fortunately farther up the creek, where liquefaction was less severe.

Bert Stoodley was at his home in Opal when the quake struck. He recounts in his memoirs:

> *When the quake occurred, on the west downstream side of the sawmill, it seemed that the entire mountain slipped down to the creek filling it to a depth of fifty to sixty feet. At a little after six in the morning a man on horseback came riding to my house in Opal and said that a slide had buried the mill and everyone there plus the 29 men upstream at the 1,000 foot elevation living at the logging camp there. He was very much*

excited and his horse was covered with lathe as though he had been ridden hard. I tried to telephone into town to let the Loma Prieta Lumber Company's secretary *Alfred Williams* know about the disaster but the phone was out of order.

Thank goodness the rider was only partly right; the up-stream logging camp, while damaged, none of the men were dead. But as far as events at the sawmill site was concerned, the news was not encouraging, only a few men outside the line of the slide had escaped injury.

Later that morning a donkey engineer rode in and told us that he had risen early to fire up his donkey engine's boiler which was located below and outside the line of the slide, but was in plain sight of it. Suddenly the ground began to shake violently. The operator of the donkey had to grab the stay rods that held the boiler to the frame of the sled in order to remain standing. After a few seconds there was a great roar to the west, trees began to sway as if the wind was blowing. Suddenly the whole hillside began to slide down towards the creek bottom, some of the trees toppling while others moved down the hill in a standing position. After it quieted the engineer left his engine and went up to where the mill building would have been if it had been rebuilt. There were no cabins on the first bench, there was nothing but tangled roots, limbs, mud, rock and tree trunks.

Digging for bodies began at once and several were found the first day. The cabins, being on higher ground behind the mill, were not buried very deep among the rubble. One man was found in the debris of his cabin with the door knob still in his hand. On the trail that circled around the back of the facilities we found the body of *James Walker* and at his heels the yellow dog that followed him everywhere, both flattened against the hillside by the flow of earth and rock. Someone said "if poor Jim had had but five seconds more time he would have been safe."

Just below the lower end of the sawmill shelf the mud and trees that slid down the side of the gulch there formed a fifty- to sixty-foot-high mud barrier that extended from side to side. Soon a thirty-foot-deep lake would result burying everything *under the mud and water.*

All but two of the lives lost in Santa Cruz County to the earthquake were at the Hinckley Creek mill. The quake caused damage everywhere, with the most severe in Watsonville and up the San Lorenzo Valley, but the county considered itself fortunate that so few people lost their lives in the temblor. Indeed, the worst damage was that done to the Southern Pacific Railroad's narrow-gauge subdivision through the mountains. Work was set to begin on the enlargement of the tunnel under the Summit when the earthquake struck. About 400 feet in from the northern portal, the tunnel had shifted sideways. This severed telegraph and telephone communication across the mountains and made rail travel between Laurel and Wrights impossible. The F. A. Hihn Company, as a result, decided to postpone the reopening of its mill at Laurel until the rail line to Santa Cruz was restored and Southern Pacific's plans for the route through the mountains were made clear.

The Summit area also suffered heavily from the earthquake, although no lives were lost. The area had endured two disastrous fires in just over six years, yet the events of April 18, 1906, brought further catastrophe to the brave settlers of the Santa Cruz–Santa Clara county border. The April 19 *Surf* reported:

> *Evidences of destruction were more vivid in the country, if possible, than in the city.*
>
> *Rocks had risen in the fields in places, huge boulders upheaved from the bed of subterranean streams. On the road over the mountains great fissures were met in many places, and these gaps in the earth were some of them from three to five feet wide. Bridges were all damaged more or less. In some cases the abutments had settled and spread apart from the main bridge, and in others the bridge was crushed and crumpled together. As the shocks continued during the afternoon the sound of falling trees in the forest could be heard, and one huge tree lay across the road below the former Hotel de Redwoods, this famous hostelry having collapsed from the quake. Many farmers were met on the way, and from*

> the tales he heard, the violence of the earthquake appears to have been heavier towards the summit than on the coast. The tremendous pall of smoke from burning San Francisco hung over the Santa Clara Valley, while the frequent shocks and gaping wounds in the breast of Mother Earth made a nerve-testing combination such as comes but once in any man's lifetime. The highway seemed to him impassable for vehicles in many places, yet teams were on the road making their way through somehow.

The road between Los Gatos and the Summit was impassible due to fissures and slides. Meanwhile, the long bridge on the Morrell Cutoff midway between Summit Road and the Hotel de Redwoods was destroyed, further limiting communication in the Summit area. For the few that headed south through Gilroy to reach Santa Cruz, they found their path blocked by a collapsed bridge over the Pajaro River. The Southern Pacific Railroad's bridge across the river was also damaged, but locals nonetheless placed planks across its length to allow them to cross it.

The *Surf* on April 21 provided more details of the destruction on the Summit:

SEEN FROM THE SUMMIT.

The Vacant Spaces Felt the Force of Nature's Convulsion.

Speaking of the observations and information gathered on his trip over the mountains, J. P. Cooper says:

The shock was terrific over all the district on the other side of "Mountain Charley's" on the summit. Though no one was seriously injured, houses were demolished, some being split in two and fell apart.

Peculiar enough, the wineries of Emil Meyer and the Fidel place escaped injury.

Frank McKiernan, son of Mountain Charlie, was going up when the shock came. Though a stalwart athlete, he was knocked to his knees and then dashed against the bureau, barely escaping serious injury. His house stood the shock without damage, but his well was "churned" so that the water has not been drinkable since.

The road up to McKiernan's place is in excellent condition, but from McKiernan's to Los Gatos the road is full of sinks and fissures, and new springs were started in many places. The road is passable, though, and teams are now making good time over the mountains, by the Scotts Valley road.

H. Morrell's house was broken into two parts and demolished. The new Arthur Sears' place was completely wrecked. The Fowler place was badly shaken, the house twisted and cracked. The barn at the brow of the hill was almost wrecked, as the ground sank several feet.

This condition prevailed in many places on the hillsides, as many buildings were wrenched out of shape by the sinking of the ground.

At the Dr. Spranger place the house went down with a crash. The Clough house was probably the worst damaged of any in the Highland district. Miltamont, the Miller place, was badly wrecked.

The same story applies to nearly every place, few houses escaping serious damage. West's house, at Laurel, was strongly built on large redwood stumps five feet high, but was torn from the underpinning and thrown to the ground.

Hiram Morrell also lost his only cow. To quote Charles Aiken: "Farmer Morrell had pastured his cow for the night on the luscious grass that lie to the northwest, and like the early worm that got caught by the early bird, 'was never seen again.'" The quake caused a lateral displacement which moved the east side of Morrell's property eight feet to the north, leaving a crack eight feet wide for his cow to fall into. For forty years, the Schultheis family's fence demonstrated this shift in the earth.

Several other notable buildings suffered damage within the vicinity of the Summit. The Terrace Grove Hotel along the west side of Soquel San Jose Road just to the south of Hotel de Redwoods required structural

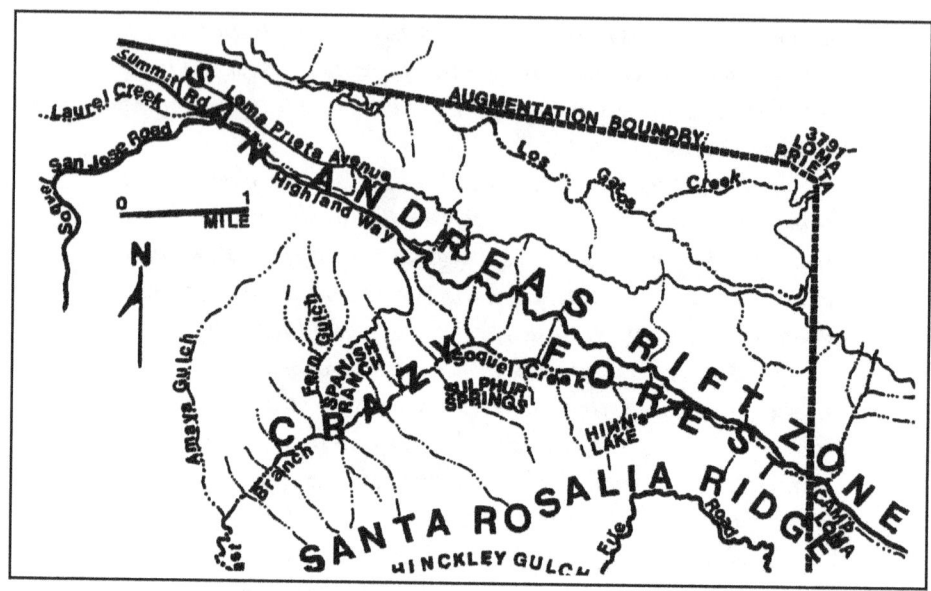

FIGURE 2.1 THE SAN ANDREAS RIFT ZONE THROUGH THE AUGMENTATION

repairs, during which a third story was added and its large basement was remodeled. Arbor Villa at the corner of Summit Road and Loma Prieta Avenue was more badly damaged—the Wright family shut down the hotel and rebuilt the structure into a private residence for the family. At the junction of Miller Road and the Miller Cutoff, the former Tre Monte Hotel, then serving as a mental hospital, shifted off its foundations. It was later realigned using jacks. High above Burns Creek, Aiken's fruit orchard was rearranged. The owners of many other homes and businesses in the Summit area, who had endured two disastrous fires in seven years yet still hung on, finally threw in the towel and moved away.

The earthquake left its imprint across the upper timber tracts of the Augmentation. Whereas before the temblor the trees were in ordered rows, after they were thrown into clusters haphazardly. Meanwhile, the rifting caused by the earth's movement opened new springs in some places and drained ponds in others. On Aiken's land, several springs fed into a newly-formed basin which quickly swelled, creating a large lagoon. Along the East Branch of Soquel Creek near Highland Way, an earthen dam formed creating a small lake. According to several sources, the water was stocked with fish and enjoyed by Hihn with his rod and reel until his death. The lake survived until the mid-1930s, when a storm finally washed the dam away.

A detailed retrospective on the impact of the earthquake on Aptos Creek Canyon, which was almost entirely devoid of humans at the time, appeared in the *Surf* on October 20:

WITH THE EARTHQUAKE ON THE APTOS.

How It Obliterated Roads; Builded Dams; Created Ponds; Moved Trees; Emptied Lagoons; and Raised a Rumpus Generally.

Geological testimony bears witness that the coast counties of California are among the latest works of Nature in continent building, and the jolt received on the ever memorable 18th of April proves that the job isn't complete yet.

Geological formations are freaky all through this region, and the resultant features of physical geography are without parallel.

A curious phenomenon in world building was the construction of the Aptos region, wherein several thousand acres of territory were placed as in a pocket from the continuous and surrounding country.

For some thousands of years it lay undisturbed, growing meanwhile one of the finest forests of redwood timber.

Twenty years ago the axe and the sawmill, and the railroad invaded, in the name of the Loma Prieta Lumber Company, and they skinned its sides as bare as they were when first uplifted from the ocean into the atmosphere. During the days of lumbering there was noise and bustle in the canyon. Homes were built and a thriving school district and voting precinct established.

The finish came to the timber sooner than expected. The mill was removed, the inhabitants forsook the place, the tiny orchards and gardens abandoned, and the works of man left to decay in the returning silence of primeval days.

No highway ever ran up to Aptos [Creek]. There are deer

trails along the ridges and fishermen's paths along the stream. These and the rapidly overgrowing skid roads of the lumberman are the only means of traverse.

* * *

This prelude is explanatory of the fact that months passed before any verified reports of the earthquake visitation were made in this section.

On a fishing trip early in the summer, Branch Wallace of Glen Haven district, with his brothers-in-law Geo. Avers and Sam Scott, came across the earthquake's trail, and it was as his guest and under his guidance that the writer a few weeks later visited the locality. It was a daybreak start from the Wallace residence, with team up and over the new Capitola Park grade to the end of the road on the crest of the ridge that separates Bates Creek, a tributary of the Soquel, from the easterly fork of the Aptos.

The dense morning fog does not obscure the sight enough to prevent realization of the fact that this Capitola Park road is one of the easiest mountain grades, and one of the grandest drives in the county.

The team is left on the summit and the downfall began ever a fairly good forest trail, which leads ultimately to the abandoned mill site. From the sawmill a railroad ran up the canyon about three miles, on which the logs and wood were hauled. This road, long since abandoned, has passed into the picturesque period. Fresh forest growths have hid the stumps and covered most of the scars made in the landscape by the axman and the fire fiend, and the Aptos creek is one of the most beautiful brooks, as well as one of the best fishing streams, in the county.

Gradually the growth of shrub and vine encroaches upon the former railroad right of way, until only a trail is passable, and then overhanging alders and wild berry vines clasp the entire way, and for a considerable distance a passage is tunneled through, half bent, or on hands and knees. Winter rains have brought down slides, and in places Alpine climbing must be resorted to. The creek murmurs and me-

anders gracefully a hundred feet below, and one misstep, or one sliding rock, or one breaking bush, can land you by its side in a twinkling.

A few fishers and hunters are lured up this canyon, but the thirst of exploration is really the only sufficient incentive.

Shortly after leaving the mill site, a trestle crosses the creek on a curve, at a bend in the stream, making what surgeons would call a "compound" crossing, the creek flowing easterly and again westerly under the trestle. The railroad then hugged the westerly bank of the creek about two thirds of the way up to Monte Vista. There was another trestle crossing about thirty feet above the stream, and here is where the earthquake commenced to do things. This trestle and bridge is a total wreck. Timbers snapped off, iron rods twisted like green withes, and the bridge span dropped into the bed of the brook.

From here onward, the rent or split in the mountain that caused the disaster at Hinckley Gulch and did so much damage in the Eureka Canyon is plainly visible. For half a mile the westerly bank for a height in places of two hundred feet is stripped bare and looks like the shining side of an avalanche.

There is no more railroad track to be seen, except scattered ties lying in and alongside the stream.

The timber left here was not heavy, but the few scattered pines and madrones were tumbled over and tossed about and sent plunging headlong towards the bottom of the canyon.

In places the right, or easterly bank, appears undisturbed. At others the jar evidently brought both banks together and formed dams in the bed of the creek. The first of these is perhaps thirty feet high and about thirty feet wide at the top. It stopped the flow of water entirely for a few days, but now the stream has made an outlet and as time goes on will develop a series of beautiful cascades and pools. This pond is about fifty yards in length.

Where this pond ends another dam begins. Not as high, nor as wide, but the backwater or pond extends a longer distance.

By the time this is passed, we have reached the site of what was once called Monte Vista, where the canyon spreads out, giving glimpses of the Highland orchards and vineyards and the stream forks.

At this point a third dam. It is impossible for a stranger to estimate accurately, but it would appear that the bed of the stream for some distance had probably been raised from twenty to thirty feet by the debris. In the open space here there is a huge moraine, not unlike the one on Deer Creek, although not as deep. This came down the westerly fork of the stream, which it chokes and fills and clogs and dams with varying degrees of depth and density for two miles. (This estimate of distance we took from a hunter met at this point who was familiar with the locality. Trudging and climbing over it under an August sun, it seemed fully twice these figures).

Up here, known to a few hunters and woodsmen, was a body of water covering between two and three acres called "White's Lagoon." It is dry. Its bottom was cracked by the earthquake as a kettle might be. Augmented by the hunters, our party of seven sat midday on a promontory fully forty feet above the former bed of the creek and quietly surveyed the work of thirty seconds, which had completely transformed the face of Nature in this locality.

A little to the left was a huge clump of bushes, with wonderfully broad leaves for a bush. Ah! ha! Not a bush, but the top of a great maple tree, roots, trunk and branches all down below, imbedded in the oozy earth, its more slender branches and topmost twigs visible. Closer inspection showed that all the apparent shrubbery in sight was simply tops of trees. As at Deer creek, the camera fails to catch any adequate conception. It is beyond the scope of any lens. It is beyond the range of physical vision. It is only the eye of the imagination aided by a full view of the locality that can comprehend the magnitude and majesty of the instantaneous movement which wrought these results. A marvelous manifestation of that invisible Power which existed before even the mountains were brought forth, and which endures world without end.

Several other individuals recorded their observations of the impact of the quake on Aptos Creek. Stoodley and others recall that there was once a large lagoon directly above White's Lagoon along China Ridge prior to the temblor. During and shortly after the earthquake, the upper lagoon drained into White's Lagoon, which itself slowly drained until it was dry. The upper lagoon never recovered and was known for several years as the Dry Lagoon. It is now gone entirely due to erosion. Stoodley also remembers several large, noticeable cracks in the ground that have long since disappeared.

One of the best-remembered natural creations of the earthquake was the Crazy Forest, which extended from Amaya Gulch east to beyond the East Branch of Soquel Creek and north to Highland Way. John V. Young wrote extensively of the forest in multiple publications and took several photographs for the *San Francisco Chronicle* in the 1930s. In the November 1941 issue of *American Forests*, he explained:

> *Hard by Loma Prieta Peak, highest point in the Santa Cruz mountain range, seventy miles due south of San Francisco, at the headwaters of Soquel Creek, the Crazy Forest lies sprawled across a vast expanse of green wooded ridges, one of the largest virgin redwood stands remaining in the world—and the only one that grows crooked....*
>
> *Zigzagging through the eastern portion of this virgin stand runs the ragged tangle of topsy-turvy trees that men have come to call the Crazy Forest.*
>
> *Clearly delineating the San Andreas fault, that crack in the earth's surface along which most of the coast's major quakes have occurred, this fifty-acre strip of forest giants was knocked into a Brobdignagian jackstraw pile when the great shake of 1906 slammed across the mountains just at dawn. The temblor hurled some trees, sturdy saplings when Christ was born, to destruction in Soquel Gorge, building a log jam that remains today.*
>
> *It laid other redwoods flat; then from their recumbent forms new trees have sprung, and through years of struggling for light have formed dense clusters of redwood towers in ordered rows along the massive carcasses of their parents.*

> *It threw still others by the hundred aslant, to come to rest with their tops entwined with the limbs of their neighbors to form vast, incredible tents two hundred feet above the earth. Some contrived to stand alone but with a drunken list to their trunks.*
>
> *The quake opened crevices in the steep banks of the Soquel slope and tributary Amaya Creek, gave birth to leaping springs in rocky crannies. Some of these springs sparkle today, surrounded by enormous ferns. Old logging roads and trails, hopelessly blocked by crevices and fallen trees, have by virtue of the springs and the ferns become fairy lanes of greenery, mossy under foot, shaded overhead, fragrant throughout.*
>
> *For fourteen years after the quake, a lake remained where a log jam blocked the creek, until erosion from a forest fire on the eastern slope filled the lake bed with mud. The lake is a morass today, from its murky depths arising the gaunt white skeletons of tall redwoods trapped by the waters and ravaged by the insects.*
>
> *Elsewhere in the mountains the Southern Pacific has long since repaired the damage the quake did to its rails and tunnels from Los Gatos to Santa Cruz; the villages of Wrights and Burrell have straightened their twisted fences, rebuilt their homes and covered their scars.*
>
> *Only the Crazy Forest remains as it was that morning, brooding over the prank Nature played on it, watching a logging crew gnaw at its northern boundary, waiting for the ax and the bandsaw to relegate it, too, to oblivion.*

The Crazy Forest had no one location, but rather was spread across a large area. On a hand-drafted Forest Service "Recreational Desirability" map of the Soquel Unit, dated 1937, it is located three miles to the east of Fern Gulch along the south side of the East Branch of Soquel Creek. This placed the forest within the vicinity of today's Camp Loma, slightly to the east of the railroad flatcar bridge that provides access to the Soquel Demonstration State Forest off Highland Way. However, after a number of exploratory hikes throughout the area, I could not find any evidence of it.

Several persons that I interviewed that had seen the forest placed it along the south side of the East Branch of Soquel Creek but further to the west of the Forest Service's placement on its map. Others that I talked to place the forest along the north side of the creek within the vicinity of Rattlesnake Gulch a mile to the west of Camp Loma. One of the old timers emphatically placed it in Laguna Gulch, now known as Ashbury Gulch, a mile or so to the east of Fern Gulch.

The only conclusion from these contradictions is that the Crazy Forest was not located in one spot—its location was in the eyes of the beholder. Because the entire stretch of the East Branch of Soquel Creek is parallel to or on top of the San Andreas Rift Zone, it stands to reason that the ground would not shake hard enough to send the trees off into "crazy" directions in only one area, but rather along its entire length.[29]

The Loma Prieta Lumber Company recovers its donkey engine from Hinckley Creek

Two weeks after the earthquake, Hinckley Creek was still dammed by a logjam up creek. The *Surf* reported on April 30, 1906:

At Hinckley.

The Water has Backed For a Mile.

Work of excavation with the hydraulic pump started yesterday.

O. C. Moore was at Hinckley yesterday at the former site of the Loma Prieta mill, where the slide occurred during the earthquake.

Mr. Moore says the fill in the canyon has caused the waters of Hinckley creek to back for a mile, forming a lake fifty to sixty feet in depth up against the slide.

A donkey engineer works the rotary pump, the water used coming from the lake, and it will be some days before the seven bodies covered by sixty feet of debris will be recovered.

> *Mr. Moore was in the gulch when the earthquake occurred yesterday at 4 o'clock and said the rumbling was terrific.*

Submerged beneath the murky waters impounded behind the mudslide was a donkey engine that was needed to assist in the cleanup of the area. Several attempts were made to reach it with ropes, but they all failed. In desperation, the Loma Prieta Lumber Company hired a marine diver, G. O. Abrahamsen of the Union Iron Works of San Francisco. It took three dives over four days for a line to be attached to the engine, which was then pulled out by a second donkey engine sitting up on the access wagon road. Their total charges were:

self and assistant	$48.00
First dive	$20.00
Second and third descents	$20.00
Railroads fare, San Francisco to Capitola, and return	$11.20
Expressage	$15.60
TOTAL COST	$114.80

During my early exploratory trips into Hinckley Gulch, I usually entered on the old wagon road that carried the wagons to and from the mill. Sitting below the road's end resting against the side of the gulch between the road and Hinckley Creek was a four-foot diameter, spoked iron wheel that must have weighed around a ton. According to old-timers, the wheel was mounted on a donkey engine to serve as a counterweight to the mainline's drum. When the diver found the engine, he either removed the wheel because of its weight or it had come loose when the engine was submerged. For years it was used as a means to cross the creek until the storm of January 4, 1982 completely buried it under debris.

At some point after the storm, a contest was held to try and locate the so-called 'lost engine of Nisene Marks.' During this competition, several youths rediscovered the wheel and claimed it was part of the lost engine. The judges agreed and granted them prize money for its discovery.[30]

More destruction along Aptos and Hinckley Creeks

The *Surf* on May 8, 1906 reported further destruction along Aptos and Hinckley Creeks caused by the earthquake. It stated:

>### CREEKS DAMMED
>
>#### Slides on the Aptos and Soquel streams.
>
>#### Two Lagoons Beyond Monte Vista Are Dry—Work at Hinckley
>
>*The Aptos Creek, towards the mouth, does not contain much running water, caused by a number of land slides along its course, especially in the vicinity of Monte Vista and Hells Gate, where slides at places completely dammed the creek.*
>
>*Two good sized lagoons—White's and Buzzard's, above the old site of Monte Vista, are entirely dry—something unheard of for this time of the year—caused by seepage through the fissures.*
>
>*The work of removing the debris by the hydraulic system in Hinckley creek moves slowly, and it will be some time before the bodies of the seven unfortunate men are recovered.*
>
>*The mill, if rebuilt, will be about two miles above the old site, and the road will be along the top of the western ridge.*
>
>*Soquel Creek is also impeded at several places by large landslides, and the water of the creek is very dirty.*[31]

The Loma Prieta Lumber Company's slow recovery

The earthquake immediately halted all of the Loma Prieta Lumber Company's operations along Hinckley Creek and it would be over a decade before it fully recovered from the disaster. Besides the loss of machinery and the destruction to its timberlands, the company also lost several workers in the temblor and were struggling to recover their bodies a month after the quake. On May 12, 1906, the *Mountain Echo* reported:

SEVEN OF NINE BODIES STILL MISSING AT HINCKLEY CREEK MILL SITE

Even with the aid of hydraulic machinery, the Loma Prieta Lumber Company has as yet been unable to recover the bodies of the seven missing men. It is now but 10 days short of a month since the quake. The Loma Prieta Lumber Company officials claim that the earth in the hillside is extremely hard to move, but they expect to locate the mill very soon.

Bert Stoodley in his memoirs gives more details regarding the search for the buried victims:

> the frantic relatives continued to urge the company to ever greater efforts to recover the bodies. Two bodies were recovered the first couple of days, but it took almost a month to find the rest. One of the cooks was found with his head still in the stove, he was in the process of putting biscuits in the oven. All of the men in the cookhouse were killed except for one—he escaped by exiting through the creek-side door, the rest left by the front door and were caught in the sliding mud. According to reports of the tragedy, eight of the nine bodies were recovered. The ninth man, Charley June, the Chinese cook, was thought to have run off after the ground stopped shaking never to be seen again.

This quote includes an obvious dismissiveness regarding June's likely death. If he ran off, how did he get out of the gulch and where did he go? Why wasn't he seen in the county again? He would have had to flee the cookhouse while the ground was still shaking, escaping out the creek-side door, which is suspicious since the cookhouse's only known survivor fled out the same door and did not see him. Once outside, he would have either climbed the precariously steep hillside to the ridge or climbed down and crossed the creek, which would have been nearly impossible due to the mudslide that destroyed the mill.

The most likely truth is that June was buried in the slide alongside his companions but nobody cared to look for his body once the other eight

A Great Calamity 1906

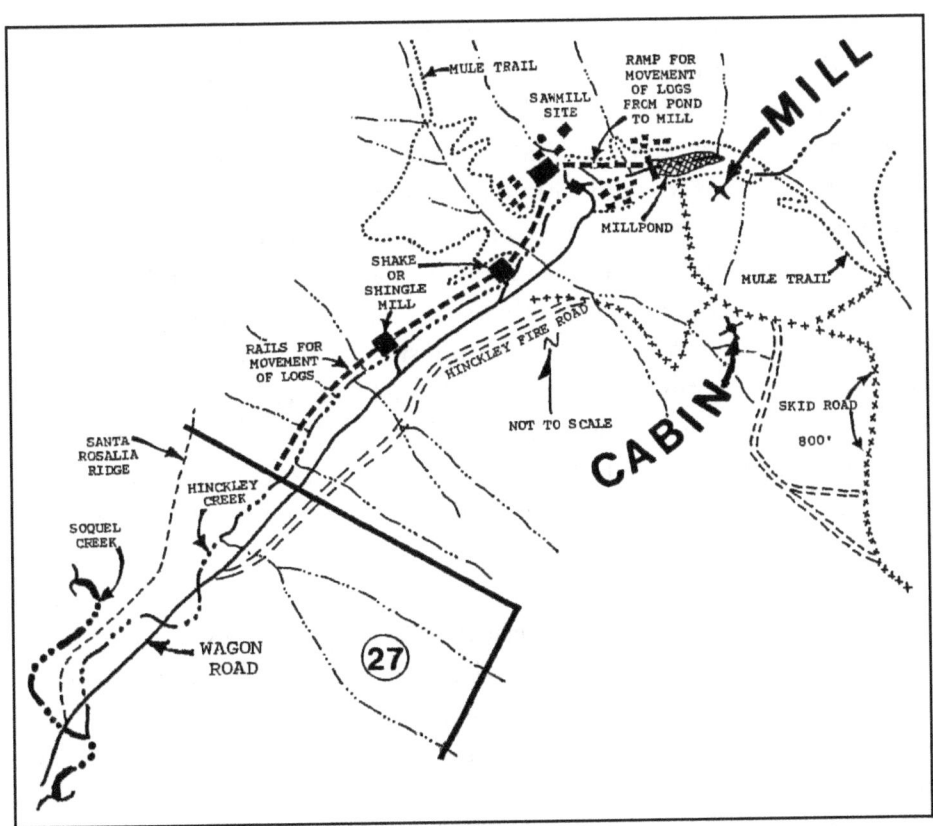

FIGURE 2.2 LAYOUT OF THE LOMA PRIETA LUMBER COMPANY'S MILL ON HINCKLEY CREEK AT THE TIME OF THE EARTHQUAKE

were recovered. Anti-Chinese sentiment was strong in the early 1900s and his death would have been easy to ignore. According to Earl LaPorte, June's body was in fact recovered late in 1906 during cleanup of the mill site. Crews were using a donkey engine to remove a boulder only to discover it was a mud-encrusted June. His ultimate fate was not disclosed but it seems likely he was buried nearby in an unmarked grave, his body's discovery not reported to any authority at the time.

Previous descriptions of the slide at the mill site suggest that an entire side of Santa Rosalia Ridge collapsed into Hinckley Creek, but there were actually two smaller slides. The southern slide was just below the mill and created the logjam that impounded the creek and created the lake that extended a mile upstream, destroying the milling facility. The other slide was beside the millpond and crashed into the cookhouse and bunkhouse.

By the beginning of June, eight bodies had been recovered and the logjam had been carefully dislodged, allowing the lake to slowly drain. Salvage teams moved in to recover what they could from the muddy creek bed. Little of use was recovered from either the main mill or from the smaller shake and shingle mills downstream. Cruisers exploring the damage between the mills and the camp a mile and a half upstream found their route blocked by several slides, with other slides blocking the creek. During one of my exploratory hikes between the mill site and the logging camp, I came across a string of logs lying in the creek, each the same length and roughly two feet in diameter that obviously were on their way to the millpond when the quake occurred. Although there were no deaths at the worker camp upstream, there was extensive damage, enough that any attempt to reactivate the camp would be futile.

At the time of the earthquake, the Loma Prieta Lumber Company's top management consisted of President Timothy Hopkins, who made decisions from his office in San Francisco, and Vice President and General Manager A. C. Bassett, who no longer lived in Santa Cruz County. The men had many ideas and in the years before the earthquake, they had wanted to log an eight-mile stretch of Pescadero Creek, as well as some land in Big Basin through their Pescadero Lumber Company. However, just before setting up their mill in 1900, they were approached by Henry L. Middleton of the Union Lumber Company, who convinced them to pool their assets together and form the Big Basin Lumber Company. As they once more prepared to set up a mill, they were interrupted again, this time by the Sempervirens Club, who bought the land and established the California Redwood Park, now Big Basin Redwoods State Park. The negotiations regarding this park, as well as continued efforts by the partners to harvest the timber along Pescadero Creek, meant that they had little time for the disrupted operations of the Loma Prieta Lumber Company on Hinckley Creek.

Locally, the highest-ranking officer of the company was its secretary, Alfred Williams. He was supported by Bert Stoodley, the bookkeeper, and Bert's assistant, Oscar Chase, as well as the logging superintendent, Fred Severance. This group of men, in consultation with Hopkins and Bassett, came to the conclusion in summer 1906 that, while a new mill on Hinckley Creek was necessary, it would never reach a capacity to effectively compete with the F. A. Hihn Company's mill at Laurel. Thus, they began searching for new places near unharvested timber that could support a lumber mill.

Meanwhile, in the gulch, management decided to build a new, smaller mill on higher ground from the former mill. Several locations were considered, but they finally settled on a place directly above the millpond near the 720-foot elevation point on the southeast bank of Hinckley Creek. They reasoned that, after the mill was operating, logs from the main millpond could be pulled up to the mill and placed in a smaller millpond before being processed. Remains of this second mill still exist above the creek. When hiking along the Hinckley Fire Road, turn left at the old cabin across the meadow and toward the creek. Just before descending to the creek, you can see the remains of the complex in the trees to the right of the trail, including the small millpond.

The cost of rebuilding the mill and the need for a larger, more profitable mill elsewhere meant that the company was in dire need of funds. They turned to the company's shareholders, but a bylaw prohibited the issuing of additional stock. Therefore, following several meetings, it was decided to amend the rules so that the investor pool could grow. Of the 3,257 existing shares, each valued at $100, 1,380 were owned by Hopkins and 600 by Bassett, who together controlled the company. After the mid-1906 meetings, another 325 shares were sold, of which Hopkins bought 310, J. S. Severance 10, and C. H. Redington 5. According to Stoodley's ledger book, this meant that the company's shares were divided as follows:[32]

Timothy Hopkins	1,690 shares
A. C. Bassett	600
John T. Porter Company	500
E. J. Sanborn (Alvin Sanborn's widow)	300
Stephen T. Gage	277
Warren R. Porter (John's son)	100
Helen A. Sanborn (Alvin's daughter)	100
J. S. Severance	10
C. H. Redington	5

The F. A. Hihn Company purchases a shingle mill from Samuel Rambo

Although its operations were not directly impacted by the earthquake, the F. A. Hihn Company was still in a bind after April 18, 1906. The quake had severed the Laurel mill's rail connection to San José with the collapse of the Summit Tunnel. The route to Santa Cruz, after some quick remediation, was cleared by early July, but shipping was more difficult and less profitable that way. In late May, the company purchased Samuel H. Rambo's shingle mill that had been operating for many years in Boulder Creek.

Rambo was a businessman operating a mercantile and lumber store in Boulder Creek. To supply his lumber business, he operated several mills in the San Lorenzo Valley, having made his first purchase of land there in the early 1880s. Around the turn of the century, he decided that it was time to exit the lumber business and began selling several of his mills, the first of which was this shingle mill purchased by the Hihn Company. J. B. Richards of the Watsonville Lumber Company was responsible for the deconstruction of the mill and its transfer to the headwaters of the West Branch of Soquel Creek near Laurel within Tract 16 of the Augmentation. The mill had a capacity of 50,000 shingles per day and around 20 men were expected to work at the mill once it reopened. With this mill supplementing the larger mill, which could not ship at optimum capacity, life at Laurel slowly resumed.

Elsewhere, the company also sought a new timber tract to harvest that would be less impacted by repairs and upgrades to the railroad. The company finally found a suitable property on King's Creek owned by a Mr. Newman. The location was ideal because the Dougherty Extension Railroad ran at the bottom of the hill and Southern Pacific Railroad officials had planned before the earthquake to take over the privately-owned narrow-gauge railroad and standard-gauge it. The Hihn Company bought stumpage rights from Newman and promptly began preparing the site for a mill.[33]

Hester Creek School opens on the Summit

In summer 1906, parents living within the vicinity of Soquel San Jose Road met in the home of R. S. Griffith. They were concerned that their children had to walk over a mile and a half in the rain during the winter months in order to reach the closest high school, which was located on Skyland Road above the road's junction with Miller Road. As a result of this meeting, the parents petitioned Santa Cruz County Superintendent C. S. Price to form a new school district and construct a high school. Both were quickly approved. Residents then pooled their resources and skills to build a 26' by 30' one-room schoolhouse at a cost of $200.

The new school, named Hester Creek School, was located at 15155 Stetson Road, on the west side of Soquel San Jose Road just below Smith Valley Road within today's Hester Creek Farms property. It opened on September 1 with Miss C. Tempelten as its first teacher. The school remained operating until 1949 when it was merged with the Summit, Burrell, and Highland Schools to form the Loma Prieta Joint Union School District. The building was sold to become the Hester Creek Community Church, but has since been demolished.[34]

Reconstruction of Hinckley Creek mill almost completed

After a difficult eight months following the earthquake, the Loma Prieta Lumber Company's mill on Hinckley Creek was nearly ready to reopen in January 1907. At the beginning of the month, the timber framework was completed. Machinery, both recovered and new, had been stored along the road to the mill at turnouts and convenient places awaiting installation. Winter weather, though, delayed final installation of the machinery.[35]

The Loma Prieta Lumber Company leases 1,000 acres of timberland on Mill Creek near Swanton

The *Surf* reported on January 14, 1907:

> **LOMA PRIETA LUMBER CO.**
>
> **Planning Operations on a Large Scale for Coming Season.**
>
> *It transpires today that the Loma Prieta Lumber Company, through A. L. Davelay of Boulder Creek, has secured the timber on a 1000 acre tract on Mill creek, and also made purchase of the [Samuel] Rambo mill on Scott's Creek, which will be moved to Mill creek, and is expected to be ready for cutting lumber by the 1st of April.*
>
> *The mill will be located about a mile above the Swanton postoffice on the coast, and a new town will probably spring up at this point, as about 175 men will be employed, and the run is expected to last for about six years.*
>
> *The new mill on Hinckley creek belonging to this company is nearly complete, and will be ready for sawing by the first of next month, unless delayed by the rains.*
>
> *With these two mills in operation, the Loma Prieta Company will be a more important factor in the lumber market than ever before. Shipments will be made from Mill creek on the Ocean Shore railway, as soon as it is in operation, or if the opening of the road is delayed, the lumber will be hauled to Santa Cruz by team.*

The acreage secured by the Loma Prieta Lumber Company on Mill Creek had been logged thirty years earlier, but because of its isolation and the difficulty of transporting the lumber, only the smallest and most easily handled timber was cut and shipped from the creek.[36]

Mills open for the season

Around mid-May 1907, after the rains had slackened and the ground began to dry, the Loma Prieta Lumber Company opened its new mill on Mill Creek. The former Rambo mill on Scott's Creek was relocated in February and construction was completed around May 18. A. L. Davelay was appointed superintendent of the 75 men constructing the facility. Because the Ocean Shore Railroad had as yet failed to build a branch line up Scott Creek to Swanton, all milled lumber was hauled by wagon south. It is unknown whether the lumber was transferred to railroad flatcars at Davenport or hauled directly to the Southern Pacific's Union Depot in Santa Cruz.

Meanwhile, the F. A. Hihn Company's mill faced several obstacles. Although construction of the facility was completed in March, the necessary machinery from the Laurel mill was stuck in Laurel due to an especially wet late winter and early spring. And with such low traffic along the railroad line between Laurel and Felton, combined with a poor economy, Southern Pacific work crews took their time making the necessary repairs to the track. By the time the machinery finally made its way up above Boulder Creek to the bottom of Kings Creek, where the machinery was then hauled up the creek 2.5 miles to the confluence of Logan Creek, it was nearly the end of summer and the company only had a few months to operate until shutting down for the season.[37]

The Loma Prieta Lumber Company moves the Hinckley mill to Aptos Creek

On May 18, 1907, despite having just completed construction of its new mill on Hinckley Gulch, the Loma Prieta Lumber Company decided to relocate the machinery from this mill to the former mill on Aptos Creek beside the former village of Loma Prieta. There are several reasons why the company decided to do this. The Southern Pacific Railroad still had a railroad line to the former village which meant lumber could be delivered from the mill to customers on short notice, which was needed as San Francisco continued to rebuild after the earthquake. Indeed, the former lumber yard with all of its railroad spurs was still intact and usable. Also, the millpond was full after a wet winter and spring, and several support structures were sitting vacant around the pond, including a cookhouse and bunkhouses. On the other hand, the Hinckley was a broken place. Pulling logs to the millpond across muddy and earthquake-damaged skid roads would be difficult, demoralizing, and potentially unprofitable. And newspapers at the time do not mention any support facilities at the mill, suggesting none had been built by the spring of 1907. Instead, the company decided to collect whatever it could from the gulch and transport it by wagon to Opal, where it would be transferred to flatcars and taken to the mill at Loma Prieta for processing. It was not an ideal solution, but it seemed to be the only option at the time.

Two weeks after making the decision, Timothy Hopkins, president of the Loma Prieta Lumber Company, approached Frederick Hihn, chairman of the F. A. Hihn Company, to lease an easement through Tract 10 in the Augmentation. Hopkins hoped to save money by hauling logs directly over Hinckley Ridge to the old mill, but this required the company to pass through Hihn's property. On May 29, an agreement was made between the two men. It allowed the Loma Prieta Lumber Company to place and operate a donkey engine on Hihn's land 1,500 feet south of the junction between the Spignet Divide and Hinckley Ridge. This placed it at the headwaters of today's Big Tree Gulch in The Forest of Nisene Marks, about one mile southwest of the West Ridge Trail Camp. The company was also allowed to lay piping from Spignet Gulch to the engine to provide it with a water supply. Lastly, the company was permitted to build a skid road from the point where logs would enter the tract to where they would leave it at the boundary of Tract 9. The value of any trees on Hihn's land that had to be removed for one of the above purposes would be paid to the Hihn Company.

Hihn was personally worried about the future of the trees in Big Tree Gulch. It contained some of the largest redwoods left in Santa Cruz County and Hihn enjoyed them for their natural beauty. He wanted to protect the four largest trees in the gulch, as well as several smaller ones nearby, by gifting the land to the county for use as a park. But the gulch's isolation made the plan impractical, so he held onto the hope that it would

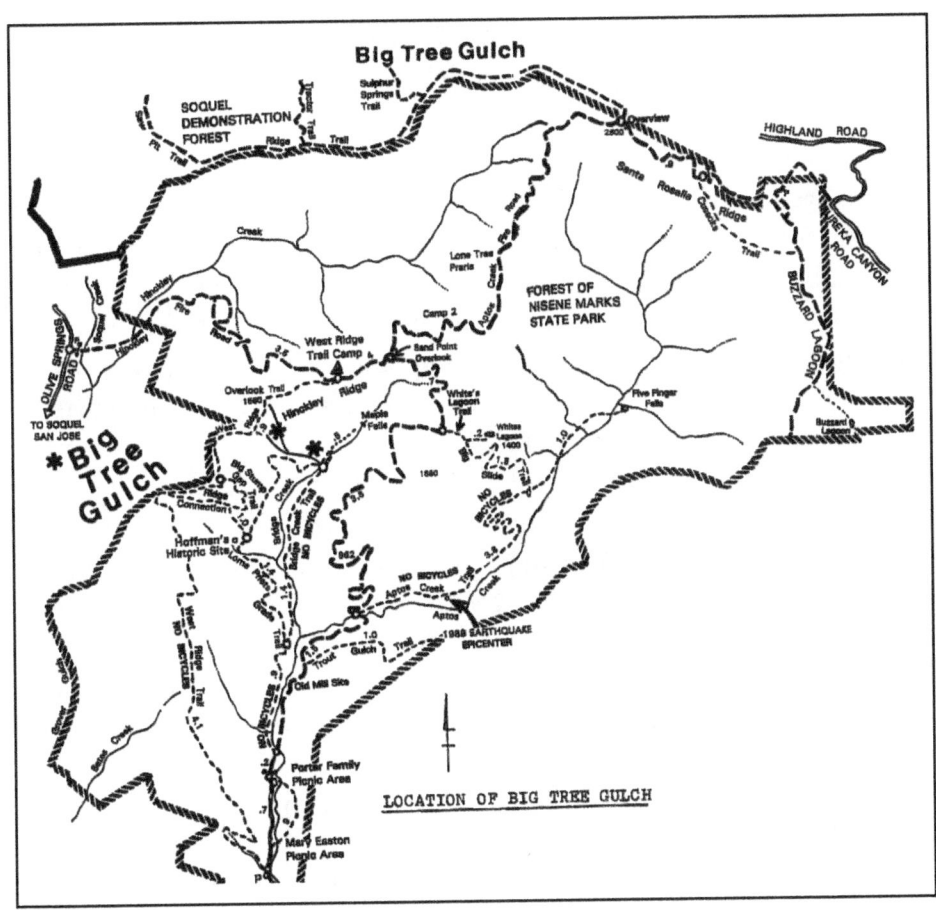

FIGURE 2.3 LOCATION OF BIG TREE GULCH ON BRIDGE CREEK WITHIN THE FOREST OF NISENE MARKS STATE PARK

one day be preserved.

Returning to the agreement, in exchange for the easement and other provisos, Hopkins agreed to allow the Hihn Company to "build, maintain and operate a skid road, a pole road, a railroad, a wagon road, or any combination" of right-of-way through the Bridge Creek section of Tract 9. Furthermore, he allowed the company to install telegraph or telephone lines between the headwaters of Bridge Creek and Loma Prieta Station. Lastly, the Hihn Company was allowed to transport logs to the lumber yard at the Loma Prieta mill so that they could be loaded onto Southern Pacific flatcars. The agreement between Hopkins and Hihn was to last five years.[38]

The Southern Pacific Railroad cuts back the Loma Prieta Branch to Spring Creek

According to Southern Pacific Railroad records, the Loma Prieta Branch was cut back from a terminus 4.78 miles north of Aptos, at the former site of Monte Vista No. 1, to the 4.27-mile marker at Spring Creek, around the end of June 1907. This change reflected the fact that the fourth bridge over Aptos Creek had been destroyed in the 1906 earthquake, thereby making travel to the track's official terminus impossible. The railroad agreed to keep the track here rather than truncate it further to the 3.7-mile marker in the former village of Loma Prieta, because the Loma Prieta Lumber Company hoped to haul logs over Hinckley and China Ridge and one of the potential collection points was the bottom of Spring Creek. If all went according to plan, logs would be high-wired over the ridges and down Spring Creek, where they would be loaded onto waiting flatcars either parked on the main track or on a spur. In exchange for maintaining the branch line to Spring Creek, Timothy Hopkins agreed to supply firewood from his Tract 8 property to the railroad for the duration that the Loma Prieta Lumber Company was harvesting timber in Hinckley Gulch.

Hopkins chose a section of uncut redwood along Long Gulch just to the north of the Rancho Aptos boundary as the source for the firewood he would provide to Southern Pacific. An 800-foot-long spur line was installed along the gulch, probably using rails and ties salvaged from the abandoned 0.51 miles of track north of Spring Creek. The path of this spur can easily be found today as the first part of the West Ridge Trail, accessible shortly after crossing the vehicular bridge in The Forest of Nisene Marks State Park.

Hopkins employed a crew of four or five Chinese workers to cut the timber and prepare the cords for shipment. They lived in three or four small cabins that sat about 200 yards to the north of Long Gulch on the Aptos Creek side of today's Aptos Creek Fire Road in a clearing now occupied by the Mary Easton Picnic Area. At the time, this location became known as China Camp and Long Gulch was nicknamed China Canyon.

After the trees were cut and the bark was removed, pack mules hauled the four-foot-long cords down to the Long Gulch spur where boxcars were waiting to be loaded. Before the cords were transferred to the cars,

A Great Calamity 1907

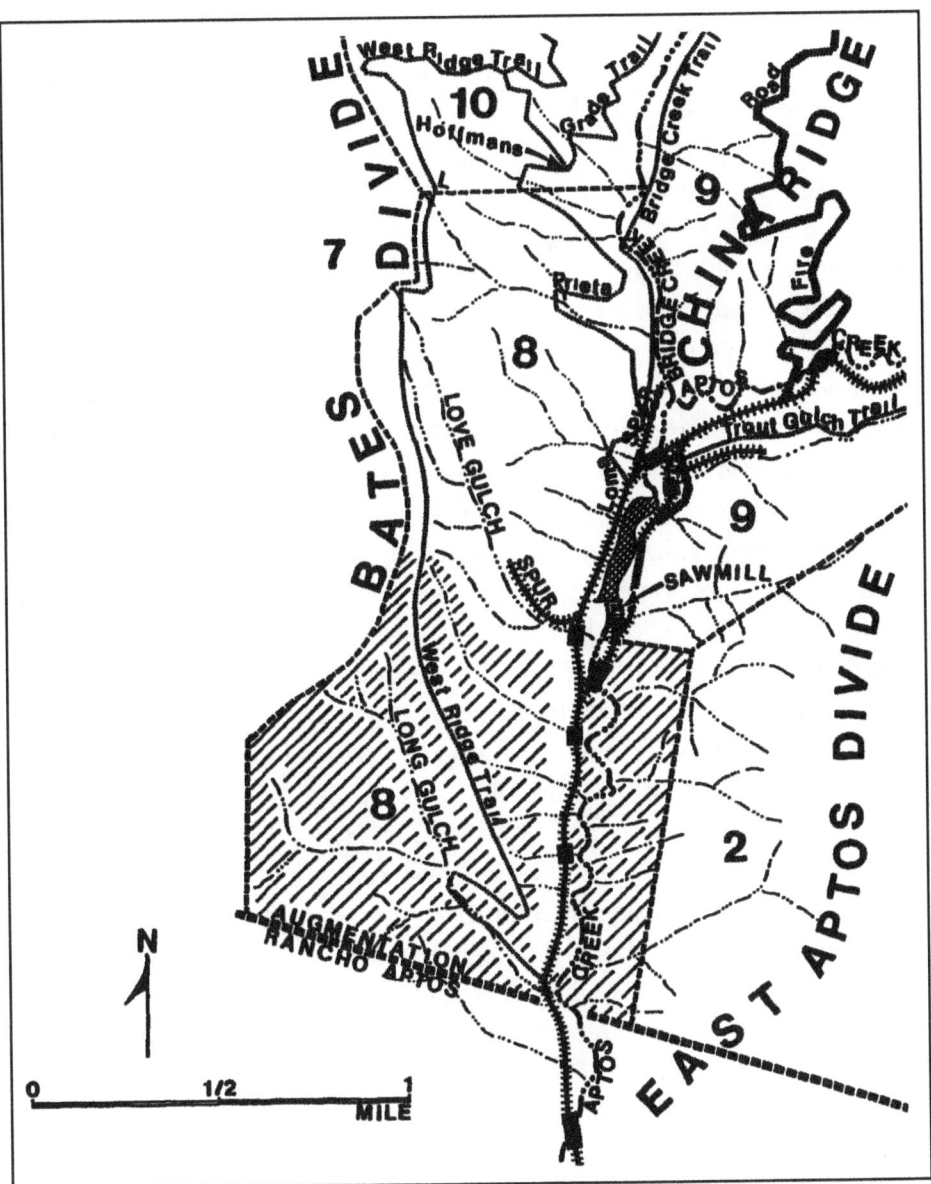

FIGURE 2.4 SOUTHERN PACIFIC TRACKAGE ON APTOS CREEK, 1907

they were cut in half—to two feet long—so that they could be used in locomotive boilers as firewood. A donkey engine was installed beside the spur to quickly cut the cords on site. The cords were then taken to train yards throughout the area where they could be used to bring under-repair locomotive engines up to proper pressure before the fuelwood could be replaced with oil in the firebox.[39]

The Panic of 1907

On March 13, 1907, the value of shares traded on the New York Stock Exchange plummeted. It was the presage of more financial woes to come. Over the following months, the flawed and poorly-regulated banking and credit sectors panicked and the United States fell into a depression. On October 22, the Knickerbocker Trust Company of New York was forced to suspend operations, prompting banks across the country to attempt to withdraw their cash reserves from New York City banks. The federal government called on John Pierpont Morgan, the nation's leading financier, for help. By the force of his personality, Morgan secured the cooperation of his fellow bankers, who combined their resources to import $100,000,000 in gold from Europe to restore confidence and end what came to be known as the Panic of 1907. Although the panic is said to have ended on November 6, its impact continued until June 1908 and beyond. The passage of the Aldrich–Vreeland Act on May 30, 1908 established the National Monetary Commission, which led five years later to the formation of the Federal Reserve System.

On the Central Coast of California, the Panic of 1907 led to a short-term collapse of the lumber and lime industries. At the same time, Southern Pacific shelved its plan to take over the Dougherty Extension Railroad, standard-gauge it, and extend it up to the F. A. Hihn Company's King's Creek mill. Even its in-process job of upgrading the South Pacific Coast Railway's narrow-gauge track across the Santa Cruz Mountains was delayed. This meant that all wood products shipped out from the Hihn Company's Laurel mill would continue to be shipped south to Santa Cruz and then transferred to standard-gauge trains heading to Pajaro and beyond.[40]

Mills open for the season

With California slowly recovering from the Panic of 1907, local lumber companies hoped to turn some profit in 1908. Both of the F. A. Hihn Company's mills—on King's Creek and at Laurel—started up in late winter at near full capacity. The Laurel mill in particular was in a position to benefit from a railroad connection to the Bay Area following the reopening of the Summit Tunnel to Wrights in September 1907. The line was now standard-gauged and the Hihn Company quickly upgraded its trackage to support the new gauge. However, direct market access did not mean increased profits, since the lumber market was still in a slump. After operating for less than a month, the Laurel mill shut down in early June, with the *Sentinel* reporting that "the present low price of lumber has made it inexpedient for the Hihn Co. to run both of their two mills." The company also resumed cutting splitstuff on Gold Gulch near Felton and along Valencia Creek within Tracts 2 and 5 in the Augmentation to supplement its income.

Meanwhile, the Loma Prieta Lumber Company resumed its operations for the season. The Ocean Shore Railway was still not extended beyond Davenport, so wagonloads of lumber were shipped to Davenport, where they were likely loaded onto flatcars of the Coast Line Railroad, a subsidiary of Southern Pacific that had reached Davenport in early 1908. In Hinckley Gulch, crews cut splitstuff, which were hauled to the Opal lumberyard for export or further processing. At the old Aptos Creek mill, the boilers from Hinckley Gulch were finally in place to begin milling timber brought over from the gulch. Throughout the late winter and early spring, logs cut from the gulch had been hauled out by wagons, transferred to Southern Pacific flatcars at Opal, and then shipped to the millpond on Aptos Creek. But this laborious process was about to change.

When the Loma Prieta Lumber Company's management made their decision in late 1907 to pull the remaining logs from Hinckley Gulch to their refurbished mill in Loma Prieta, they surely did not envision the difficulties and expense that they would and did encounter. It took me over eleven years of periodic searching to discover the overland route that the logs took. It was Rick Hamman who informed me that the logs were pulled over Hinckley Ridge, and several old-timers confirmed it in interviews, but I did not know where to begin my search. Both the Hopkins–Hihn agreement and the truncation of the Loma Prieta Branch

FIGURE 2.5 ROUTE LOGS TRAVELED OVERLAND FROM HINCKLEY GULCH TO THE LOMA PRIETA LUMBER COMPANY'S MILL ON APTOS CREEK

by Southern Pacific, discussed above, provided clues. Little by little, piece by piece, clue by clue, I discovered the route from the gulch to the bottom of Spring Creek, where the logs were loaded onto waiting railroad flatcars. The following are my findings:

Hinckley Ridge Pond: The logs began their journey about a quarter mile north of Sand Point, which is along today's Aptos Creek Fire Road. Here at an elevation of 1,500 feet, there is a depression in the ground that the road curves around to continue its journey up the ridge between the headwaters of Hinckley and Bridge Creeks. In this depression is a small pond which the Loma Prieta Lumber Company used to temporarily deposit its logs from Hinckley Gulch and the surrounding hillsides. To ensure the pond maintained sufficient depth for the operation, water was piped into it from nearby springs. Beside the pond, cutters using donkey engines cut the logs into smaller sizes so that they could continue on their journey. Other donkey engines were used throughout the area to drag logs to the pond, with some logs so far away that several engines had to be used in relay.

Point A: After the log was cut to its proper size and weight, it was pulled by cable northward for about 1,000 feet. A portion of the path the logs traveled can still be identified. It begins on the north side of the Aptos Creek Fire Road at the top of the sharp U-shaped curve around the pond. From there, the path can be followed for several hundred feet until it disappears into vegetation. Beyond this, a donkey engine sat on a narrow shelf at about 1,600-foot elevation. Once there, logs were mounted onto a highline cable measuring 2,800 feet long, which carried the logs across several gullies until reaching a slight ridge near the West Ridge Trail Camp west of Sand Point at 1,400-foot elevation. The gullies were separated by narrow, steep ridges, one of which exceeded the clearance for suspended logs. As a result, the lumber company made a cut through the ridge, roughly 40 feet deep, 15 feet wide, and 75 feet long. To find this cut today, follow the Hinckley Basin Fire Road a short distance from Sand Point, where the road makes a sharp turn. Instead of turning south, continue northwest from the top of the curve through low vegetation along a narrow ridge. After about 650 feet, you will encounter the bottom of the cut.

Point B: When logs arrived at the donkey engine, they were dragged by another donkey engine to the vicinity of today's West Ridge Trail Camp. The journey between the cable and the camp was about 1,200 feet. Unfortunately, its exact path is unclear since Mother Nature and the construction of the Hinckley Basin Fire Road and the West Ridge Trail have obliterated all evidence of the logging operation here.

Point C: The next donkey engine was seated 4,800 feet to the southwest at the top of Big Tree Gulch. This was the engine that Frederick Hihn allowed the Loma Prieta Lumber Company to place on his land in the 1907 agreement. Although both ends of the route were at approximately 1,400-foot elevation, the cable was forced to drag logs up to 1,560 feet to surmount a ridge blocking a direct line between the two ends. Much of this route is paralleled today by the West Ridge Trail, while the staging area for the donkey engine at the top of Big Tree Gulch is still discernible as an open, circular area surrounded by trees and low vegetation. Just to the south of the staging area there is an outcropping of rocks known to early surveyors as "Granite Point."

Point D: The next donkey engine was situated 5,000 feet away across Bridge Creek on China Ridge near 1,200-foot elevation. Logs were dragged the first 2,600 feet of the distance from the top of Big Tree Gulch to near the bottom, at 700-foot elevation. The first 1,000 feet of this journey was through a narrow, rocky channel while the remainder was along a wide, sloping area formed by the gulch's stream.

Point D: The rest of the journey of the logs to the top of the ridge was aerial and the donkey engine's cable became a highline. A staging area was maintained here to prepare logs for the ascent up the steep hillside. The point where this occurred can be found by following the Loma Prieta Grade Trail beyond Hoffman's Historic Site. Where the trail makes a sharp right turn back toward Bridge Creek, instead of following the trail, continue north. After a short descent, there is a level meadow that was artificially widened for the staging area.

Point E: Once the logs made the ascent to 1,200-foot elevation on China Ridge, they were assembled in a large, level clearing which today forms part of the Aptos Creek Fire Road about halfway between Aptos Creek and Sand Point. From there, the logs were dragged over the top of the ridge to the headwaters of Spring Creek.

Point F: From the top of Spring Creek, one final cable dragged and suspended logs 3,800 feet down the gulch to the railroad grade (**Point G**) on the south side of Aptos Creek. From there, the logs were loaded onto waiting flatcars and taken to the millpond further down the railroad grade.

The entire journey from above Hinckley Gulch to Aptos Creek spanned around 3.5 miles. To allow donkey engine operators and assembly crews to communicate effectively across this vast and complicated system, telephone wires were suspended from tree branch to tree branch across China and Hinckley Ridges. Some of these wires can still be seen today with a keen eye.[41]

Forest fire at Olive Springs

On March 15, 1908, a fire broke out near Olive Springs just south of the Loma Prieta Lumber Company's timberland. The *Surf* reported on the following day:

Twenty acres burn near Olive Springs

Fire Warden Welch and a number of men fought fire for five hours yesterday and saved valuable timber land for the Loma Prieta Company and as a result, a warrant has been issued charging William Smith with setting fire without a permit.

Welch noticed the fire and with a dozen men started from Soquel Creek and went to the scene of the big blaze.

They were on what is known as the "hog's back," the division between the Hinckley and Soquel creek gulches and from two to seven in the afternoon fought hard and continuously against the spreading of the fire, which was in the wild lilac,

> etc., but as fast as they put it out it came spreading up the hill.
>
> Mr. Welch decided to investigate and went down the very steep mountain side, where he found William Smith, who had been setting the fire to burn off the brush so that he could plant out a vineyard.
>
> The fire was within fifty feet of the timber of the Loma Prieta Lumber Company at a place where they are getting out a big lot of shingle bolts.
>
> At this point Welch and his crew fought the fierce flames by back firing and if they had not been there, there was no way to keep it from spreading to the timber and which would have burned without doubt, from olive to Sulphur spring, amidst the fine lot of virgin timber of that section.
>
> As it was, over twenty acres of brush land were burned over, but Smith will have to stand for breaking the state statute.

Smith owned a triangular section of Tract 27 in the Augmentation that was situated on the East Branch of Soquel Creek north of Santa Rosalia Ridge, where Roger Hinckley and John Shelby had built and operated a water-powered sawmill in 1858.[42]

The Loma Prieta Lumber Company establishes a eucalyptus nursery on Tract 9

In early spring 1908, the Loma Prieta Lumber Company began planting eucalyptus trees within Tract 9 in the Augmentation in an attempt to regrow profitable timber in an area logged over thirty-five years earlier. The trees that formed the nursery were planted in the vicinity of the Compound, west and across Aptos Creek from the mill. An article dated April 1, 1908 from an unknown newspaper, possibly the *Santa Cruz News*, explains:

> ### Eucalyptus Forest to cover the Cut-Over Region of Aptos Creek and its Tributaries
>
> *The Loma Prieta Lumber Company is extensively experimenting with the planting of eucalyptus trees on land at the*

> *old Loma Prieta mill beyond Aptos.*
>
> *Mr. A. C. Bassett states that they have planted thousands of trees of different varieties of the eucalyptus for timber purposes on the lands from which they have already removed redwood and which, if they had planted fifteen years ago would be worth at present $500 an acre. Mr. Bassett also states that this section is the best land along the coast for the raising of eucalyptus trees, and especially at the place where they are experimenting, as the hardy eucalyptus require moisture, which is there, as well as a rich soil. The undergrowth there is just rank enough for the proper shade required, and which they do not have further south.*
>
> *One of the main varieties planted is the Rostrata, or red Gum, a hard wood timber, especially adapted for interior finishing, flooring and furniture; also the Corynocalyl, a sugar gum, which makes fine timber.*
>
> *Another variety is the Globulne, also a hard wood. Another is the "Iron Bark Black Butt," and the Maraliofiro, a valuable wood, as well as the blue gum.*
>
> *They are also experimenting with the She oak, a hardy tree from New Zealand, a red wood, especially good for use in the making of mallets, etc.*
>
> *The Melanoxyli is a species of acacia used principally for the manufacture of gun stocks and furniture. The experiment will no doubt prove successful, and Mr. Bassett states that his company will continue the planting of these trees over their vast areas of timber land already cleared. He also believes that this will be done on a large scale everywhere in this section so adapted to the growth of these trees.*

At the time that the Loma Prieta Lumber Company was experimenting with eucalyptus, people thought that they could be as valuable as redwood. Yet as time passed, it became clear that eucalyptus was mostly good at absorbing water and acting as a wind screen. Thus, they were often planted alongside railroad rights-of-way and roads to keep them as dry as possible, and they were planted in fields across the Central Valley to quickly soak up water from seasonal floods and protect crops from the wind. Unfortunately, eucalyptus cannot survive a frost and are as quick to die as they are to grow, so most people turned to other trees by the middle of the twentieth century.

The value of eucalyptus as a timber source was also quickly disproven. As the cut timber dried out, it warped and twisted into shapes, making it useless for anything but firewood. But the Loma Prieta Lumber Company did not realize this immediately. After an extensive search for the ideal variety of eucalyptus in late 1908, the company settled on a species in early 1909 and planted several in the nursery. However, the hot summer of 1909 led to the deaths of many of the trees before they could sufficiently take root. In December, a harsh frost that brought temperatures on Aptos Creek to 18°F killed off more of the young trees. The lumber company announced in spring 1910 its plan to plant as many as 30,000 new seedlings, but they clearly came to their senses and stopped the project shortly afterwards.

In the ensuing years, it became clear that a small number of seedlings had survived and spread beyond their designated area. They matured into full-sized eucalyptus trees and were never harvested. All attempts to remove them have failed, so eucalyptus can still be found today in The Forest of Nisene Marks State Park on either side of the creek in the vicinity of the mill site.[43]

The F. A. Hihn Company opens a shingle mill on the East Branch of Soquel Creek

At some point in the spring of 1908, the F. A. Hihn Company opened a shingle mill on Tract 11 in the Augmentation along the south side of the East Branch of Soquel Creek. The mill was located on the flat area that today is the parking lot for the Soquel Demonstration State Forest off Highland Way. There is evidence within the vicinity of the parking lot of three millponds: two shallow ponds above the mill site and a larger pond located below it near the bridge over Soquel Creek. Products made at the mill would either be transported over Rider Road (now Buzzard Lagoon Road) or over a rough, narrow, dirt road that becomes Eureka Canyon Road at Grizzly Flat. The products would then continue to Watsonville, where they could be shipped to customers via rail.[44]

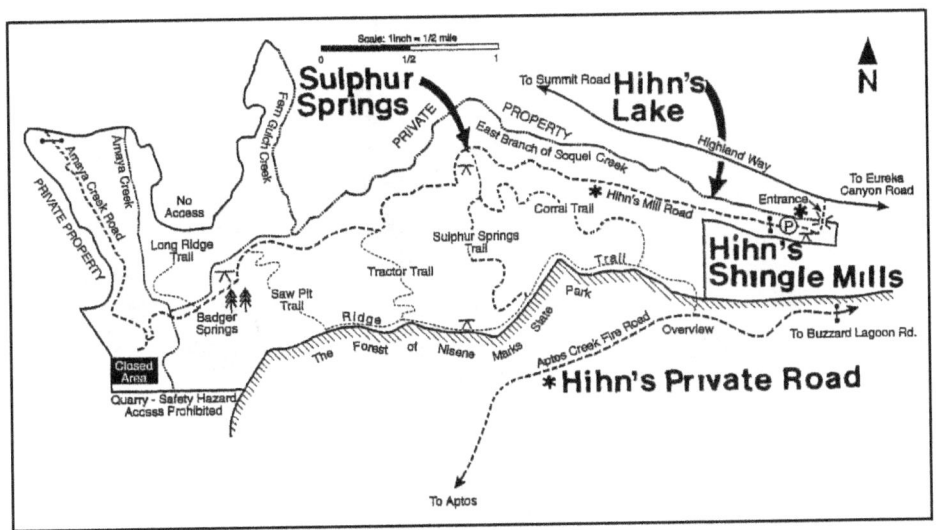

FIGURE 2.6 LOCATION OF THE F. A. HIHN COMPANY SHINGLE MILL AND OTHER FEATURES ALONG THE EAST BANK OF SOQUEL CREEK

The Arden Forest

On December 8, 1899, the Santa Cruz Bank of Savings & Loan foreclosed on Grover & Company's mortgage for 1,098 acres in Tract 7 in the Augmentation. Bad management and the financial crisis of the mid-1890s had led to the company's collapse. In 1897, the company was taken over by John Harvey Logan, J. L. Schwartz, and H. E. Makinney, who were joined by J. W. Forgeus of the Capitola Park Company in late 1899. Over the following five years, 304 acres of the property were sold by the bank to various people, with most parcels coming from the southern end of the tract. H. M. Howard was one such buyer, who acquired 11.997 acres about midway up Grover Gulch. On March 15, 1904, the bank sold the remaining land—around 794 acres—to Forgeus.

Around this time, the Capitola Park Company, a San Francisco-based company, bought stumpage rights to the western 453 acres in Tract 10 from the F. A. Hihn Company. Information about the sale is based on a map found in the Map Room at the University of California, Santa Cruz. Later survey information stated that the potential yield of this land was 24 million board feet of lumber, making it one of the highest per acre yields

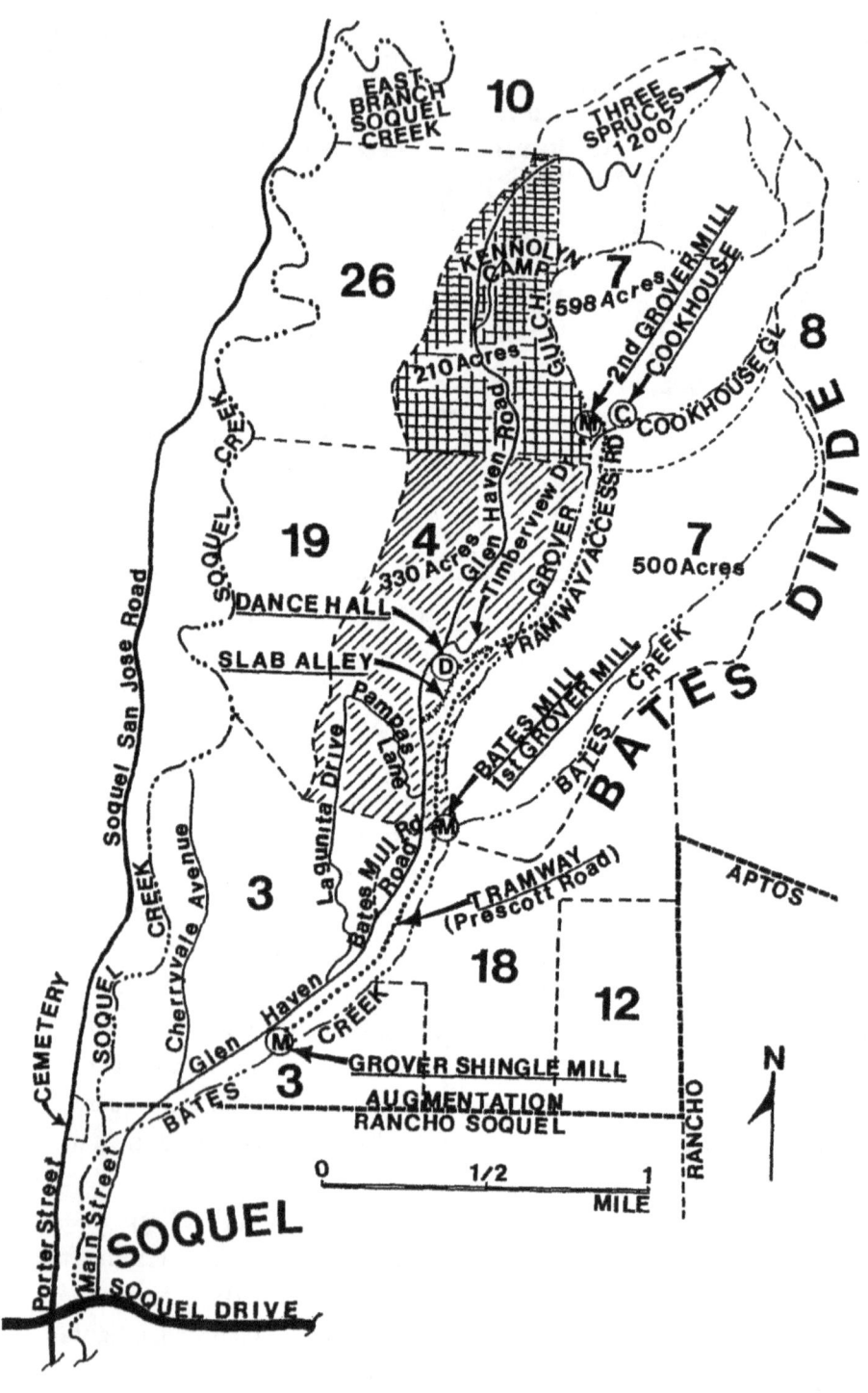

FIGURE 2.7 HISTORICAL ACTIVITIES AROUND TRACT 7 IN THE AUGMENTATION

of anywhere in the Augmentation. Financing the harvesting of this timber was a problem, though, so the company turned to Forgeus.

On December 9, Forgeus sold 732 acres of his land in Tract 7 to the Capitola Park Company. The newly acquired property was undeveloped and lacked natural beauty since its trees had been clearcut by Grover & Company only a decade earlier. As a result, the company had to find creative ways to increase the value of the land so that it could turn a relatively quick profit, thereby providing the company the funds it needed to harvest the timber in Tract 10.

Tract 10 had been a headache for Frederick Hihn for over fifteen years. In 1889, he had surveyed a railroad grade to Tract 10 and beyond, but he never built it. A decade later, the F. A. Hihn Company made an agreement with Timothy Hopkins to cut timber in the eastern acreage of Tract 10 and haul it over Tract 8 to Bridge Creek, where it would build a lumber mill and ship timber south over the Loma Prieta Branch of the Southern Pacific Railroad. But that agreement fell through on October 31, 1904, and was not renewed. The Hihn Company decided that all the timber north of Tract 10—specifically Tracts 1, 6, 11, and 25—could be taken to Laurel and processed there. But Tract 10 remained isolated and too distant from any easy transportation route. By 1904, the company was content to leave the problem of the western half of Tract 10 to someone else.

The earthquake in 1906 stalled the F. A. Hihn Company's plans to harvest timber outside Tract 16 near Laurel. Instead, it shifted its primary focus to its new mill on King's Creek. Meanwhile, the company entered a new agreement with Hopkins in 1907 by which the Loma Prieta Lumber Company could cross through the eastern half of Tract 10 in exchange for which the Hihn Company could cross through Hopkins' Tract 8. As before, the Hihn Company delayed exercising its option. This may have been pragmatic—if both the Loma Prieta Lumber Company and the Hihn Company were assembling lumber at the Aptos mill, it would be difficult to keep the products separated. It would also potentially overwork railroad crews and cause disputes between mill workers of both companies. Instead, the Hihn Company waited and watched. Its option to build a right-of-way through Tract 8 remained valid until May 1912 and the activities of the Capitola Park Company in Tract 7 attracted the Hihn Company's interest.

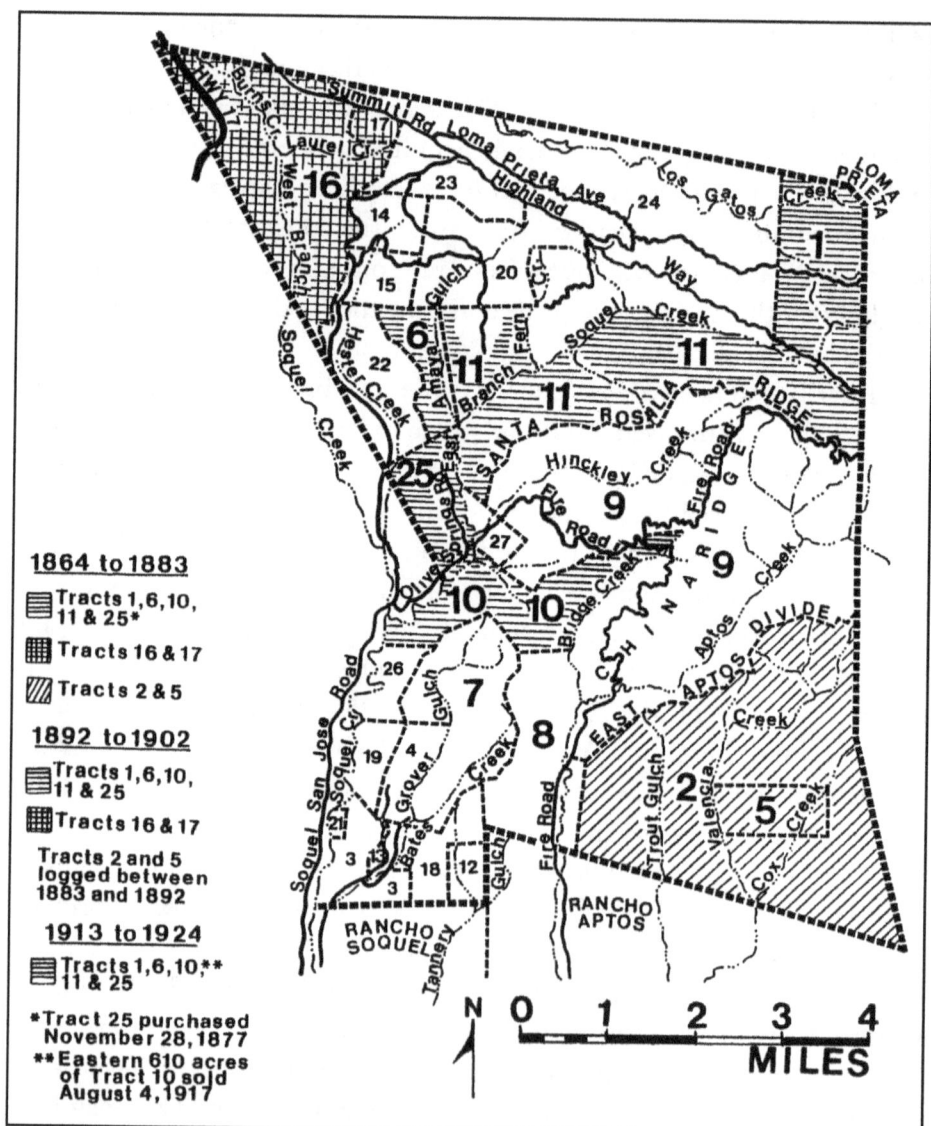

Figure 2.8 Summary of Hihn family lands within the Augmentation

Tract 7's only real value was that it was only two miles by way of the old Grover wagon road to Soquel San Jose Road. Therefore, the Capitola Park Company decided to build a residential subdivision. It hired Lloyd Bowman to survey a 115-acre site within which 62 home sites would be located. Bowman was instructed to survey for homes, roads, and the location of all necessary utilities. This acreage would be the first of potentially four different housing subdivisions within Tract 7, with each new area becoming available once the previous section sold. Meanwhile, the Capitola Park Company sought out a potential partner in its property scheme.

On August 11, 1908, Forgeus sold 20 of the 62 acres he retained in Tract 7 to the Capitola Park Company, probably to round out a corner of the residential subdivision. The following month, on September 2, the company sold all its property in Tract 7 to the Capitola Investment Company, which shared the same board of directors. On October 7, the property was bought by Morton L. and Carrie M. Cook, who mortgaged the 637 acres not set aside for housing to the Anglo–California Trust Company on October 10. The bank officers who held the mortgage were Louis Sloss, J. C. McKinstry, and Mortimer Fleishhacker.

The name chosen for the subdivision was Arden Forest, after an extensive woodland in Warwickshire, England that served as the setting for William Shakespeare's *As You Like It*. Bowman used the theme to name the two roads in the property Rosalind and Shepherd, after two of the play's main characters. The parcels ranged in size from one acre to six, with the average being 1.82 acres. Three neighbors to the east of the subdivision in Tract 4, F. Speroni, Pat Kelly, and J. W. Lunbeck, allowed Bowman to upgrade the old Grover tramway into a road that would allow access to the subdivision from the south via Prescott Road. Slab Alley Road, which crossed Grover Gulch's creek to the west of the subdivision, was also sold to the property developers to allow more direct access to Glen Haven Road. Other rights-of-way were permitted by the neighbors to the south and east, including E. R. Borland, W. V. Stafford, and I. T. Stowe.

When Bowman laid out the subdivision, he was also advised by the Capitola Park Company to set aside a logical route for a railroad line through Tract 7, as well as through neighboring Tract 4, if necessary. This would function to connect the company's planned mill in Tract 10 with Hihn's long-unbuilt railroad grade to Capitola. Bowman was instructed to obtain easements from all the properties within Tract 4 through which the proposed railroad would pass. Presumably, the mill would be constructed near the northwestern end of Tract 10, atop Hinckley Ridge, where railroad

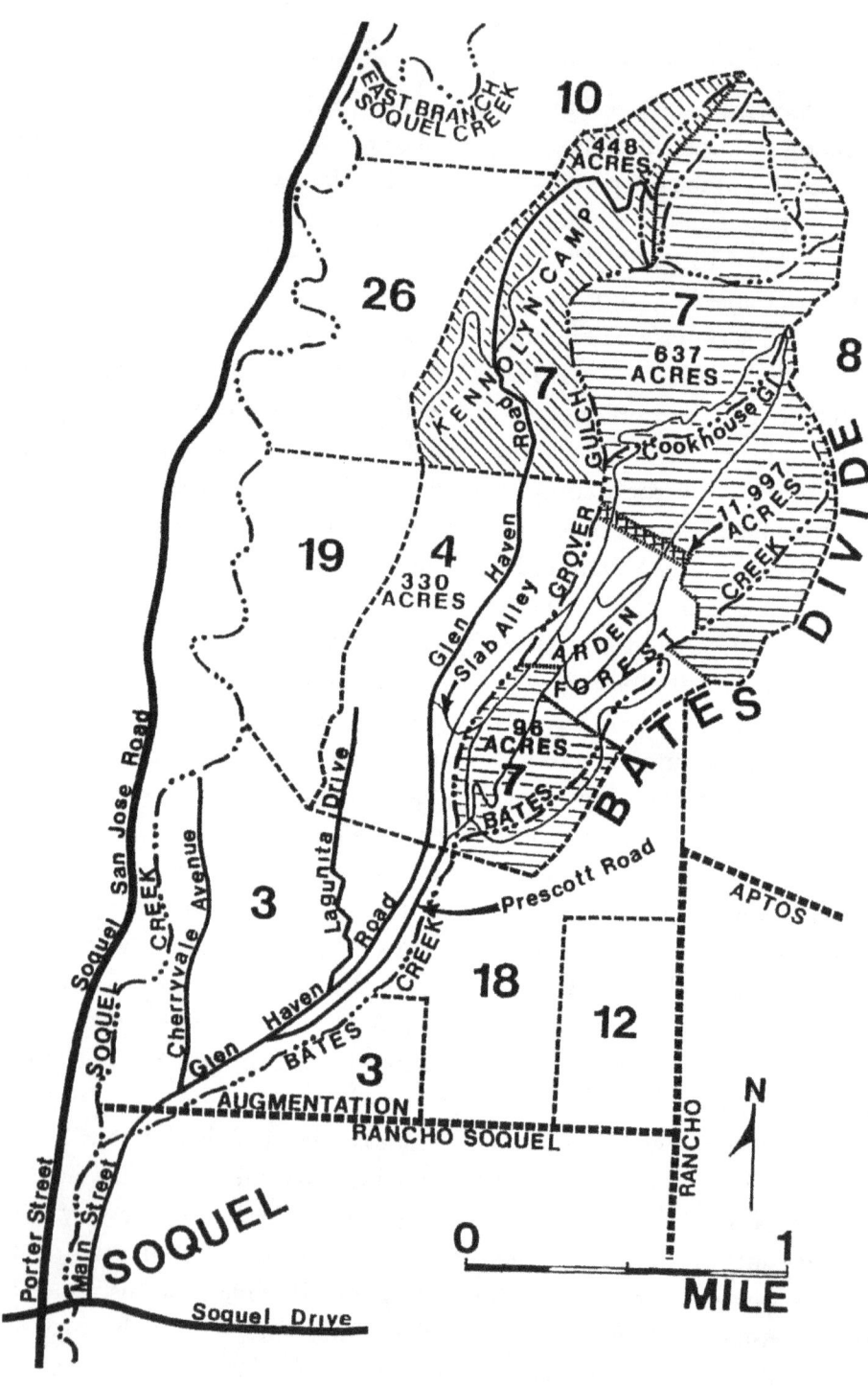

FIGURE 2.9 THE ARDEN FOREST SUBDIVISION WITHIN TRACT 7

A Great Calamity — 1909

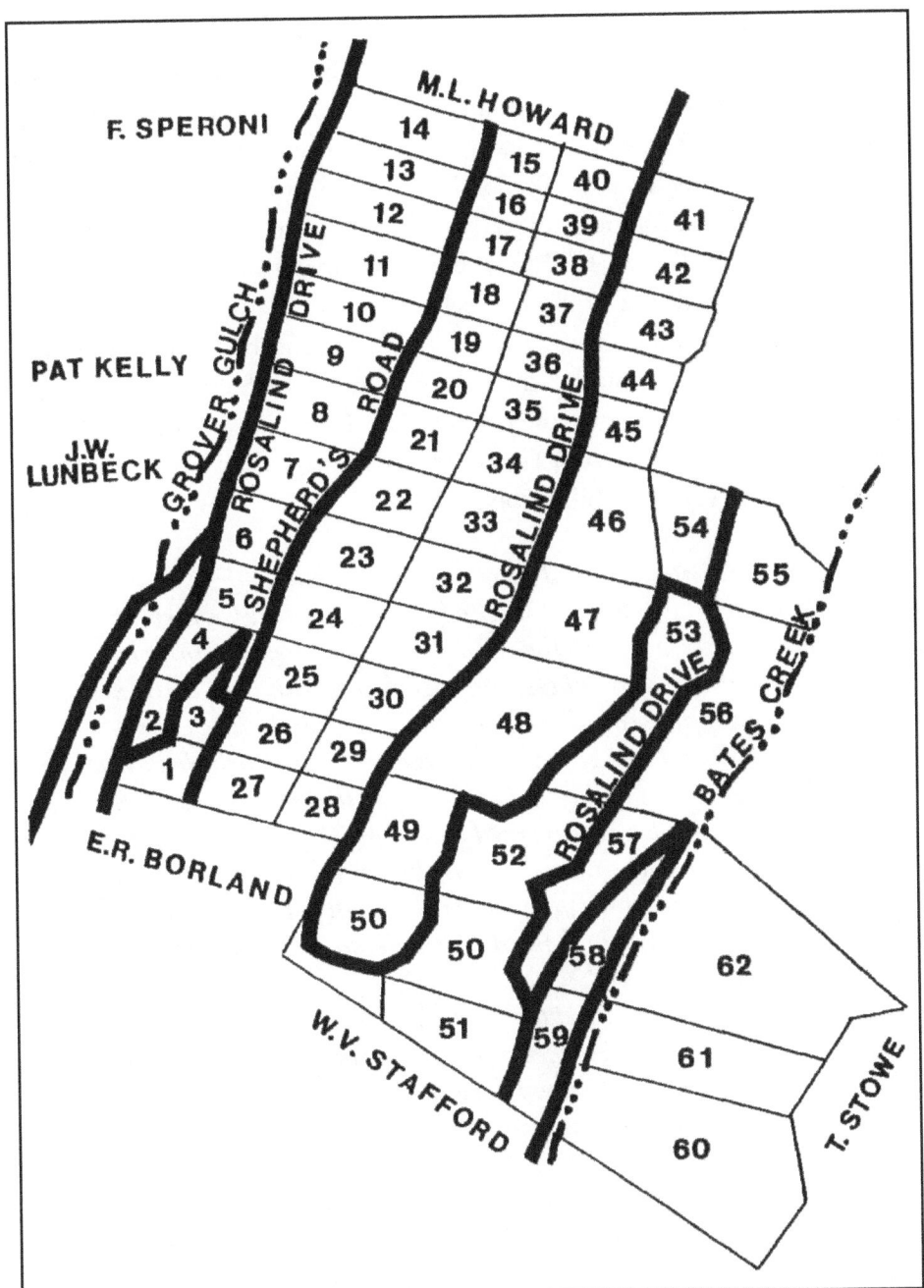

FIGURE 2.10 RESIDENTIAL LOTS WITHIN THE ARDEN FOREST SUBDIVISION, WITH PLANNED ROADS, WATERWAYS, AND THE NAMES OF NEIGHBORS

flatcars would be loaded with lumber or splitstuff and then taken down the railroad, possibly using gravity, along the boundary of Tracts 4 and 7 to the edge of the Augmentation. There, a fully built railroad on Hihn's set-aside grade would take the timber products to the Southern Pacific Railroad station at Capitola. Such a plan would also benefit the F. A. Hihn Company, which could extend the ridgetop rail line further east into its own 610 acres of timberland in Tract 10. This would avoid many of the problems the company faced with the Loma Prieta Lumber Company.

With all the plans in place and buyers arranged, the Cooks submitted their petition for approval of the subdivision to the Santa Cruz County Board of Supervisors in January 1909. The following is the full list of conditions provided by Carrie Cook, which accompanied Bowman's map, entitled "Arden Forest Subdivision No. 1":

> *The hereunto attached map of the land owned by the undersigned Carrie M. Cook, who is the proprietor thereof, following is a list of the deeds and agreements signed by Grover family members and their backers that gave them ownership of the lands now owned by Morton L. and Carrie M. Cook that comprise the Arden Forest. Also included are statements concerning the meaning of the symbols used on the enclosed map as surveyed by Lloyd Bowman. The symbols used to indicate the streets, highways and roads that are offered for public purposes are brought to the supervisors' attention, especially those that are offered with the following conditions attached.*
>
> *If the same be accepted as public roads by any municipal authority in charge of the territory covering this tract, the undersigned and her assigns reserve and shall have the following rights, and the dedication of said roads subject thereto:*
>
> - *The sale and exclusive right to use same roads for public utilities of all kinds and character including more particularly (without intending to exclude anything).*
> - *The exclusive right to lay, construct and maintain thereon, thereunder and across the same, pipes and other*

contrivances, wires poles and other mechanical contrivances and or capable of being used for the transmission or delivering or other handling of water, oil, gas, electricity, or any other substance that may itself or by means of appliances be conducted or transferred through, along, across, over or under roads, also the exclusive right to lay, construct and maintain thereon tracks, including switches, turnouts and other incidental appliances usual and incidental to railroads however the railroad stock may be propelled, and for the purpose of maintaining and conducting railways and running cars and other rolling stock thereon however propelled, and whether for passengers, freight or both, or for any other purpose, and also the sole and exclusive right to erect and maintain poles or other mechanical appliances thereon, thereunder and thereover for the purposes of carrying wires or other appliances for transmitting electric power, light or other elements or materials or appliances, constituting or usual in or incidental to the maintaining of public utilities for sale or otherwise, including the overhead appliances for railroads, telephones, telegraphs, trolley lines for mechanical purposes of all kinds and character, and any other similar purpose.

<u>And on the further condition...</u>

- *All sand, water, stone, oil, minerals or other commercially valuable substances that may be hereafter come on, along, under or over said roads, all trees of every kind and description that are now growing or may hereafter grow on the said roads, are reserved by the undersigned and shall continue to be her property despite the use of any portion of said territory for roads and the acceptance thereof for roads shall be on the condition that said ownership shall remain in the undersigned as to said accepted portions of said property forever, and on the further condition that the property here shown shall be relieved from all obligations of every kind and character, and be the property of the undersigned with the same effect as if this map had never been made or recorded, in case the undersigned uses the property shown as.............purpose than roads or transfers the same or any part thereof to a third party prior to the actual acceptance by the mentioned authorities on the conditions named herein, together with the assumption of the condition and of all obligations.........have the same, as herein provided.*

Said Carrie M. Cook hereby certifies that she is the owner of the tract of land and delineated on the map hereto attached: that said tract has been laid out into lots and the lots numbered according to my interests and that said map fully and faithfully represents said tract, its name and its subdivisions; and that no other signature is necessary to pass title to said property.

In witness whereof, the said owner has hereunto set her name and seal, this ___ day of _____,1909.

Carrie M. Cook

In early February, the Board of Supervisors rejected Cook's petition. As a result, the Cooks forfeited the failed subdivision as well as the other 637 acres they owned in Tract 7 to the Anglo–California Trust Company. The firm immediately began seeking a buyer for the property, but nothing would be forthcoming. At the same time, without access to its timberland, the Capitola Park Company gave up its stumpage rights to Tract 10, causing the land to revert to the F. A. Hihn Company.[45]

The F. A. Hihn Company opens negotiations with the A. P. Hammond Lumber Company to sell its retail business

Frederick Hihn was 76 years old the day the earthquake struck in 1906. He was in San Francisco conducting business and witnessed the destruction in the city. Between his holdings in Santa Cruz County and those elsewhere in the Bay Area, Hihn lost nearly $100,000 in the catastrophe. It was becoming too much for the energetic businessman who had been Santa Cruz's entrepreneurial soul for fifty years.

In February 1909, Hihn still held a significant stake in the F. A. Hihn Company, the Hihn Investment & Building Company, the Hihn Water Company, the Capitola–Hihn Company, The Santa Cruz Water Company, and the Soquel Water System Company. It was the first of these companies that he decided to wind down. Acting on behalf of his children and their spouses, who jointly controlled the company, Hihn reached out to the A. P. Hammond Lumber Company, one of the largest lumber-producing concerns on the Pacific Coast. Hihn was not looking to deprive his family of its valuable land—he wanted to sell the company's retail lumber yards, which had spread across the Bay Area over the past decade.[46]

The Loma Prieta Lumber Company ends pulling logs from Hinckley Gulch to the mill on Aptos Creek

After two summers of hauling logs from the headwaters of Hinckley Creek to Spring Creek and down to the mill on Aptos Creek, the Loma Prieta Lumber Company abandoned operations around October 1909. The process was too time consuming, and it was determined that it ran at a financial loss to the company. With the end of operations to Spring Creek, timber cutting activity also ended on Long Gulch. The timber cut here had been used as firewood for locomotives continuing up the grade to Spring Creek, so without the need for extra firewood, there was no reason to cut it. The Long Gulch spur was soon cut back to the main railroad grade.

By the end of the year, the Loma Prieta Lumber Company's mill on Aptos Creek had been converted to cutting shingle and shake bolts. Timber cut from the upper reaches of Hinckley Gulch was hauled over the ridge on the backs of pack mules and then taken to the mill, while timber cut on the lower end of the gulch was loaded onto wagons and taken to Opal, where it was cut at the planing mill on site.[47]

The F. A. Hihn Company finalizes sale of its retail business to the A. P. Hammond Lumber Company

On October 25, 1909, the *Surf* reported:

> **LARGE LUMBER DEAL.**
>
> **The F.A. Hihn Company to Convey Control of their Lumber Business to the A. P. Hammond Lumber Company.**
>
> **One of the largest concerns on the coast, the deal will involve great advantage to the lumber business of this section.**
>
> *Negotiations which have been in progress more or continuously since last February for the sale of the F. A. Hihn Company's lumber business to A. P. Hammond Lumber Company, one of the largest lumber manufacturing concerns of the Pacific Coast, was practically concluded today.*
>
> *The Hammond Company has mills in Washington, Oregon and Northern California and has yards in the principal cities as far as Los Angeles.*
>
> *The F. A. Hihn Company retains as interest in the business, but the management will be with the Hammond Company.*
>
> *This deal places the control of the redwood timber of the coast practically in the hands of five men, and will doubtless lead to stability of prices and increase of production. The F. A. Hihn Company have been large lumber cutters for many years in the Valencia canyon, at Gold Gulch and at Laurel, and has yards in this city, Watsonville and Salinas.*
>
> *As to whether this deal involves the untouched lumber on the Soquel we are not informed.*

The following day, another article appeared in the *Surf* clarifying the details of the arrangement between the F. A. Hihn Company and the A. P. Hammond Lumber Company:

THE HIHN–HAMMOND COMPANY.

Details of the Big Lumber Deal, the local employees will not be disturbed.

The A. P. Hammond Lumber Company, in the deal with the F. A. Hihn Company, have taken over the Hihn Company's lumberyards at Santa Cruz, Hollister, Spreckels, Salinas, Watsonville and in Castroville. They also take over the planing mills at Hollister, Watsonville, and in Santa Cruz.

The corporation does not take the Hihn sawmills in the county, as they have extensive plants with a capacity of a million and a quarter board feet per day. Their mills for pine lumber are at Astoria and Mill City, Oregon, and for redwood lumber, at Samoa in Humboldt County.

Their yards are mostly in Southern California at Los Angeles, Pasadena, Riverside, Imperial Valley and all the principal Southern California towns.

F. M. Fenwick of San Francisco, the secretary of the A. P. Hammond Lumber Company is here at present, but states that there will be no change in the management of the local concerns.[48]

Chapter 3

~

Along the Ridgetop Rails

The Loma Prieta Lumber Company and F. A. Hihn Company's operations

The year 1910 was looking brighter for both of the major lumber companies operating within the Augmentation. The Southern Pacific Railroad's route through the Santa Cruz Mountains had been standard-gauged and reopened in 1909, meaning that the F. A. Hihn Company mill at Laurel could now haul its timber products out to market. The company planned to end operations along Kings Creek that year, after which it would move its large boilers back to Laurel. The Laurel mill, meanwhile, resumed cutting timber at its shingle mill and smaller-scale lumber mill. The Hihn company, with its Hihn–Hammond retail sites across the Bay Area, was set to have a stellar year.

The Loma Prieta Lumber Company knew it could not compete, but it still anticipated a better year than the three that had preceded it. The Mill Creek mill on the North Coast was finally able to benefit from the Ocean Shore Railroad. The tracks had been opened to Swanton in mid-1909, so it is possible that the company began shipping out from Swanton then, but 1910 was the first full season where it could benefit from the track extension. Through agreements with the Southern Pacific Railroad and Timothy Hopkins, a spur was installed at the Santa Cruz Union Depot to allow Ocean Shore freight trains to haul their timber products directly to the Loma Prieta Company's lumberyard on Pacific Avenue.

Meanwhile, the company planned to resume hauling timber from Hinckley Gulch over the ridge to the Aptos Creek mill or to Opal. The saws would cut shake and shingle bolts exclusively. The tedious process barely turned a profit due to the amount of time required and the low yield. The company also came to the realization that it was running out of sources of lumber and other timber products. It owned nine lumberyards and two planing mills across the Bay Area, but the Mill Creek operations and the splitstuff cut in Hinckley Gulch would not be enough to fully restock these locations. The Loma Prieta Lumber Company was running on fumes and likely only had a few years left before it would be forced to dissolve.

The F. A. Hihn Company was in a similar position. By the end of 1910, the timber on its Kings Creek property was exhausted and crews began dismantling the machinery in early September. Most of it was moved back to the mill at Laurel, but even that location was beginning to see the end as most of the accessible timber on the nearby tracts was close to exhaustion. The company predicted that the Laurel mill only had a few more years before it, too, would close for good.[49]

The Molino Timber Company is incorporated

On May 31, 1910, the Molino Timber Company was incorporated in the hope of reversing the financial and operational decline of the Loma Prieta Lumber Company over the previous three years. At the start, the goal of the company was to harvest the timber on several thousand acres of Loma Prieta Lumber Company land within the Augmentation in preparation for planting eucalyptus trees. Bert Stoodley, one of the incorporators, recalled in his memoir that the company had a capital stock of $20,000: "Al Williams had been chosen president as he was in a better position to deal with the L. P. L. Co. than any of the others. Oscar Chase was Vice-President and I was Secretary. All five were directors as well as stockholders." The other two founding members were Fred Daubenbiss and Fred Severance.

Stoodley gives a detailed history of the founding of the Molino Timber Company and its operations within the Augmentation in his memoir. He recalls:

> *One Saturday afternoon early in January, 1910, five men were enjoying the heat of fir block in the big wood heater in the office of the Loma Prieta Lumber Company at Opal, Calif.*
>
> *The office stood in the front row of buildings facing the ocean with an unobstructed view of the bay and the mountain beyond it. A strong southwest wind was driving the rain against the window panes and froth from the waves breaking just under the bluff was being carried several hundred feet inland, resembling a snow storm. It was too early to light the large hanging lamp which hung from the ceiling near the center of the room. Yet it seemed near night with the low, dark clouds outside and the walls and ceiling of the office painted a deep green.*
>
> *Al Williams, the Company's secretary, turned partly around from the roll top desk in the corner near the window with one leg hanging over the arm of the chair, nursing a cigarette and facing the group; Fred Severance, the logging superintendent, just in from his woods camp and drying his overcoat, alternatively front and back, next to the stove; Fred Daubenbiss, deliveryman for the Company store (next door), his team of mules snugly put away in the stable and through work for the week; Bert Stoodley sat at the high standing desk on the revolving stool and Oscar Chase at the typewriter table by the front window turned now and then to add his two cents worth to the conversation.*
>
> *Thus, being all introduced, we will proceed...*
>
> *The conversation for a time was about local happenings but gradually shifted to more general affairs. During a lull someone remarked that he had had what seemed to him a good idea, "Why not combine our small savings and open a business which would yield us all a profit but yet allow us to keep our jobs?"*

This sounded like something constructive and immediately discussion started. What kind of business, and where?

Well, Castroville Creamery was for sale. Oscar's brother-in-law, Frank Topham, blacksmith at Milpitas, is enthusiastic about orange growing down near Porterville. Has bought forty acres down there (so Oscar tells us). Lumber yards are proposed but no town near here is in need of another yard.

A distant relative of Oscar's in San Francisco, whose name is Davenport, is building a boat for coast-wise trade and wishes to sell shares in the new craft. It will be named the "Davenport" as that family has been in the shipping business for years and their boats have paid good dividends. The village of Davenport Landing (now Old Davenport) was named for the family.

Fred Daubenbiss' nephew, Jim Swan, of Soquel, has had glowing reports from Southern Idaho and wishes to go up there to scout out the possibilities. It sounds so good that we made up a small fund to pay his traveling expenses. He made a very good study and sent us reports every two or three days. Openings for creameries, for a store handling farm machinery, and the best: a store for selling seeds, fertilizer, grain and stock feeds. These around Weiser, Caldwell and Boise. He thought so well of it that he located there.

But we later agreed that something nearer home was what we should have [focused on. Perhaps something we all knew about, something, say, like the lumber business.]

The Loma Prieta Lumber Co. had a vast acreage of oak and madrone timber, and also considerable redwood unfit for lumber. The logger had passed these redwood trees by. There was, at this time, a steady demand for fuel wood. Redwood for the apple dryers in Watsonville, oak and madrone for the wood dealers in the surrounding towns, and peeled tan oak for the Chinese laundries in San Francisco. As a start, someone suggested that we buy stumpage from the Loma Prieta Lumber Co. and hire a few woodchoppers to make up fuel wood. When dry it could be sold at a profit.

The newly-formed company began hiring the woodchoppers on June 1 and by fall, they had a large cache of wood products available to sell. The directors quickly set out to dispose of as much as they could to recoup their initial investment and other costs. Their timing was exceptionally good. The Loma Prieta Lumber Company realized at the end of the season that the cruising reports for the Mill Creek timber tracts had been grossly overestimated. The mill only had one season's worth of timber left and then would be shut down.

Meanwhile, the company's Hinckley Gulch hauling operation was proving just as profitless as it had in previous years. The reasons for the failure were many, but at the top of the list was cost versus profit. The cost was high due to both distance between the gulch and the mill on Aptos Creek, and the difficult terrain that the mules had to travel over. In addition, it was expensive to transport shake and shingle bolts to wagons and then railroad cars at Opal. Timothy Hopkins and A. C. Bassett were done with the project. They abandoned the remaining timber in Hinckley Gulch and wrote it off as a loss for tax purposes.[50]

The Southern Pacific Railroad abandons 0.57 miles of the Loma Prieta Branch

At the beginning of 1911, the Loma Prieta Lumber Company was in the process of reassessing its options regarding its remaining timber in the Augmentation. Taking advantage of the change in mood, the Southern Pacific Railroad made the decision easier. In early spring, the company sent crews to the end of the Loma Prieta Branch and promptly abandoned the 0.57 miles of track from the former village of Loma Prieta to the end-of-track at Spring Creek. The new terminus was 3.7 miles north of Aptos Station near the confluence of Bridge and Aptos Creeks, just north of the village site. This meant that the long curving railroad bridge at the bottom of China Ridge was finally removed, or rather the rails, ties, and usable timber were stripped—the remaining pilings and crossbeams were left behind. The railroad company also took the opportunity to dismantle most of the remaining spurs, including those up Love Gulch, Bridge Creek, and within Loma Prieta itself.

With the mainline cut back to Loma Prieta, it no longer made sense for the train to cross Aptos Creek to reach the old station. Most of the buildings in the former village were boarded up, and some were torn down for their lumber. Therefore, and with Timothy Hopkins' permission, a new station was built further to the south on Tract 8, just south of the Directors' Cottage in the Compound. This site today is the level ground on the west side of the Loma Prieta Grade Trail south of the Porter House site sign. Several large second-growth redwood trees now occupy the location.[51]

The Molino Timber Company builds a railroad to the top of China Ridge

The Loma Prieta Lumber Company was on the verge of collapse in early 1911. All activity within the Augmentation had ceased and the Mill Creek operation was in its final year. Crews on Aptos Creek were busy finding places to store equipment for future sale. And then suddenly Warren Porter returned to the scene following his stint as Lieutenant Governor of California. He returned to a despairing company with Timothy Hopkins and A. C. Bassett clearly out of their element, and Alvin Sanborn's heirs—his widow, E. J. Sanborn, and daughter, Helen Sanborn—hardly involved at all. Thus, he was eager to hear what the directors of the Molino Timber Company had to offer.

The directors had not been sitting idle. Their first short year of timber operations had been successful and they were eager to expand their operations. Bert Stoodley explains in his memoir:

> *This success in the wood business in a small way led to more ambitious plans. Why not contract with the Loma Prieta Lumber Co. to make up into split stuff the fifteen million feet of redwood timber that had been abandoned in the upper Hinckley Creek canyon?...*
>
> *Our tentative plan was to build up the old Southern Pacific grade from the sawmill to the mouth of Spring Creek. This would be easy as the rails and ties had been removed by the railroad company and there would be little dirt to move.*

From here to gain an elevation of 600 feet we would lay a line straight up the hillside to the top where we would station a donkey engine to raise and lower cars.

We could avoid this incline by building switchbacks into Spring Creek...but three miles more of track would be required—several tons of rail, many ties and much grading. There were many steep spots where a great deal of dirt would have to be moved. Also every train trip would be increased six miles, which would cut down the number of cords we could deliver in a day with the train. And almost all of this would have to be written off when the job was done. We were satisfied that an incline was our answer.

The first step was to figure out a list of prices at which the split stuff could be delivered at Loma Prieta. A price schedule was finally figured out, making sure that the spread between our delivered price and the current market would allow the L. P. L. Co a desired profit (or it might be considered stumpage). Three major items had to be considered: manufacturing the split stuff, packing it to the railroad on mule back, [and] freight to Loma Prieta. Besides this there was a certain amount of "overhead" to be considered—expenses which unexpectedly cropped up. The size of the job and the probable cost of equipment made us shiver, but we were hopeful.

About the only definite item on which we could rely was the cost of manufacturing. These costs were pretty well settled.

Mule packing would depend on what kind of bargain we could arrange with the packer.

Railroad building was an unknown factor. The total cost of the railroad must be laid against the entire job for its salvage value, after the contract had been completed, would be relatively small. Surveying, grading, rails, ties, and rolling stock would all be large items but we hoped to pick up considerable material along the way which would help defray the cost.

Each member of the company, as he paid into the treasury $100, received one share of the capital stock, and each member was putting in all of the money he could spare. Not all took up their stock for lack of funds. The remainder had *to be borrowed. For some reason, it seemed to me that I was always the one to borrow money. I interviewed bankers until I was tired and I knew all of their objections. Nevertheless, we <u>did</u> borrow enough money to keep going. Indeed, I marvel at the amount of credit we were able to obtain. One day I figured up how much indebtedness I was personally responsible for, should the others fail to pay, and I found it was more than $50,000. Did this give me goosepimples? But we had to keep on. Some way, we muddled through. I believe I became an expert in persuading a bank finance board to loan us money. Before its dissolution, I found myself with nearly half of the stock and of course the value of assets had gone far beyond the $20,000 original capital. All profits had been left in the Company; no one had drawn anything out of it in its seven years of existence.*

One last obstacle the Molino directors had to overcome was convincing the F. A. Hihn Company to let their railroad pass through its land. China Ridge veered for four-tenths of a mile into the Hihn Company's Tract 10, from the north fork of Bridge Creek to Sand Point. The Molino Timber Company sent surveyors ahead to plot the railroad grade through the area and see if any profitable timber would need to be cut. They presented their findings to the Hihn Company, which promptly approved the right-of-way without charging Molino.

Confident that all of the preparatory work was done, the Molino board approached the directors of the Loma Prieta Lumber Company. Stoodley recalls: "The Board of Directors took it under consideration and after a week or two gave us their answer. They would let us [do] the job but were skeptical if it would work. Wishing to get some stumpage out of that abandoned timber, they were very cooperative. We were free to use, without cost, any equipment the Company owned, donkey engines, wire cable, tools, etc." The Molino Timber Company became an informal subsidiary of the Loma Prieta Lumber Company and was treated like a subcontractor. In addition to allowing the firm to use its physical resources, which were otherwise going unused, Loma Prieta allowed Molino to sell its splitstuff at all of the parent company's lumberyards. Such a relationship greatly eased the burden of responsibility on Molino's management.

With the formalities completed, Molino was able to start building its railroad and incline in the summer of 1911. Stoodley explains:

> *Arnold Baldwin, formerly county engineer, was hired to do the surveying. He was a good man and his charge moderate.... Split stuff makers and wood choppers were set at work picking up what timber was available along the right of way. Grading was started at once.*
>
> *Motive power would be needed soon. Locomotive salesmen were on the job at once. Baldwin, Brooks, Shay, Climax and Heislers were all urged as the proper engine for our road. Some were straight rod engines; others geared as the Shay, Climax and Heisler. We finally decided on an eleven-ton Shay, which was to cost us about $2,750 delivered (the price was advanced within a month or two after our order was placed. Later it would have cost us over $3,000).*
>
> *A thirty-inch gauge was chosen—less grading and sharper curves permitted. Also ties four feet long could be used; we picked out many ties from the regular four-foot cordwood. The engine would burn wood or coal.*

The Shay style of locomotives is named after Ephraim Shay of Haring, Michigan, who designed it in the mid-1870s. It was specifically designed for working in rough and steep terrain, such as logging, mining, and quarrying, and could handle sharp turns and poor roadbeds. Shays are not fast locomotives, but they are powerful and relatively lightweight, which made them ideal for operating over relatively low-quality rails. The Shay purchased by the Molino Timber Company in fall 1911 was one of four built according to the Lima Locomotive Works' Plan No. 2203, and the only to be customized to operate on a 30-inch-gauge track.

Stoodley continues:

> *Young firm of engineers in San Francisco, Dodge & Prausnitz, represented a German firm and from them we bought the rail—16-lbs to the yard and in 15-ft lengths. This was shipped*

> from a town close to Berlin, Germany: Essen, where the great iron works are located.
>
> Dodge & Prausnitz also supplied us with trucks for our flat cars—twenty four-wheel trucks on which we built ten flat cars 16 feet long. These trucks were shipped from Koppel, Pennsylvania, by the Orenstein-Arthur Koppel Co. They were link and pin couplers with hand brakes. We could not afford to equip the engine and cars with air brakes and we never had any trouble in controlling the cars with hand brakes together with the "steam jam" on the engine...
>
> The Shay worked the upper line for seven years without any major repairs. Gears on such an engine take much wear and, as I recall it, they had to be replaced every two or three years, in spite of using much grease. The boiler needed no repairs. Neither did the two engines, 15-horse power each, mounted on the right-hand side. With a gear of three-to-one this gave us a power of 90 horse power on the drive wheels and every wheel was a driver on this type of locomotive.
>
> We built [a] short side track and shipped in the necessary timber for the flat cars. Here the carpenters built the cars. After the bumper and drawheads had been attached and the painting done, the cars were moved over to the main line, and were ready for service.

The flatcars were four feet wide, the same width as the railroad's ties and the locomotive, which made the cars much more maneuverable on sharp turns and narrow cuts. The wooden flatbeds were custom made at Schillings' Camp in a small building connected to the Loma Prieta Branch by a short spur. In subsequent years, more flatcars were built and added to the fleet, reflecting increased production along the ridge.

> From the Southern Pacific Co., we had permission to lay a third rail between their rails; thus, we were able to run down their tracks to about Schilling's Camp, which gave us much space for piling wood and split stuff. Our rail a little off center between the S.P. rails was not as tall as the railroad's 56-lb rail which caused our carloads of stuff to tilt a little toward

the center but at slow speeds we had no trouble. As one stands facing a Shay locomotive, it will be seen that the boiler is off-set some to equalize the weight of the two engines mounted on the right-hand side, vertically.

Construction on the section of track between Schillings' Camp and the top of the incline began around June 1911. Southern Pacific, recognizing the important new project occurring along the Loma Prieta Branch, upgraded Schillings' Camp into a formal train station named Molino. As soon as Baldwin finished surveying a section, crews moved in and began grading it. Homer Kinsman of New York was in charge of building the line and gave a lot of his own time to the task, coming in on weekends to push the track onward. Stoodley later remarked: "without Homer's dedication and interest in the job, it never would have been completed within the time it was." When Kinsman reached the bottom of the incline, he had a short spur built that could serve as temporary storage for empty cars before they were pulled up the incline. Beside this, his crew erected a 75-foot-long bridge across Aptos Creek, which served as the bottom of the incline. To build the remainder of the incline, a zigzagging path was carved into the hillside to allow mules and work crews to access the right-of-way. Meanwhile, at the top of the incline, an area was being prepared where a steam donkey could be installed to haul rolling stock up and down the hill.

Stoodley explains:

We installed one of L. P. L. Co.'s big donkey engines (sometimes called a "road engine") at the top of the incline, borrowed some of their heavy steel cable and built a strong track up the hillside to the top of the hill, and prepared to lower the loads and bring back the empties by steam power.

The total vertical lift was 610 feet and the distance between the Aptos Creek bridge and the top of the incline 2,250 feet of track. A house was built at the top of the incline for the engineer, [Joseph John] Rossi. He and his wife [Sena] lived there about 8 months of the year; we shut down during the winter months. Mrs. Rossi, in a few months, became quite

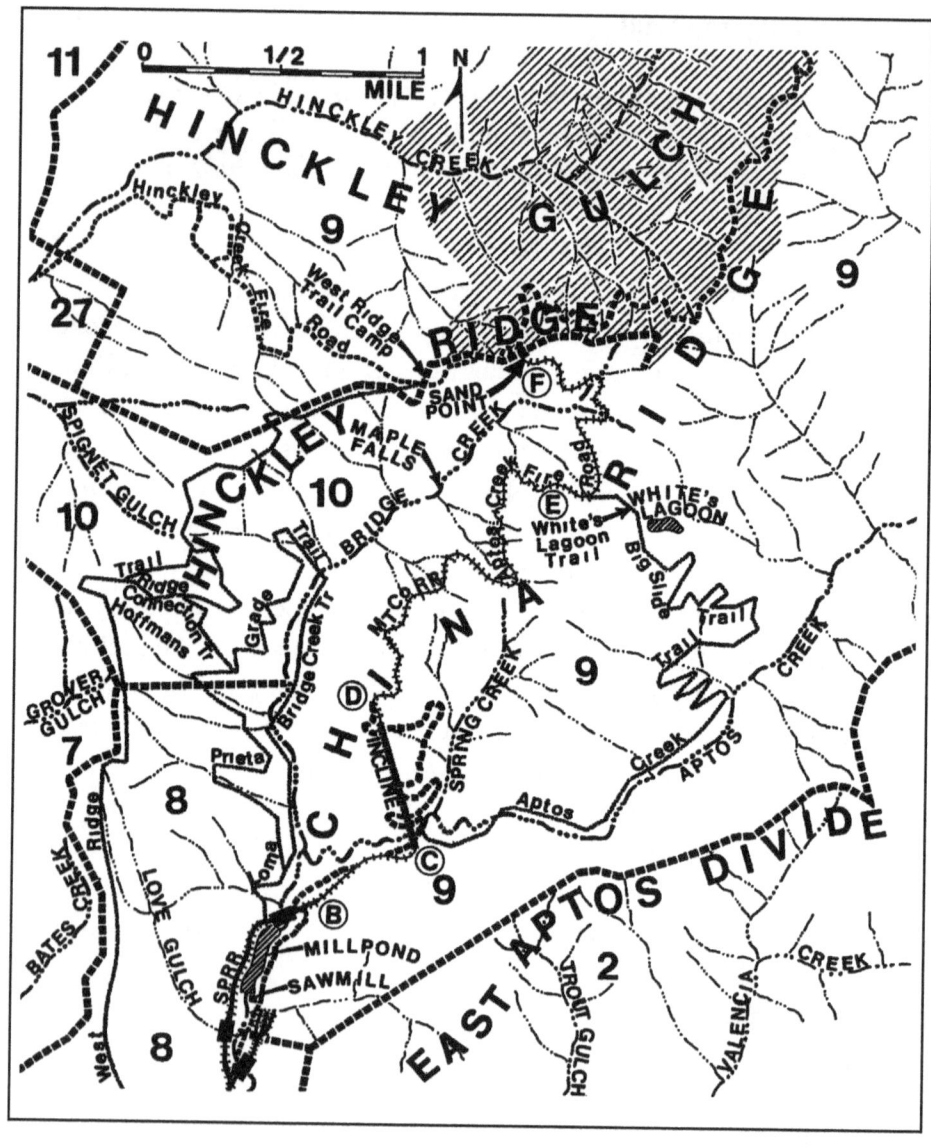

Ⓐ Temporary storage area for splitstuff (elevation 260 feet)
Ⓑ End of the Loma Prieta Branch (elevation 320 feet, 1.0 miles from Ⓐ)
Ⓒ Bottom of the Incline (elevation 360 feet, 0.5 miles from Ⓑ)
Ⓓ Top of the Incline (elevation 970 feet, 2,250 feet from Ⓒ)
Ⓔ White's Lagoon Trail (elevation 1,400 feet, 2.0 miles from Ⓓ)
Ⓕ Sand Point (elevation 1,600 feet, 1.0 miles from Ⓔ)

FIGURE 3.1 ROUTE OF THE MOLINO TIMBER COMPANY'S RAILROAD ALONG CHINA RIDGE BETWEEN THE APTOS CREEK MILL AND SAND POINT

skillful in handling the engine, and could raise and lower cars as well as her husband.

Sena Rossi's son, Walter F. Stanard, was also trained to use the machinery and assisted frequently in managing Camp 1. At other times, he served as fireman on the Shay when it went out and then he worked as a brakeman when it coasted downgrade to the camp.

The wire rope which handled the loads was 1 ¼" diameter, made up of low steel material, six strands of 19 wires each. This made a very flexible line, and amply strong. The steepest part of the incline was 67% grade. Riding the incline was supposed to be prohibited but this order was usually disregarded. The contour of the hill was such that as soon as the cars left the summit, they were out of sight of the engineer and he had to depend upon signal bells in controlling the cars.

The signal system for the incline was two wires rather loosely hung on low poles beside the track. Touching these two wires together would ring the bell at the engine. A code was arranged and posted at the foot of the incline and at the hoist.

To guide the lowering line as it was paid out, corrugated rollers were placed between the rails at the proper places. These required no care excepting daily oiling. [These] were cast in the Santa Cruz foundry with their chairs (bearings machined) and they were set on the track in places indicated

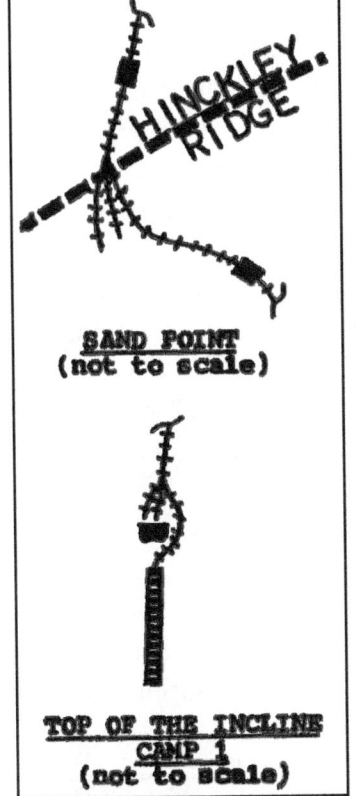

FIGURE 3.2 CLOSE-UP VIEWS OF THE TRACK CONFIGURATIONS AT SAND POINT AND THE TOP OF THE INCLINE

> *to carry the swaying rope and guide it between the rails.*
>
> *It might be mentioned that there was a possibility that the entire line might "creep" down the hill, especially in winter when the ground became wet. For this reason, the track was anchored to the earth securely at several different places.*

After the donkey engine was anchored in place, it assisted in the construction of the remainder of the incline. Already constructed flatcars were loaded with building materials and pulled partially up the incline. This was fortunate since there were several places where small bridges and cribbing had to be installed across deep depressions, and some of this building material was heavier than what a mule could carry.

This area at the top of the incline was branded Camp 1. In addition to the large donkey engine, Stoodley notes, "space was graded for a switch yard, for sorting and setting out the loads, and picking up the empty cars for the trip back into the woods. There was a blacksmith shop here, a storage shed to keep freight dry, and an additional 'rip track' where cars could be set out if repairs were needed." The Molino directors made the decision early on to build an enclosed structure for the donkey engine and Shay locomotive since they were by far the company's most valuable possessions. Both pieces of machinery could sit safe and dry throughout the winter months awaiting the start of the next season.

Several portions of the incline's right-of-way can still be found today with little effort. To locate the bottom section, walk northeast along the Aptos Creek Fire Road for a half mile from the Trout Gulch Trailhead. Instead of crossing Aptos Creek, turn right and cross the shallow drainage ditch, on the other side of which is the former railroad grade. Continue following this railbed until it suddenly ends about 30 feet above the fire road. Here was where the old Loma Prieta Branch's 300-foot-long curving bridge began and just to the left is where the incline began its steep ascent up China Ridge.

The top of the incline is just as easy to find, although it involves a 1.5-mile-long journey up the switchback of the Fire Road. Just as the road begins to leave Spring Creek Gulch and enter the Bridge Creek drainage basin, to the left is a rather noticeable groove in the side of the ridge. To the right and up the hillside about fifteen feet is the site of Camp 1, which can be reached around the next curve of the road. Beware of poison oak, which can be thick in this area.

By mid-November, the incline was completed and ready for the Shay. The company's directors were cautious when it came to their locomotive because they could only afford one. Stoodley recalls that the "Lima Locomotive Works sent a man to see that the Shay was in perfect working order before we need to accept it." Once accepted, it was moved to the bottom of the incline. Stoodley recounts: "When the time [came] to haul it up the incline, to make sure that there be no accident, we attached two cables to the locomotive and two donkeys at the top of the incline to haul it up." Once at the top, the final parts of the locomotive were assembled, including the bell and whistle. The Lima Locomotive Works' engineer supervised its final preparation and ran a final test firing of the boiler at Camp 1. Satisfied, he made several short trial runs of the locomotive within the confines of the camp and then it was stored in its shed until the start of the next logging season.[52]

The Woodwardia Hotel opens

The last major resort established in the Summit area was built by Joshua Jeremiah Rucker and his wife, Dora Sue Clark, in 1911. They named it the Woodwardia Hotel after the many giant ferns of the same name that flourished throughout the mountains beneath the redwoods. The hotel was located 0.65 miles from Summit Road, about halfway between that road and Mountain Charley Road on today's Old Santa Cruz Highway. The exact spot of the hotel is easily identified along the road's east side: at the point where the road makes a fairly short but sharp curve in order to avoid a large second-growth redwood tree, the hotel was off to the right. Today the location is covered with small redwoods and many ferns.[53]

Land transfer from George Olive to Elizabeth Olive concerning Tract 27 in the Augmentation

On August 23, 1911, George Olive, realizing that his health was deteriorating and his passing was imminent, in a gift deed passed title to the 126 acres he owned in Tract 27 in the Augmentation to his wife Elizabeth. Olive died three days later, on the morning of August 26 at the age of 82.[54]

The Molino Timber Company agrees to transport splitstuff for the F. A. Hihn Company

The scale of operations along China Ridge caught the attention of the F. A. Hihn Company, which had approved the Molino Timber Company's grade through Tract 10 earlier in the year. The company soon realized that it could benefit from this new operation, specifically from the presence of a railroad along the ridge. As a result, the Hihn company sent cruisers to Bridge Creek to assess the remaining uncut timber within the eastern 610 acres of Tract 10. The cruisers concluded that the timber south of Maple Falls could be cut into logs and hauled to a lumbermill downstream. The timber north of the falls could be cut into splitstuff and hauled to the top of the ridge, where Molino could haul it out. The only problem with this plan was that the company did not have a mill along Aptos Creek and all of the company's machinery was currently being used at Laurel.

With no better option, the company approached the Loma Prieta Lumber Company's management and offered to lease the latter's abandoned mill on Aptos Creek. Timothy Hopkins was uninterested. Frederick Hihn had long been a rival of the Loma Prieta Lumber Company and the idea of Hopkins' firm leasing its facility to a former rival did not sit well with any of the directors. Thus, Hopkins replied with a counteroffer: Loma Prieta could purchase Tract 10 from the F. A. Hihn Company. After months of internal deliberation and ineffective negotiating, Hihn's directors decided against selling the land and instead concluded that they would turn all 1,063 acres of Tract 10 into splitstuff.

The problem of getting the splitstuff out of the western 453 acres of Tract 10 was easy to address. It could be taken out by truck or wagon through Spignet Gulch and then down the county road. But the terrain in the eastern 610 acres along Bridge Creek was more problematic. In early 1912, the company approached the Molino Timber Company to negotiate use of the railroad it was building to Hinckley Gulch. The firm agreed to pay a reasonable hauling fee to bring the splitstuff from Sand Point to the transloading station at Molino. Stoodley remarked later that "there was some question about our collecting freight charges because we were not organized as a common carrier. However, we took a chance on it."

The Molino deal did not solve the bigger issue of getting the splitstuff to Sand Point, though. It was a little over 1.75 miles from the bottom of Tract 10 to Sand Point and the area included very steep terrain, especially directly below the point. The solution the company came up with was the same as that of Molino: build a narrow-gauge railroad. Yet this would be more difficult than it had been for Molino since the Hihn company would have to bring the rolling stock in first and then build the line, as needed. They set to work preparing the area as Molino began extending its line toward Sand Point.[55]

Land transfer from Elizabeth Olive to James Olive concerning Tract 27 in the Augmentation

Following the death of George Olive, his widow, Elizabeth, realized that she did not want the responsibility of running the Olive Sulphur Springs Resort. On March 1, 1912, in a gift deed, she passed title of the 126 acres she owned in Tract 27 of the Augmentation to her son James.[56]

The Molino Timber Company extends its railroad to Sand Point

Construction of the Molino Timber Company's narrow-gauge railroad atop China Ridge began in earnest in spring 1912. Following its agreement with the F. A. Hihn Company, the timber company's first goal was to reach Sand Point. Pieceworkers had been cutting timber along the planned railroad grade since the previous year, stacking piles of splitstuff beside the route to be picked up once the railroad was extended there. Other pieceworkers climbed to the top of the ridge to cut timber there. Thus, by early summer, between 60 and 80 men were employed by Molino to work various duties in the Augmentation.

Bert Stoodley says the following about how the railroad was graded and operated beyond Camp 1:

> The grading beyond the incline for five miles was kept at a four percent grade (four feet to 100 feet of track) and the grade was always in favor of the loads. We tried teams and Fresno scraper but with roots and rock to contend with, we found it cheaper, per foot of track, to use pick and shovel work. There was not too much heavy cutting to do as our road ran near to the top of the mountain, but there was considerable cribbing to build in spots and a few bridges. We had to use mainly young redwoods for these and they, being mostly sap timber, would, we knew, last for only a few years but we hoped the job would be completed before these timbers rotted. Landings were built at frequent spots along the track where the mule loads of split stuff could be dumped and loaded on the flat cars for the mill yard. Since each landing would be used only a short time as the adjacent timber was manufactured, they were cheaply constructed but answered the purpose.
>
> We used ground-throw switches instead of the tall switch stands as they were not so expensive and no lamps were required as we did no running after darkness came. Kinsman designed the frogs and had them built and welded in our blacksmith shop.
>
> A telephone line was built along the railroad and a portable telephone carried on the engine. This line was a grounded line (single wire) and the portable 'phone was fitted with a pole and hooks which, in case of need, could be hooked over the wire and the engineer or brakeman talk at once with any station. There were regular stations at the mill yard, at the hoist and end-of-track wherever that might be at the time. There were also occasionally temporary stations for one purpose or another as short spur tracks were built for local loadings. I remember that at Camp Three for a time the telephone box was hung on a large redwood stump with a broad sheet of redwood bark as a roof to shelter it from rain in case we had an unexpected shower. The insulator pins were nailed to tree

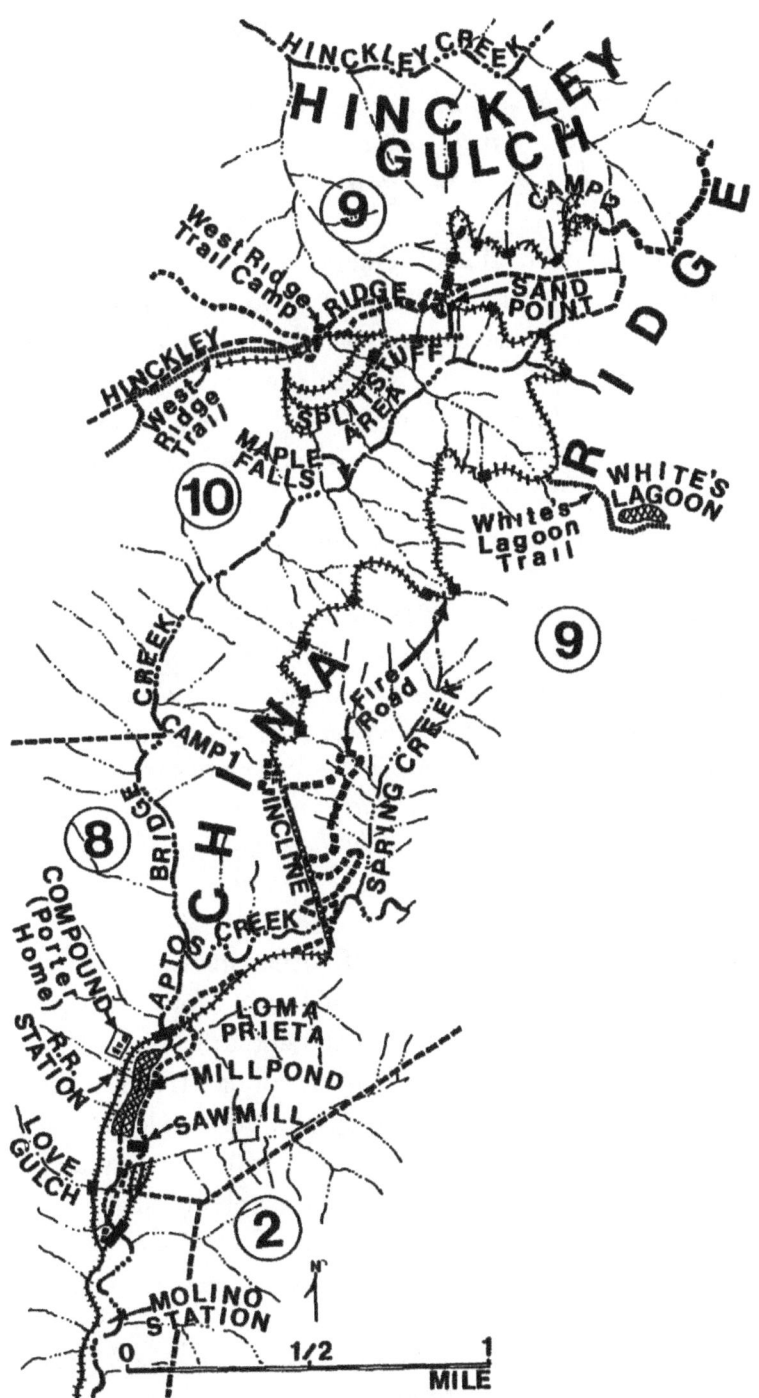

FIGURE 3.3 ROUTE OF THE MOLINO TIMBER COMPANY'S RAILROAD FROM THE APTOS CREEK MILL TO CAMP 2 ABOVE HINCKLEY GULCH

> *trunks or stumps—sometimes the insulators were suspended overhead from a branch—all to avoid setting poles if possible. However, a few poles had to be used.*

Daily operation of the donkey engine and locomotive used a tremendous amount of water, a resource that was not readily available on the ridge. Therefore, "it was necessary to carry water from Aptos Creek to the top in barrels. The man operating the switch engine on the lower end of the railroad, between the foot of the incline to the sawmill yard, which was a little more than a mile, filled the barrels and signaled the engineer when filled and ready to go."

At the bottom of the incline, the operator had other duties, as well:

> *He also moved the loads from the lowering line and hooked up the empties to go back up the mill. On this run at the lower end, this one man was able to take the cars to the mill yard and unload them as fast as the train could bring them in from the woods. For this switching at the lower end of the line, we used an old Maxwell automobile fitted with flanged wheels. The grade was gentle here and this homemade gas locomotive did the work very well.*

A few years later, once profits had sufficiently increased, Molino bought a gasoline-powered rail car from the Hall–Scott Motor Car Company of Berkeley, which proved to be a much better and safer vehicle for the task.

Back along the ridge, a total of ten trestles or half-trestles were required to reach Sand Point. The cribbing was composed of at least ten large logs stacked atop each other to create a retaining wall. The remnants of some of these can still be viewed along the Aptos Creek Fire Road.

Operating the railroad could be dangerous, so Molino crews adopted a system that ensured maximum safety and efficiency. Stoodley explains:

> *The train was operated with a two-man crew, the engineer and a man who was a fireman on the trip into the woods, and a brakeman on the outgoing train with loaded cars—usually from four to six cars. The engine was always on the downhill*

end of the train so that a car could not break loose and run away back toward the hoist. This was not really good practice for pushing the empties back to the timber, as the head cars, owing to the very crooked track, were often out of sight of the engineer. Any obstruction on the track would mean a derailment. However, I do not recall that this ever happened. If any of our company were going into the timber, we usually rode the head car.

The braking system on the cars was similar to that on any railroad: a brakestaff, ratchet with a wheel on the top. A chain connected the staff with the brake beam underneath. It made an effective system in the absence of air brakes. A team jam on the engine made quite a braking system with the gears helping to slow the speed.

Two or three of us were riding in one morning, on the head car as usual, and as we rounded a curve there was a bob cat trotting along ahead of us between the rails. He had probably been out scouting for a belated breakfast; he jumped off the track, not hurriedly however, and went up the hill into the woods. Some deer were usually to be seen near the small lagoons in the vicinity of the White's Lagoon trail.

As soon as the railroad reached Sand Point, probably in mid-summer 1912, men from the F. A. Hihn Company set to work preparing a camp. A donkey engine was mounted near the 350-foot drop-off to the headwaters of Bridge Creek, where it would pull material up to the camp. Finding the exact spot where the engine was anchored is not difficult. It was mounted a short distance to the north of today's Sand Point Overlook sign along the Aptos Creek Fire Road. There is a large rock here that has had its face worked with pick and shovel, above which was installed the engine.

The camp was large enough for one or two spurs where flatcars could park while being loaded with splitstuff. Additional space was provided so that splitstuff could be lifted to the grade to await loading. Molino workers may have assisted in setting up the camp, at least in relation to grading and installing the spurs. While this delayed the company's drive to Hinckley Gulch, the added income the Hihn operation would provide more than made up for the delay. Stoodley notes that, "soon after the road was completed to Sand Point and was operational, Hihn's timber was made up into splitstuff and we hauled it out."

At Molino Station—the southern end of the line—the former Schillings' Camp was enlarged into a transloading station where passing Southern Pacific trains could collect splitstuff for shipping out. Quickly, however, production outpaced shipments and stacks of splitstuff, both Molino's and Hihn's, began lining the right-of-way to the north all the way to Loma Prieta Station nearly a mile to the north. Keeping straight which splitstuff was from which company also became a logistical nightmare for the directors of both companies.[57]

The F. A. Hihn Company begins shipping splitstuff from Bridge Creek

Even before the Molino Timber Company extended its railroad track to Sand Point, the workers of the F. A. Hihn Company were busy preparing the area at the headwaters of Bridge Creek below. Because the timeline of events is speculative at best, most of the history of the operation will be recounted here.

When one stands at the Sand Point Overlook sign at 1,600-foot elevation, it is difficult to accept that directly below—about halfway between the point and Bridge Creek—pieceworkers produced splitstuff while a narrow-gauge train collected the material. The drop from Sand Point appears to be almost straight down, only 500 feet to the top of the creek, while slightly to the west the distance is 700 feet. But the area encompasses over 100 acres and spans a quarter of a mile from south to north and half a mile from east to west. Exploring this section of steep hillside proves that first impressions can be deceiving and gives credit to the old adage 'seeing is believing.'

I name this part of Tract 10 in the Augmentation the Splitstuff Area. It is comprised of an upper and a lower section separated by a very steep, 200-foot hillside. The upper area extends from just below Sand Point to slightly beyond today's West Ridge Trail Camp. While steep in most areas, there are places that are level enough to give pieceworkers space to produce splitstuff. The lower area, which is smaller, is a narrow gulch enclosed by three steep sides. From this area's steep northern wall, it slants for 500-600 feet toward Bridge Creek before suddenly dropping ten feet straight into the creek.

Running through the center of both the upper and lower sections is a small creek that has its beginning along the top of Hinckley Ridge between Sand Point and the West Ridge Trail Camp. The creek's three branches are all easily identified as they pass through the upper section, with the center branch the most prominent. In the lower section, the confluence of the three branches creates a marshy area during the rainy season.

The first time I entered the Splitstuff Area, it was from Bridge Creek. I had worked my way down from the junction of the Aptos Creek Fire Road and White's Lagoon Trail to the creek and then followed an old trail along Bridge Creek's north side until I entered the lower section. Lying on the ground were two bucket-shaped wire mesh containers—later I found out that they were put over the smokestack of a donkey engine to contain sparks and reduce the possibility of starting a fire. To my right, away from Bridge Creek, there was a bridge of logs that crossed a marshy area, beyond which was a cut that provided access to an area at a higher elevation. The marshy area appeared to be a former millpond, although it was bereft of logs when I found it. As I continued north away from Bridge Creek, I reached the steep back hillside that separated the lower from the upper section. I stopped here and headed back to my car—I was tired and the journey back was long.

On my second exploration, I entered the area just to the east of the West Ridge Trail Camp. After a journey of about a quarter-mile, I entered a world that both enthralled and perplexed me. Here was an area containing many large logs and piles of what appeared to be splitstuff and the residue produced from the activity, all scattered about in a helter-skelter pattern. In addition, there were roads, roads in every direction, also in a helter-skelter pattern. What was their purpose? Were they built to carry splitstuff out of the area by wagon? I asked myself, if the splitstuff was removed by mule, where were the trails? After making several visits to the area I noticed that there were few stumps that matched the size of the majority of the logs that lie about waiting to be turned into splitstuff. I also noticed that one

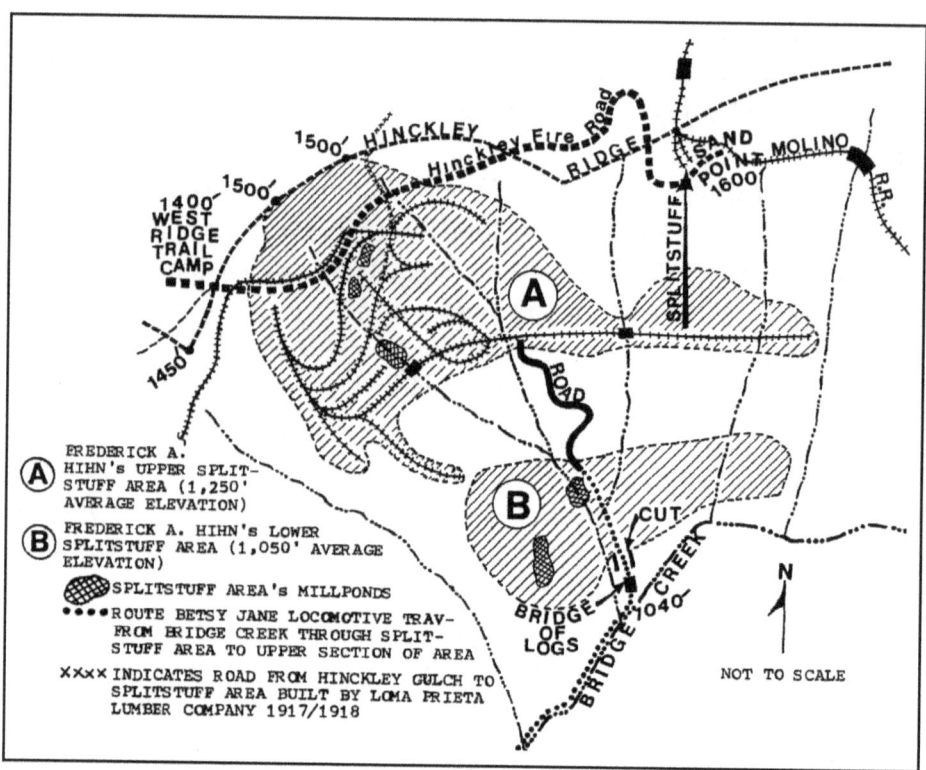

FIGURE 3.4 THE F. A. HIHN COMPANY'S TRACKAGE IN THE SPLITSTUFF AREA AT THE HEADWATERS OF BRIDGE CREEK BELOW SAND POINT

end of each log was beveled which indicated that they were all pulled into the area from another area. Down on the lower section, beside the piles of splitstuff that I had overlooked during my first visit, there were several logs with beveled ends pointing away from Bridge Creek, which indicates that they had been pulled into the area from the vicinity of the creek. After several more trips into the area, and after closer examination of the piles of what I first thought were splitstuff waiting to be loaded onto some sort of transportation, I realized that the piles were in fact the residue produced from a splitstuff production.

I discovered the Splitstuff Area before I learned of the situation between Timothy Hopkins and the F. A. Hihn Company. Had I known, it would not have taken me eleven years to realize what I had found. The reason why I was there in the first place was that I was searching for the route that the Loma Prieta Lumber Company used to pull its logs from Hinckley Gulch to the mill on Aptos Creek in the late 1900s. When I discovered the Splitstuff Area, I felt that I was close to finding the route. But after further explorations, I realized that here was just another mystery that needed to be solved.

I found many interesting things in the Splitstuff Area throughout my explorations. I found places where pieceworkers had installed small logs into the hillside in order to have level ground on which to work. I found the remains of a ladder that a feller used to climb up to a springboard so that he could saw a tree. I found several logs that had been partially worked, showcasing the skill of the pieceworkers who had abandoned the log. Indeed, after years of exploring, I always left with the eerie feeling that one day long ago, someone blew a whistle and sent everyone home, telling them not to return.

While the make-up of the Splitstuff Area perplexed me from the moment I first entered it, the roads were by far the most confusing feature. It was during my second visit to the upper section that I discovered a road that connected the upper and lower areas. It was narrow, steep and very twisting, with turns far too tight to pull logs over. What was its purpose? There was also a second road that was to remain a mystery for several years. It headed east from the point where the latter road reached the upper section and continued for a good quarter-mile, ending about 350 feet directly below Sand Point. Throughout the area, I found five millponds, three in the upper section and two in the lower.

There was also one last mystery that I had to answer: what was the purpose of the road that crossed the Hinckley Creek Fire Road from Tract 9 into Tract 10, about a quarter-mile in length? This road, located just to the east of the West Ridge Trail Camp, appeared to be so placed that logs could be pulled from one side of Hinckley Ridge to the other. Why? And who pulled them—the F. A. Hihn Company, the Loma Prieta Lumber Company, or the Molino Timber Company? What was most perplexing was the fact that the 2,400-foot-long cable that was used by the Loma Prieta Lumber Company to carry logs from the back of Sand Point to the vicinity of the West Ridge Trail Camp ended within the vicinity of this road. What was going on here?

The answer is fairly obvious in hindsight: the F. A. Hihn Company brought its locomotive to Bridge Creek and built an isolated, 36-inch-gauge railroad. Where the *Betsy Jane* had been for the previous fifteen years is a bit of a mystery. After the operation on Gold Gulch south of Felton wrapped up in the late 1890s, the company moved on to Laurel. But there is no evidence that the locomotive was used in Laurel except possibly as an overqualified donkey engine. Rumors that the locomotive was moved to the King's Creek mill following the 1906 earthquake lack evidence. The Porter 0-4-2 saddleback locomotive may have simply sat in storage for much of this time, awaiting a new use by the F. A. Hihn Company. What does seem clear is that it was stored in Laurel at the beginning of 1912, possibly in a state of disassembly.

This disassembled state made the locomotive easier to relocate to Bridge Creek. From Laurel, there were three possible routes for it to take. First, there was the Southern Pacific Railroad's line, which was longer but by far the easiest route. Second was a meandering path up Schultheis Road, down Summit Road, down Soquel San Jose Road, and then up Olive Springs Road to Spignet Gulch just south of Sugarloaf Mountain. Third was Hotel de Redwood (Redwood Lodge) Road, which was a more rugged but direct route to Soquel San Jose Road. Because both of the roads were unpaved, narrow, and sometimes steep, the heavier parts, such as the locomotive's boiler, must have travelled via railroad.

The tense relationship between Timothy Hopkins and the F. A. Hihn Company meant that the parts were not taken all the way to Loma Prieta or Molino, but rather unloaded at Opal. This explains why Bert Stoodley never mentions hauling *Betsy Jane* in his memoir or oral history. At Opal, the parts of the locomotive were loaded onto heavy wagons and taken up Soquel San Jose Road and then Olive Springs Road. From there, the wagons made their way up an old skid road to the top of Hinckley Ridge. This road can still be found on the boundary of The Forest of Nisene Marks, opposite the top of the Big Stump Gap Trail along the West Ridge Trail.

From the top of the ridge, the disassembled locomotive was hauled down to Bridge Creek. The elevation at the top of the ridge was 1,100 feet, while three-quarters of a mile below it was only 450, so it was a steep descent. It was another three-quarters of a mile upstream, ascending 250

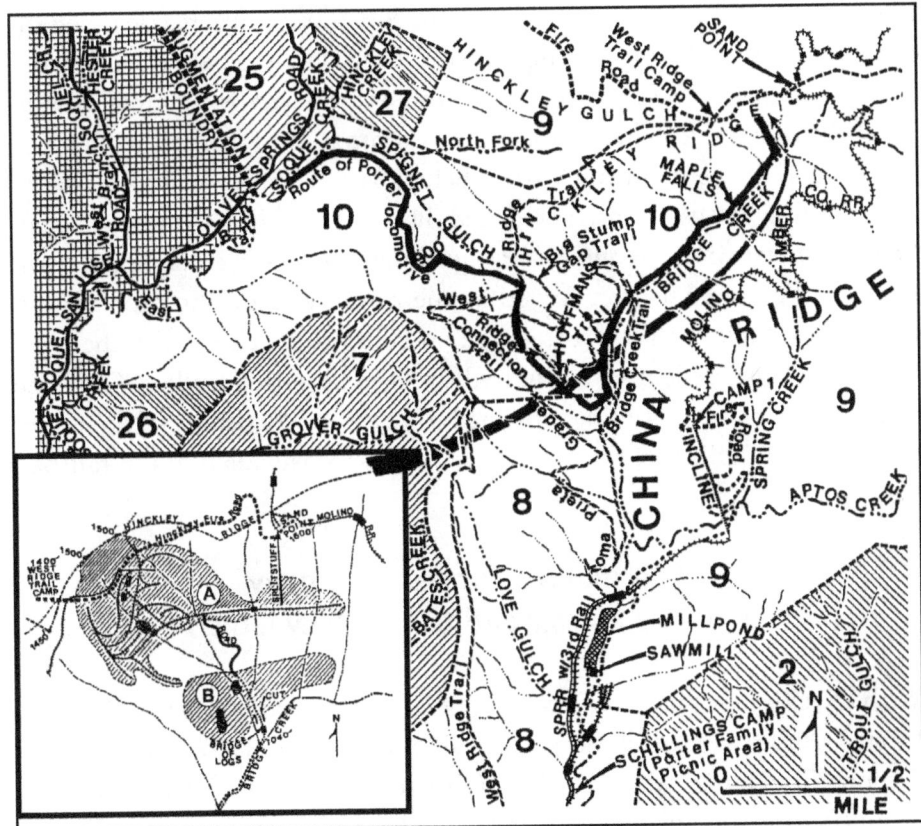

FIGURE 3.5 THE ROUTE OF THE *BETSY JANE* TO THE SPLITSTUFF AREA

feet in elevation, to the base of Maple Falls, where the parts were hauled 30 feet to the top. Long cables were installed on the east side of the falls to perform this task, several of which remain in place today. Finally, the locomotive parts were hauled the last half-mile northeast of the falls to the lower section of the Splitstuff Area at 1,040-foot elevation.

When I explored the narrow ravine between the top of Maple Falls and the entrance into the Splitstuff Area before the storm of January 4, 1982, I found several areas where logs had been placed across the creek. These log bridges, which the storm washed away, indicated that something large and heavy had used them. It was *Betsy Jane*, which was dragged across the bridge using donkey engines. Just below the Splitstuff Area, a cut had been made to allow the machinery to reach a section of already-prepared railroad. Once all the parts were on site, the locomotive was reassembled on the track, ready to begin hauling splitstuff to the landing below Sand Point.

How much of the railroad's trackage was prepared by the time Molino finished its track to Sand Point in mid-summer 1912 is unclear. What is certain is that the main track from below Sand Point to where the *Betsy Jane* was dragged was constructed, and that the F. A. Hihn Company began hauling splitstuff up to the Molino grade as soon as it could. This main track in the upper section served as the primary feeder line for the rail network and it was the only trackage on Bridge Creek to justify the erection of bridges, which were required to cross two deep gullies. Over the next five years, the network expanded to reach most corners of the upper section, while splitstuff from the lower section was hauled to the railroad via mule teams.[58]

The Molino Timber Company extends its railroad to Hinckley Gulch

With the closure of its Mill Creek lumber mill at the end of 1912, the Loma Prieta Lumber Company was placing all of its chips in 1913 on the Molino Timber Company and its perilous railroad along China Ridge. As such, Molino's directors made it a priority to extend their railroad one mile beyond Sand Point to the planned Camp 2 above Hinckley Gulch. Late the previous year, pieceworkers had cleared the right-of-way of saleable timber and moved into the gulch itself. Nonetheless, it was not easy to grade the railroad to Camp 2.

A quarter mile beyond Sand Point, two trestles were required before the right-of-way reached a small sink pond that the Loma Prieta Lumber Company had used prior to the earthquake. Arnold Baldwin graded the route west around the pond to avoid the need for a fill or cribbing. Today, travelers on the Aptos Creek Fire Road can easily identify the path that the railroad took around the pond.

The Molino Timber Company built Camp 2 at the 1,700-foot-elevation point for two main reasons. The first was convenience—there were many standing old-growth redwoods at the top of the ridge here. The second was that the area had sufficient space to support a camp that needed to operate

Along the Ridgetop Rails   1913

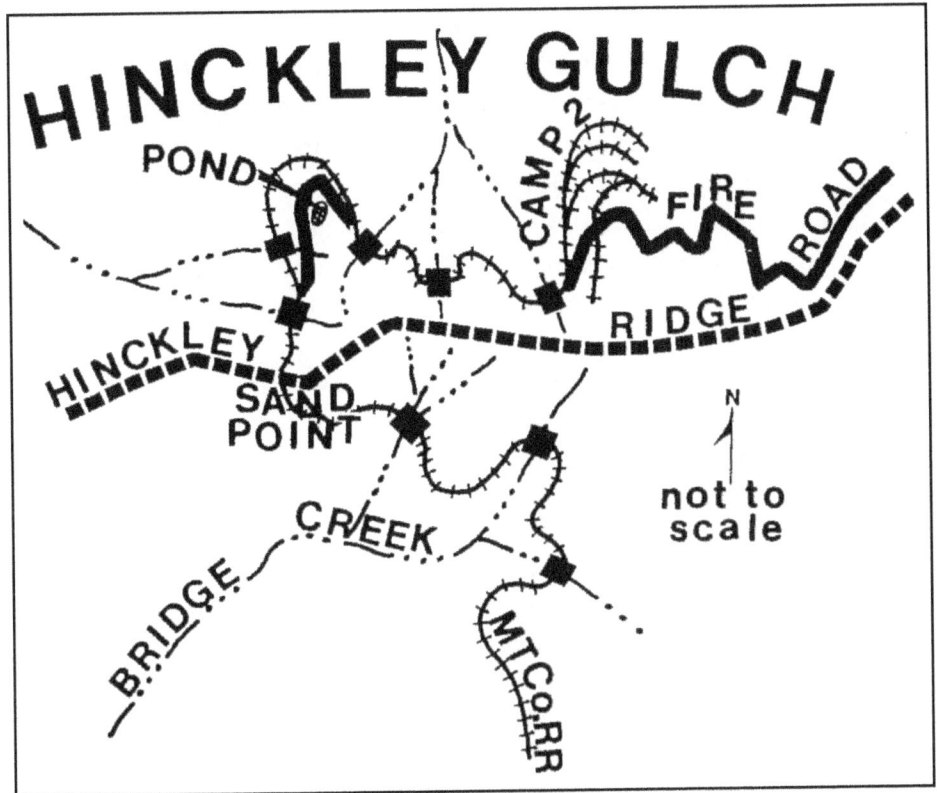

FIGURE 3.6 ROUTE OF THE MOLINO TIMBER COMPANY'S RAILROAD FROM SAND POINT TO CAMP 2 ABOVE HINCKLEY GULCH

largely autonomously from Camp 1 and Molino Station. The location of Camp 2 was just north of where Hinckley Ridge meets China Ridge. Today, it is not along the Aptos Creek Fire Road, but rather slightly downhill and to the west of it. About nine-tenths of a mile from Sand Point and just beyond the sixth sharp bend in the road, the railroad grade diverts to the left and stays relatively level when compared to the slowly ascending road. In reality, Camp 2 sprawled on either side of the railroad grade, up to the top of China Ridge and down to near Hinckley Creek, encompassing an area of around 30 acres.

One aspect of Camp 2's history that does not sit well with modern readers was its nickname: 'Jap Camp.' Most old timers, including Bert Stoodley, when discussing Camp 2 use this name, and it was a frequent term at the time for people of Japanese descent. Other equally inappropriate words were used to describe Black and Chinese workers who were occasionally hired to work in the Augmentation. The reason 'Jap Camp' came to refer to Camp 2 is because the Molino Timber Company primarily hired Japanese pieceworkers to cut timber into splitstuff, and it was they who lived in the camp.

Japanese pieceworkers did not work for wages—they were paid for the amount of product they produced. After negotiating with Molino, the workers accepted the terms offered. Stoodley explains in his memoir:

> *Some of the split stuff making was done by individuals who preferred to work by themselves. Territory was assigned to these but there was sometimes dissatisfaction when some man thought he did not have as good timber on his assignment as his neighbor.*
>
> *Much of this work was done by Japanese contractors who built and handled their own camps. It was surprising how many sacks of rice hauled on the train and unloaded at these camps, and how many wooden kegs of "Jap sauce." This was imported and I never knew how it was made. The kegs held about 5 gallons each and were bound with stout hooks, also made of some kind of wood—not iron hoops.*

The workers would often build a cabin near a spring, if one was available, and work for a number of years in the same locality. In hot weather, they would rise at daylight and work until it was too hot to continue, then rest in the shade until late afternoon, and then work until darkness set in.

While many of the pieceworkers operated in this way, a number lived in Camp 2 working on logs pulled in by donkey engines. The workers at the camp were supplied with logs hauled from as far away as Hinckley Creek. The creek was 1,000 feet below the camp and up to 30 men cut logs here before they were taken to the top of the ridge. Many of the paths that the logs traveled are still visible today.

Pack mules were the primary means by which splitstuff was taken up to Camp 2. About 2,000 feet upstream from the Hinckley Creek pieceworker camp was a waterfall about 35 feet high. A second, shorter one was located about 700 feet further upstream. While mules could circumvent the first, they were stopped from continuing upstream by the second unless they traveled far up the side of the gulch and then headed back down to the creek. There was little reason for mules or pieceworkers to travel downstream since the Loma Prieta Lumber Company had more or less clearcut the gulch to this point a decade earlier. Thus, operations were confined to the area between the creek camp and the bottom of the upper falls. Eventually, though, workers crossed Hinckley Creek and began harvesting timber from its northern side. Because of the steepness here, workers had to either pitch the splitstuff down to the creek, lower it by rope, or use a wooden chute. The accumulation of this material along the creek presented a problem of how to get it up to Camp 2.

The solution Molino crews found was to run a highline across Hinckley Gulch. The 1.5-inch-diameter, mile-long cable ran from Santa Rosalia Ridge to the top of China Ridge directly above Camp 2. When I first discovered that a cable heavier than two Shay locomotives had been strung across Hinckley Gulch, I immediately wondered how they got it up there. I discussed the problem with several knowledgeable engineers. They explained that the cable would have been carried up the incline to Camp 2 and then wound around the drum of a heavy-duty donkey engine. Then the cable would have been pulled across the gulch with a thinner cable. The area that was selected as the anchor point on Santa Rosalia Ridge was at the southwest corner of a quarter-mile-long shelf that extends out into Hinckley Gulch. This is across from the end of Braille Trail in the Soquel Demonstration State Forest today. The elevation on the northern side was 2,000 feet, while it was slightly lower on the southern side. The center of the highline cable sat directly above Hinckley Creek, 700 to 800 feet overhead.

With the cable now suspended across the gulch and the block in place, a special carriage that they had designed for them was mounted on the cable at Camp 2. The carriage was about four feet long and had four grooved wheels, two on top, the other two on the bottom. The top wheels were for riding on the cable, the bottom two were for a line that had a sling attached at its end. Also, there was a "load line" attached to the carriage which was used to run the carriage out to the block at the center. When the block was reached, the carriage would lock itself automatically and the line with the sling would be lowered by pulley to the creek below.

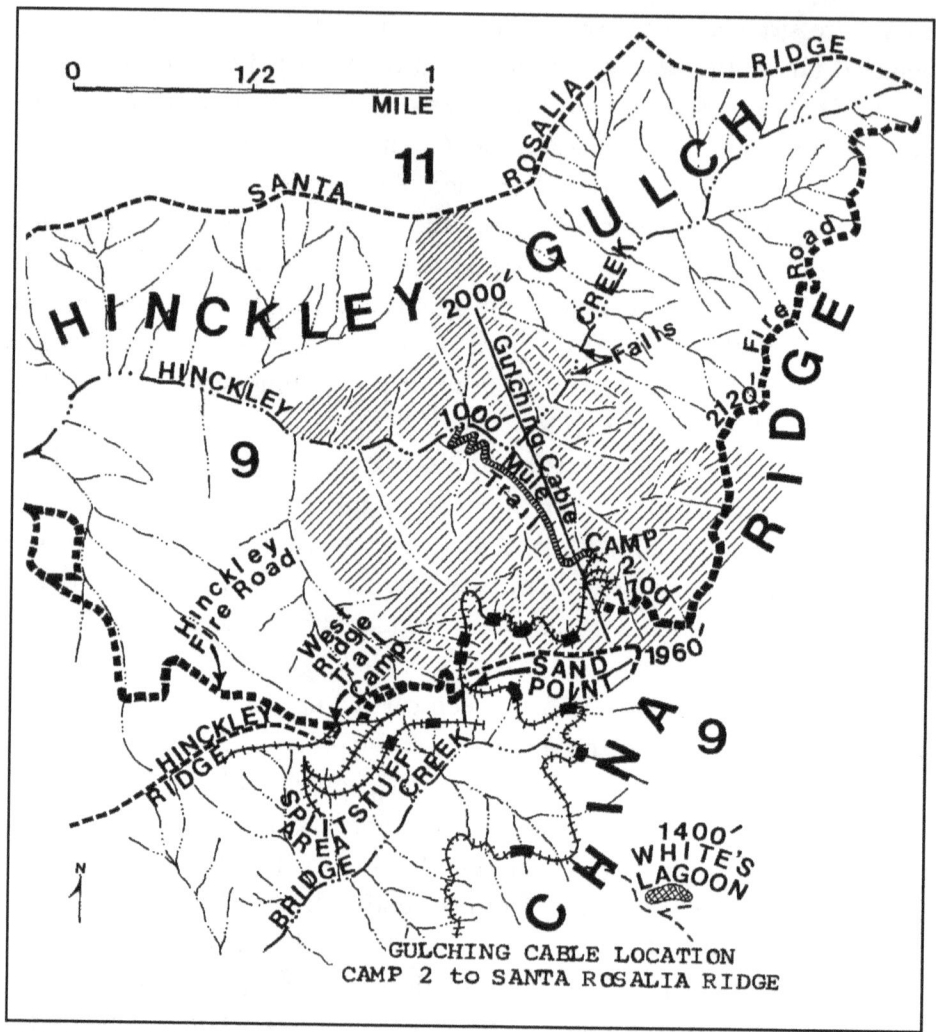

FIGURE 3.7 THE MOLINO TIMBER COMPANY'S HIGHLINE SETUP OVER HINCKLEY GULCH BETWEEN SANTA ROSALIA RIDGE AND CAMP 2

Pieceworkers would bring the splitstuff to the creek camp and stack it into pallets. These would then be attached to the sling. Once ready, a signal was sent to the donkey engine operator at Camp 2, who would pull the material straight up to the highline. When the sling hit the line, it would unlock from the block and begin a slow, gravity-led descent down the line to Camp 2. Above Camp 2, a second block triggered a similar action as the first and lowered the pallet to the ground. Stoodley, who called this system 'gulching,' noted, "while this was not a cheap arrangement to operate, it was included as just a part of the job."

While the cable and carriage solved one of their problems, they also created several others. First, there was how to get the mules down to Hinckley Creek from Camp 2. While the cable was being suspended, Molino contracted the King brothers to run the mule operation. Workers had to dig and blast a switchbacking trail down the gulch's steep side until reaching Hinckley Creek. It was so narrow that mules could not wear their saddles because the hooks that extended out from them would hit against the side of the gulch. On the left, there was a sheer 200-foot drop to the creek, while on the right was solid rock. The highline was used to bring supplies to the creek camp. According to Stoodley, "The pack saddles had been carried out and dropped to the creek in the same way and all mule feed, hay and other supplies had to be sent down in the same manner." Indeed, most of the workers and all of the mules remained in the gulch for the entire season, only emerging at the arrival of winter.

The second problem was that the donkey engine that drove the highline burned away a lot of water during a day's operations. During spring and early summer, there was enough water in Hinckley Creek to fuel the engine at Camp 2. But most of the time it had to be brought in on the railroad. Thus, the railroad was forced to supply water for both the incline's engine and the highline's, more than doubling its reliance on water from Aptos Creek.

The highline created a more immediate problem, as well. Periodically, the latching block at the center of the highline cable needed to be oiled. Stoodley recounts: "A sort of bos'n's seat was rigged to the carriage and a man sent out to do the oiling. To sit in that…frail support and look down nearly a thousand feet to the creek bottom was not too pleasant a sensation, and there were few volunteers for it."[59]

Frederick Hihn dies

In the aftermath of the San Francisco earthquake in 1906, Frederick Hihn had become a different man. He was traumatized by the event, having been in San Francisco at the time and witnessed many of its horrors. Over the subsequent seven years, he entered a state of semi-retirement and divested himself of many of his business obligations. He helped negotiate the sale of the F. A. Hihn Company's retail lumber business to the A. P. Hammond Company and otherwise stepped back from the day-to-day operations of his family's company.

By 1912, he was suffering periodic bouts of an illness that rendered him homebound. At the time of his birthday on August 16, 1913, he seemed to have recovered somewhat, but relapsed shortly afterwards. On August 23, Santa Cruz County's most famous pioneer and one of its wealthiest citizens passed away. In its obituary of Hihn, *Evening News* provided a summary of his life:

> *F. A. Hihn, the well-known Santa Cruz capitalist, died at his home on Locust street at 3:30 o'clock this afternoon of pneumonia. Mr. Hihn was eighty-four years old one week ago today.*
>
> *Many a rare old battle has F. A. Hihn fought with the destroyer and each time he emerged a smiling winner.*
>
> *But it was noted at his eighty-fourth birthday anniversary a week ago today that he had lost hope of ever having his children and grandchildren about him at another such gathering. Though he had been ill for some time he became worse that night and pneumonia developed. This was the immediate cause of death.*
>
> *Frederick A. Hihn was born on the 16th day of August, 1829, at Holzminden, Duchy of Brunswick, Germany. He was one of a family of seven.*
>
> *He was educated in his native town and graduated from its high school.*
>
> *In April, 1849, he sailed for California, attracted by the reports of the discovery of gold.*
>
> *He reached San Francisco in October, 1849, and for a time worked in the mines.*
>
> *He became a hotel proprietor at Sacramento, but quit it after the fire of 1851, coming to Santa Cruz in October*

of that year.

Having knowledge of several languages Mr. Hihn built up a large mercantile business here.

In November, 1853, he married Miss Therese Paggen, a native of France, of German parents. The issue of this marriage was Kate C., Louis W., August C., Fred O., Theresa and Agnes.

In 1857 he made his family home on Locust street, where he died today.

Soon after arriving in Santa Cruz Mr. Hihn devoted himself to real estate and other investments and his properties extend all over the county and take many forms. He was rated a multimillionaire.

He assisted in the organization of the City bank and the First National; he owned Capitola, owned the Hihn water system; owned great business frontage on Pacific avenue; and was interested in many milling enterprises.

With the advance of years he lost none of the clarity of mind which distinguished his early life and was in many respects the most remarkable man this section of California had produced.

His death sparked a dispute among his widow and children over his estate, which would linger in the courts for four years.[60]

The F. A. Hihn Company closes its mill at Laurel

The F. A. Hihn Company's Laurel mill continued to cut lumber through the 1913 season from timber harvested in Tract 16 of the Augmentation. However, in early 1914 cruisers reported that there was not enough standing timber for another season. In response to this, the mill was shut down and dismantled. As had been the case with the Valencia Creek and Gold Gulch mills, pieceworkers were sent to Tract 16 and adjacent tracts owned by the company to turn the remaining usable timber into splitstuff. This operation continued until at least 1917.[61]

The Molino Timber Company continues producing splitstuff in Hinckley Gulch

By the beginning of its second season in the gulch—and the third season since it had started cutting timber in the Augmentation—the Molino Timber Company had worked out most of its problems. Every day, weather permitting, except Sundays and the winter months, Molino's Shay led four to six cars down the grade from Camp 2 and Sandy Point to the top of the incline. This happened at least twice a day, and sometimes as many as four times a day if production levels justified it. At the incline, each car was positioned so that the Rossis could attach a cable to it. In the first two years that the ridgetop railroad operated, laden flatcars were lowered one at a time. However, improved processes and increased market demand justified lowering multiple cars at a time. Still, cars were lowered with extreme caution.

Riding cars up or down the incline was officially forbidden, but the rule usually went unenforced. Early on Monday mornings, workers would catch the first cars as they were hauled up to the top of the incline, while on Saturday nights, they would ride them back down. Specialists and directors, too, would catch a lift on the incline to avoid hiking the long switchback to the top of the ridge. Bert Stoodley describes riding the cars up the incline:

> *On the steepest part of the grade, in riding down on a car, one seemed suspended in the air. In my own case, I usually rode on the rear end of the car, ready to jump off in a hurry if anything happened.*
>
> *This proved entirely practicable and, excepting for one accident when two cars broke loose and ran back down the hill, we had no trouble. In this instance, cars were being lowered with a number of men returning from working. All of the men succeeded in jumping off without injury excepting one, Tony Sweet of Aptos, a man along in his sixties, who was thrown off severely injured. We had him in the hospital for about two months.*

Most workers rode the topmost car for the obvious reason that it was the easiest to jump from if the cable snapped. Stoodley later noted of the incident above that, when they went to look for the runaway cars, they found the wooden beds in splinters but could never find the wheels. The force of gravity on the cars operating up and down the incline was incredibly strong.

At the bottom of the incline, Bernard Klink was in charge of assembling cars to be hoisted to the top of the incline. These 'empties' were in fact stocked with supplies and barrels of water collected from Aptos Creek. Two to three cars at a time were connected together and hoisted up the line by the large donkey engine at the top. Once at the top, they were strung together into a four to six car train and attached to the Shay, which was always connected to the lower end of the train. The Shay then pushed the train the six miles to Camp 2, and the process was repeated.[62]

A. C. Bassett and Alfred Williams die

On March 31, 1914, A. C. Bassett retired as vice president and general manager of the Loma Prieta Lumber Company. At the same time, he relinquished his seat on the boards of several other companies. Bassett was 76 years old at the time and his health was starting to decline. He moved to Gilroy, purchased the local Loma Prieta lumberyard there, and bought a majority stake in the Gilroy Mercantile Company. He hoped to spend his twilight years running this company as a hobby. Bassett did not enjoy his retirement for long, though. On May 14, he died from post-operation complications.

At the next directors' meeting of the Loma Prieta Lumber Company, Timothy Hopkins, Warren Porter, E. J. Sanborn, Helen Sanborn, Stephen Gage, C. H. Redington, and Fred Severance elected Bassett's son, Harvey, as general manager, while Bert Stoodley was appointed secretary. With this new position Stoodley found himself holding the same position in two companies. As head bookkeeper, his salary had been $100 monthly. Now, as Loma Prieta's secretary, his salary increased to $175. Oscar Chase took over Bert's former position as head bookkeeper for the Loma Prieta Lumber Company. Hopkins, meanwhile, became the undisputed head of the company.

The *Evening News* printed Bassett's obituary on May 16:

A. C. BASSETT, PIONEER RAILROAD AND LUMBER MAN, GOES TO REST

With the passing of A. C. Bassett, for many years vice-president and general manager of the Loma Prieta Lumber company, one of the best figures in this portion of California has gone the way from whence there is no returning. When the Southern Pacific company owned a mileage of 125 miles from San Francisco to Monterey, A. C. Bassett was its superintendent and a very popular man he was. He was a close friend of the old guard in the directorate of the Southern Pacific and Central Pacific Railroad company and worked for the latter company when the gap between Sacramento and Ogden was being closed. He gave up railroading to go into the lumber business and associated himself with Timothy Hopkins in the Loma Prieta Lumber company. For the past twenty-five years he has been the general manager of the company and has guided its fortunes from the start when the company owned thousands of acres of standing timber in this county.

During the civil war, Mr. Bassett was a civil engineer and helped build railroads for the confederacy.

Recently he gave up active business and retired with the hope of enjoying life. He remarked to friends in Santa Cruz just a few weeks ago that he hoped the end would be sudden when it came. He died at his Union street home in San Francisco Thursday night.

Surviving him are two children, Harvey Bassett who succeeded to his father's business and a daughter, Miss Amy Bassett. He was born in Ohio 76 years ago.

The newspaper appears to have made a mistake regarding Bassett's Civil War services, however, since the *Oakland Tribune* published an anecdote from his life on May 25 entitled

WHEN BASSETT MET BUCKNER

A. C. Bassett, the lumberman who died here a few days ago af-

ter close business relations for a number of years with Timothy Hopkins, was fond of telling his friends of how he first met General Simon B. Buckner, the Confederate general who died several months ago in Kentucky. It was at the outbreak of the Civil War while Bassett was a telegraph operator on the old Louisville & Nashville Railroad line. Bassett had a small station office near the southern line of the Blue Grass State. Buckner's men came in and seized the place, also making Bassett a prisoner after he had declared himself in sympathy with the North. He was finally taken before Buckner, who offered to give him work as an operator if he would join the South.

"Better do it, young man," said Buckner, "for when this trouble is over we will be the best part of this country."

Bassett said he couldn't champion the southern cause and was given three hours to get out with his personal effects.

Some months later the same Buckner met a signal defeat at Fort Donelson at the hands of Grant and Bassett was an operator for some of the latter's troop trains.

Two days after Bassett's death, on May 16, Molino Timber Company president and Loma Prieta Lumber Company secretary Alfred Williams died of stomach cancer at his home in Santa Cruz. The *Evening News* lamented:

ALFRED WILLIAMS IS SUMMONED

Secretary of Loma Prieta Lumber Co. follows his associate, A. C. Bassett, in death.

Well known and well liked lumber man had been suffering for long time.

Strangely and closely following the demise of his old time friend and business associate in the affairs of the Loma Prieta Lumber company, A. C. Bassett, death this morning laid its cold hand on Alfred Williams, secretary of the company at his home on Jordan street. The end had not been unexpected, on account of the recent serious illness of the well known man.

> He had been a patient sufferer with acute stomach trouble for a period of years.
>
> The deceased was an extremely popular man in a business way and socially and Santa Cruz suffers a distinct loss in his death. He was born at Rio Vista on the Sacramento river, fifty-three years ago. Before coming to Santa Cruz county a quarter of a century ago, Mr. Williams was in the lumber business in Pasadena. It was there that he was married. Coming to Santa Cruz he became the manager of the big lumber interests of Grover and company and had an interest in the Little Basin Lumber company. About fifteen years ago he took up his work with the Loma Prieta Lumber company and has been with them ever since.
>
> Surviving the deceased is the wife and two daughters, Mrs. A. F. Cowden and Miss Irene Williams.
>
> The funeral services will be held Monday afternoon at the home. Rev. E. C. Philleo, former pastor of the Presbyterian Church here to which Mr. Williams belonged, officiating. The interment will be made in Odd Fellows' Cemetery.

His son-in-law, Dr. A. F. Cowden, was elected by the Molino Timber Company's board to replace him, while Oscar Chase was elected the new president of the company.[63]

Bert Stoodley brings the Notley Barrel & Box Factory to the Loma Prieta Lumber Company's mill on Aptos Creek

Even though he was secretary of both the Loma Prieta Lumber Company and the Molino Timber Company, Bert Stoodley found himself with a lot of time on his hands in late 1914. As a side project, Stoodley decided to buy a recently defunct barrel and box factory from the Notley Company of Notley's Landing in Monterey County. Prior to the acquisition, he asked permission from Timothy Hopkins to set up two small mills beside the abandoned Loma Prieta Lumber Company's mill building on Aptos Creek. Hopkins agreed and the purchase was finalized. Stoodley hired Jim Fisher to help him set up the two mills, which could turn out shakes, shingles, and apple boxes.

With the spare parts from Notley's mills and the deteriorating parts from the Loma Prieta Lumber Company's mills, Stoodley and Fisher were able to assemble a lumber mill capable of producing 12,000 board feet of lumber daily. Once more, Stoodley approached Hopkins, this time to ask if the millpond's dam could be disassembled and its logs cut into lumber. Draining the pond would also free all the sinker logs that had been sitting below the surface for up to twenty-nine years. Hopkins gave permission, but required Stoodley to pay a stumpage fee to the Loma Prieta Lumber Company. Because it was almost winter, Stoodley waited until the next year to begin the task.[64]

The Loma Prieta Lumber Company closes its planing mills

With no new sources of lumber, the Loma Prieta Lumber Company had been importing lumber to its yards to keep its planing mills afloat. However, the price of lumber had become too expensive by late 1914 to make a profit, so the company decided to permanently close its two planing mills. In Watsonville, this meant that at least 50 men were put out of work, while around half that number were given notice in Santa Cruz. The company also began selling and ending its leases on its lumberyards throughout the Bay Area. It retained a small number of yards to sell the splitstuff from Hinckley Gulch, but reduced its footprint considerably.[65]

The Loma Prieta Lumber Company's millpond dam on Aptos Creek is dismantled

In early spring 1915, Bert Stoodley and Jim Fisher began dismantling the dam of the Loma Prieta Lumber Company's millpond on Aptos Creek. They cut the large logs that formed the dam as well as the sinkers found at the bottom of the millpond into lumber at the small mill Stoodley had purchased the previous year from the Notley Company. Stoodley later claimed that he did not make much of a profit from the venture, but he did gain much experience in the manufacture of shingles, shakes, apple boxes, and rough lumber.

After all the logs were processed, Stoodley and Fisher began making shingles and shakes at the mill from bolts provided by the Molino Timber Company. As independent contractors separate from the timber company, they charged a fee for this service, which helped make up for the poor return from the lumber operation.[66]

The Molino Timber Company extends its railroad to Camp 3

After two seasons operating out of Camp 2, the Molino Timber Company made plans in spring 1915 to shift operations further up Hinckley Gulch. Probably from late 1914, workers began clearing the railroad grade between Camp 2 and the planned location for Camp 3. This new site was two miles to the north and the route to it followed an increasingly narrow shelf above the eastern side of the gulch. A short distance from Camp 2, the hillside begins to fall steeply toward Hinckley Creek, with grades of up to 75 degrees in places. Some of these hillsides were 50 to 200 feet high. Dynamite was required to blast large stumps and rock outcroppings out of the right-of-way. As before, track layers followed behind the graders and piles of splitstuff lined the route as pieceworkers moved ahead.

A small number of logs were left behind by pieceworkers to be used for cribbing and trestles, sixteen of which were required beyond Camp 2. Most of these crossed shallow gulches and streams, and several still remain in place today. Grading crews were also forced to make six cuts along the right-of-way north of the camp. Only two cuts were required for the section between Camp 1 and Camp 2, one at the top of the incline and one near Sand Point.

Molino also needed to relocate the highline across Hinckley Gulch. The anchor on Santa Rosalia Ridge remained in place, but the donkey engine was moved north to Lone Tree Prairie, which today is a waypoint along the Aptos Creek Fire Road. When Molino's crews first identified this location, they found three tall redwood trees with their tops broken off in an area that was otherwise deforested. The Loma Prieta Lumber Company had come through this section prior to the earthquake but left these trees due to their condition. All three still remain today, the largest directly on the fire road and the other two just to the west of it, all in the vicinity of Sheep Camp Meadow two miles from Sand Point. To get the donkey engine up to the top of the ridge, it was

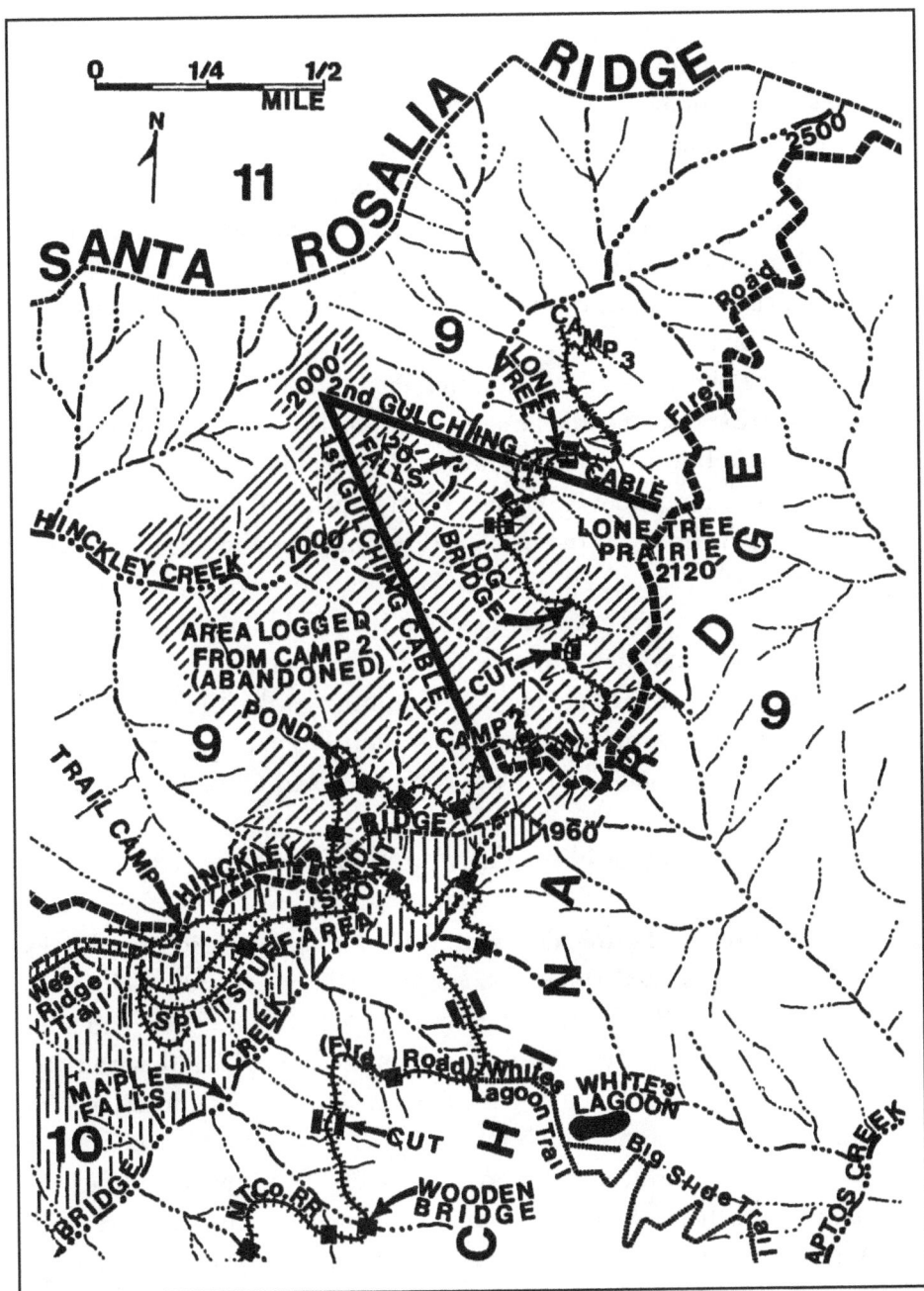

Figure 3.8 The Molino Timber Company's second highline setup over Hinckley Gulch between Santa Rosalia Ridge and Lone Tree Prairie

loaded onto a flatcar and taken by railroad to below Lone Tree Prairie, still attached to the highline. A crude road was carved 370 feet straight uphill to the site and the engine pulled itself to the top using a secondary cable.

Below on Hinckley Creek, the highline's new path situated the center of the cable directly over a clearing formed above the upper waterfall. This waterfall had proven an impediment to workers being able to harvest timber upstream of the old creek camp, so the new camp's location above the waterfall meant that most of the headwaters of Hinckley Creek were now accessible to pieceworkers.

Where the highline's path intersected the railroad route, two spurs were installed where splitstuff could be assembled and loaded onto flatcars. Camp 3 was located slightly further to the north. It occupied a narrow shelf at about 1,800-foot elevation, and was 900 feet from Hinckley Creek. Unfortunately for crews, the nearness of the creek did not make it any easier to harvest timber there—there was a 200-foot drop just to the northwest of the camp. Unprocessed timber was taken to the camp from the highline landing to be cut into splitstuff and then shipped out. Worker cottages, called 'shanties' by Bert Stoodley, lined either side of the railroad tracks. One or two short spurs with accompanying landings were installed to park flatcars and aid in loading. By late summer, Camp 3 was completed and Camp 2 shut down.[67]

The Valencia–Hihn Company is incorporated

Following Frederick Hihn's death in 1913, a dispute arose over his estate. The court assigned three referees to settle the matter: Charles W. Hammer, Orrin S. Blodgett, and Ralph W. Heins. The heirs and their representatives agreed that the F. A. Hihn Company's land within the Augmentation, encompassing some 5,098 acres, should remain intact. With the assistance of the company's bookkeeper, A. S. Jansen, they incorporated the Valencia–Hihn Company on August 10, 1915, transferring to this new firm from the F. A. Hihn Company all of the unlogged acreage in the Augmentation as well as the right-of-way known as the Hihn Railroad Grade through Rancho Soquel between the Capitola railroad station and the Augmentation's southern boundary.[68]

Chapter 4

~

The Residue of Success

The dispute over the Frederick A. Hihn estate and the role of the Valencia–Hihn Company

On January 4, 1916, Charles Hammer, Orrin Blodgett, and Ralph Heins submitted their estimate on the value of Frederick Hihn's estate. According to Hihn's will, the estate was to be divided between Hihn's widow, who was to receive half, and his six children, who would receive one-twelfth each. However, by 1916, the situation had changed and the estate was to be divided between the following:

- Therese Hihn (*née* Paggen), Hihn's widow
- August Charles Hihn
- Katherine Charlotte Cope (*née* Hihn)
- Agnes Younger (*née* Hihn)
- Frederick Otto Hihn
- Ruth Ready, daughter of Theresa Hall (*née* Hihn), who was living with her aunt and guardian, Agnes Younger

- Teresa Agnes Hihn, daughter of Louis William Hihn, who was represented by her mother, Harriet Israel

Louis' son, Eulice William Hihn, had died in 1915 leaving behind a surviving child, Jack Eulice William Hihn, who was not considered in the inheritance.

Excluding the value of the unlogged land in the Augmentation, which had been transferred to the Valencia–Hihn Company in 1915, the referees estimated the value of the estate to be approximately $3,000,000. The value of the Valencia–Hihn Company land, meanwhile, was estimated at

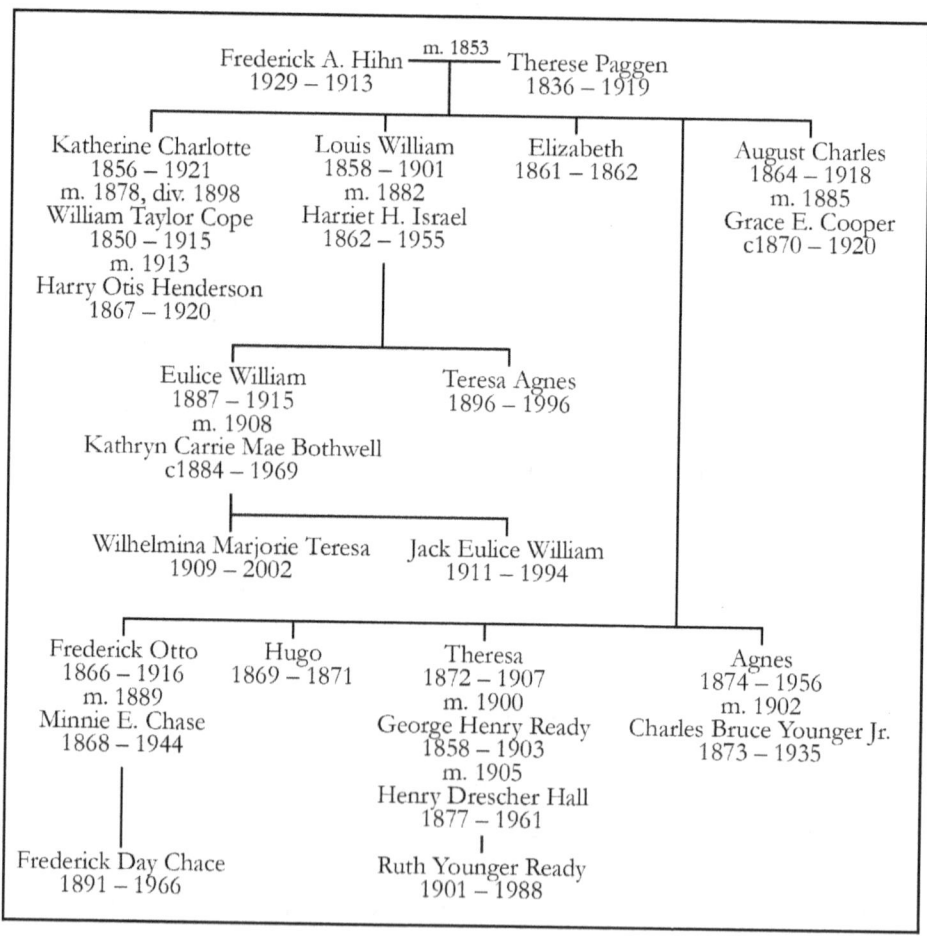

FIGURE 4.1 THE FREDERICK A. HIHN FAMILY

$102,750, or $20.15 an acre, while the value of the timber was set at $3.50 per 1,000 board feet. The referees declined estimating the value of the tan oak, live oak, madrone, pine, and less usable redwood in the property, although they stated that it had some value, as well.

Hihn's widow, Therese, disagreed with the referees' findings and filed suit against her children, grandchildren, and the estate's assistant secretary, A. S. Jansen. She wanted the entire estate, including that of the Valencia–Hihn Company's land, revalued. To accomplish the latter part of this demand, the Valencia–Hihn Company hired the A. W. Elam Company, a logging, engineering, and estimating company headquartered in San Francisco, to survey the property in the Augmentation and establish a value. The company hired a local logging engineer, Horatio N. Ormsbee, to supervise the survey team.

Ormsbee was born in Michigan on March 26, 1884. When he arrived in Santa Cruz County is unknown, but he was first hired by the Elam Company in 1914 and remained with them until 1917. In a report published around 1946, he described himself as "a forest engineer and surveyor. I am also an owner and administrator with an intimate knowledge of the Soquel Augmentation Ranch for the past twenty years. I have cruised timber (in this and in other areas), surveyed boundaries, and located forest roads. I have also had charge of various developments and improvements in the subject area, including water supply, lake building, and some timber management."[69]

The Santa Cruz Land Title Company simplifies description of land sold in deeds concerning the Augmentation

For fifty-two years, every deed written concerning the sale of land in the Augmentation included the following statement in one form or another:

> *All that real property situated in Santa Cruz County, known as the Augmentation Rancho, set apart to [name] in severalty by the final decree of the District Court of the Third Judicial District of the State of California, in and for the County of Santa Cruz, in the action of FREDERICK A. HIHN ver-*

sus HENRY W. PECK et al. and entered on the 14th day of September 1864, and being particularly described as Lot No. _____ in the report and maps of the commissioners of said Rancho, in said action, which said decree, report and maps are hereby referred to for particular description as follows...

On February 10, 1916, the Santa Cruz Land Title Company finally recorded District Judge Samuel B. McKee's 1864 decision in the Santa Cruz County Book of Deeds. This made the process of filing future land sales in the Augmentation substantially simpler since they would no longer need to refer to the lawsuit and subsequent decree. According to local legal analyst Earl Livingston of Ben Lomond, the reason the decree had never been recorded was that the County Recorder's Office expected further lawsuits and disputes over the decision, so it felt it was prudent to delay filing the decision. Then it simply forgot to register the decision after enough time had passed.[70]

The Molino Timber Company pauses operations on Hinckley Creek

For the Molino Timber Company, 1916 began as planned. As soon as the ground began to dry and harden, the Shay locomotive was taken out of storage, given a maintenance check-up, and then sent to Hinckley Gulch to pick up the accumulated cords of splitstuff produced over the winter. Soon, all operations were up and running along the line's entire eight miles. But then, in late spring, disaster struck.

The latch for the highline's carriage and sling, which raised and lowered splitstuff bundles from Hinckley Creek to Camp 3, stopped working. Without it, the carriage could not automatically stop at the center of the line. All attempts to repair the mechanism failed, halting all highline shipments arriving from the upper creek camp. Molino teams quickly searched for alternatives to get the splitstuff to the railroad grade. They brought in extra donkey engines and tried pulling pallets of splitstuff up the hillside. But this severely damaged the products. Adequately protecting each load proved too expensive and time consuming, two luxuries

The Residue of Success   1916

Molino did not have. As a result, the company halted most of its operations to reconsider their options.

After several months where the only activity in the Augmentation was Molino sending its remaining splitstuff and that produced by the Valencia–Hihn Company down to Molino Station, Oscar Chase and Bert Stoodley informed Timothy Hopkins that the company would be terminating its contract with the Loma Prieta Lumber Company at the end of the year.[71]

The Southern Pacific Railroad completes a survey of the Loma Prieta Branch

In June 1916, the Southern Pacific Railroad completed a survey of the entire Loma Prieta Branch between Aptos and the former village of Loma Prieta, a distance of 3.7 miles. The primary purpose of this, paired with an earlier preliminary survey conducted in 1915, was to replace records lost in the fiery aftermath of the 1906 earthquake in San Francisco.[72]

The A. W. Elam Company submits report on the Valencia–Hihn Company's land in the Augmentation

On July 15, 1916, the A. W. Elam Company completed its report on the Valencia–Hihn Company's 5,098 acres in the Augmentation, comprising all or part of Tracts 1, 6, 10, 11, and 25. It should be noted that the report puts smaller survey lots into large blocks, of which there are seven. Several sections of the report have no bearing on this book and have been omitted. Of the sections relating to timber, I have arranged Horatio Ormsbee's findings into the five tracts mentioned above.

> *This timber land, comprising five thousand and nine acres* [corrected to 5,098 acres to include the 99 acres Ormsbee missed in the eastern section of Tract 10] *is situated in Santa Cruz County, California and is a portion of the Soquel Augmentation, an old Spanish grant.*
>
> *It lies about seven miles north of Capitola on the Coast. Capitola is four miles east of Santa Cruz, and the line of the*

Southern Pacific passes through Capitola. There is a good highway from Capitola to the timber.

Method of Examination

As the timber lies in an old Spanish Grant on which there is no Government survey, the tract was divided into lots containing forty acres or more or less, as the boundaries would permit, these lots being grouped for convenience into blocks. The main creeks were taken as the base lines and the cruise lines run as nearly at right angles to them as was consistent with the topography. The base lines were run with a transit, and stadia elevations taken as a basis for the topographic map.

Two runs were made through each lot, and 20 percent of the timber tallied as a basis for computing the total timber. Instruments were used to determine the diameter, height and taper of the timber. The scale was compiled from our own volume tables of California timber.

A topographic map was made, with a fifty foot contour interval, to accompany this report, and the factors governing logging, milling and operation of the timber noted.

Timber

The timber consists of Redwood, Fir, Tan Oak, Chinkapin Oak, Madrone and some of the lessor hardwoods. A few good sized Sycamore were seen.

Redwood

First in commercial value, and is a good grade of timber for this locality. As a run it does not get so large as some of the Humboldt County, California redwood, but on the whole this is a fine body of timber.

In places there is evidence of dry rot in fallen logs, etc., and in different portions of the tract there is evidence of defect caused by fire, scars and overmature timber. The bulk of the timber, however, is good, thrifty wood and will average with any of its age and class in the State.

The timber will grade into lumber about as follows: #1

Clear 25% and Sappy Clear 10% totalling 35% while #1 Common is 30%, #2 Common 25%, and #3 Common 10%.

It splits exceedingly well, much better than the northern Redwood, and will furnish the best of split timber.

Fir

A very small percentage of the stand is Fir, and it cuts little figure. There is considerable defect in it, and there are also some very fine trees. There is not enough Fir in the tract to supply the necessary amount needed to mix with the Redwood for local trade, for dimension, etc.

Tan Oak

Tan Oak operations have been carried on in the tract at different places for some years back. The Tan Oak is of all ages, and there is considerable second growth oak on the tract. The small oak was noted separately. The bark is very heavy on the old oak, and it is a well known fact that the Tan Oak of this district contains a high percentage of tannic acid and is much desired by the tanneries.

Other Timber

The other Oak, Madrone, etc., is scrubby and fit for fuel only, and was established as such.

Former Cuttings

There has been no lumbering operation carried on in the timber except occasional cutting for split timber, shakes, posts, etc., to supply local need. It has not been extensive enough to damage the tract for a lumbering operation.

There is considerable wind thrown Redwood lying on the ground in good condition and still valuable for splitstuff.

Lumber and Wood

The Tan Oak as aforesaid has been operated extensively, and at the time of this examination Tan Oak was being peeled on the tract by a contractor.

Markets

This timber is very accessible to market; in fact, it is one of the most accessible Redwood tracts on the Coast.

Everything of value can be disposed of.

It is near the fruit growing districts of the Santa Clara Valley, the country surrounding Watsonville, and the Santa Cruz district. The Little Soquel Valley, in which the timber lies, furnishes a small local market, and will develop. Capitola, a small summer resort, is but seven miles away, and that with Santa Cruz will help to take wood refuse, etc. The adjacent local market is one of the best.

Plan of Operation

In order to operate this tract in the most efficient manner in the opinion of the writers of this report, it would be best to build a single band mill at the timber along Soquel Creek's East Branch, where several sites are available for pond and yard sites.

The logging should be done by donkey engines to a narrow-gauge logging railway built from the mill through the timber, with short chutes to reach odd corners, but the bulk of the timber can be logged directly to railway well located.

There are two practical methods for bringing the lumber from the mill to market: (1) by motor truck to the Southern Pacific Railroad at Capitola, and (2) by the construction of a railroad to the mill from a point on the Southern Pacific near Capitola.

- ***Using motor trucks:*** *There is a good road all the way to the timber with easy grades, nearly all in favor of the traffic. The only adverse grade is one about four percent, which is not an obstacle to motor truck hauling. A very little expense would put the mills at the timber into touch with Capitola with a first class truck road, on a scant seven mile haul.*
- ***Installing a railroad:*** *From a point on the Southern Pacific about a mile east of Capitola, a standard gauge railroad could be constructed to the mill without great difficulty, the distance being about seven miles. The grade*

could be located above the cultivated lands in the Soquel Valley, thus avoiding expensive rights-of-way.

We estimate that the road could be built for not over $42,000. If this was done, we would recommend making the entire logging railway standard gauge, in which case an additional locomotive would not be necessary, as the logging locomotive would be able to take care of the haul to the mainline.

Lumber could be loaded at the mill onto cars of the Southern Pacific, thus eliminating the need of equipment. A great advantage in favor of the railroad is the avoidance of the expense of rehandling and also the fact that lumber can be marketed during the rainy season, when trucks would sometimes be tied up.

The element of uncertainty in this plan is the cost of right-of-way, and on that account we have rendered our report on the basis of motor truck haul from the mill to Capitola, and a narrow gauge railroad from the timber to mill.

The Bridge Creek unit is the only portion of the tract that would be at all difficult to bring to the mill by logging railway but grade could be developed into it.

This Bridge Creek unit could be operated by the Loma Prieta Lumber Company, whose logging railway crosses one end of it. If, however, it could not be sold to them at an advantage it could be operated with the rest of the timber, but it would be best their way.

In the purposes of this report the whole tract will be considered logged to a single band mill on the East Branch of Soquel Creek, as outlined above. The details of the logging plan are shown on the topographic map accompanying this report.

Timber Estimates

The timber on each lot or subdivision has been estimated separately, the amount of each species being recorded on the timber map accompanying this report. The following table shows the number of thousands of each species in each block.

The table also shows the number of cords of Tan Oak Bark, Tan Oak Wood, Hardwood and Soft Wood, and the number of Redwood and Fir piles, computed separately. All trees of a diameter from 14 to 18 inches are figured as piling.

A provision of some timber sales contracts required that logging debris be piled in the logged area rather than being left where it fell for its disposal, usually by burning. Also, sometimes the United States Forest Service in timber sale contracts required the purchaser to move logging residue to a landing or other specified location. The Elam report includes in its definition of 'pile' all trees that had a diameter from 14 to 18 inches. The following is a summary of the Elam Company's timber estimates:

TRACT 1
Cruised area: 107 acres
Total area: 1,200 acres
Yield: 1,743,000 board feet
Average yield per acre: 16,290 board feet
Down timber: 0 board feet

TRACT 6
Cruised area: 442 acres
Total area: 442 acres
Yield: 12,964,000 board feet
Average yield per acre: 29,329 board feet
Down timber: 728,000 board feet

TRACT 10 (Spignet Creek)
Cruised area: 453 acres
Total area: 453 acres
Yield: 24,863,000 board feet
Average yield per acre: 54,885 board feet
Down timber: 1,035,000 board feet

The Residue of Success 1916

TRACT 10 (Bridge Creek)
Cruised area: 610 acres
Total area: 610 acres
Yield: 21,771,000 (14,000,000) board feet*
Average yield per acre: 35,690 (22,951) board feet*
Down timber: 569,000 board feet
  * (Total after logging was halted in Tract 10)

TRACT 11
Cruised area: 3,022 acres
Total area: 3,513 acres
Yield: 124,237,000 board feet
Average yield per acre: 41,111 board feet
Down timber: 2,432,000 board feet

TRACT 25
Cruised area: 464 acres
Total area: 853 acres
Yield: 2,985,000 board feet
Average yield per acre: 6,433 board feet
Down timber: 41,000 board feet

ESTIMATES:
Total area: 7,071 acres, of which 5,098 was cruised

Redwood and fir:
Average yield (from redwood): 36,988 board feet
Total yield (from standing redwood): 188,563,000 board feet
Total yield (from dead and down redwood): 5,235,000 board feet
Total yield (from fir): 7,256,000 board feet
Total yield (from redwood and fir): 201,054,000 board feet

Other trees:
Total yield (from tan oak bark): 3,222 cords
Total yield (from tan oak wood): 6,638 cords

Total yield (from hard wood): 10,695 cords
Total yield (from soft wood): 12,578 cords
Total yield (from redwood piles): 12,578,000 board feet
Total yield (from fir piles): 1,157,000 board feet[73]

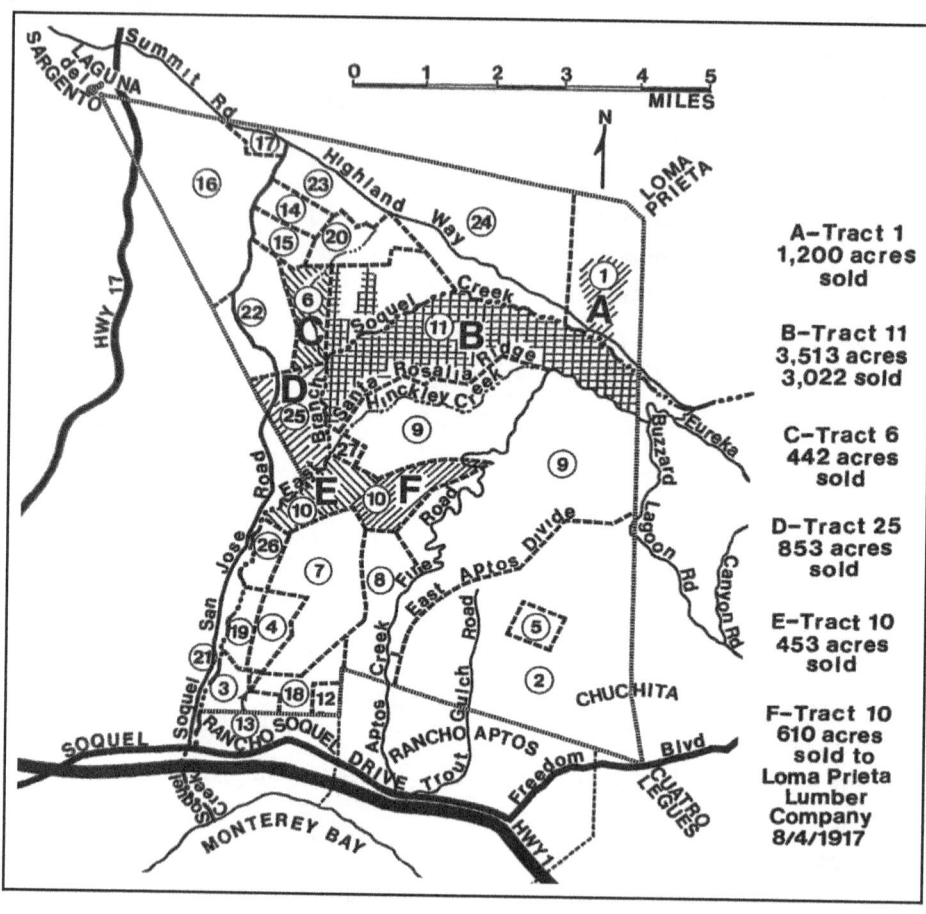

FIGURE 4.2 AREAS CRUISED BY THE A. W. ELAM COMPANY

Agreement between the Valencia–Hihn Company and the Loma Prieta Lumber Company concerning Tract 10 in the Augmentation

In an attempt to head off a judicial ruling that would negatively impact the timber-harvesting operations of the company, the directors of the Valencia–Hihn Company decided in fall 1916 that the best course of action was to sell the 610 acres along Bridge Creek in Tract 10 in the Augmentation. The Elam report had found that it still contained about 14,000,000 board feet of timber along its lower section, plenty to interest a potential buyer.

The obvious candidate to purchase the property was the Loma Prieta Lumber Company. At the end of the 1916 season, Valencia–Hihn ceased all operations within Tract 10 and its representatives met with Timothy Hopkins to hammer out the details of the sale. The matter of Therese Hihn's lawsuit notwithstanding, a memorandum of agreement must have been made between the two parties, since Hopkins began preparations to rebuild the old mill on Aptos Creek shortly afterwards.

At the same time, Hopkins advised the Molino Timber Company's directors to push on with their harvesting of the upper reaches of Hinckley Gulch. Rather than find some way of restoring the broken highline rig, he advised them to extend the railroad track all the way to the headwaters of Hinckley Creek, so that mules could directly load splitstuff onto waiting flatcars. However, this plan would not produce enough money to make the cost of extending the line worthwhile. Thus, Hopkins also recommended that trees large enough to turn into lumber be left for now. Once the new mill was up and running, he would find a way to transport logs cut in the Hinckley to the new mill. This idea excited the directors and they agreed.[74]

The Frederick Hihn Estate is divided

On December 12, 1916, Charles Hammer, Orrin Blodgett, and Ralph Heins submitted to the court their plan relating to the settlement of Frederick Hihn's estate. As expected, Hihn's widow, Therese, was to receive half of the estate, with the remaining half being split six ways between Hihn's children or their senior heirs. Before the actual divisions could be defined, though, the court had to resolve Therese Hihn's lawsuit against her children, which meant assessing the findings from the Elam report. The matter of the sale of the Bridge Creek land to the Loma Prieta Lumber Company was also ongoing and had to be settled.

Over his lifetime, Frederick Hihn had acquired or gained a stake in many businesses across California, many of which he still owned at the time of his death. These all had to be divided between his heirs as a part of the settlement. The referees separated the assets into two categories denoted by the letters "A" and "B." The properties and facilities that made up the "A" category would, if retained, provide the heir with an income. Items in the "B" category would not provide an income, if retained, but if sold would provide the heir with a one-time payment. The approximate value of the "A" category divisions was $182,000, while the "B" items were worth about $60,000 each. Therefore, the market value of each division that the heirs would bid on was about $242,000.

Before the six heirs, excepting the widow, could make their selection, they had to submit a bid, with the highest bidder then being allowed to make the first choice. The selections made by the heirs were made in the following order:

- Agnes Younger, with a high bid of $21,000, made the first selection. She selected the Shasta and Commodore Hotels in San Francisco, properties in Fairview Park, property in Santa Cruz, and minor holdings elsewhere in San Francisco and Fresno County.
- Louis Hihn's daughter, Teresa Hihn, represented by her mother, Harriet, made the second choice with a bid of $20,000. She selected land in the eastern part of Tracts 2 and 5 in the Augmentation, property on Pacific Avenue in Santa Cruz which was occupied by O'Conner, Strikeman & Moore, properties within the township of Aptos, and personal property consisting of lumber, shingles, split-stuff, old railroad iron, ties and bolts, and many additional items, all of which ultimately proved worthless on the open market.
- August Hihn made the third choice with a bid of $12,000. He selected land in Gold Gulch and on Rancho Zayante, property in Rancho Rincon, property at the northwest corner of Pacific Avenue and Lincoln Street in Santa Cruz, the Hihn–Hammond Company's lumberyard in Watsonville, and several lots in Santa Cruz.
- Frederick Day Hihn made the fourth choice with a bid of $4,500.

Frederick was the only son of Frederick Otto Hihn, who had died on March 20, 1916 from a heart aneurysm. He, with the aid of his mother Minnie, selected property on Pacific Avenue in Santa Cruz, land and a building on Walnut Avenue tenanted at the time to a Miss Holsey by Woolworth & O'Brien, property in Hollister, and land in Tract 16 in the Augmentation near Laurel.

No further bids were made, leaving Katherine Henderson and Ruth Ready without a choice. They were allocated the following:

- Henderson was given several properties in Camp Capitola, the Soquel Water System, Grove Place, the Capitola reservoir, and several other properties.
- Ready was given land and facilities in the western half of Tract 2 in the Augmentation, properties in San Francisco and Castroville, land in Aptos, and several other properties in the county. She was also given a number of farm animals and other items, all relatively worthless on the open market.

On February 23, 1917, to enable the execution of Hihn's will, the F. A. Hihn Company was formally dissolved. Following this, August Hihn, Katherine Henderson, Agnes Younger, Ruth Ready, Teresa Hihn, and Frederick Day Hihn sold their shares in the Hihn Water Company and Santa Cruz Water Company.[75]

The Southern Pacific Railroad's property in Tract 9 reverts to the Loma Prieta Lumber Company

On March 25, 1899, the Loma Prieta Lumber Company had transferred 15,150 square feet of land in Tract 9 in the Augmentation to the Southern Pacific Railroad. The transfer included the lumberyard, the three spurs within the yard, and the right-of-way between the yard and Aptos Creek. The reason why the railroad wanted this property remains unclear, but it was part of a wider scheme to own the right-of-way of the Loma Prieta Branch outright. By the mid-1910s, the lumberyard had been mostly abandoned and Bert Stoodley was running a small shingle and box mill on the site.

In late 1916, Timothy Hopkins, in preparation for rebuilding the Aptos Creek mill, sued Southern Pacific to return possession of this land to the Loma Prieta Lumber Company. The railroad offered no defense, so the Santa Cruz District Court awarded the property to its prior owner in a decision given on January 30, 1917.[76]

The Molino Timber Company extends its railroad to the headwaters of Hinckley Creek

As soon as the ground was dry enough to lay track in the spring of 1917, the Molino Timber Company began extending its narrow-gauge railroad 3,000 feet from Camp 3 to the headwaters of Hinckley Creek. Unlike with previous extensions, most of this right-of-way was probably already clear of timber since Molino spent the second half of 1916 harvesting all accessible redwood trees in a desperate attempt to make up for the loss of its highline rig. Crews had also likely spent the late winter and early spring at the headwaters of the creek preparing splitstuff that could be hauled out as soon as the railroad was extended.

Any search for the railroad right-of-way beyond Camp 3 should not begin at the camp site. Although there is some graded railroad bed beyond the camp, most of it was buried in a landslide in February 1982, with a large lagoon formed to the north of the slide at the top of the creek. It was not until 1983 that I was able to find traces of the railroad line on the west bank and determine the approximate route it must have taken to reach this place.

When the Molino line left Camp 3, it set off in an easterly direction along the gulch's wall. A short bridge was needed to cross a seasonal stream and then the track continued, meandering around a tight curve as the elevation gradually increased. The track reached a steep gully and continued up it as far as possible, about 200 feet, until the gradient became too steep. At this point, the track switched and headed back toward Hinckley Creek. The track made a sharp curve to the north, crossed a short bridge over another stream, and then made a hard eastern turn up another gully. It climbed

The Residue of Success 1917

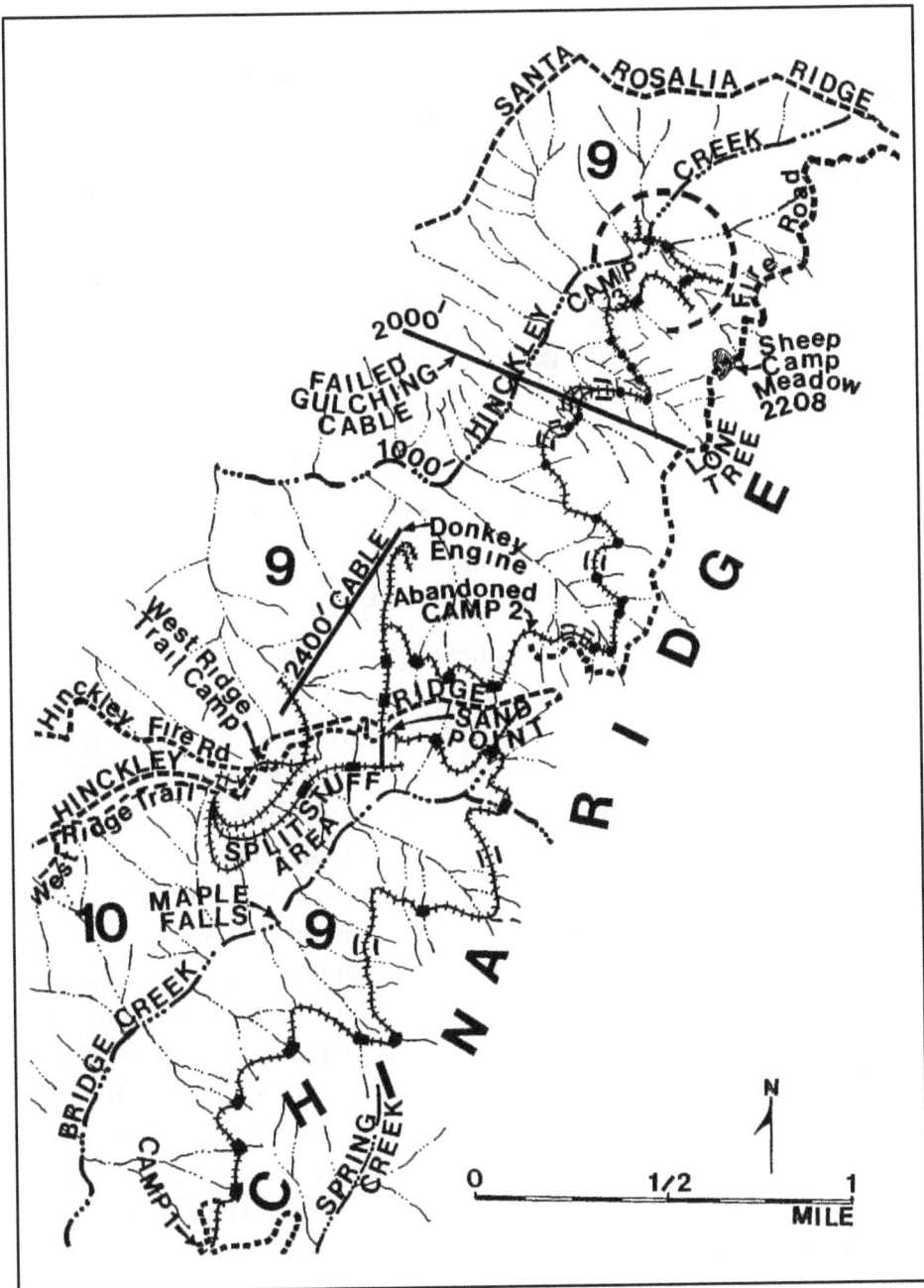

FIGURE 4.3 ROUTE OF THE MOLINO TIMBER COMPANY'S RAILROAD FROM CAMP 1 TO BEYOND CAMP 3 ON HINCKLEY CREEK

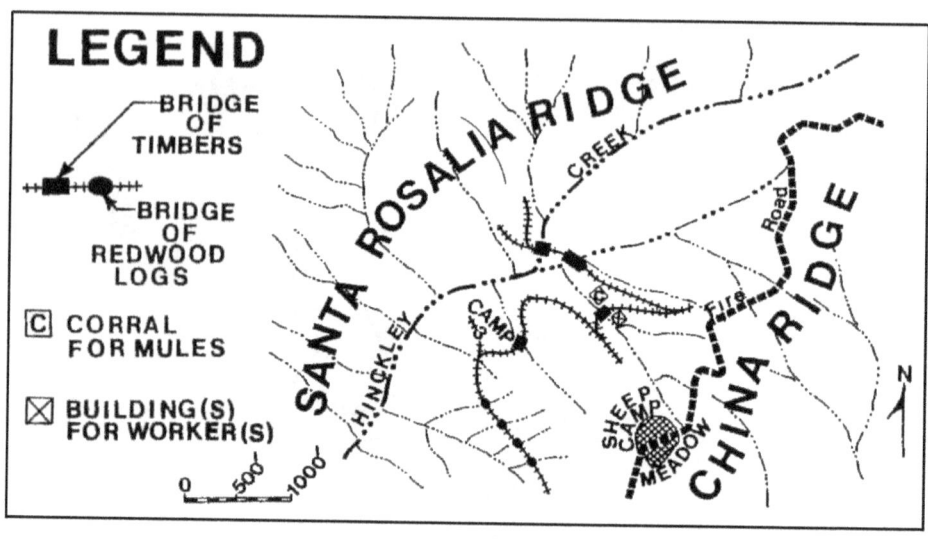

FIGURE 4.4 THE MOLINO TIMBER COMPANY'S RAILROAD TRACKAGE AROUND THE HEADWATERS OF HINCKLEY CREEK

this for about 500 feet until the gradient again became too steep. The track once more switched and ran down the middle of a seasonal stream bed until reaching a larger tributary of Hinckley Creek. Here, a long bridge was built, followed immediately by a shorter bridge over Hinckley Creek itself, before the track finally reached the flat loading area on the west bank.

This landing provided sufficient space for mule teams to deposit their splitstuff, much of which was cut from trees harvested from the west bank of Hinckley Creek. Following Hopkins' recommendation, smaller logs that could be cut into timber were also dragged by donkey engine to the landing and loaded onto flatcars. By the middle of the summer, these could be cut by the Loma Prieta Lumber Company at the reopened Aptos Creek mill.

Some proof of this right-of-way still exists, although it is difficult to access and find. On China Ridge, north below Sheep Camp Meadow, the 200-foot-long roadbed remains and can be reached with minor difficulty. The route from there to the next gulch, including several timbers with nails from the bridge, can be found along the railroad bed. Evidence of two structures also survives just beyond the bridge ruins. Immediately to the east, part of a large structure can still be identified, including bricks used in a fireplace. Across the right-of-way from it, many posts still hold

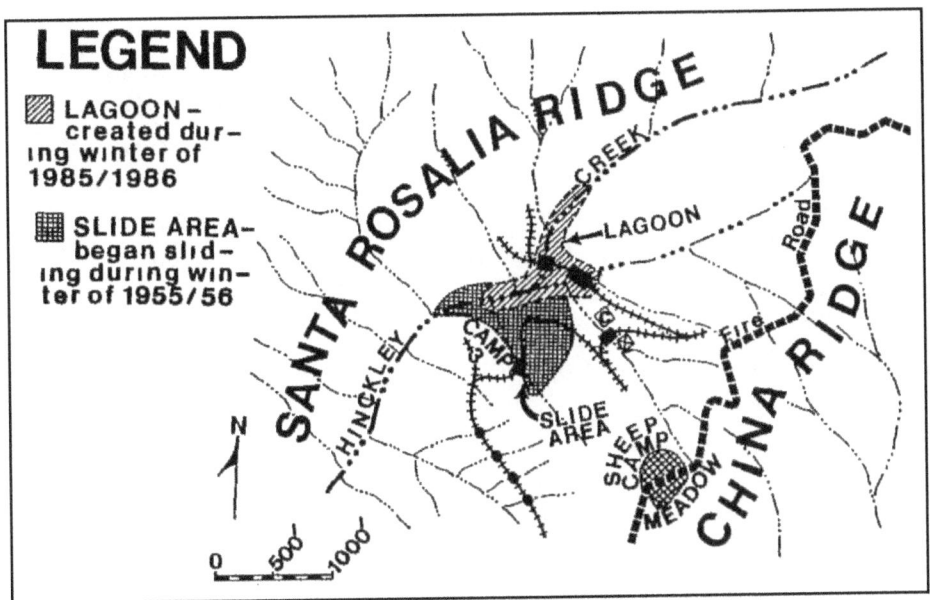

FIGURE 4.5 CHANGES TO THE AREA AT THE HEADWATERS OF HINCKLEY CREEK

barbed wire, once used to fence in a large mule corral. Following the grade further becomes more difficult. Some remnants of the abutment for a long bridge over Hinckley Creek can be found on the east bank, just before the lagoon. On the west bank, the impressions of two spurs can still be discerned with careful observation.

The Molino Timber Company was now operating many miles away from Molino Station in a remote wilderness populated only by the company's workers and wild animals. Bert Stoodley came to understand this isolation personally one day in the late summer of 1917, when he found himself out in the forest a bit too late in the afternoon. He recounts in his memoir:

> *One day, after spending the afternoon in the timber, I arrived back at Camp Three too late to ride back to the hoist on the train. I had forgotten to tell them to wait for me. It was a walk of five or six miles to the hoist. Someone suggested that I could try riding down on a small push-car used when the road was built to carry ties and rails. The flanges of the wheels seemed*

rather badly worked but I hoped they would stay on the rails. The only brake was a short board wedged between the tread of a wheel and the frame of the car. I started out about four o'clock and drifted along all right until I came to a sharp curve near Jap Camp. Here the car jumped the outside rail and took off down through the brush and briars with me as an unwilling passenger. The car came to a small sapling which it attempted to climb but kept on going for 20 or 30 feet further. I sat up after a bit and took account of the situation. The car stood nearly on end with the two head wheels halfway up the sapling. I had cuts and bruises but no bones broken. I crawled back up the bank and started limping toward the hoist which was still fully four miles away.

At the hoist, the engineer had no steam. Not expecting to have any further use for the engine that day, he had "blown off" the boiler and was washing it out. That meant that I had a mile and a half still to walk and I was sore—physically and mentally. Down the incline was worse than the mile plus from the foot of the incline to the mill yard. Here I had the Loma Prieta Lumber Co. watchman, "Tex" Cathey, take me to Aptos with the Company's Fairbanks-Morse motorcar and at Aptos my automobile was parked ready for the ride home. I had a very late dinner that night.[77]

The Loma Prieta Lumber Company rebuilds the Aptos Creek mill

Shortly after the court granted the Loma Prieta Lumber Company its former land in front of its mill on Aptos Creek in January 1917, Timothy Hopkins set to work preparing the area for a new facility. Machinery such as headrigs, edgers, and trimmers were ordered since the company's were either being used elsewhere or unusable. Until the parts arrived and a final decision was made regarding the sale of the eastern portion of Tract 10 in the Augmentation, Bert Stoodley was allowed to continue running his shingle and box mill.

The new equipment was not the only thing that had to be prepared, though. The company also had to rebuild the dam for its millpond, which Hopkins had allowed Stoodley to dismantle two years earlier. This second dam would not equal the first one in quality, height, or length. The first dam was nearly 300 feet long, 26 feet high at its center and was constructed mostly of large redwood logs, each nearly identical in size, beveled, and notched properly. This second dam would consist of boards nailed between large posts with a simple spillway in the center to allow water to escape.

By early summer, enough equipment had arrived that Stoodley had to wind up his operation. The area needed to be cleared to allow the new facility to be built. Landings were constructed where the lumber from the mill could be stacked. Tracks between Molino Junction and the mill were completely overhauled with a third rail added to support the narrower gauge of the planned railroad up Bridge Creek.[78]

The trustees of the F. A. Hihn Company offer to buy right-of-way through Tract 8 of the Augmentation

Frederick Hihn's granddaughter, Ruth Ready, was awarded in the inheritance settlement several acres of unlogged land at the headwaters of Trout Gulch within Tract 2 in the Augmentation. The area had been abandoned by Hihn in 1884 when he decided to relocate his mill from Aptos to the confluence of Valencia and Cox Creeks. Through luck, the trees had survived a large forest fire in 1903 as well as damage from the 1906 earthquake.

Harvesting Ready's uncut timber and cutting it into splitstuff became a priority following the inheritance settlement since the area was within reach of the Loma Prieta Branch and it was unclear how much longer the Southern Pacific Railroad would retain the branch line. Frustratingly for Ready's guardian and the trustees of the F. A. Hihn Company, the only reasonable way to access Tract 2 was through Timothy Hopkins' Tract 8. The trustees also wanted to sell Hopkins the eastern 610 acres of Tract 10 along Bridge Creek.

On June 20, 1917, Ready's guardian and the trustees submitted the following proposition to Hopkins regarding access to the railroad tracks within Tract 8:

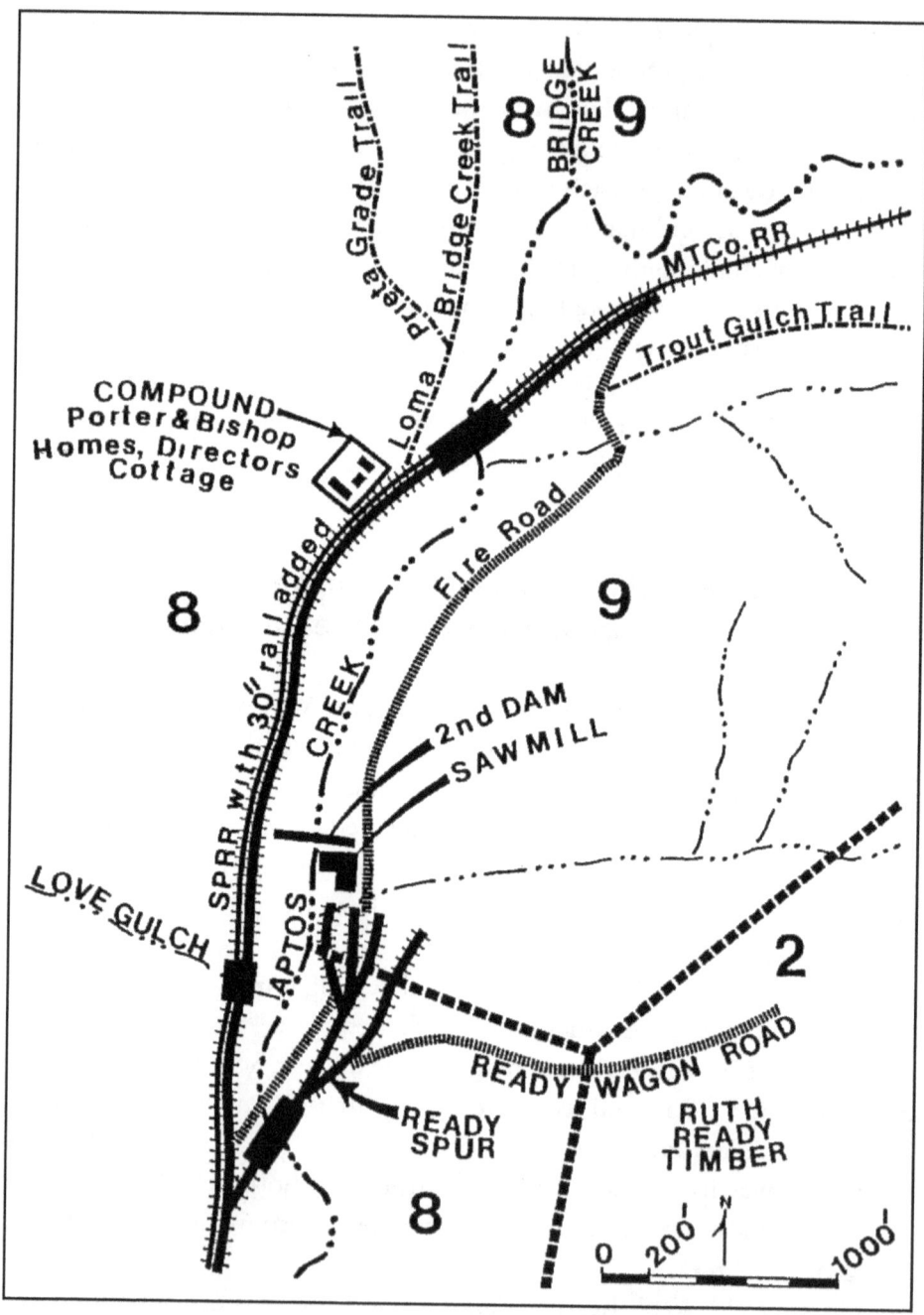

Figure 4.6 Proposed wagon road from Ruth Ready's Tract 2 to the railroad spur in Timothy Hopkins' Tract 8

> *In the event that the Loma Prieta Lumber Company avails itself of the right to purchase from the Valencia–Hihn Company, a corporation organized under the laws of the State of California, the eastern portion of Tract 10 of the Soquel Augmentation Rancho, given it by the option executed by Valencia–Hihn Company to said Loma Prieta Lumber Company, and dated June 20th, 1917, and at the time of said conveyance in such option provided for being made, to convey to said trustees, a right-of-way for a wagon road 40 feet wide, from an appurtenant to the property belonging to the F. A. Hihn Company at the time of the company's dissolution and being a portion of Tract 2 of the Soquel Augmentation Rancho, to the southerly end of the old mill yard at Loma Prieta, where a spur track is to be located as hereinafter, together with ground sufficient for a spur tract or switch for cars upon which timber or timber products from said property belonging to said F. A. Hihn Company at the time of its dissolution and being a portion of Tract 2 of said Soquel Augmentation Rancho, may be loaded, and also sufficient space along said spur tract to conveniently pile two hundred cords of wood or split material at any one time for the period of ten years from the date of such convenience. Said Timothy Hopkins shall be paid, for each standard cord transported over said right-of-way, the sum of fifty cents.*

Hopkins declined the offer since it would negatively impact his own plans to use the mill and lumberyard.[79]

Therese Hihn's lawsuit and Frederick Hihn's estate are settled

On June 30, 1917, the court settled Therese Hihn's suit against her children regarding the value of Hihn's estate. A month later, on July 31, the Santa Cruz District Court accepted the division of Hihn's estate according to the advice of the three referees.[80]

Land transfer from the Valencia–Hihn Company to the Loma Prieta Lumber Company concerning Tract 10 in the Augmentation

With the matter of Frederick Hihn's inheritance resolved, the sale of the eastern 610 acres of Tract 10 in the Augmentation to the Loma Prieta Lumber Company could proceed. The sale was agreed on August 4, 1917, for a total cost of $53,250, to be paid in four installments. The first, due immediately, was for $35,145, with three additional payments of $6,000 each due on July 1, 1918, January 1, 1919, and July 1, 1919.

The Valencia–Hihn Company retained the right to harvest tan oak bark until January 1, 1918, and the tan oak trees until September 1. In or-

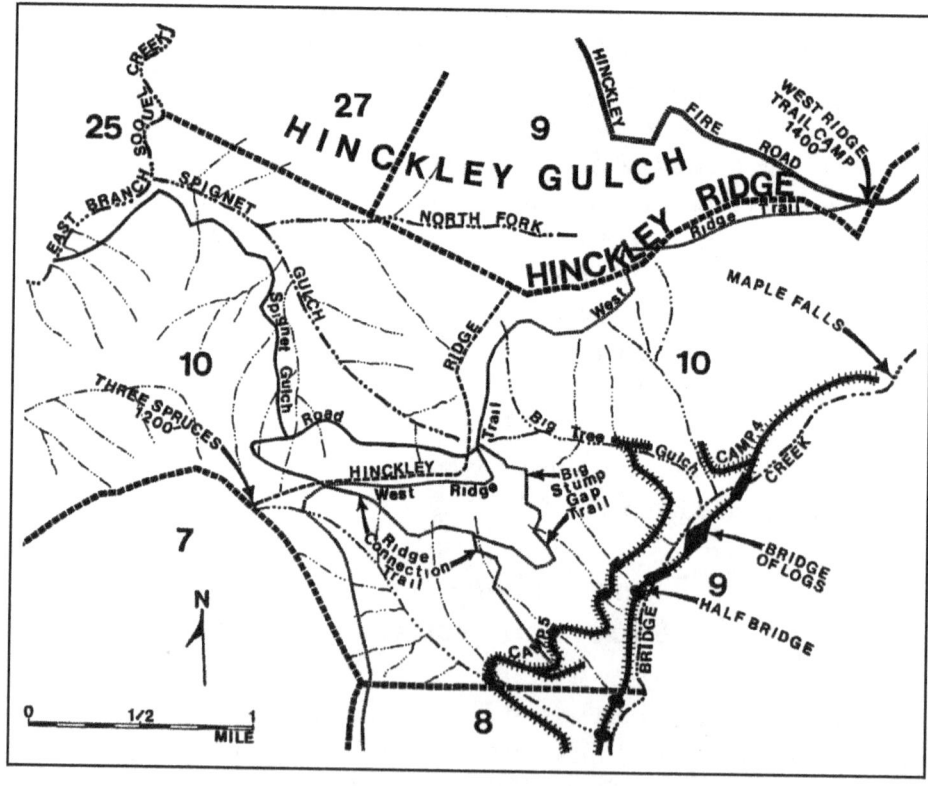

FIGURE 4.7 SPIGNET GULCH ROAD AND CONNECTING TRAILS IN TRACT 10 OF THE AUGMENTATION

der to accomplish this, they also were allowed to build roads or railroads as necessary. Shortly after the agreement was signed, peelers were sent into the tract to collect the bark. But rather than use wagons or trucks, the peelers had mules haul the bark to the vicinity of Big Tree Gulch, where it was stacked to await the arrival of a railroad line to the site.

Harvesting the tan oak timber was a different matter. Many years earlier, the F. A. Hihn Company had built a road from the East Branch of Soquel Creek up Spignet Gulch to the top of Hinckley Ridge in order to access a shingle mill. This road then descended to Bridge Creek, adhering closely to today's Big Stump Gap Trail and the Ridge Connection Trail. Portions of the West Ridge Trail also show signs that it was once a road used by large vehicles. It is highly probable that these roads were also used by the Valencia–Hihn Company to remove the tan oaks from along Bridge Creek in 1917 and 1918. Assuming this is true, the company used wagons or trucks to carry the product to Olive Springs and then out to market.

One final clause in the contract required all of the land to be sold back to the Valencia–Hihn Company once the timber was harvested. Curiously, this clause was never acted upon—the property remained with the trustees of the Loma Prieta Lumber Company.[81]

The Loma Prieta Lumber Company begins grading railroad along Bridge Creek

Even before the Loma Prieta Lumber Company acquired the eastern part of Tract 10 in the Augmentation, it had begun grading for a railroad to the boundary of the property. Following negotiations the previous year with the Molino Timber Company, Timothy Hopkins planned to dismantle the China Ridge railroad and use the rail and ties to build a narrow-gauge route up Bridge Creek to Maple Falls. Trees cut from further upstream, including those remaining in the Splitstuff Area, would be sent downstream to the railroad. Going forward, the only timber to be cut into splitstuff would be that which was unsuitable for lumber.

Molino likely began dismantling the line first by removing excess sidings and spurs from along its length, allowing Loma Prieta to begin installing third rails in the trackage within the lumberyard at the Aptos

Creek mill. The timber company, however, continued to use the railroad to the headwaters of Hinckley Creek until the end of the 1917 season.[82]

Valencia–Hihn Company begins harvesting timber in Tract 2 of the Augmentation

By declining access to the mill site on Aptos Creek, Timothy Hopkins forced the Valencia–Hihn Company to search for other ways of getting Ruth Ready's timber in Tract 2 of the Augmentation to the Southern Pacific Railroad's grade on Aptos Creek. The timberland at the top of Trout Gulch covered about 700 acres. Around late August 1917, the company decided that the next best option was to build a road south from the timber to the boundary of the Augmentation and Rancho Aptos, in the vicinity of today's steel bridge and George's Picnic Area. The owners of the land through which the road would need to pass gave permission for a right-of-way and pieceworkers quickly moved into Tract 2 to begin cutting timber.

The Valencia–Hihn Company approached Southern Pacific and requested a spur be installed on the east side of the Loma Prieta Branch above Aptos Creek. This spur would receive splitstuff from Tract 2, which was transported by wagon. The railroad designated the spur site Ready Station in official documents, a name that remained on the books until the abandonment of the Loma Prieta Branch.

Today, the site of Ready Station is George's Picnic Area. It was named after George Haire, an avid outdoorsman who had a special affection in his later life for the Augmentation. The road that was used to transport splitstuff from Tract 2 remains intact as an escape road, accessible just to the east of the steel bridge.

Probably beginning in 1918, logs were also shipped to Ready, albeit to a second spur installed further to the north. These logs were transported via highline from Tract 2 to log-loading stations beside the spur. While the number of stations in the area is unknown, the remains of one are still visible just north of the steel bridge about midway between the creek and road. Traces of the spur track can also be found on the ground. Once the logs were loaded onto flatcars, they were taken north by train to the Loma Prieta Lumber Company's mill on Aptos Creek, where they were processed

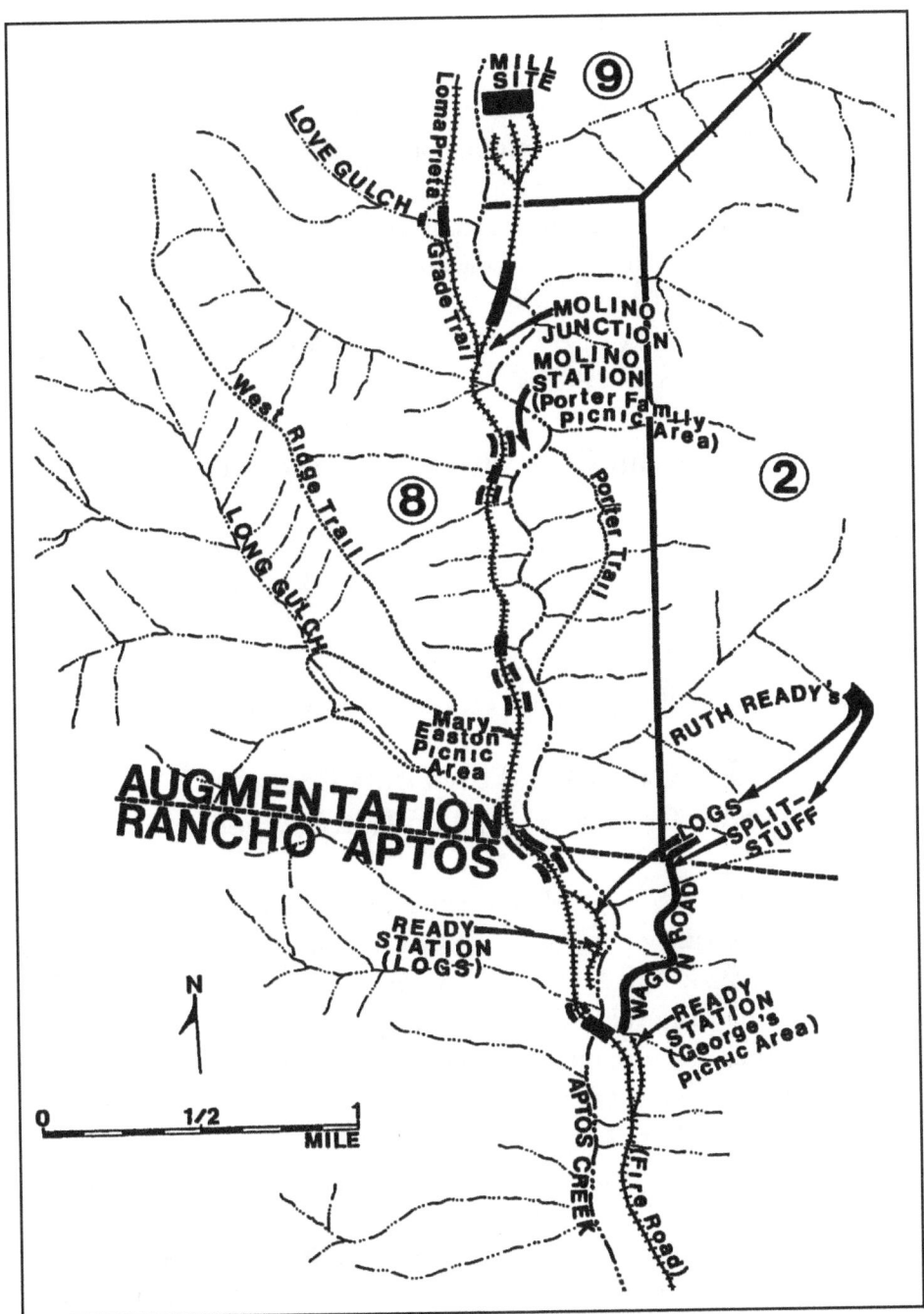

Figure 4.8 Route of logs and splitstuff from Tract 2 to Ready Station

into lumber. After the 1920 season, an agreement was made with the San Vicente Lumber Company to process the logs. At the time, San Vicente had nearly exhausted its own timberland so was eager to have a customer.

Because Ruth Ready was a minor, Southern Pacific lowered its standard freight rate for hauling logs. The operation also benefited from cheap labor, since many laborers shifted to working for the Valencia–Hihn Company once timber-cutting operations elsewhere in the Augmentation ended. It is unknown how long the harvesting effort in Tract 2 lasted, but it was certainly over by the end of 1922, when the San Vicente Lumber Company shut down its mill in Santa Cruz.[83]

The Valencia–Hihn Company sells Laurel mill's machinery

In late 1917, the Valencia–Hihn Company sold the machinery that had been used at the Laurel mill between 1902 and 1914 to the California Fruit Growers' Association. The organization sent it to Mather in Tuolumne County, where it would remain until 1925. Included in the sale were large redwood frames built from single logs, which were used to make boxes.[84]

Camp 4 and the Loma Prieta Lumber Company's mill on Aptos Creek open

Around November 1917, the Molino Timber Company, under the direction of Timothy Hopkins, abandoned its trackage between Hinckley Creek and the former Camp 2. The Loma Prieta Lumber Company determined that the cost of operating the railroad over these two miles of track did not provide a sufficient return once maintenance costs were calculated. Most of the rails and ties were put to immediate use to build the new Bridge Creek railroad 1.85 miles from Loma Prieta to Maple Falls.

This new railroad broke off from the Loma Prieta Branch between the Porter House and the bridge over Aptos Creek. Beyond the house, the track adhered closely to Bridge Creek throughout its entire length. The route included four small wooden bridges and three half bridges over gullies and along steep hillsides. At the third half bridge, the line entered Tract 10. Today, the railroad route closely follows the Bridge

The Residue of Success — 1918

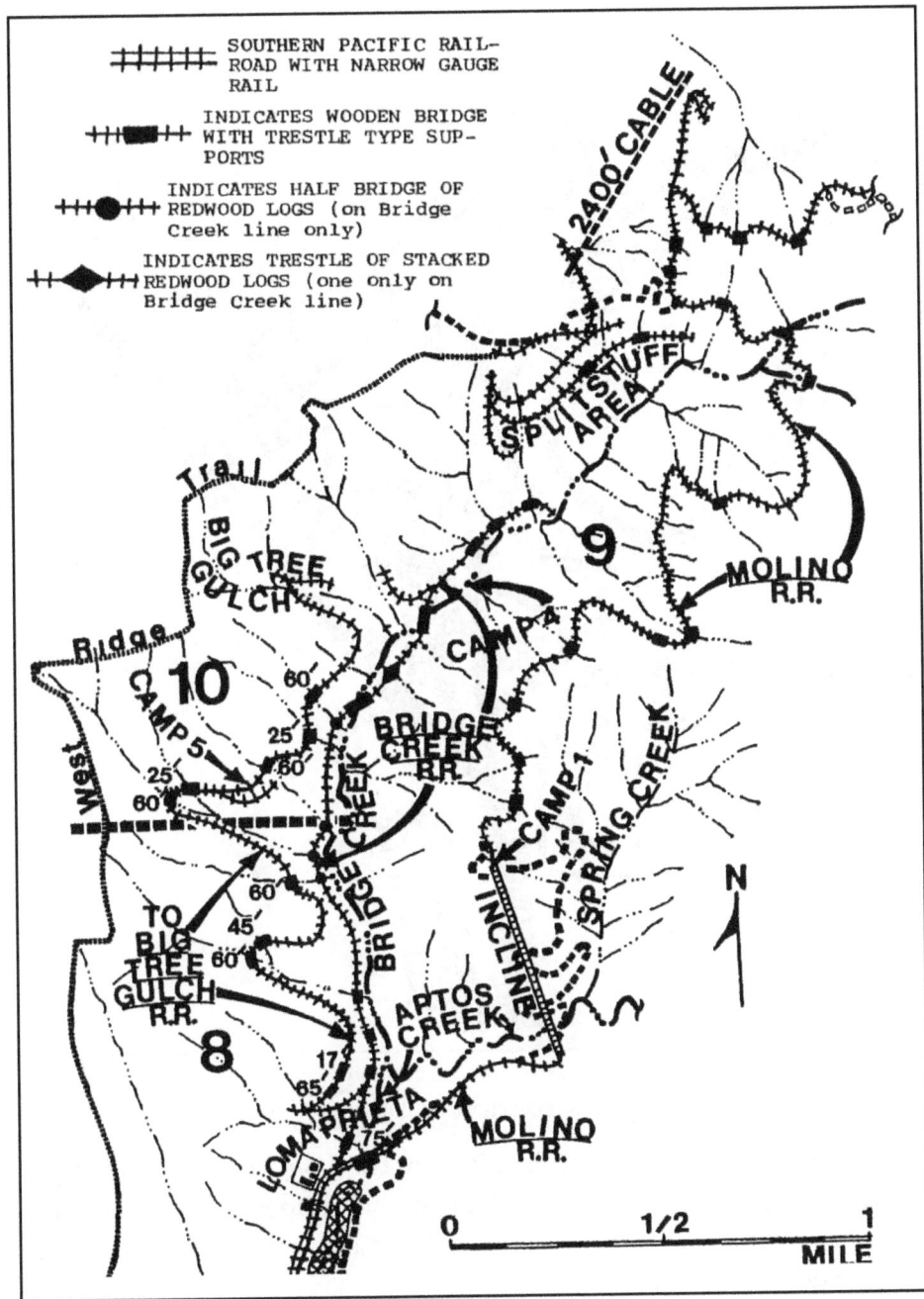

FIGURE 4.9 OVERVIEW OF THE LOMA PRIETA LUMBER COMPANY'S RAILROAD TRACKAGE ALONG BRIDGE CREEK TO CAMPS 4 AND 5

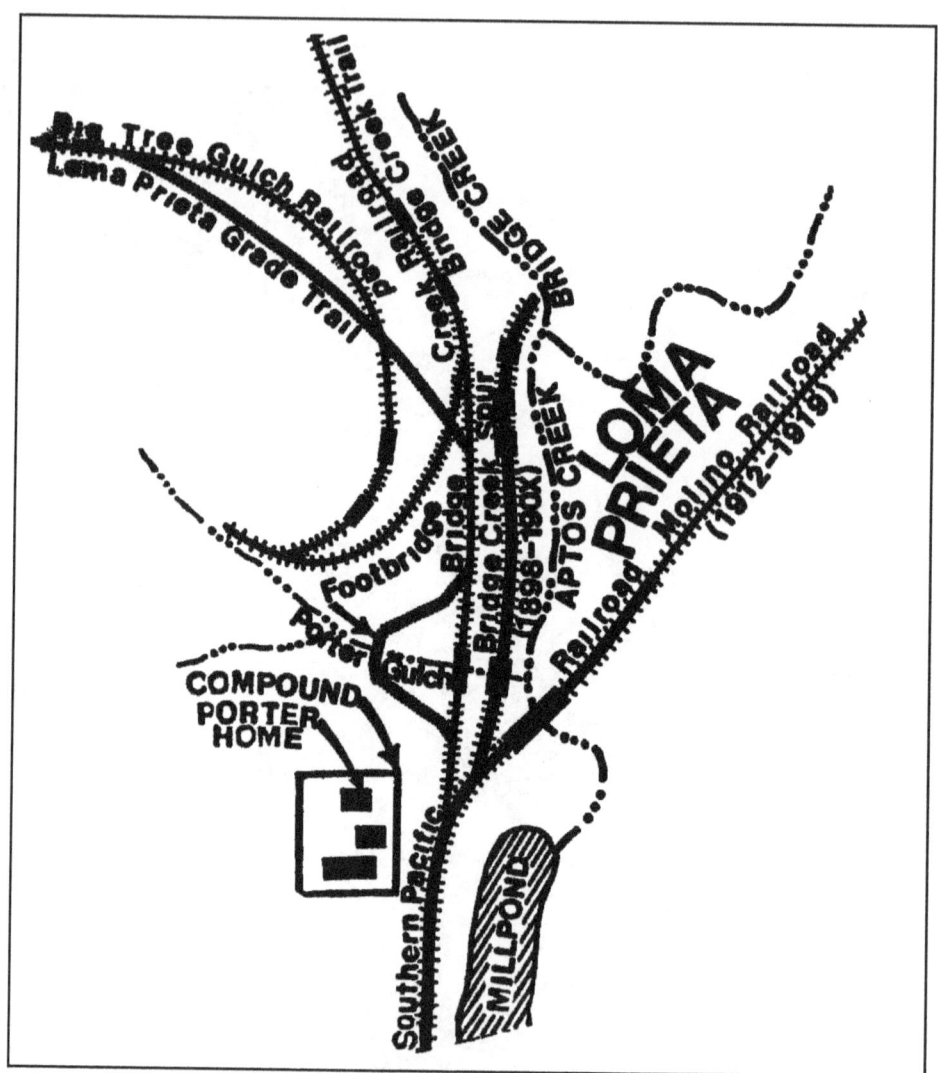

FIGURE 4.10 SOUTHERN PORTION OF BRIDGE CREEK TRACKAGE

Creek Trail from where it breaks off from the Loma Prieta Grade Trail. Although most of the remains of the third half bridge are now gone, the boundary of Tracts 8 and 10 is located just north of where the Bridge Creek Trail crosses the creek.

After the line entered Tract 10, still on the west side of Bridge Creek, the next quarter mile required only a single half bridge to continue north.

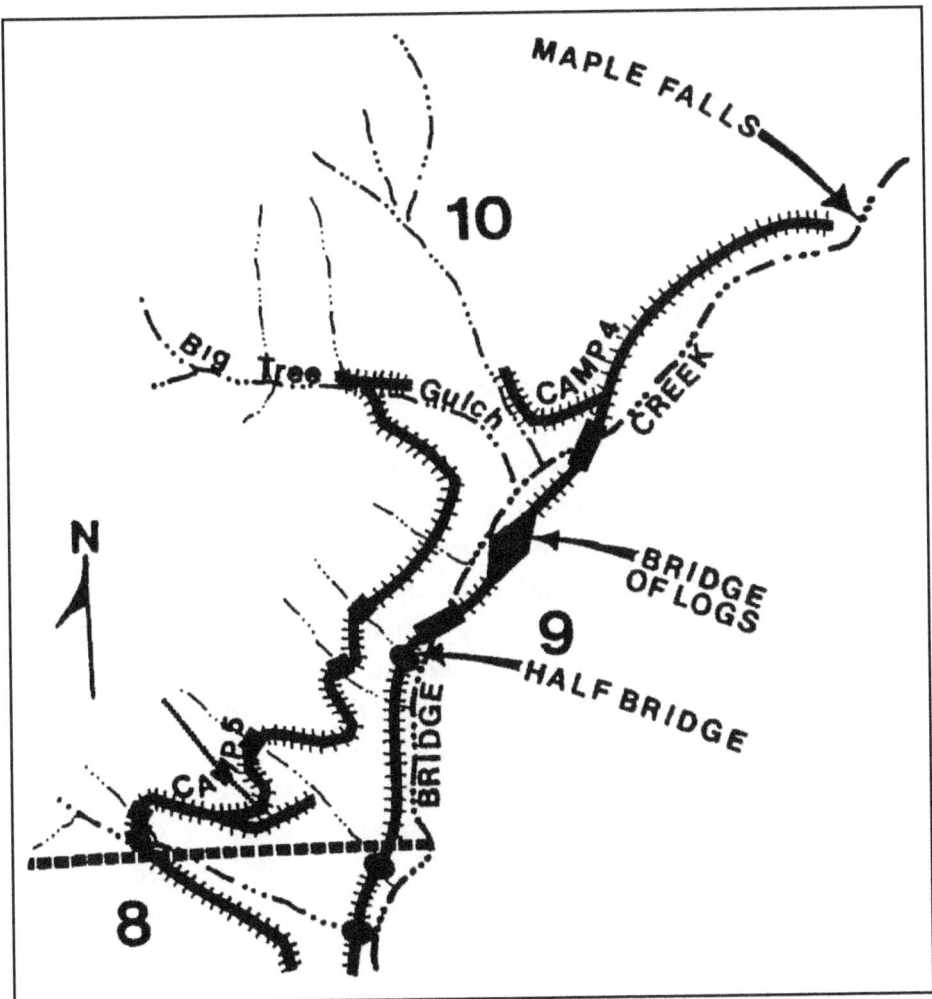

FIGURE 4.11 NORTHERN PORTION OF BRIDGE CREEK TRACKAGE

Then the railroad crossed Bridge Creek for the first time over a long, high bridge. Just beyond this point, in a short section within Tract 9, the railroad encountered a broad, saucer-shaped depression. Rather than cross the depression with an expensive bridge, grading crews stacked a pile of large logs until a sufficient height was achieved. More logs were then suspended over the depression and balanced on the pile of logs, creating a cheaply-built but surprisingly stable bridge. The remains of this crude structure are today one of the most iconic features in The Forest of Nisene Marks State Park.

Just beyond this bridge, the gulch widened enough to allow for a camp, which became known alternatively as Camp 4 or Bridge Creek Camp. The camp sat at about 600-foot elevation, while the Porter House at the bottom of the line was at 300 feet, meaning the railroad between those two points had a grade of about four percent. The railroad crossed Bridge Creek again at Camp 4 along a long, low bridge. A 100-foot-long spur was installed to the west of the bridge up a narrow gully. This allowed logs to be lowered from the hillsides above directly onto waiting flatcars. Throughout this area, faint impressions of rails and ties can still be found in the soil.

Before the January 4, 1982 storm, evidence of the line beyond Camp 4 could still be found. Following the February 1986 storms, only a few traces remain. It now requires an extensive search to find even the most minute trace of the northern portion of the Bridge Creek railroad. Indeed, the route beyond Camp 4 is not known with certainty. Did it remain on the west bank of Bridge Creek, or did it cross it again? Were more bridges needed? Whatever the answers, it did eventually reach the bottom of Maple Falls, where logs were lowered from atop the falls into waiting flatcars.

With limited operations still planned for the 1918 season along China Ridge, the Loma Prieta Lumber Company required another locomotive. Using the *Betsy Jane* was not an option, unfortunately. Still stuck in the Splitstuff Area, it was also a 36-inch-gauge and the new Bridge Creek trackage was set at 30 inches, since that is what the Molino line used. Instead, the company began to search for a new locomotive to buy.

The company concluded almost immediately that it wanted a Shay since the operational record of the Molino's Shay was so spectacular. Having two Shays also meant that parts could be exchanged between them, lowering maintenance costs. Loma Prieta soon found a 14-ton oil burning Shay that had been used by the Empire City Railway Company in the Sierra Nevada at Strawberry. The total price was $4,000 and it was brought intact by Southern Pacific to the Aptos Creek mill.

While supportive of these new operations along the Loma Prieta Branch, Southern Pacific only saw profit in running two to three trains to the mill each week. This was insufficient for the needs of the workers, though. They needed food, supplies, mail, and newspapers daily. As a result, Loma Prieta bought a standard-gauge, 4-ton Fairbanks-Morris rail speeder. Immediately upon arrival, it was put into use, operating between Aptos and the mill. As the need arose, it functioned as a switch engine and was used to move logs and lumber in the lumberyard. It would also take workers to Aptos on Saturday evenings and return them to the mill late the next day.

On January 17, 1918, the *Surf* announced the completion of the Bridge Creek railroad.

Loma Prieta Logging Road

Two Miles of the New Line is Finished

Two miles of the new line of the Loma Prieta logging railroad has been finished. It starts at the high bridge of the Loma Prieta branch of the Southern Pacific and follows the west branch of Bridge Creek. At the lower end is a spur track that goes up a branch of Bridge Creek for a mile. The new road will be about four and a half miles long.

The old road started with an incline and hoist, was seven miles long. Two miles of this roadbed has been taken up and used in the new line.

The old road as it wound in and out toward the summit of the mountain was one of the finest scenic roads in the county.

By early April, according to Bert Stoodley, the Loma Prieta mill on Aptos Creek had opened, meaning that Camp 4 was also active. Fallers, buckers, pieceworkers, and support crews erected shacks and temporary shelters all along the creek and hillsides here. Beside the tracks, landings were situated for loading logs and splitstuff.

When I first explored Camp 4 in August 1980, six of the original shanties were still standing. While they were unsafe to enter, they added character to the picturesque scene. Fortunately, I took a number of pictures of the shanties and pleasant surrounding scene. When I returned to the camp later, to my disappointment, some misguided youths had pushed the six shanties down leaving only piles of rubble. Camp 4 remained in this condition until 1982, when the remains of the six shanties along with most of the surrounding vegetation were washed away in the storm. Along with the devastation at the camp site, many sections of Bridge Creek, from its headwaters to Aptos Creek, were reconfigured. Then, to add insult to injury, the storm of 1986 reconfigured the gulch again, removing many of the logs and fallen trees that had survived the earlier storm.[85]

The Molino Timber Company begins sending logs to Bridge Creek

With the completion of the railroad line up Bridge Creek to Maple Falls and the opening of the Aptos Creek mill, the Molino Timber Company could finally begin sending logs out of Hinckley Gulch. It was not an easy task, though. Over the final months of 1917, before the railroad line beyond Sand Point was truncated, Molino had been busy shipping mid-sized logs to the millpond on Aptos Creek via its China Ridge railroad. That operation ended in November and all remaining logs had to be dragged by donkey engine and then highlined to the Splitstuff Area.

The method for getting the logs from Hinckley Creek to the Splitstuff Area was in no way straightforward. By 1918, most logs were coming from the southern slopes of Santa Rosalia Ridge, across Hinckley Creek from the Molino railroad. This was a substantial distance for logs to travel, especially without a railroad to collect them. Yet the railroad line beyond Sand Point had been shortened at the end of the previous year, so trains could no longer take these logs to where they needed to go. Instead, they were dragged up to and along the former railroad grade or up hillsides until they reached the sink pond north of Sand Point, where the logs were deposited until they could continue their journey to the south.

From the sink pond, the Molino train took the soaked logs along a new, 1,000-foot-long spur atop a long shelf to the north of the pond. At the end of this, the track forked to allow multiple cars to unload logs. Several donkey engines were installed here. Most were responsible for pulling logs from Hinckley Creek and its tributaries to the top of the shelf. The smaller logs were sent on flatcars down the incline, while the larger joined those harvested from upstream. The biggest engine on the shelf was attached to a 2,400-foot-long highline that stretched to another shelf to the southwest

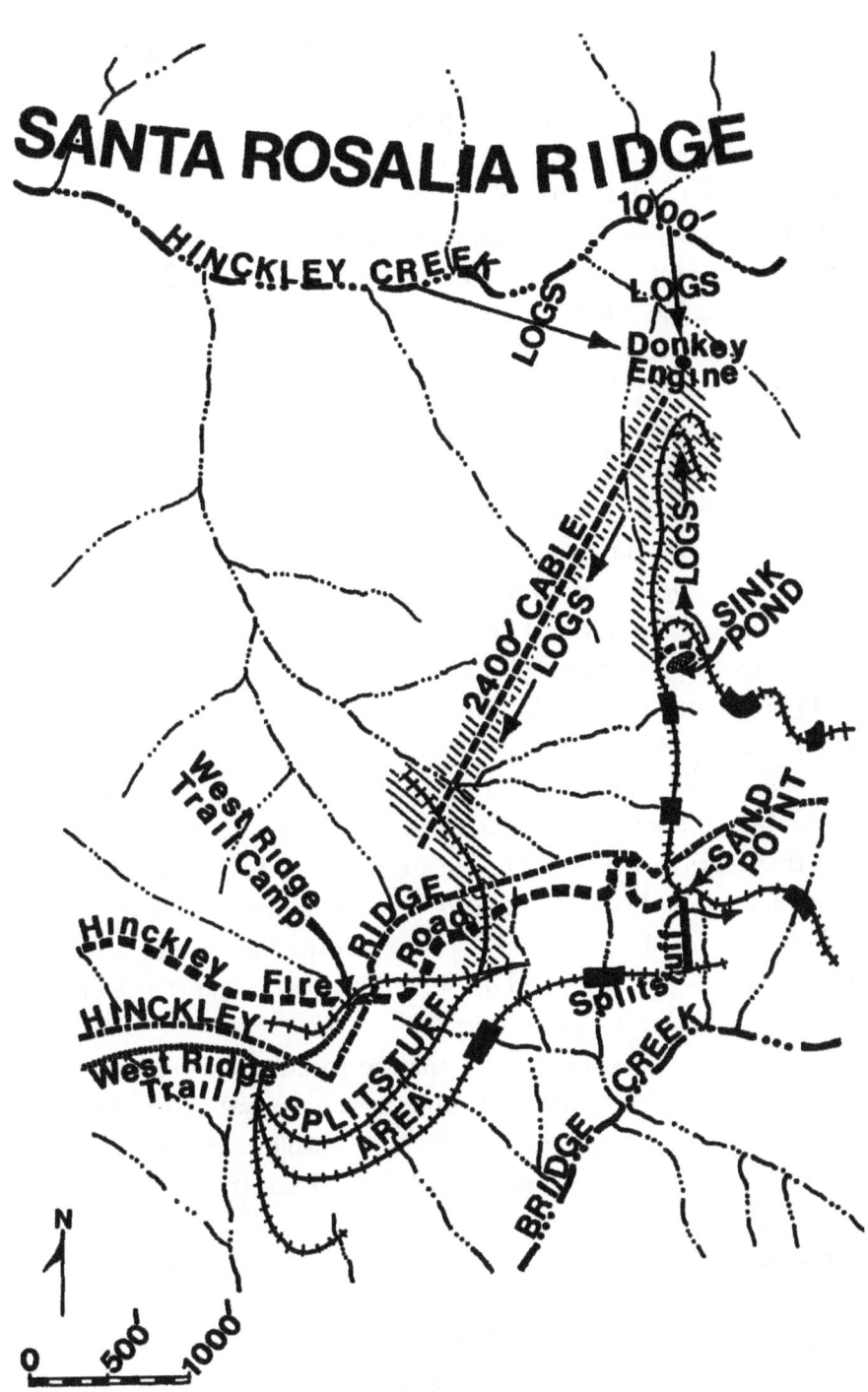

FIGURE 4.12 HIGHLINE ROUTE OF LOGS TRANSPORTED FROM HINCKLEY GULCH TO THE SPLITSTUFF AREA

near today's West Ridge Trail Camp. Logs too large to be taken down the incline were mounted onto the end of the cable and carried over several gulches and ridges to the top of the Splitstuff Area.

At the other end of the highline, flatcars waited along a long spur. Workers set the logs on the flatcars and secured them, and then detached the overhead cable. Once several cars were arranged, *Betsy Jane* headed south, crossing today's Hinckley Fire Road before descending to the headwaters of Bridge Creek in the Splitstuff Area. There, pieceworkers began their task of cutting the log into splitstuff for eventual transport up to Sand Point and down the railroad grade and incline to Molino Station. If all went according to plan, the railroad along Bridge Creek would be extended to the Splitstuff Area, and all logs could then continue their journey south to the Aptos Creek mill to be turned into lumber.

When I began exploring the area at the back of Sand Point in my attempt to solve the mystery of the spur's purpose and who built it, I found lying about the area between the sink pond and Hinckley Creek a helter-skelter pattern of large logs with their butt ends pointing towards the top of the shelf. I also found many broken cables hidden under debris and growing vegetation. If the logs were pointing in the opposite direction, this would indicate that they had been prepared for the journey to the Loma Prieta mill on Hinckley Creek that had operated before the 1906 earthquake. However, the fact that all of the logs were positioned to be dragged up the hill suggests that they were being taken to the shelf to be processed.

Bert Stoodley provided an explanation for all the cable debris in his memoir: "One of the major problems that continually arose in the forest causing delays was the smaller diameter cable that the Loma Prieta Lumber Company's general manager, Harvey Bassett, had to buy for the logging donkey engines to use. Instead of regular cable, he could find only elevator cable, which was smaller in diameter. This elevator cable would usually break at the most inopportune time, usually when a large log was being pulled up to the railroad." He noted more generally about the operation that, "because it was war time, labor was scarce and many times inefficient, plus the turnover was high, making labor problems from first to last a headache. Both mill and logging supplies such as lubricants, belting, and wire line were often delayed and an occasional shutdown resulted. Oil for the two Shay engines was hard to come by."[86]

Allen Rispin moves to Capitola

Born in Petrolia, Ontario on August 26, 1872, Henry Allen Rispin acquired a large fortune when he married Annette Blake in 1901. She was the daughter of Isaac E. Blake, a California oil pioneer and, at one time, president of United Oil Producers.

Rispin had been interested in the Capitola area for over a decade. Caught up in the hype of the Ocean Shore Railway, he had bought 84 acres of land from Henry Daubenbiss in early 1907. The property sat directly on the route of the proposed Ocean Shore & Eastern Railway line, and Rispin hoped the railway would situate its Capitola Station within his property.

When the Ocean Shore scheme faltered, Rispin contemplated building a summer home on the property, but felt the land "was bordered by the rubbish heaps of the little town of Capitola." He erected a small country cottage instead. For the next six summers, Rispin and his family returned to Capitola to hunt, swim, fish, hike, ride horses, and sell small lots from the property. The Rispins briefly left California in 1915 and moved to Denver, Colorado, but they returned fulltime in the summer of 1918. For the next eleven years, Rispin would become a visionary in the Capitola community and the guiding light in the development of the Capitola Heights subdivision.[87]

Storm destroys Splitstuff Area and Camp 4

From the beginning of the summer through early September 1918, the Loma Prieta Lumber Company had been making good progress harvesting timber at the headwaters of Hinckley Creek and along Bridge Creek, with crews working throughout both watersheds. Labor and supply shortages due to the war had caused ongoing headaches, though, and sometimes operations had to temporarily shut down as replacement parts were sourced. The frequent discovery of spot rot in logs was a bigger issue that resulted in up to twenty-five percent of some logs being trimmed away to remove the signs of the disease. As a result, the mill only produced three to four million board feet of lumber in 1918, a far cry from the glory days of the Loma Prieta Lumber Company.

The summer of 1918 had been unusually hot and dry, so the clouds that arrived in the first days of September were a welcome arrival. The average rainfall for September between 1890 and 1917 was 0.62 inches, with the highest on record being 2.37 inches, which occurred on September 29, 1894. In contrast, from the evening of September 11 and the morning of September 12, 1918, an average of 5.80 inches fell on Santa Cruz County. In the mountains, it was substantially more, possibly as much as 20 inches. Two days later, the *Surf* published the following article on the subject:

> *The unprecedented rainfall of the last few days was due to a pocket formed by a high ranging [wind] north and south of the Rocky Mountains, which interfered with the free circulation of the air, there being no outlet for the prevailing western winds, which supercharged with humidity to such an extent that an enormous 'leak' was developed, which deluged that part of the coast lying between San Luis Obispo and Eureka. Santa Cruz seems to have been the center of this 'leak' and consequently got the full benefit of the rainfall.*

The storm caught the Loma Prieta Lumber Company utterly unprepared. Its three locomotives—the Molino Timber Company's Shay, the new Shay on the Bridge Creek railroad, and *Betsy Jane*—were all sitting out in the open, exposed to the elements. While the two Shays managed to avoid the worst of the storm, *Betsy Jane* was not as fortunate. Earlier in the day, the aging Porter saddleback locomotive had pushed a couple of loaded flatcars into place for lifting up to Sand Point. When the storm struck, it was still sitting below Sand Point with the cars attached. Sand Point had always been prone to sliding, but the F. A. Hihn Company had miraculously avoided any serious slides in its several years operating at the headwaters of Bridge Creek. Yet as the rain began to fall, the earth below the locomotive slowly slid away. Both locomotive and flatcars joined the mud and rocks, ending their journey about 100 feet below the ruins of the railroad grade. *Betsy Jane* came to rest in the same position it was before the storm: upright, facing toward today's West Ridge Trail Camp.

Damage to the locomotive was not the only loss suffered by the Loma Prieta Lumber Company in the Splitstuff Area: the facilities within the area were ruined sufficiently for the company to abandon five million board feet of split material already cut and ready for delivery. There was possibly an equal number of logs sitting throughout the area waiting for the pieceworkers to begin working on them.

The China Ridge track of the Molino Timber Company fared better. The western side of the ridge was not prone to slides, so the railroad remained intact and the Shay, though left outside, suffered no serious damage. What was impacted, however, was the donkey engine at the top of the incline. James W. Alves spent 26 days illegally camping in The Forest of Nisene Marks in the early 1980s in search of remains from the various logging operations. In a letter he wrote to Rick Hamman, he stated that he found "the rusting hulk of the donkey engine at the top of the incline. It fell down about 70 yards from its anchored position in Camp 1. Most pieces have been taken off by stupid people, boiler about 50 inches in diameter, vertical tire tube. [In] some place[s] the lagging is coming off [the] rusted hulk." Assuming James is correct—I was unable to verify his discovery in my own explorations—the donkey engine that had endured for six years went over the side.

With the loss of the engine, as well as the destruction of the Splitstuff Area, the viability of the ridgetop railroad was put into doubt. Around November 1918, Timothy Hopkins announced the end of timber operations in Hinckley Gulch. The machinery at Sand Point and Camp 1, as well as all of the remaining track along the ridge, would be dismantled and taken down the incline to be used in Tract 10.

To the southwest along Bridge Creek, the new railroad there experienced an insurmountable problem when the long, simply-built wooden bridge over Bridge Creek south of Camp 4 was destroyed by the rainstorm. Camp 4 itself was also heavily damaged. With the bridge gone, access to the camp was blocked and Loma Prieta quickly decided that it was a better idea to abandon the trackage and shift it further up the hillside than continue operations at creek level.

The end of World War I on November 11, 1918 meant that cheap labor would soon return to Santa Cruz County, but replacement parts and machinery were still in short supply. At the same time, an overwhelming malaise was settling upon workers, who saw the end of the Loma Prieta Lumber Company in sight.

BETSY JANE: THE LOST LOCOMOTIVE

Sometime between September 11 and 12, 1918, *Betsy Jane*, a locomotive that had been purchased in 1886 to run on the Valencia Creek railroad of Frederick Hihn's Aptos Milling Company, fell from its grade at the headwaters of Bridge Creek and disappeared into legend.

My first contact with the "lost locomotive" occurred in the Special Collections Room of the McHenry Library at UC Santa Cruz. In early 1979, during one of my many research sessions, I came across a statement made by an old-timer which provided me with one of the first rumors of a locomotive located somewhere within The Forest of Nisene Marks. Because I had just begun my explorations and research, the statement made little sense; therefore, I entered it into my notes but promptly forgot about it.

For years, rumors have persisted that there is a locomotive lying somewhere in The Forest of Nisene Marks. Many of the rumors place it somewhere in Bridge Creek Gulch. One important question had to be asked to find the solution to this mystery, though: what were the fates of the three locomotives that operated in and above Bridge Creek? Faced with wild rumors, misleading and conflicting stories, and further questions, I began to doubt if such a locomotive ever existed. But curiosity and perseverance pushed me to find the answer.

Stories concerning the lost locomotive existed decades before California Parks & Recreation ranger Nils Bergman claimed to have found it. Bergman was Nisene Marks' first unit ranger and even before the property was purchased, he began familiarizing himself with the land. He hiked and drove along all of the existing roads, and rode horseback to many hard-to-reach places. In the early 1960s, it was much easier to explore the park than it is today since there was much less vegetation and the storms of the 1980s had not yet destroyed the old railroad rights-of-way and logging trails.

Bergman also met with several old-timers who had worked for the

The Residue of Success 1918

Molino Timber Company and the Loma Prieta Lumber Company in the vicinity of Sand Point and the Splitstuff Area. They told him that there were several rail speeders left in the area by their former employer. Bergman set out to find these speeders with two helpers. They drove up to Sand Point and then down to the vicinity of the yet to be established West Ridge Trail Camp. From there, they headed off in three directions. Bergman went east towards Sand Point through the Splitstuff Area, noticing with curiosity the many logs distributed throughout the area on what he began to suspect was an old railroad bed. With each step he took eastward, he was more convinced of his suspicions until he found himself directly below Sand Point, where evidence of the line apparently ended. When he looked down from there, about 100 feet below the railroad grade, he saw a locomotive.

The locomotive sat in an upright position with only its front end exposed, the rest buried under dirt and rocks. When the locomotive made its journey down the hillside, it obviously did not tumble since the large smokestack was still mounted on the boiler. After a closer inspection of the exposed front end, Bergman noticed that the bell appeared to be the only item missing. This had been taken earlier by a former employee of the Loma Prieta Lumber Company and was sitting on his front porch.

Bergman decided to keep his discovery a secret in order to deter souvenir hunters. He also decided that he would not tell anyone, even his supervisor, until the "time was right." Having made his decision, Bergman covered the front of the locomotive with vegetation, obscuring it from casual observers. He eventually did tell his supervisor of the find, but refused to disclose its location. He wanted to hear what they would do with it. He never got an answer and never told anyone, even at the time of his death. I know this for a fact because I met one of his close relatives in the mid to late 1980s and he was ignorant of the locomotive's location, and we were less than two miles from Sand Point.

Rick Hamman states that there were two locomotives known to have operated in Santa Cruz County in which their disposition is unknown. The first is the original *Betsy Jane* that was designed and built in San Francisco for the Santa Cruz Railroad in late 1874. It was shipped out of Pajaro in January 1884 to be scrapped or used in one of Collis Huntington's railroads in Central America.

The second *Betsy Jane* had operated along Valencia Creek and Gold Gulch outside Felton until 1898. It may have been used at Laurel afterwards, possibly as a stationary engine to run the cable pully. Suggestions that it operated at Kings Creek are unsubstantiated. When the Splitstuff Area opened up, *Betsy Jane* was moved there.

The adventurous and curious who hiked the mysterious old grade of the Loma Prieta Branch before the state park was established would tell of a locomotive that was sitting in Aptos Creek just to the south of the Loma Prieta Lumber Company's mill site near Molino Junction. Others claimed to have observed it resting below Sand Point. At one time, a car was driven up to Sand Point and pushed over the side just to the west of today's Sand Point Overlook sign. As the years passed, vegetation began to partially hide the car, disguising what it actually was. Therefore, to many, this was the lost locomotive.

As the years passed, the rumored location of the locomotive shifted to along Bridge Creek between Aptos Creek and Maple Falls. Hamman once informed me it was in the gulch just north of the Porter House on the Loma Prieta Grade Trail. Meanwhile, Bergman continued to tell people that he had found it without saying where it was. Most of his stories were implausible and his listeners and supervisor began to doubt the story. Was Bergman playing a game? Had he forgotten where the locomotive was hidden? Or did he make the whole thing up?

Over an eleven-year period, every time I heard a new rumor or got an urge to explore, I would head off into The Forest of Nisene Marks. Thanks to the many false rumors, I explored many sections of the park that I surely would not have visited otherwise. During these explorations searching for the engine, I discovered the Splitstuff Area and the route that the logs traveled from Hinckley Gulch to the Loma Prieta mill on Aptos Creek in 1908-1909.

In the mid-1980s, I interviewed three men who had interviewed Bergman at some point. The following are some of their findings:

Larry Green lived in San José at the time I met him. He had hiked the park's trails for a number of years. Because of his interest in railroading, he sought out Bergman in 1965 and asked about the lost locomotive. When Bergman answered, his expression suddenly turned serious: he stated that he knew where the locomotive was located, that it was in good condition, it was well hidden, and he was not going to tell where it was until his supervisors decided what they were going to do about it. Because of his reluctance, several of his supervisors thought he was hallucinating when he found what he thought was a locomotive. It was for this reasoning that the Parks & Recreation Department decided not to do anything about recovering the locomotive. Bergman stated that he was promised by authorities at Fort Ord that they would provide a large helicopter to move the locomotive to wherever he wanted it moved to. Clearly, he never took them up on the offer.

Doug Richter was a resident of San Bruno when I met him. To accompany his fervent passion for railroading, he had many years of practical experience in the profession. Wanting to solve the mystery of what type the locomotive was, and naturally where it was located, Richter gathered several friends, all knowledgeable in railroading, then scheduled a meeting with Bergman. Before they met, Richter and his friends prepared a list of questions in such a way that, without a knowledge of locomotives, Bergman could not make up his answers. He could only relate what he had observed. As he answered Richter's questions, it became obvious that he knew little or nothing about railroading, especially locomotives. When they asked where the engine was located, he did not answer, but he drew a picture of what he observed while looking down at the engine from what he thought was a railroad bed. The picture he drew resembled in every detail Hihn's locomotive.

After the interview, Bergman invited the four interviewers to a tour of the park to seek out the locomotive. He claimed that after so many years—he had found the engine in 1964 while the interview took place in 1971—he had forgotten its exact location. Before they arrived at the Splitstuff Area, Bergman took the four to several other locations. This was obviously done to confuse Richter and his friends. One of the areas visited required a difficult hike from the Aptos Creek Fire Road at the top of the incline and today's White's Lagoon Trail down to the top of Maple Falls. After a climb back to the fire road, the group finally reached the Splitstuff Area. Immediately, Richter noticed that there were still ropes with block and tackle hanging from several trees, and that obviously there had been a great amount of activity in the area earlier. While Richter and his friends were allowed to roam freely in the area, Bergman was careful to keep them away from the bottom of Sand Point.

Richter and his friends did not find the locomotive and Bergman kept his secret. Perhaps he had truly forgotten its location. When he had purportedly found it, only the front end was exposed and the locomotive sat in a slide-prone area. In the intervening seven years since its discovery, it very well could have been covered.

My third and last interview was with Bergman's former supervisor, Wayne Dennis. When I met him, he was retired and living in Felton, and had just returned from vacation. Dennis was both helpful and forthright concerning his former employee. He stated that one day, the two of them were eating their lunch while sitting on the tailgate of their truck at Sand Point. They had backed the truck up so that they were looking out at what is considered by many to be the best view in the park. The two discussed several subjects before the conversation included the lost locomotive. Bergman told Dennis that the locomotive was sitting directly below them completely covered with dirt and rock. I asked Dennis if he ever hiked down to observe the area. He answered no because his leg problem kept him confined mostly to his desk and taking such tours with his employees in a truck.

To this day, the fate of Hihn's *Betsy Jane* and the story of the lost locomotive of Nisene Marks remain speculative at best.[88]

Renegotiation of the land transfer agreement between the Valencia–Hihn Company and the Loma Prieta Lumber Company concerning Tract 10 in the Augmentation

The Valencia–Hihn Company in the summer of 1917 had sent peelers into the eastern part of Tract 10 in the Augmentation in order to collect tan oak bark. Rather than remove the bark, they stored it in Big Tree Gulch. It is clear from the letter below that an agreement had been made between Valencia–Hihn and the Loma Prieta Lumber Company for the latter to haul out the bark once a railroad was extended to Big Tree Gulch. However, no such railroad was built in 1918, as anticipated, and it was not until late

1918, after the catastrophic storm, that Loma Prieta finally made moves to construct a railroad to Big Tree Gulch.

On December 23, 1918, Valencia–Hihn's secretary, A. S. Jansen, wrote to Harvey Bassett, general manager of Loma Prieta, asking when the railroad line would be extended to Big Tree Gulch and when Valencia–Hihn could expect to receive its bark. On December 29, Bassett replied:

> *In answer to yours of December 23, regarding peeled oak wood now on this company's property at a point beyond our present railroad, [it is] my understanding that upon the completion of our road to the point where the bark is piled, we will ship the same for you over our road and load same on Southern Pacific cars at the agreed price.*[89]

August Hihn dies

On December 30, 1918, August Hihn, president of the Valencia–Hihn Company and last surviving son of Frederick Hihn, died unexpectedly. The *Evening News* reported:

A. C. Hihn Dies Suddenly; Anxiety Over Settlement of Estate Contributing Cause

> *August C. Hihn, president of the recently dissolved F. A. Hihn company since 1889, son of the late capitalist F. A. Hihn and one of the best known property owners and business men in this section of the state, passed away suddenly at his home at the corner of Chestnut and Walnut avenues last evening about 6 o'clock, following an attack of acute indigestion. Mr. Hihn had not been feeling well for the past few days. On the way to the theater Christmas night he had a fainting spell on the street and was taken to his home. Sunday he was apparently much improved and spent the afternoon with his wife and friends on the beach, his favorite spot for pleasure since his boyhood.*
>
> *The deceased was born in this city about fifty-five years ago, and from the time he was a very young man he had*

> been connected with his father and his brother, the late Fred O. Hihn, in the management of the large interests which the family had in this county and in San Francisco and other parts of the state.
>
> Since the distribution of the Hihn property following the death of his father, Mr. Hihn became the owner of considerable Santa Cruz county real estate, as well as a valuable piece of property on East street in San Francisco and valuable property in Hollister and Watsonville. He was the sole owner of the Hihn block at the corner of Pacific avenue and Lincoln street, in which is located Orchard's candy store and Walsh-Mellott's shoe store, and has an interest in the valuable timber lands belonging to the Hihn heirs and yet undivided, on Soquel creek.
>
> Mr. Hihn had not been in the best of health for some time, due mainly to the anxiety and work connected with the settlement of his late father's estate and the distribution of the property. This is believed to have had a marked effect on his condition, making his sickness more acute. He is survived by his aged mother, Mrs. Theresa Hihn, two sisters, Mrs. C. B. Younger and Mrs. H. O. Henderson, and his wife, who was formerly Miss Grace Cooper of Watsonville.

In August's stead, his nephew Frederick Day Hihn was elected president of the Valencia–Hihn Company, who abandoned his life of luxury in San Francisco to relocate to Santa Cruz. His aunt and Frederick Hihn's eldest daughter, Agnes Younger, was appointed vice-president, while H. N. Lindsay was made secretary and treasurer. Frederick Day immediately resumed his uncle's goal of finding a buyer for the company's 4,488 acres of unlogged land in the Augmentation.[90]

The Loma Prieta Lumber Company builds a railroad to Big Tree Gulch

In the aftermath of the September 1918 storm, the Loma Prieta Lumber Company shifted all of its energy to reaching Big Tree Gulch along Bridge

Creek. As soon as weather permitted, the track along China Ridge was removed and taken to the vicinity of the Porter House. All of the rails along Bridge Creek, except for a short section to allow for trains to switch, were also removed, although most of the ties were left in place. As the track was cut back, the small number of redwood trees that had survived along the rights-of-way were felled.

By the middle of spring, the track had been cut back to Camp 1 and Molino's Shay was carefully lowered down the incline, inch by inch. To help relieve the weight on the line and donkey engine, the locomotive's boiler was fired up which allowed the gears to work in reverse. With the locomotive's arrival at the mill on Aptos Creek, the Loma Prieta Lumber Company had two Shay locomotives to work the railroad line between Molino and Big Tree Gulch. For sake of convenience, Molino's Shay was designated No. 1, while the second Shay became No. 2 on Loma Prieta's roster. Before it was put into service along the Big Tree Gulch line, No. 1 was converted to oil power, just like its companion.

Meanwhile, work crews were busy grading the new railroad high up along Bridge Creek's western wall. This line would initially be three miles long, although Timothy Hopkins hoped to eventually extend it into the Splitstuff Area so that the abandoned timber there could be harvested. The route broke off from the Bridge Creek railroad line just beyond the Porter House, switching south up the hillside in a long arc into Porter Gulch. Because of the narrowness of the gulch, there was only space for four cars and a locomotive along the upper switch. The higher elevation of the railroad was necessary to avoid three wide gullies with near-vertical walls further to the north. These could not be crossed without building tall, expensive bridges. Thus, the alternative was to build the railroad at a higher elevation, where the gulches could be crossed with less effort. The result, however, was a twenty percent grade on the switchback, which the Shays could handle on their own or hauling empty flatcars, but which proved difficult to navigate with a loaded train of four cars. Without the benefit of air brakes, the engineer and brakemen had to rely on steam jams and hand brakes to navigate down the switchback.

From the upper switch, the railroad continued north with a three percent grade. The track zig-zagged up three gullies and crossed at least four seasonal streams over wooden bridges, none of which exceeded 65 feet in length. Several cuts were also required within Hopkins' Tract 8 to maintain an even and stable grade around tight corners. Just past the seventh bridge 1.7 miles from the Porter House, the railroad reached the boundary of Tract 10. Here at 620 feet above sea level, the Loma Prieta Lumber Company built its last formal logging station, Camp 5, better known today as Hoffman's Camp.

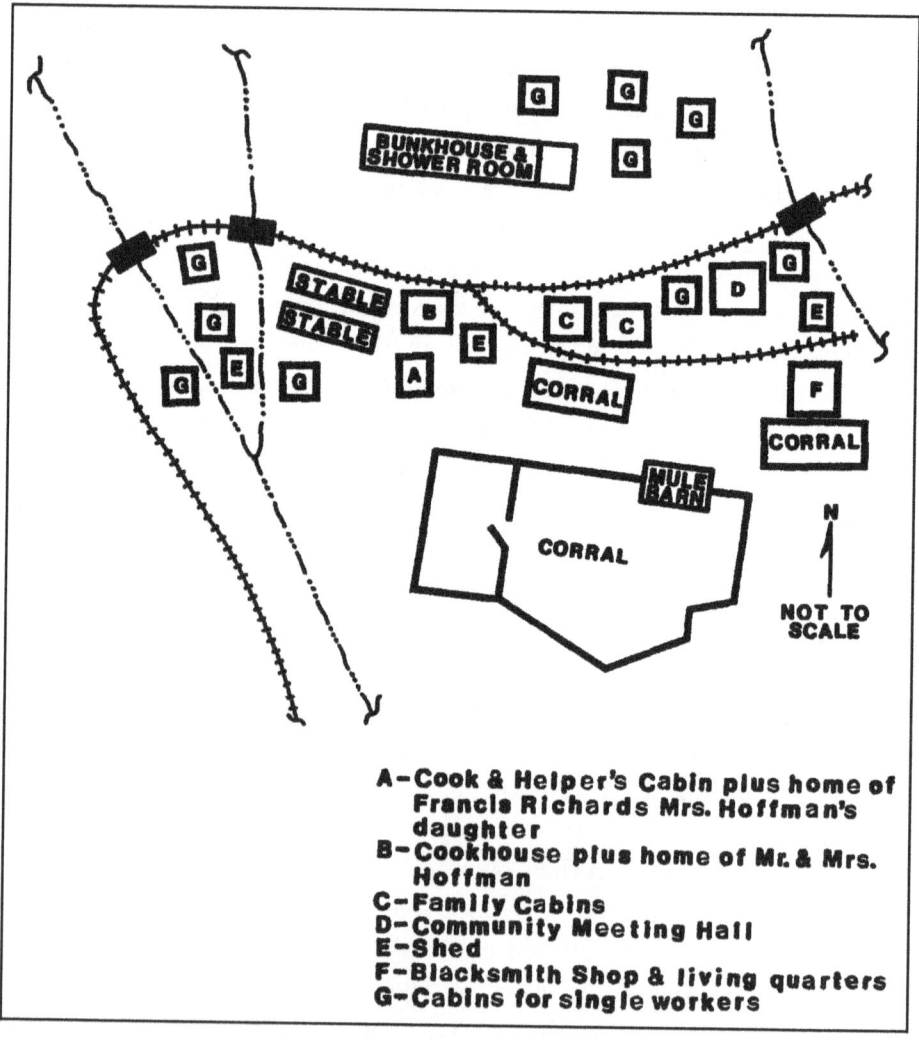

FIGURE 4.13 LAYOUT OF CAMP 5 "HOFFMAN'S CAMP"

Louis Hoffman was the camp's superintendent, whose wife was the camp's cook. He had worked for the Loma Prieta Lumber Company since the early 1900s at Olive Springs before the earthquake. He preferred to call Camp 5 "Camp Liberty," probably in reference to the recent Allied victory in World War I. His wife, meanwhile, called it "Camp Comfort." The Marks family, meanwhile, named it China Camp in the 1965 deed that transferred their lands to the state. This latter name is likely a misplaced reference to the Chinese workers who had built the Loma Prieta Railroad in the mid-1880s.

Camp 5 was unusual compared to the earlier camps built in the Augmentation. In some ways it resembled more the village of Loma Prieta than the ramshackle shanties of the woodsmen of Camps 2 or 3 on China Ridge. Hoffman's camp consisted of at least twenty-four buildings and half a dozen outbuildings. These were not intended to be permanent and lacked foundations, yet they were built well enough to remain livable to at least 1965 with several still standing well into the 1980s. The largest building was the 120-foot-long bunkhouse, which had showers and a washroom. The complex also included a cookhouse with living quarters for the Hoffmans, homes for the assistant cook and kitchen helpers, a home for Mrs. Hoffman's daughter, a community meeting hall, corrals and barns for the mules, a blacksmith shop with living quarters, and about twelve cabins built by men who did not want to live in the bunkhouse. The camp's occupants were predominately from Northern Italy and from two cantons in Switzerland, as well as a few Portuguese. Men who preferred to live in Aptos or near the Aptos Creek mill were brought in daily by railcar.

Above the camp, a spring was channeled into a large water tank that provided water for the camp's occupants, as well as for the donkey engines and two locomotives. To the south, about midway between the camp and the switchback, an acre of land was cleared for growing food. A gardener lived nearby in a cabin and delivered vegetables, fruits, and herbs to the cookhouses at Camp 5 and the Aptos Creek mill.

Beyond Camp 5, the railroad continued to follow the western hillside for another 0.6 miles, crossing over three more short bridges, until it reached Big Tree Gulch. Here, Frederick Hihn had left standing four massive old-growth redwood trees, the largest of which measured 18 feet

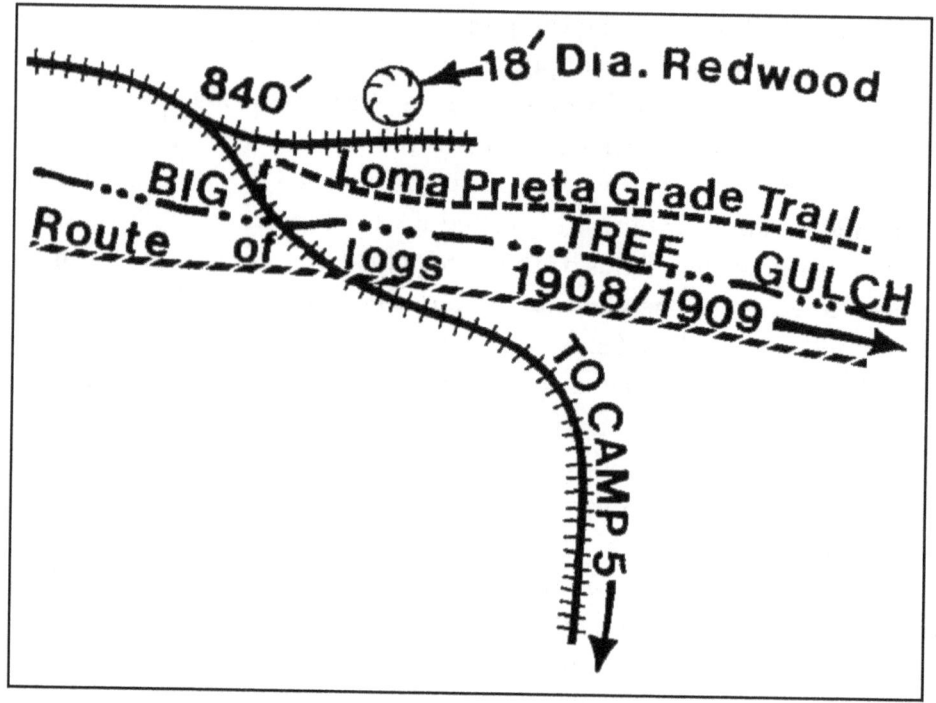

FIGURE 4.14 THE RAILROAD GRADE AT BIG TREE GULCH

across and the other three 16 feet each. It seems that after visiting the four giants, Hihn was so impressed with their beauty and magnificence that he wanted to give them, plus some surrounding land, to the county for a park. His plan to preserve the grove went for naught upon his death in 1913. The Loma Prieta Lumber Company only cared about the bottom line.

Today, the stump of the 18-foot giant can be found to the left of the Loma Prieta Grade Trail as it heads downhill toward Bridge Creek. If the stump is measured, one will find that it is only 12 feet across. That is because the bark was removed during the felling operation and weathering of the exposed stump has also shriveled its size over the years. Curiously, the tree left no second-growth cathedral grove around its stump as is common among felled old-growth giants.

The railroad line continued up the southern side of Big Tree Gulch for about 600 feet and then switched back down on the northern side until ending slightly past the 18-foot diameter giant. It is from this point that

The Residue of Success   1919

the company hoped to eventually continue the line 1.5 miles further up Bridge Creek to the former Splitstuff Area, but this plan never came to fruition. Either due to lack of funds or insufficient timber to justify the cost, the Loma Prieta Lumber Company decided to terminate its railroad in Big Tree Gulch.

Because workers would spend nearly two years working in and around the gulch, a temporary camp was formed of tents and one-man shacks. Remnants of the camp can be found several hundred feet above today's Loma Prieta Grade Trail in the gulch: one of the redwood stumps they turned into a toilet (the board they sat on was still in place as of 1992).

The Big Tree Gulch operation required the company's largest donkey engine. The monster machine measured 30 feet from ground to top of smoke stack and sat on a sled composed of two 60-foot-long redwood runners. It had a cylinder bore of 10 inches and a stroke of 14 inches. Because it was too heavy to load onto the train, it had to drag itself to Big Tree Gulch. After crossing from the Aptos Creek mill to Molino Junction, it began its climb up the Loma Prieta Branch to the confluence of Bridge Creek. Unfortunately, the engineer miscalculated and the engine toppled into the millpond. It took two weeks for the engine to be pulled out of the pond by two smaller donkey engines. Once repaired, it slowly crawled its way along the former Bridge Creek railroad route to the bottom of Big Tree Gulch.

Paul Johnston remembered the journey of the engine as it left the millpond to head up Bridge Creek. Johnston worked for the Loma Prieta Lumber Company in 1917 as an apprentice carpenter before quitting to join the Army. After he returned from service, he joined the donkey engineer on the trip up to Camp 4. When I interviewed Johnston, I was mostly interested in finding the location of the lost locomotive. However, he did recount his adventure on the donkey engine. To paraphrase him: "I held on for dear life as the donkey engineer maneuvered the engine up along Bridge Creek. While there was no need for haste, the engineer had a different idea. As soon as the donkey engine reached the stump that its cable was attached to, it would be removed then pulled manually upstream to the next stump then attached. As soon as this was accomplished off the donkey engine would go at top speed until the next anchor stump was reached."

When the engine reached the abandoned Camp 4, all of its working

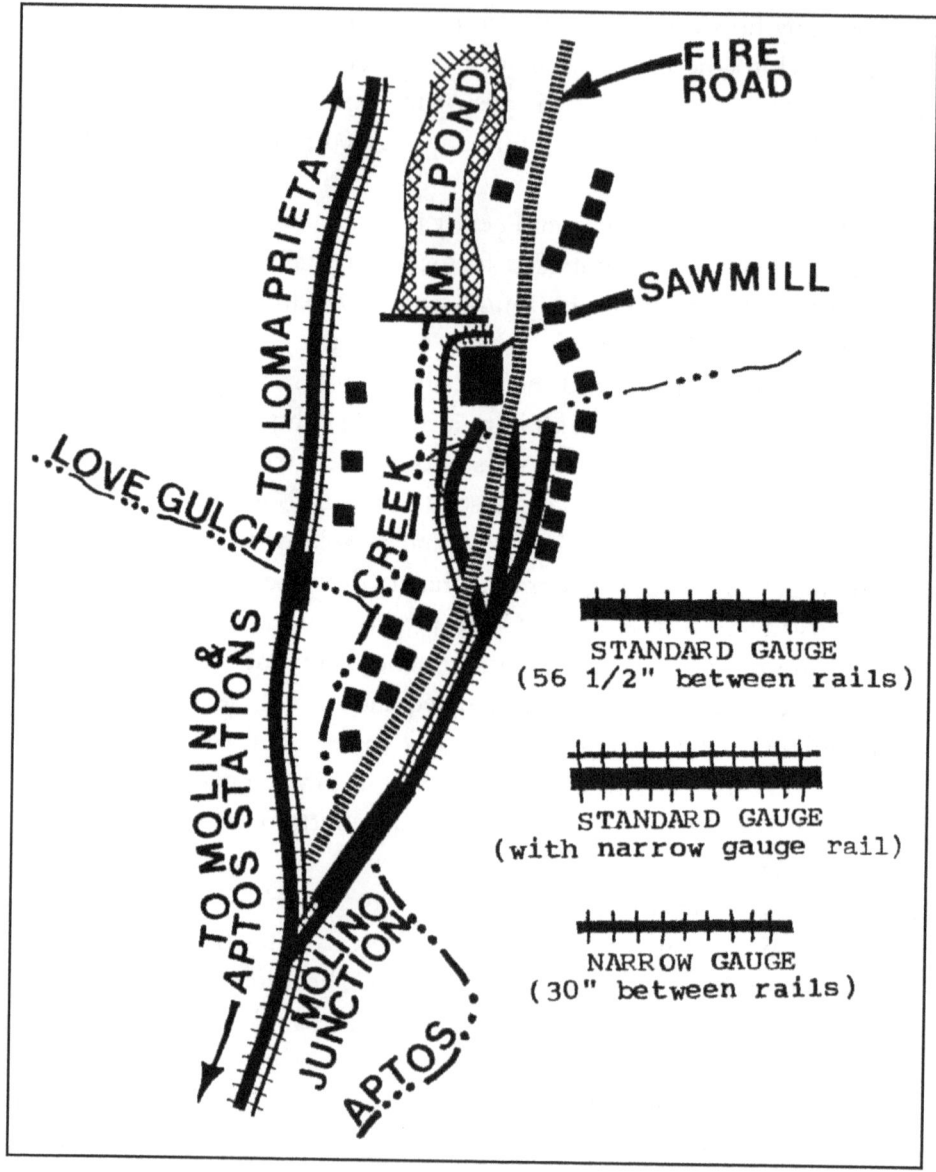

FIGURE 4.15 CONFIGURATION OF THE TRACKAGE AT THE
LOMA PRIETA LUMBER COMPANY'S MILL ON APTOS CREEK

parts were removed from the sled. They were then carried up to the top of the gulch by other donkey engines and mounted on new runners. Some former Loma Prieta employees, recounting in their interviews with Woods

Mattingley, said that two sixty-foot logs remained at the site of Camp 4 until the storm of 1982, when they were washed downstream.

All of the material that was loaded onto the flatcars could be no wider than four feet. Thus, the logs of the giants had to be cut into quarters or halves, with carefully-placed dynamite performing this task. The donkey engine was responsible for loading these logs onto the flatcars at the main landing within the gulch. The logs were then taken by one of the Shay locomotives to the millpond on Aptos Creek. Out of concern that the quartered and halved logs would sink when deposited in the millpond, a spur was added that wrapped around the western side of the mill and to the back. Here, the logs could be fed directly into the headrig's saws, bypassing the pond entirely. While Southern Pacific agreed to supply the rails and ties for this spur line, Loma Prieta had to pay the construction costs.[91]

Therese Hihn dies

A lifelong companion to her husband, Frederick Hihn, Therese Hihn died on April 21, 1919. The *Evening News* reported:

Mrs. Therese Hihn passes after 66 Years Residence

Mrs. Therese Hihn, widow of the late capitalist, F. A. Hihn, and the last of the older generation of the prominent family which has been connected with the history of this county for the past sixty-six years, closed her eyes in the last sleep at her home on Church street about 10 o'clock last evening. With her at the time were Mrs. C. B. Younger, her daughter; Mrs. C. W. Hammer and Mrs. Sophia Brooks, the latter her companion for several years past.

Mrs. Hihn's life has been one of pioneering. She was born in Paris, France, nearly 82 years ago, her name being Therese Paggen. With her parents she crossed the Atlantic ocean, then an eventful voyage of the adventuresome sort and landed in Mexico. She came to San Francisco as a young girl in 1849. There she met F. A. Hihn, who had already settled in Santa Cruz, and in 1853, in the midst of the mining excitement which then reached to every corner of the young city by the Golden Gate, she was married and immediately came to Santa Cruz to live. That was 66 years ago. Eight children were born to the couple, of whom only two now survive—Mrs. Agnes Hihn Younger and Mrs. Katherine Cope Henderson. As a younger woman, Mrs. Hihn made great use of her sense of humor, and was a very bright, witty person, in a conversational way. Many in Santa Cruz today can testify to the interesting periods of pleasure that were spent at the beautiful home on Church street, with Mrs. Hihn as hostess of the occasion.

Upon the death of her husband in 1913 Mrs. Hihn succeeded to the home and an income of several hundred dollars a month from the Coast Realty company, one of the profitable holdings belonging to the late capitalist. She has lived a quiet life since her husband's death, and has been a familiar figure, off and on, in her walks about town with her companion. She was in possession of all her faculties almost up to the time of her death, and although badly injured in a fall a few years ago, she recovered then from a broken collar bone within a few weeks and did not seem to suffer any ill effects from her experience.

Funeral services will be held tomorrow morning at the home at 11 o'clock, when Rev. E. T. Born of Cavalry Episcopal church will officiate. The family have given no formal invitations for friends to attend the services, but it is understood that those who desire will be welcome to attend.[92]

Land transfer from Katherine Henderson to Allen Rispin for Camp Capitola and Soquel Water System

On July 30, 1919, it was announced in the *Evening News* that Allen Rispin had purchased from Katherine Henderson most of Capitola and Soquel. The newspaper explained:

RISPIN BUYS NEARLY ALL OF CAPITOLA

Big Hotel Property Included in the Deal; Talk of Improvements

Negotiations were being concluded today for the transfer to H. Allen Rispin, San Francisco and Denver capitalist, of all of the properties at Capitola and Soquel owned by Mrs. Katherine Cope Henderson as successor in interest of her father, the late F. A. Hihn, who founded the town and community many years ago.

Mr. Rispin becomes the owner of virtually the entire business district and waterfront area of the town of Capitola, including Hotel Capitola and all of the cottage city and all other resort properties in connection with the place. He also purchases thirty acres along Soquel creek, between the bridge in Capitola and the new bridge near the town of Soquel, as well as 200 acres comprising the old Grove ranch near Soquel. The deal also includes the transfer to Mr. Rispin of the wharf property; 128 lots on the heights east of Hotel Capitola; water works and the electric light privileges of the resort.

Mrs. Henderson said today that she has sold out entirely everything which she owned in the Soquel and Capitola district, with the exception of her home property and the block in which it is situated, near the railroad track and diagonally across from the Southern Pacific depot. Mr. Rispin will take possession as soon as the deeds are signed. The final papers are being drawn up today.

It was impossible for The News to get in touch with the new buyer today, but it is understood from assertions made by him to prominent Santa Cruzans that it is his intention to expend several hundred thousand dollars in extensively improving Capitola as a resort and home town. This will quite probably include the construction of a modern concrete hotel as well as a natatorium, and the general permanent improvement of all of the streets. Mr. Rispin is not a stranger to the community in which he is now intended to invest large sums,

> *having been connected with C. E. Canfield some years ago in the subdividing of Capitola heights, and he has since personally purchased other property along the heights overlooking the west bank of Soquel creek, near Capitola, and is about to erect a beautiful home for himself on one of the sites along the bluff.*
>
> *Attorney Walter H. Linforth of San Francisco, Mrs. Henderson's representative, has been in Capitola for several days closing up the legal details of the deal.*
>
> *When the news of the purchase was made public in Santa Cruz this morning it was freely stated that the plans for improvement of the nearby resort will undoubtedly have a marked beneficial effect on the entire resort section lying along the northern shore of Monterey bay and including Capitola, Del Mar and Santa Cruz.*
>
> *Mrs. Henderson said to The News this morning that she was glad of the opportunity of being able to turn over the property to some one who could make the necessary improvements and was sanguine herself that the effect would be beneficial to this entire section.*

Over the next few years, on the western hillside overlooking Soquel Creek, Rispin built a 22-room mansion. Throughout Capitola, he planted trees, paved roads, and constructed the seawall that still exists today. Much of this he directed from behind the scenes.[93]

Hollywood invades Loma Prieta

In fall 1919, Republic Pictures leased from the Loma Prieta Lumber Company the Big Tree Gulch railroad and part of the Loma Prieta Branch beside the millpond to film several scenes for its upcoming silent film, *The One Way Trail*. The film starred Edythe Sterling and Gordon Sackville. According to a summary by the *Dayton Daily News*:

> *The timberland of Canada is the locale of "The One Way Trail"... The action is not unlike that of the ordinary western thriller, there being quick drawing of weapons, much gun-*

The Residue of Success 1919

play, the conflict between crime and law and order, and other things so dear to the heart of the movie fan. But the story is very different and the settings, too, are Canadian instead of Western United States. Views of the lumber mill in operation are particularly interesting. The story centers around Wanda Walker, whose father once had been sent to prison for a crime he did not commit and the effort of the real criminal to win Wanda for his own by threatening to expose him as an escaped convict. But, fortunately, there is the brave limb of the Canadian mounted police on hand to thwart the arch-conspirator and criminal and to bring retribution for his crimes upon his head. And there is Wanda, second only to him, to fight for the father and the man she loves.

The film was released in February 1920 to relatively little fanfare. In its review of the film, the *Evening News* wrote on November 29, 1920: "The most spectacular and natural scenes were those taken at the Loma Prieta mill, showing actual milling and logging operations, as well as railroad operations."

The film did feature one unique event: the only recorded train wreck on the Loma Prieta Branch. A staged disaster was created for the film, seemingly sacrificing one of the two Shay locomotives for the scene. After the scene was filmed, the locomotive was righted, its cab repaired, and it returned to service.[94]

The Molino Timber Company files for voluntary dissolution

On December 1, 1919, the Molino Timber Company filed for voluntary dissolution. The officers of the company at the time were Oscar Chase, Bert Stoodley, Dr. Cowden (who represented the interests of the Williams family), Fred Severance, and Fred Daubenbiss. By filing before the end of the year, the directors avoided paying their annual fee to the state. Upon the company's dissolution, Stoodley, who owned nearly half the company's stock, became a modestly rich man. He remained secretary of the Loma Prieta Lumber Company.[95]

The Loma Prieta Lumber Company
ends logging operations in the Augmentation

Throughout the 1920 season, the Loma Prieta Lumber Company continued to harvest the timber on the western hillsides of Bridge Creek within Tract 10 of the Augmentation. By the end of the year, logging crews had reached the top of Hinckley Ridge—today's West Ridge Trail and the boundary of Loma Prieta's land in the tract—and finished gathering the timber that had been left uncut beside the creek when Camp 4 shut down in 1918. Daily trains shuttled logs from the forest to the millpond on Aptos Creek. The end of operations along Bridge Creek was near, but the company's directors did not want to admit as much to their workers.

Daily life continued at Camp 5 and in Big Tree Gulch. Twenty-five to thirty people lived and worked at the camp and in the gulch, while another twenty worked at the mill. This was the height of activity in the Augmentation in the early twentieth century, although it paled when compared to the approximately 230 workers who had been employed by Loma Prieta in the mid-1890s. Still, the company had learned some lessons. The garden and two cookhouses provided workers with high quality food that was universally praised. Workers only worked an average of ten hours per day, as opposed to twelve in 1900. And their wages had increased on average from $0.13 an hour in 1902 to $0.82 an hour in 1920. At the time, this was considered a good wage and most workers were satisfied with it even if management was not.

Indeed, the directors of the Loma Prieta Lumber Company were regretting their decision to purchase the eastern part of Tract 10. According to Bert Stoodley, "from the fall of the first tree to the last the entire logging of Frederick A. Hihn's formerly owned eastern 610 acres of Tract 10 was a disappointment." There were many reasons for this sentiment. The war in Europe had increased labor and machinery costs and also made it difficult to acquire parts. The project itself was badly planned, with the Bridge Creek railroad built so close to the creek a proven mistaken when the September 1918 storm destroyed Camp 4. Furthermore, the A. W. Elam Report had failed to discover the problem of spot rot in the trees, meaning it had overestimated the value of the property when it was sold to Loma

The Residue of Success   1920 – 1921

Prieta. And then there was the fact that the company had to pay to rebuild the millpond's dam since it had earlier allowed Stoodley to dismantle it.

The first casualty came after the end of the 1920 season. The directors decided not to reopen the lumber mill on Aptos Creek for the 1921 season. Instead, all remaining logs, including those fished out of the millpond, would be sent to the San Vicente Lumber Company's mill on the West Side of Santa Cruz, just as the Valencia–Hihn Company was doing with logs cut from Tract 2. Logs that were deemed insufficiently profitable as lumber would be cut into splitstuff or cordwood at the mill. The company hoped that the savings on labor and maintenance would make the remaining operation along Bridge Creek profitable.

By the start of the 1921 season, workers knew that it was the final year of operations along Bridge Creek. Yet the directors hired the same number of workers for Camp 5 and Big Tree Gulch as the previous two years and sent fellers and buckers into the forest to cut trees and prepare them to be dragged to the railroad grade. However, as spring turned to summer, this task proved increasingly difficult since few trees remained. In reality, the company had lied when recruiting crew for the new year and not revealed to them that there was only enough work for part of a season.

The last trees were probably cut along Bridge Creek in late August. The workers then set to work dismantling and removing the machinery and everything worth salvaging in the area. The buildings were left standing, not valuable enough to take with them, but over the winter and spring of 1922, the tracks were cut back to the Porter House and the third rail was removed from the Loma Prieta Branch. All of the salvaged equipment, including the Shay locomotives, were placed in storage within or beside the abandoned lumber mill.

The end of operations along Bridge Creek in 1921 marked the conclusion of thirty-seven years of logging by the Loma Prieta Lumber Company in the Augmentation. All considered, Loma Prieta harvested timber from a total of 7,455 acres, including 6,845 acres in Tract 9 and 610 acres in Tract 10. Divided evenly, that results in 201 acres of timberland harvested each year. During the high years of production, from 1883 to 1902, the average increased to 229 acres per year. Meanwhile, in the later years an average of 156 acres per year was achieved. However, much of the timber produced in Hinckley Gulch at this time was turned into splitstuff rather than lumber. Not included in these numbers is the lumber produced from Timothy Hopkins' 1,100 acres in Tract 8 and the timber cut along Mill Creek on the North Coast between 1907 and 1912.

As the cleanup was wrapping up in 1922, Harvey Bassett had a chance encounter with Teck B. Cathey in Aptos. Cathey had just arrived in Aptos from Oklahoma with his family. He had visited the area in 1918 and liked what he saw, so settled his affairs and moved west. Bassett hired Cathey as the caretaker of the Loma Prieta mill and former village. His primary responsibility was to liquidate the company's properties and assets in Aptos and within the Augmentation. Bassett especially wanted him to sell the two Shay, a chore that would prove easier said than done. Cathey moved with his family into one of the homes at the mill, where he would reside for the next two years.[96]

Mortgage deed transfer from the Loma Prieta Lumber Company to the Peoples Savings Bank of Santa Cruz

On June 30, 1922, Timothy Hopkins, as president of the Loma Prieta Lumber Company, and Bert Stoodley, as secretary, entered into a mortgage deed in which they passed title to the Loma Prieta Lumber Company's 7,455 acres in the Augmentation to the Peoples Saving Bank of Santa Cruz in exchange for $24,700. The bank acknowledged receipt of the deed on July 8.

The history of the activities of the Loma Prieta Lumber Company over the subsequent four years is mostly lost to time. I contacted a number of historians in search of further information, but had little success. I only discovered three other deeds and an announcement of a partnership to help fill in the gap. Therefore, in order to maintain story continuity, I am forced to speculate somewhat regarding what occurred from mid-1922 until the end of 1926.

The purpose of the mortgage deed was to secure a loan from the bank in order to pay off a $24,700 promissory note made earlier to an unspecified payee. Who that payee was is unclear, but the most likely candidate is Hopkins himself, who may have borrowed heavily to buy the eastern half of Tract 10 and was rewarded with loss after loss from the endeavor. The deed granted the bank full powers of ownership of the company's land within the Augmentation until such a time that the amount was repaid. The deed also mentioned the Valencia–Hihn Company's expired right to harvest tan oak trees and bark within Tract 10, suggesting that the company had left at least some trees and bark behind which could still turn a profit for the Loma Prieta Lumber Company or the bank.

Faced with the fact that their second-growth redwoods were years away from harvesting, Loma Prieta management decided that the best course to follow was to put the land into trust then search for a buyer that was willing to wait for the trees to mature. Because it would be easier to sell if the land was debt free, they began searching for a way to pay off the debt they now owed the Peoples Savings Bank of Santa Cruz. Their solution was to try and sell the 2,500 acres the company held in Hinckley Gulch, since this area had caused the most difficulties and challenges.

The decision to sell the troublesome Hinckley Gulch land presented problems of its own, most importantly its isolation and lack of access. Regarding the latter, every person who was awarded land in the Augmentation in 1863 was given the right to have direct access to the nearest county road. Those who did not have direct access could not be denied the right to cross adjacent land to reach a county road. The Loma Prieta Lumber Company had relied on this ruling to gain access through Olive Springs Resort in Tract 27 to reach its mills along Hinckley Creek in Tract 9. This accessway still existed in 1922, but it would need improvement to attract potential buyers.

The Loma Prieta Lumber Company set to work building a new steel and concrete bridge across the East Branch of Soquel Creek that could support regular use by automobiles. Three large pipes were also installed under the bridge to control the flow of the creek and protect the bridge. The cement supports that are visible today at the crossing did not support this bridge—these were built later to support a steel bridge erected around 1949, which was later moved to the Aptos Creek Fire Road where today it spans the first crossing of Aptos Creek.

Further north along the road, three additional heavy-duty bridges were constructed. The first was a wooden bridge supported by two cement piers, which still exist today. The other two bridges were also

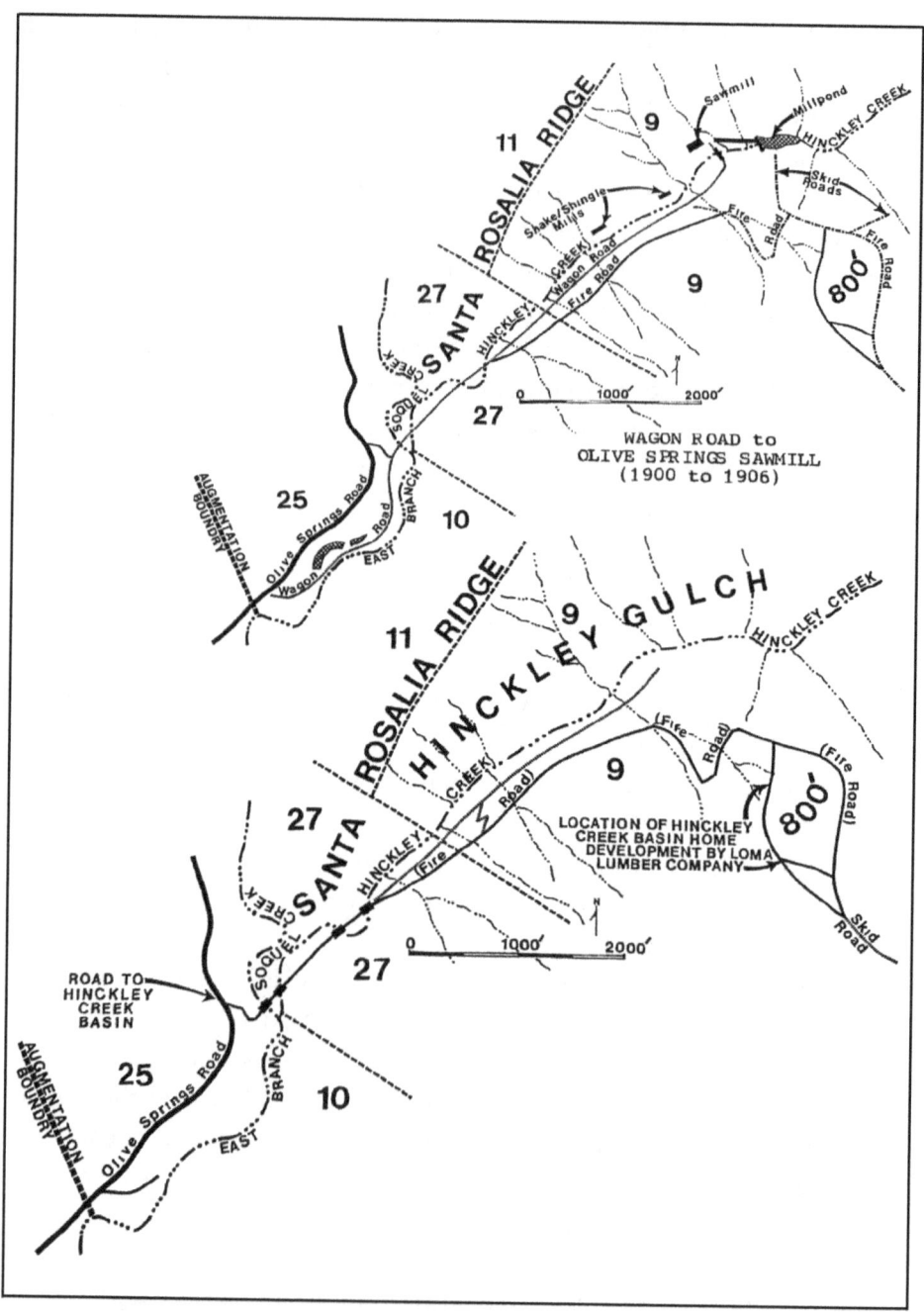

FIGURE 4.16 IMPROVEMENTS TO THE HINCKLEY CREEK ACCESS ROAD IN PREPARATION FOR THE HINCKLEY BASIN NO. 1 SUBDIVISION

The Residue of Success 1922

made of wood but have since been dismantled or destroyed, so their design is unknown. Beyond the third bridge, the road began a steep climb up Hinckley Ridge for three-quarters of a mile along a reclaimed skid road until it reached a level area at 800-foot elevation. Here, Loma Prieta management planned to establish a housing development simply named "Hinckley Creek Basin." It was hoped that the development would be the first of many in the gulch and that the sales would also repay the mortgage owed to the Peoples Savings Bank of Santa Cruz.

Meanwhile, on Aptos Creek, Teck Cathey was busy trying to repay the debt in a more traditional way: by selling everything he could of the old Loma Prieta mill. He dismantled many of the old structures, including homes, sheds, and outbuildings. He also removed most of the lighter equipment from the mill. Most of the work was done by local farmers, who came in, dismantled a building with Cathey's help, and then took it away.

Cathey and his family relied heavily on the Fairbanks–Morris rail speeder to travel between the mill and Aptos Station. He used it to bring in prospective buyers and ship out items that had been purchased. Southern Pacific had left behind a few old flatcars that Cathey could attach to the speeder to haul larger loads. He also used the speeder more generally to bring in supplies, travel to town, and bring guests to the old mill and village of Loma Prieta.

Over time, Cathey added many planks to the piles of lumber that Loma Prieta had left behind in 1921. Farmers and other buyers often preferred to buy the lumber rather than disassemble a building. Other parts that sold quickly were the lighter machinery and the narrow-gauge flatcars once used by the Molino Timber Company on China Ridge and, later, by Loma Prieta on Bridge Creek. The flatcars were broken up, with their wheels and metal parts sold for scrap and the wooden deck planks sold as lumber.

Concerning the two Shay locomotives, Cathey put them up for sale with an asking price of $700 each. While the price was fair, there were no takers. By this time, there was little need for 30-inch-gauge locomotives in the Santa Cruz Mountains or anywhere on the California coast. Only a few old-growth groves were left in the area, most of which were protected, and improvements to machinery and techniques made logging railroads mostly obsolete. So that he could disassemble the lumberyard, Cathey moved the two locomotives to a custom-built shed near the Porter House. The locomotives, however, were exposed to the elements and theft. One of the bells from a locomotive was soon stolen, and the other had been removed by Harvey Bassett and taken to his ranch in Milpitas.

The former Molino locomotive, No. 1, was eventually purchased in 1927 by the Oliver Salt Company of Mt. Eden (Hayward). According to John Sandoval, when the locomotive was fired up and allowed to run a short distance down the track between Loma Prieta and Molino Junction, the brakes almost failed. Fortunately for Loma Prieta, this did not dissuade the company from purchasing the little engine.

By the end of 1924, Cathey had cleaned up most of the mill site and moved back to Aptos with his family. However, he continued to maintain the property and kept the rail speeder at Aptos Station for this purpose. For the next two years, he ventured back to the old mill site regularly to check on conditions, straighten things up, and sell machinery and structures to interested buyers.[97]

David Mills approaches the Valencia–Hihn Company regarding unlogged land in the Augmentation

Around the end of 1922, David W. Mills of Cleveland, Ohio, approached Valencia–Hihn Company management regarding its land in the Augmentation. Presumably, Mills represented the White Motor Car Company, which among other things manufactured industrial motor trucks. It may be recalled that in the A. W. Elam Report of 1916, Horatio Ormsbee suggested that trucks were one of the two best options for extracting timber products out of the F. A. Hihn Company's land. Fast forward six years and trucking technology had improved substantially. Mills may have seen in the Valencia–Hihn Company's land a potential testing ground for his company's trucks as well as a profitable investment.

What was agreed in 1922, if anything, is unclear, but on March 1, 1924, a contract was signed between Mills and Frederick Day Hihn, Agnes Younger, and H. M. Lindsay regarding 5,970 acres in Tracts 10 and 11. Combined, these properties included 4,488 acres of unlogged timber, encompassing an estimated 166 million board feet of redwood and 6 million board feet of fir.

Mills agreed to pay Valencia–Hihn $500,000 for the land, with the first $60,000 paid by the end of the year. The remainder would be paid out periodically over the next several years at a 5.5% interest rate until the amount was paid in full. In addition to the land noted above, the undeveloped seven-mile-long Hihn Railroad Grade from Capitola to Tract 10 was included in the sale.[98]

Final year of activity on the Loma Prieta Branch

In early 1925, Southern Pacific gave notice that it intended to cease all rail traffic along the Loma Prieta Branch effective January 31, 1926. The Loma Prieta Lumber Company, with the help of Teck Cathey, realized that this was its final opportunity to shift unsold timber products and machinery out of its old mill complex on Aptos Creek. Once the mill was stripped of everything saleable, a small crew moved up to the headwaters of Bridge Creek to salvage anything left in the Splitstuff Area. The only reasonable route these workers could have used to transport the material out was along today's West Ridge Trail and then down Long Gulch to the railroad grade near today's Mary Easton Picnic Area. All of the mill's machinery and anything recovered from the Splitstuff Area was taken by rail speeder and flatcar to Aptos, where Loma Prieta rented several buildings to store it.

At Molino, Timothy Hopkins decided to harvest the remainder of standing oak and madrone on Tract 8. Most of this was located high on the east bank of Aptos Creek just below Ruth Ready's property. A two-inch diameter highline cable was installed between the top of the ridge and Molino. Pallets of wood were lowered by gravity to Aptos Creek where the load stalled just before hitting the west bank. From here, it was pulled up to the railroad grade and loaded onto flatcars parked on the spur. After a few months of this activity in the spring and summer of 1925, Hopkins abandoned the operation. The labor and transportation costs cut too deeply into the profits. Its end marked the last commercial venture on the Loma Prieta Branch of the Southern Pacific Railroad.[99]

Chapter 5

~

The Feller's Last Felling

The Monterey Bay Redwood Company incorporates

On January 24, 1925, the Monterey Bay Redwood Company was incorporated with the goal of harvesting the timber in the lands purchased by David Mills in the Augmentation. The leadership of the company was composed of Mills and five Bay Area businessmen: Charles R. Wayland of Palo Alto, and Donald M. Gregory, Clifton R. Gordan, A. DeMartini, and Winfield Dorn of San Francisco. The company's registered place of business was 1201 Merchants Exchange Building in San Francisco. The new company was capitalized at $1,350,000, split between 6,000 preferred shares and 7,500 common shares, each valued at $100.

On June 9, the *Santa Cruz News* reported:

> *The hum of industrial activity once more in the vicinity of Capitola and Soquel is due to commence in the near future, as work of the Monterey Bay Redwood Company, which yesterday purchased from the Valencia–Hihn Company the great 6,000 acre timber tract at the base of Loma Prieta, gets*

underway. The first public announcement of this transaction appeared first exclusively in the News *many months ago.*

In a deal indicated by revenue stamps used in the transaction of approximately $500,000, the Monterey Bay Redwood Company comes into ownership of the peak of Loma Prieta, the highest in the Santa Cruz Mountains, and a forest of 5,000 heavily wooded, mainly virgin redwood, with a con-

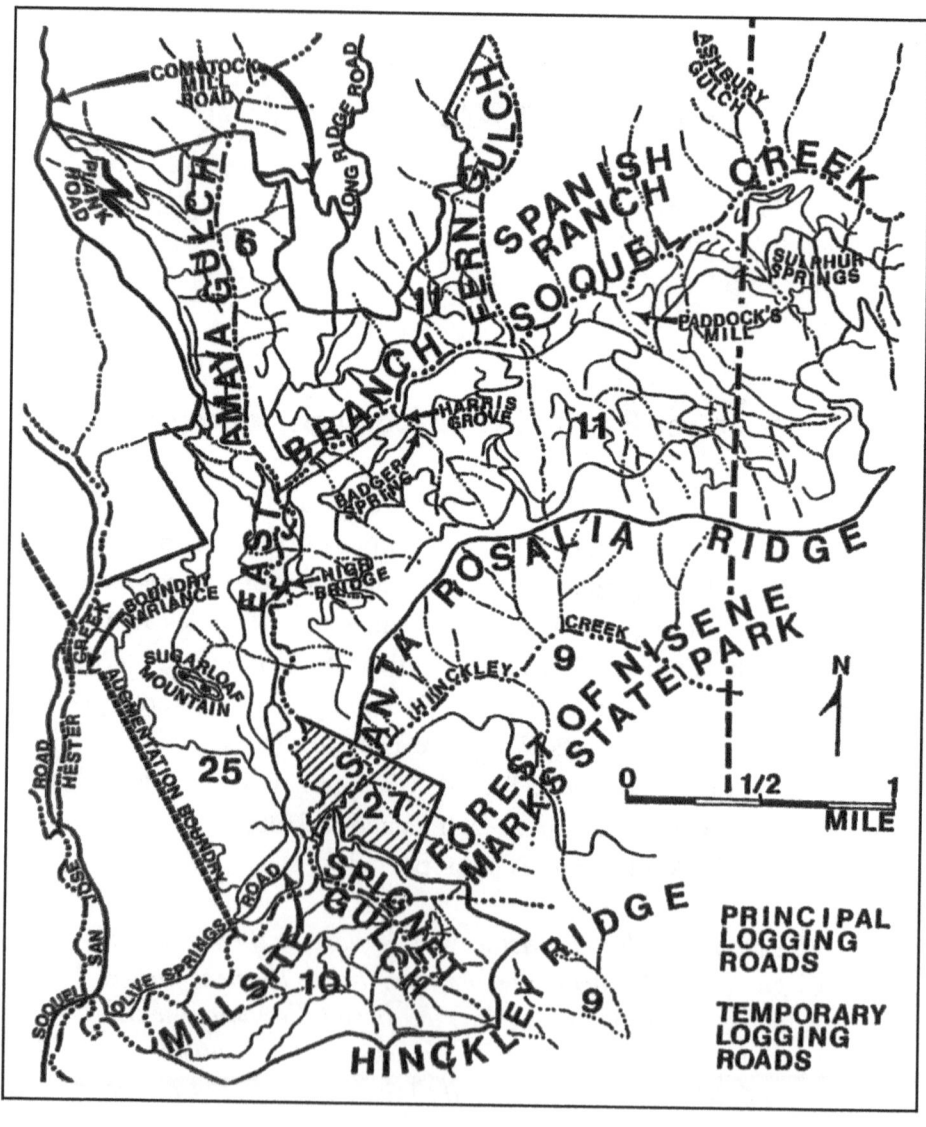

siderable stand of pine.

The forest south of Olive Springs, up the Soquel Creek gulch and into the large basin below Loma Prieta at the headwaters of Soquel Creek's East Branch, to what is known as the Hihn Sulphur Springs section, a portion of the acreage for which at one time efforts were made to set aside as a public park. This is the section seriously threatened with fire this fall.

The rate includes rights-of-way for a railroad from the

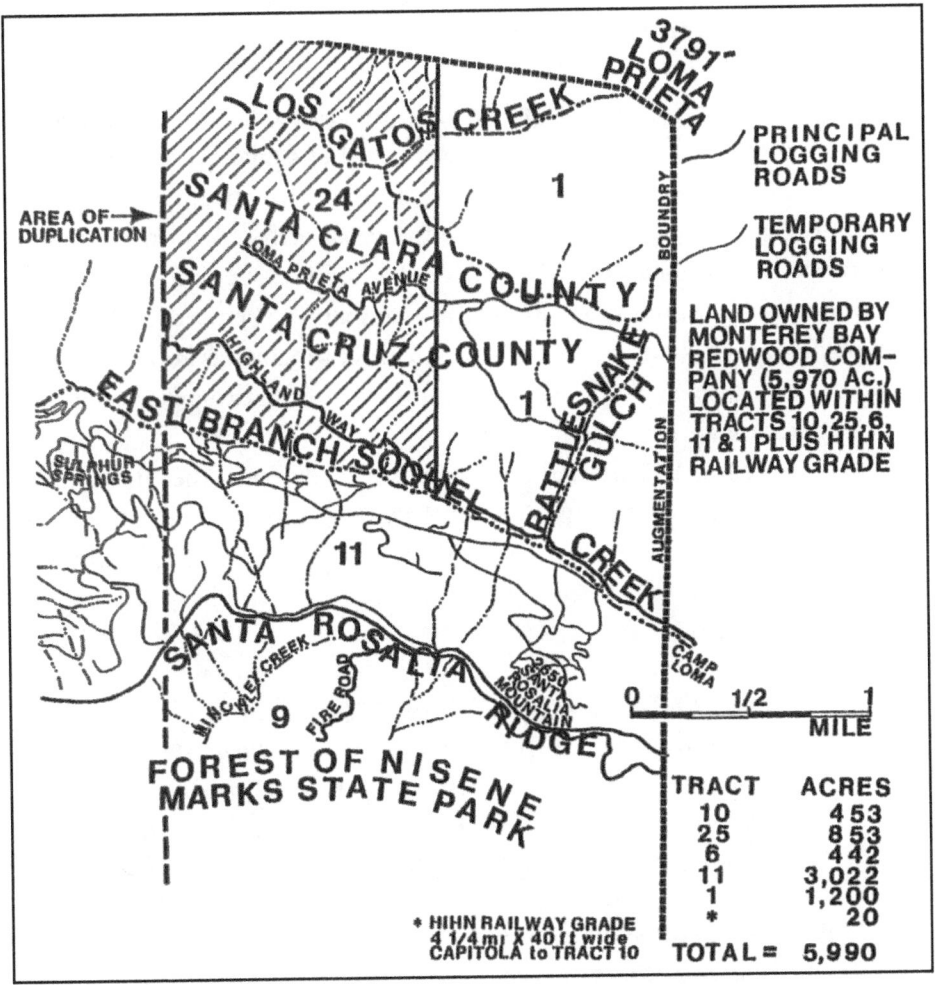

FIGURES 5.1-2 PROPERTY PURCHASED WITHIN THE AUGMENTATION FROM THE VALENCIA–HIHN COMPANY BY THE MONTEREY BAY REDWOOD COMPANY

timber holdings to a point on the Southern Pacific right-of-way at Capitola. It is understood that the new owners will locate their large mill and yards between Soquel and Capitola.

The deed was filed yesterday through the Santa Cruz Land Title Company, a $500 revenue stamp being attached thereto. Noel Patterson, local manager of the Hihn interests, has busied himself with preliminary details and arrangements for the big sale for the past many months. The Monterey Bay Lumber Company is headed by David W. Mills and a group of capitalists of local origin.

On November 10, the *Santa Cruz News* reported that the "foundation of the Monterey Bay Lumber Company's mill at Olive Springs has been completed, under the supervision of Horatio N. Ormsbee, the company's superintendent. The mill will be in operation shortly." A month later, on December 12, the *News* revealed: "A carload of 12 x 12 timbers has been received by the Monterey Bay Redwood Company to be used in their mill, now being constructed at Olive Springs. This company has about fifty men now at work on their plant, and is making every effort to get in shape for active operation early in the new year."

Machinery for the mill had been arriving throughout the latter part of the year and placed in storage. Presumably it was installed in late winter for the 1926 season. In an April 1, 1951 article in the *Sentinel*, local historian Leon Rowland explained where the machinery used at the new mill originally came from:

> The sawmill machinery which, in the Hihn mill at Laurel cut the lumber that rebuilt San Francisco after the 1906 quake and fire, has left the Santa Cruz mountains for the second time.
>
> The mill came, bright and new from San Francisco, at the beginning of the century; it operated at Laurel for 17 or 18 years; moved to Mather, in Hetch Hetchy country; came back to the redwoods on Soquel creek 26 years ago.
>
> Now it is leaving again. It presumably is going into the hands of used mill machinery dealers.
>
> James A. Harris Jr., president of the no longer operative

Monterey Bay Redwood company, says the edgers and trimmers have gone to Arcata, in Humboldt county. Where the

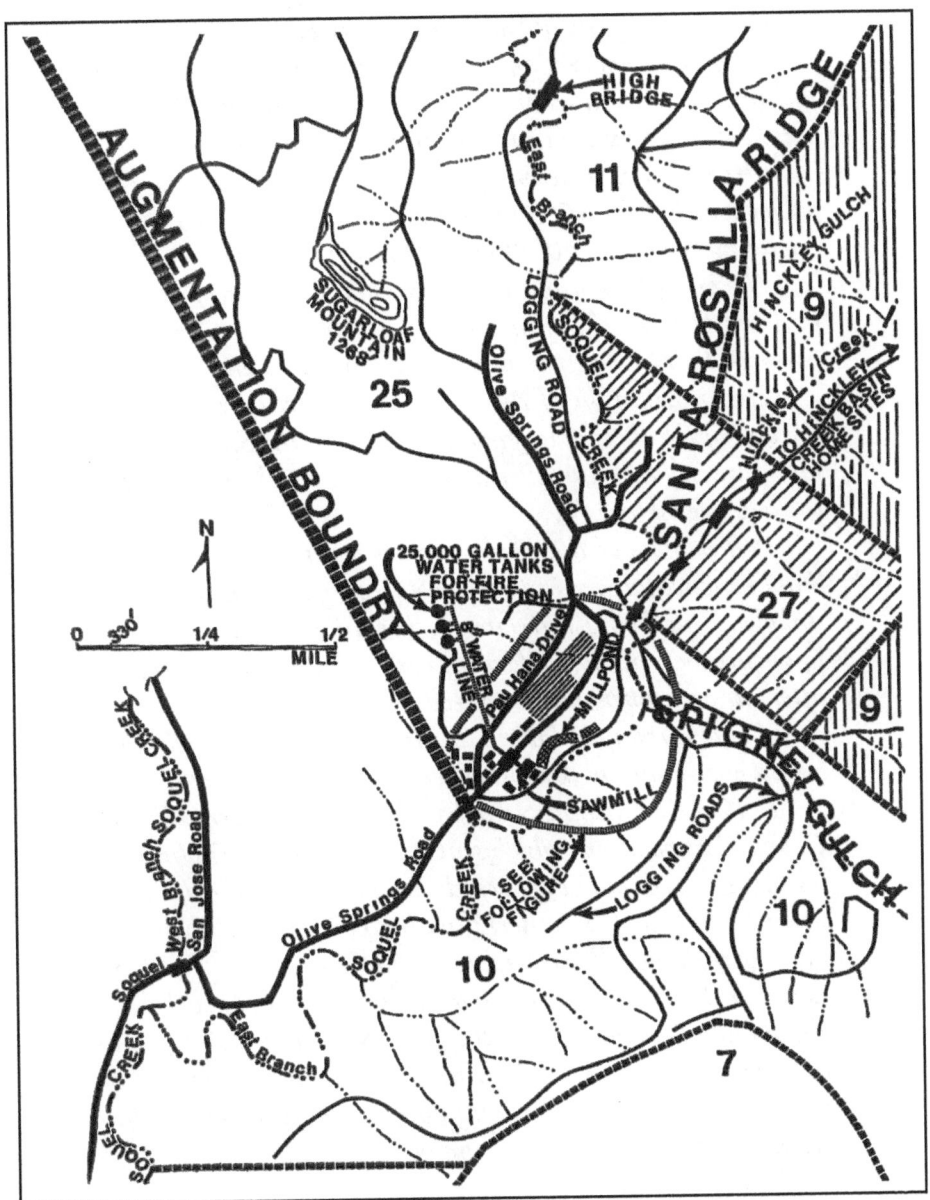

FIGURE 5.3 LOCATION OF THE MONTEREY BAY REDWOOD COMPANY'S MILLING FACILITY ON TRACT 25 IN THE AUGMENTATION

engine, bandsaw and other pieces of equipment will go he does not know.

The machinery, a Stearns mill, was bought from the Eby Machinery company in San Francisco by F. A. Hihn.

Hihn had logged off the country around Aptos and Valencia and operated on Soquel creek. His move to Laurel was to open a stand of timber virtually untouched.

The mill was a steam operated single band saw. Its capacity was rated at 50,000 feet a day, with a possibility of crowding the run to 60,000 feet if the logs ran good.

The new Hihn mill was the pride of the old German who had made himself Santa Cruz's first millionaire. He announced that his equipment would be the latest and best.

The installation of the Laurel mill virtually marked the end of the days of logging with oxen in the Santa Cruz mountains. Hihn installed donkey engines which dragged the logs over skidways.

When most of the quake-shaken downtown district of San Francisco burned in 1906 the narrow gauge railroad was still operating from Laurel north. The railroads north of San Francisco were all closed down by the quake. From Laurel car after car of lumber sped to the rebuilding metropolis.

A few years after Hihn's death in 1913 the Laurel mill ceased operations, with most of the available timber cut.

In 1917 the machinery was bought by the California Fruit Growers' association, which sent it to Mather in Tuolumne county. Even the frame of big redwood logs was sent to the new site, where it cut box material with other lumber. The next move of the sawmill was back to Santa Cruz county. In 1925 James A. Harris Jr., and David Mills, out from Cleveland, bought about 6000 acres on the upper Soquel creek. The mill they bought was that at Mather. Back it came, even to the redwood frame to operate until four or five years ago as the Monterey Bay Redwood Company.

As workers put the finishing touches on the mill in early 1926, buckers and fellers were sent out into the forest to the south of the mill. Their first

The Feller's Last Felling — 1926

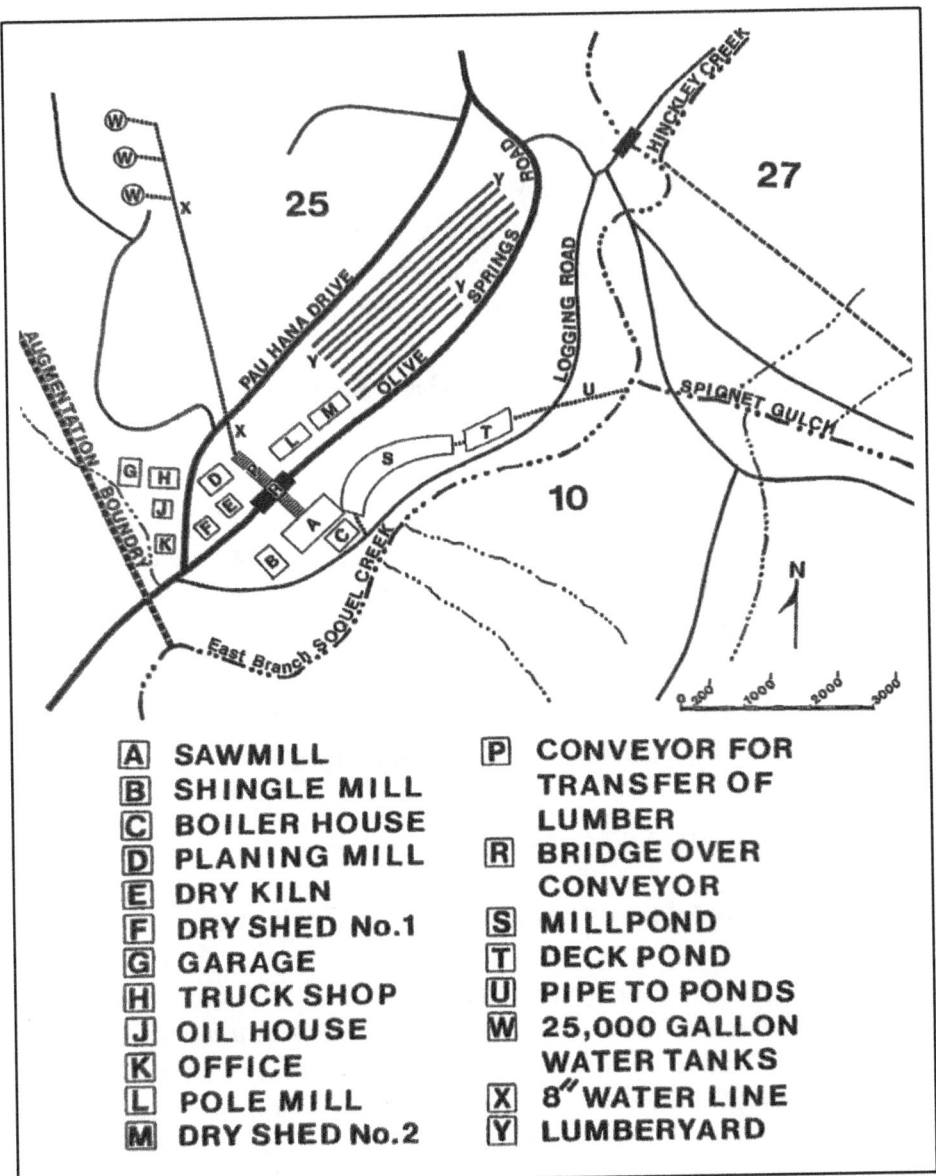

FIGURE 5.4 LAYOUT OF THE MONTEREY BAY REDWOOD COMPANY'S MILL

target was the standing timber in Spignet Gulch. The gulch was not overly steep so most logs were pulled directly to the millpond by donkey engines. One new character on the scene in spring 1926 was James Armstrong

Harris, Jr. Harris was born on October 31, 1886 in Ohio and came to California as a representative for several South Carolina investors. When the Monterey Bay Redwood Company incorporated, he purchased 2,875 shares, valued at $287,500. This gave him 99 more than Mills and a controlling interest in the company. Not long after the mill opened, Mills began to step away from the day-to-day operations of the company and Harris came to the fore. By mid-1927, Harris rose to the position of general manager and assumed leadership of all operations.[100]

Railroad traffic on the Loma Prieta Branch is discontinued

On January 31, 1926, all railroad traffic along the Southern Pacific Railroad's Loma Prieta Branch came to an end. The railroad would no longer allow any trains or cars to use the tracks, including by special request, and the tracks were no longer being maintained, although no rails or ties were removed at this time.[101]

The Monterey Bay Redwood Company's mill on Soquel Creek opens

On April 3, 1926, the *Santa Cruz News* announced:

Big Lumber Mill Soon to Operate

Following extensive plans and preparations, the Monterey Bay Redwood Company will start active operations next week, and will be turning out its normal production within a month. The company, of which David W. Mills of Cleveland is president and James A. Harris Jr is secretary-treasurer, now has in its employ seventy-five men, about half the number that will comprise the crew when it will turn out its daily capacity of 60,000 board feet. The mill is located on Soquel Creek's East Branch at the mouth of Spignet Gulch.

Former mayor John Maher will act as salesman for the company, as he has had much experience in the industry. The

> *company offices will be at the mill. President David Mills declared himself a Santa Cruzan, heading a Santa Cruz industry, in a true sense of the word. He further declared that in the company's conservative program it does not aim to strip the property of the redwood trees, and that some forty acres will comprise the drying field.*

The mill did not, in fact, open until mid-May and it only operated at an average 40,000 board feet daily capacity throughout its lifetime.

The operation used a curious blend of old and new technologies. Rather than using a railroad, the mill relied on White Motor Car Company trucks to bring logs to the millpond. To run the old 9-foot bandsaw, the company used a new vibrationless steam engine. Logs were still soaked in a millpond fed by water from the East Branch of Soquel Creek and in the mill, rough-cut lumber was edged and trimmed using a circular saw rig dating back to the late 1880s. However, from the mill, the lumber passed under Olive Springs Road via a modern Green Chain conveyor system to a planing mill for finishing, to kilns for drying, or to the lumberyard. Finished products were either stacked in the lumberyard for shipment to the Southern Pacific station at Capitola or loaded into White Motor Car Company trucks for delivery to various Bay Area retail outlets.[102]

Land transfer from the Loma Prieta Lumber Company to the California Pacific Title & Trust Company concerning Tract 9 in the Augmentation

On June 4, 1926, negotiations between the Loma Prieta Lumber Company and Horatio Ormsbee, who represented Charles T. Park, concluded with the sale of Hinckley Gulch. Park lived in Alpena County, Michigan and likely never set foot in California. Harvey Bassett and Bert Stoodley, acting for Timothy Hopkins and the other directors, transferred 2,500 acres, which included a right-of-way through Tract 27, to Park. The agreement included the following:
- A right-of-way through Tract 27, which was owned by Elizabeth J. Corcoran. The clause stated: "Being the most convenient route to reach

the Loma Prieta Lumber Company's land in the 'Hinckley Creek Basin' known as Tract 9." The description of the route stated that it crossed the East Branch of Soquel Creek on a concrete bridge supported by steel supports, and then continued over Hinckley Creek on a small wooden bridge followed by two crossings through the latter creek before reaching Tract 9.

- All other rights-of-way that the Loma Prieta Lumber Company may have over and across the lands of Tract 27 and the lands sold by the Valencia–Hihn Company to the Monterey Bay Redwood Company on June 9, 1925.
- A 40-foot-wide right-of-way for a road leading across the lands of the Loma Prieta Lumber Company and Timothy Hopkins (Tract 8) from the easterly boundary of the latter's land in order to reach Highland Way, to be located along the ridge between the East Branch of Soquel and Aptos Creeks. Essentially, this gave Park the right to use the Molino Timber Company's railroad right-of-way and build what later became the Aptos Creek Fire Road to the north.
- The right to use any road south of Hinckley Gulch that had been built to support the Molino Timber Company's railroad.
- The Loma Prieta Lumber Company reserved the right to use the former railroad grade across Park's land and reserved the right to use any road or roads that Park may construct across the easterly and southerly portion of his land.

The day after the deed was signed, Ormsbee, acting for Park, sold the newly-purchased property to the California Pacific Title & Trust Company of Santa Cruz. The quick turnaround seems to have delayed the registration of both deeds. Ormsbee's signature on the second deed was not acknowledged until August 26. As a result, Stoodley did not sign the first deed until September 14. The latter was only acknowledged by the County Clerk on November 12.

As soon as the gulch was firmly in the hands of the title and trust company, Park and Ormsbee formed a partnership with the former's lawyer, F. H. Riebanack. Because Park did not live in California, he gave Ormsbee and Riebanack power of attorney over all of his California affairs. Immediately,

Ormsbee set to work preparing the property for sale. He later recounted: "I opened up existing roads, fixed some old loggers' cabins, did fire trail work, and surveyed the gulch's boundaries. There was no cutting of timber during this period."[103]

The Monterey Bay Redwood Company moves up the East Branch of Soquel Creek

In the winter of 1927, the Monterey Bay Redwood Company was undergoing change. A corporate document dated February 1 revealed that the directorate and base of operations of the company had shifted since it was incorporated two years earlier. The corporate offices were now located at the mill on Soquel Creek. James Harris had become a director with 2,875 shares, alongside David Mills (2,776 shares), B. F. Bates (417 shares), W. O. Scholtz (350 shares), and J. M. Bordy (337 shares). Presumably these latter three men were some of the South Carolina investors whom Harris had convinced to buy shares in the company. Between the original investors and Harris' group of entrepreneurs, the company was able to remain financially viable for the year.

Meanwhile, as the activity of the Monterey Bay Redwood Company along the East Branch of Soquel Creek moved north away from the mill, the road used by the trucks to reach the standing timber continued for a mile and a half until it reached the mouth of Amaya Gulch. For the first quarter of a mile from the mill, the terrain was fairly level, but then the grade increased to about 2.5% for the next three-quarters of a mile. The top of the grade was a little over 100 feet above the creek bed. The road beyond this point required a bridge over Soquel Creek, which became known to workers as the High Bridge.

The structure was designed and constructed by John Dahlgren, the 'woods boss' responsible for planning and building all of the roads within the lumber company's property. The bridge had no guard rails and was just wide enough for one-way traffic. The roadway on the bridge consisted of planks laid side by side, requiring extreme caution and care by the truck driver in both directions. The bridge's planking, even in dry weather, was difficult to maneuver but extremely so in wet weather when the planks were slick and slippery from the mud that earlier trucks had left behind. When a truck approached the bridge from the south, the driver had to come to a complete stop, shift into low gear, make a sharp left turn to get onto the bridge, and then an equally sharp left turn to leave it.

North of the bridge, the terrain became too steep for trucks to directly access most stands of timber. As a result, highlines were rigged across the creek to transport logs from the hillsides to the beds of waiting trucks. Where a highline could not reach a truck, a short road was graded to a temporary landing, where the logs could be loaded directly onto trucks. For the next three years, almost all logging activity was in the vicinity of Amaya Gulch or along the East Branch of Soquel Creek in the direction of Badger Springs and Fern Gulch.[104]

Land transfer from the California Pacific Title & Trust Company to Allen Rispin concerning Tract 9 in the Augmentation

Sometime in 1927, Allen Rispin acquired ownership of Hinckley Gulch. I have searched with no success for the document that confirms when and if this reclusive oil millionaire acquired exclusive ownership of the gulch. What is known is that he either owned or was in charge of the development of the gulch in the late 1920s. Rispin seemed interested in the gulch both because of the planned Hinckley Creek Basin housing development and the year-round water supply the gulch could provide to Soquel and Capitola.

Rispin made a substantial down payment on the $75,000 sale price of the gulch and then immediately began spending money on improvements. He spent $30,000 on building new roads, improving existing roads, erecting two bridges across Hinckley Creek, and developing an artificial lake. The lake sat at the 800-foot elevation and he planned to construct his housing development around it. There would be a total of 61 lots in the subdivision, which he registered as Hinckley Basin Unit No. 1. The first structures erected were salvaged buildings left behind by the Loma Prieta Lumber Company.

To plan for potential forest fires, Rispin constructed a wooden flume that could deliver water from a tank located a mile and a half up the gulch.

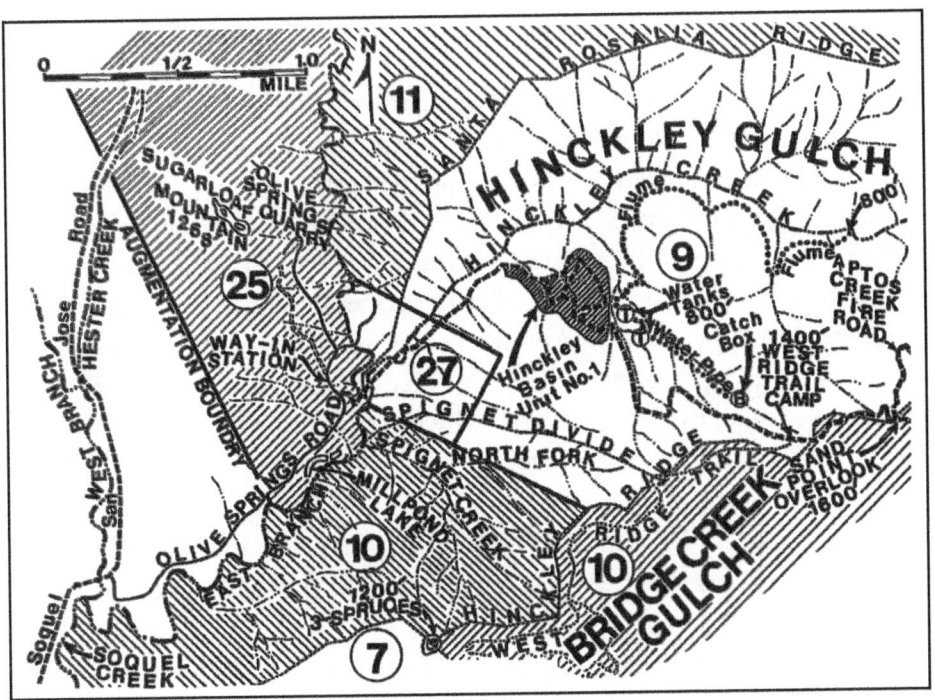

FIGURE 5.5 LOCATION OF THE HINCKLEY BASIN UNIT NO. 1 SUBDIVISION WITHIN TRACT 9 IN THE AUGMENTATION

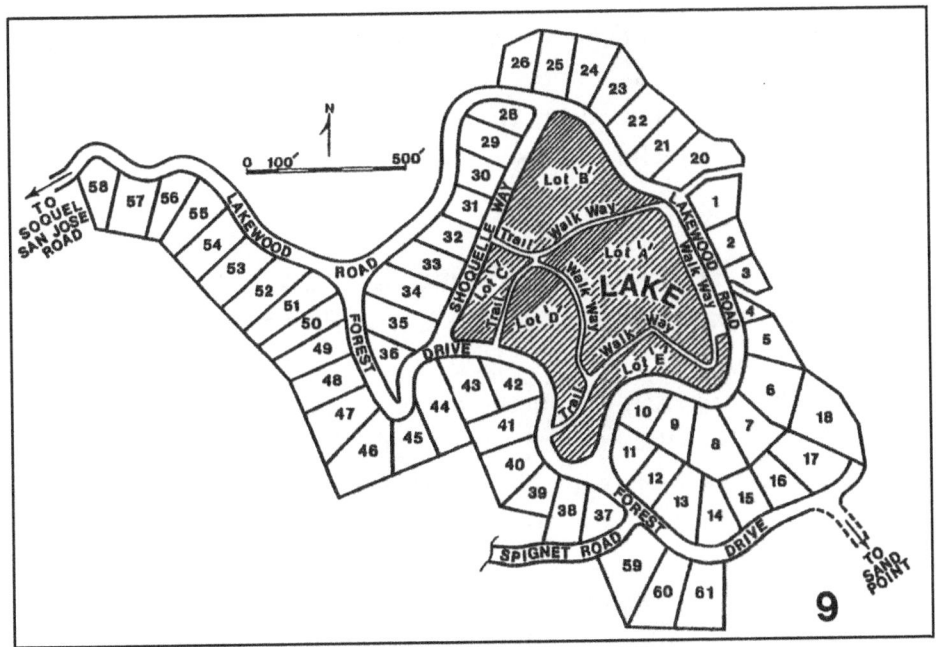

FIGURE 5.6 LAYOUT OF THE HINCKLEY BASIN UNIT NO. 1 SUBDIVISION

The source of the flume's water originated within the headwaters of the gulch that lies just below today's West Ridge Trail Camp at the 1,400-foot elevation along Hinckley Creek Fire Road. Down at the 1,200-foot level in the gulch, a large catch box was set in the creek from which a steel pipe picked up the water collected and carried it down to the first of two water tanks. The two tanks were located at the upper end of the housing development. The upper tank was built in order to increase provide a surplus water supply that could be released in the event of a fire. It also provided water, via gravity, to the lower tank, which could release water into the lake to maintain a constant water level.[105]

The Loma Prieta Lumber Company settles its debt to the Peoples Savings Bank of Santa Cruz

On June 1, 1927, the Loma Prieta Lumber Company paid back in full the $25,700 that it had borrowed from the Peoples Savings Bank of Santa Cruz. The timing of this with Allen Rispin's purchase or lease of the property in the same year suggests that either Rispin, or Charles Park, Horatio Ormsbee, and F. H. Riebanack, or the California Pacific Title & Trust Company had paid enough to the Loma Prieta Lumber Company for the latter to settle its debt. With this sale, Loma Prieta was free of Hinckley Gulch, which had caused the company so many difficulties for over twenty years.[106]

The Southern Pacific Railroad files for abandonment of the Loma Prieta Branch

On November 30, 1927, the Southern Pacific Railroad Company and its parent, the Southern Pacific Company, formally filed an application to abandon the Loma Prieta Branch with the Interstate Commerce Commission. According to the request:

> *The applicants represent that all of the lumber tributary to the branch has been shipped out, and that there is no freight that might require shipment over the railroad, so far as they*

can ascertain. The line has not been operated for the past two years, for the reason that no business was offered. The route does not pass through any towns or villages, and no passenger traffic has been handled. It appears that the branch line has served the purposes for which it was built, and that the expense of its continued maintenance and operation would be a needless waste.

On January 20, 1928, the commissioners authorized the line's abandonment. At the time, the branch measured 3.298 miles and included four stations: Aptos, Ready, Molino, and Loma Prieta. Southern Pacific was informed that the branch would be officially abandoned from February 19, 1928.[107]

Last Watsonville Mill & Lumber Company assets sold

On January 18, 1928, the lumberyard of the Watsonville Mill & Lumber Company at the corner of Third and Pine Streets in Watsonville was sold to Walter J. Foster. This was the last active facility owned by the company, which had been operating as a subsidiary of the Loma Prieta Lumber Company for decades. Indeed, shortly after the death of Charles Ford in 1890, the sign above the yard was replaced with a Loma Prieta sign. Nevertheless, the sale of the property marked the end of a company that had its origins sixty-six years earlier with John Bernard Brown and his small logging venture in Eureka Canyon.[108]

The Monterey Bay Redwood Company defaults on its payment

The Monterey Bay Redwood Company was never the most financially secure company. Despite the Bay Area and South Carolina investors, the company still had not sold all of its shares by the spring of 1928. In 1927, the company had split its annual $50,000 payment between March and September, only to request a waiver for the latter payment. Before the next $50,000 was due on March 1, 1928, the company attempted to secure a bond on the property, but was denied. Thus, it failed to send any money to the Valencia–Hihn Company. This left it in debt $250,000—half the original amount—plus interest. Valencia–Hihn began to consider its options: whether to stretch out payments or foreclose on the property.

The first option was preferable, so Valencia–Hihn informed the lumber company on September 18 that it must pay $50,000 by November 1. Going forward, only $15,000 every six months would be required, thereby reducing the annual total by $20,000. Beginning in 1932, the semi-annual amount would return to $25,000, and in 1933 increase to $30,000. In exchange for this lenient policy, the interest rate would increase one percent to 6.5%. The Monterey Bay Redwood Company agreed to the new terms and made its $50,000 payment on schedule, reducing the total amount it owed to $200,000 plus interest.[109]

The bridge across Aptos Creek to the former village of Loma Prieta burns down

According to Teck Cathey, around the end of 1928, the bridge across Aptos Creek between the Compound and the former village of Loma Prieta burned to the ground. Urban legend attributed the fire to John Huber, better known as John Hubbard, who purportedly fell asleep in his cabin below the bridge with a cigarette still burning between his fingers. Both his cabin and the bridge burned down as a result. While the fire may well have been the result of a vagrant or squatter living in Huber's old cottage, it could not have been the fault of Huber himself because he had died over a decade earlier.

Huber was perhaps Loma Prieta's most colorful character. He had lived in the village from its earliest days in the 1880s and, unlike everyone else, remained when major logging ended in 1899. The stories concerning Huber are many, some with elements of truth, others entirely untrue or greatly exaggerated. Warren Porter's grandson, Edward P. Pfingst, recounted one such story:

> *John Huber was a Civil War veteran that was shot through his jaw at Gettysburg, leaving his face badly scared. John hid his disfigurement with a beautiful auburn red brush of whis-*

kers. He lived in Loma Prieta from the early 1880s until his death in late 1918. He was an excellent lumberman. It is said that he could stretch a line on a ground, and he could fell a tree right on the line, a feat he performed.

John received a pension from the government, therefore he found it unnecessary to hold down a regular job. He lived in several locations in Loma Prieta, the last being under the bridge that crossed Aptos Creek in the center of the town. The location of this last home gave the name Huber or Hubbard's Bridge to the structure, a name that stuck for years after it burned down.

Over the years, rather than ride the train in and out of Loma Prieta, John preferred to walk. In the morning he would head for Aptos to pick up the San Francisco Bulletin, an evening paper. He always got to Aptos early enough so that he could pass the time of day in various saloons. Sometimes he would head back to Loma Prieta with his paper so 'exhausted' that he would stop at certain favorite areas along the railroad track to sleep his 'problem' away. There were two spots between Aptos and Loma Prieta that he favored to rest at and 'relieve' himself. These areas became known as 'Huber's Rest Areas.'

In a letter dated January 24, 1908 from the Department of the Interior to John Huber, it is revealed that during his lifetime, Huber maintained a mysterious and inconsistent air:

In your above cited claim for pension, you allege that you were born at or near Lancaster, Ps., while the records of the War Department show that the John Huber who served in Company 'L', 6th U.S. Cavalry, from October 28, 1862, to April 28, 1864, and who rendered a prior service in Company 'G', Wisconsin Infantry, was born in a foreign country [the Gettysburg campaign occurred during the June and July period of 1863].

You should explain this discrepancy under oath, and state the name and the place you gave as the place of your birth at each enlistment. You should state, also, whether you ever signed your name other than John Huber while serving in Company 'G,' 3rd Wisconsin Infantry.

In the *Surf* of December 31, 1918, a short article revealed that Huber had requested that he be buried at the Catholic cemetery in Santa Cruz and that enough money be taken from his estate to provide for a brass band at the funeral. This last request was honored, with the band playing rousing tunes all the way to the cemetery. In his will, Huber bequeathed money to the Saint Francis School for Boys in the Pajaro Valley and to the Sisters of Holy Cross at Santa Cruz for orphans. John Huber, or Hubbard was truly one of Loma Prieta's and possible the entire Aptos area's more colorful and interesting characters.[110]

Santa Cruz County opens a quarry on Sugarloaf Mountain

The first area that the Monterey Bay Redwood Company logged completely of its standing redwoods was the land on and surrounding Sugarloaf Mountain in Tract 25 of the Augmentation. According to Robert Lincoln, Jr., sometime in late 1928 or early 1929, Santa Cruz County officials approached the company with a proposal that they be allowed to quarry the east side of the mountain. After a contract was signed between the county and company, operations began.

For the next twenty-four years, the county or a subcontractor quarried rock from Sugarloaf irregularly, providing a small amount of much-needed revenue to the Monterey Bay Redwood Company. As more land was clearcut of usable timber, additional acreage was added to the quarry until it encompassed about 283 acres along the mountain's east side toward the East Branch of Soquel Creek.[111]

Proposal to create Loma Prieta State Park

As an increasing number of logging operations in the Santa Cruz Mountains wrapped up at the end of the 1920s, environmental groups began agitating for the creation of state parks to protect timberland from future logging.

The Feller's Last Felling   1929

One of the largest proposals, which would have impacted about twenty percent of Santa Cruz County's total land area, was for a Loma Prieta State Park, which would have had at its heart much of the Augmentation including both the Loma Prieta Lumber Company's lands and the disparate properties owned by the Valencia–Hihn Company and the Hihn family. The *Evening News* reported on May 24, 1929:

> *Proposals to have Loma Prieta and the wooded canyons and streams about it set aside as a state park received unanimous approval of directors of the San Jose chamber of commerce in resolutions passed today.*
>
> *The table-shaped mountain is one of the most ideal sites for a state playground under requirements of the $6,000,000 state park program, voted by California last November, the directors stated in a letter to William E. Colby, chairman of the state park commission.*
>
> *The territory about the peak, about 12 miles square, which it is hoped to include into the proposed state park lies partly in this county and partly in Santa Cruz county. Similar action as that taken in San Jose is proposed by organizations in Santa Cruz and Watsonville.*
>
> **Considered Ideal**
>
> *Since the purpose of the state bond act is to set aside large tracts of scenic beauty in this rapidly growing state for playgrounds and outing spots, the Loma Prieta proposal fits every requirement, the directors stated in their letter to Chairman Colby. Besides being located near the populous bay district, it is easily accessible and will be increasingly accessible with the development of state and county roads in the section.*
>
> *Extracts from the letter of the directors to Colby follow:*
>
> *"The peak of Loma Prieta stands near the southern end of the Santa Cruz mountains, and will be directly on the route of the Skyline boulevard when that state road is completed. From its top is a wonderful view of ocean, valleys and redwoods. About it are heavily timbered slopes and canyons covered with virgin and second growth redwoods, oaks, manzanita, ferns and flowers.*

Easily Accessible

"Since it is about 60 miles from San Francisco and about that distance from Monterey, it should be an ideal and easily accessible playground for the bay district, with the completion of the Skyline boulevard. At present easy approaches exist from any of the surrounding cities and towns—San Jose, Gilroy, Morgan Hill, Campbell, Los Gatos, Alma, Santa Cruz, Capitola, Soquel and Watsonville.

"While the Skyline boulevard will be pushed into the district within a few years, another state-county highway has already been built from the southeast—the Hecker highway, now giving access to the Santa Clara county park about Mount Madonna. This park is contiguous to the proposed Loma Prieta state park, providing added territory for campers and hikers.

Since the Hecker highway over the mountains from Gilroy to Watsonville is part of the Yosemite-to-the-Sea state highway, it can be seen that the proposed state park would be easily accessible to residents of the interior valleys as well as those of the populous bay district.

"It appears to be one of the most logical sites for a state park that exists—if accessibility from populous areas to a natural park site is the criterion, as we understand it is."[112]

Black Tuesday and the start of the Great Depression

As the Roaring Twenties neared its end, many across the United States were convinced that the prosperous times would go on forever. But beneath the surface, there were signs of trouble coming. Special aspects of the economy had begun to decline in 1927. Growth was in fact being produced by wild speculation in the stock market. On September 3, 1929, stock prices reached their highest levels ever. The day after, a slow decline began. On October 24, the decline accelerated. Leading bankers tried without success to stem the tide. On October 29, today known as Black Tuesday, a record 16,410,030 shares were traded as huge blocks of stocks were dumped for whatever profit they could bring. By December 1, stocks traded on the New

York Stock Exchange had dropped in value by $26 billion. In an attempt to reassure the public, the day after the crash, President Herbert Hoover told the nation that "the fundamental business of the country, that is the production and distribution of commodities, is on sound and prosperous basis." Hoover's assessment would soon be proven wrong.

The Monterey Bay Redwood Company paid its agreed amount of $15,000 on April 1, 1930. But when the next payment came due on October 1, the directors of the Valencia–Hihn Company received a letter from James Harris instead. Harris stated that in the aftermath of the stock market crash, lumber prices had plummeted to a point where it was nearly impossible to even give lumber away. The company could not make its payment. On October 24, Valencia–Hihn agreed to split the Monterey Bay Redwood Company's payments into smaller, more frequent amounts: $5,000 was due on November 15, another $5,000 on December 15, and a third on January 15, 1931. In the end, the company made the second and third payments well ahead of schedule, saving the company for the time being.

Allen Rispin was not so lucky. The majority of his wealth was tied up with the stock market. When the market collapsed, he went from millionaire to pauper almost overnight. Because he was unable to make the agreed monthly payments, ownership of Hinckley Gulch, including all of his improvements, reverted back to Charles Park and Horatio Ormsbee. This placed the two men in their own perilous situation since the tax burden for the 2,500-acre property also reverted to them. They quickly set to work finding a way out of this situation.[113]

Clarence Srock and his one-man mill

In 1930, two unemployed men, Clarence Srock and his friend James Bishop, wandered up the abandoned Loma Prieta Branch from Aptos to begin a new chapter in the history of the old Loma Prieta Lumber Company's mill. Srock's father, Johann, was a German immigrant who had settled in Wisconsin to work as a lumberman. In 1910, the family moved to Fresno and Srock took up work with the Atchison, Topeka and Santa Fe Railway Company as a fireman. He remained with the company until the start of the Great Depression, when he was laid off. Looking for employment, he headed north and ended up in Aptos, where he met Bishop.

When they arrived at the old Loma Prieta mill, they immediately became interested in the machinery that was still strewn across the former lumberyard and mill building. They were surprised to find so many buildings still standing. After they explored the mill and the former village, they decided that they would like to live on the property and wrote to Harvey Bassett asking for permission to work as watchmen. Bassett replied shortly afterwards and allowed them to live on the property as unpaid employees. Srock and Bishop each found abandoned cabins that were not too worse for wear and moved in. The men wanted to survive on their own devices. They planted wheat for bread and even made their own soap.

Their lives were enjoyable but difficult in the rugged wilderness. Bishop eventually tired of mountain life and left around 1932. Srock stayed, though, and began considering ways that he could use the old machinery to run a small mill, just as his father had done in Wisconsin. He decided to first turn the sinker logs that lined the bottom of the millpond into lumber, but in order to reach them the dam had to be torn down. To accomplish both tasks, he needed a power source. He brought in a Stanley Steamer and then attached sawmill blades to its 30-horsepower engine. With his mill now ready to cut logs, he needed something to pull the logs from the bottom of the pond to the mill once the dam was down. For this he brought in a Model-T Ford. With his Stanley Steamer as the mill's engine and the Ford as his donkey engine, he began tearing the dam down board by board.

It soon became apparent to Srock that the old Stanley Steamer did not have sufficient power to power the mill. Some timber such as that used in the dam and the smaller pieces lying around the area could be cut, but the engine could not cut the large, heavy sinker logs. Thus, he began rummaging through the Loma Prieta Lumber Company's leftovers and discovered to his delight the remaining 14-ton Shay—LPLC No. 2. He brought the small locomotive to the mill yard, removed its boiler, and then shoved the frame with its wheels and cab still attached off the 320-foot-long bridge into Aptos Creek. The locomotive sat upright in the creek for decades, but over time its frame and wheels were covered with silt and vegetation leaving only the cab exposed. With this new source of power, Srock began his attack on

The Feller's Last Felling — 1930

the many large sinker logs that lined the bottom of the pond.

By the late 1930s, Srock had finished cutting all sinker logs and other debris in the vicinity of the old Loma Prieta mill and he was desperate to find something else to process. His gaze turned to the nearby bridge over Aptos Creek. Down came the pilings, bents, crossbeams, and ties until only a few remnants remained, which can still be seen along Aptos Creek with a keen eye. Srock continued milling the bridge and other local sources of timber until late 1938, when early winter rains forced him to shut down operations.

Soon, Aptos Creek rose to new heights and Srock could do little but watch as the floodwaters washed away the vehicle bridges across Aptos Creek at Molino Junction and the bottom of the former incline. After the storm, Srock relocated the mill to a property he and his father had purchased on Park Avenue in Soquel. He brought the Shay's boiler with the mill, but left the rest behind.

When World War II began, Srock filed as a conscientious objector and then enlisted in the Army's medical corps, leaving his father to operate the mill. Johann died before the end of the war and the mill sat idle. Upon his return, Srock resumed milling on Aptos Creek as a one-man operation. The operation barely eked out a profit, with his average income totalling no more than $75. Still, it attracted interest, with one local newspaper noting that it was one of the "most unusual sights to be seen in Santa Cruz County, if not in all of California."

In order to supply his mill with logs, Srock periodically ventured to the old Loma Prieta mill, cut down a second-growth tree, and hauled it by truck to his mill in Soquel. At his mill, an overhead pulley system allowed him to move the log from the truck to the saw without any assistance. Srock had engineered the mill's saws to perform multiple tasks at once. In one operation, as a slab was removed from a log, he could also cut the slab to a desired width. Meanwhile, trimmers mounted at right angles on the rig could slice the main log into pieces of lumber. Using this system, he said he could turn out 2,000 board feet of lumber a day "when I have a mind to." Another mill owner said, "this is a good day's work for a crew of men."

By the mid-1950s, Srock had reduced his business to focus on special orders with only a small quantity of extra logs held for use in last-minute orders and for financial security. This operation continued through the 1960s, although when he finally stopped milling lumber is unknown. Srock died on May 16, 1976.[114]

The Monterey Bay Redwood Company builds a plank road to reach the headwaters of Amaya Gulch

Near the end of the 1930 season, the Monterey Bay Redwood Company had harvested most of the timber south of its mill on the East Branch of Soquel Creek, as well as the lower two-thirds of Amaya Gulch, the north side of Sugarloaf Mountain, and within Spignet Gulch. Beyond the 1,000-foot elevation point, though, the truck crews ran into a problem: trucks could go no further up Amaya Gulch.

Although there was a fairly flat, sloping area at the top of the grade, there was a short, extremely steep section just below it. Not even a cable winch could bring trucks to the upper landing. The first potential solution crews came to was to pull the logs over the troublesome area to Comstock Mill Road, where trucks could take the logs down Stetson Road and then Soquel San Jose Road before hauling them up Olive Springs Road to the mill. But this route would require the trucks to use public roads and also these roads were narrow and twisting.

Instead, crews decided to build a road with a lower grade. They laid redwood planks perpendicular to the slope and pulled trucks along this road using a donkey engine mounted at the top of the grade. Once loaded, the trucks were lowered down the plank road in the same way, minimizing the wear and tear on the trucks' brakes. The plank road was probably built after the end of the logging season in 1930, so it was not used regularly until the 1931 season.

The location of this plank road is easy to identify today. After a mile and half hike up Amaya Creek Road, you will encounter a steep switchback. The planks were originally installed straight up this hillside.

Nearly a mile beyond the High Bridge and slightly less than half a mile from Amaya Gulch, the fellers reached a gulch that provided a year-round water supply from an easy-to-reach spring. It was located just to the south of the main truck road. The source was named Badger Springs, possibly after Joseph Badger, a New York lumberman who was a registered voter in Soquel in 1888. Throughout this area, highlines were used to bring logs to the road. The road through this area had a surprisingly gentle gradient, allowing vehicles to operate between the mill and the timberland year-round.

By the early 1930s, most logs were taken to the mill via yoked flatbed trailers pulled by tractors, although trucks were used as well to transport smaller logs from beyond Badger Springs. On a flat area at the confluence of Badger Springs and Soquel Creek, the lumber company built Badger Camp. The camp consisted of three small wooden shacks. Water was provided to the residents from a tank that was supplied by an elevated springbox constructed along the south side of the main road. The box was kept in good repair from the late 1920s through the 1940s, first as a source for the donkey engines, which used large amounts of water in their boilers daily. Over time, the water was used personally by workers and in the radiators of trucks and tractors operating in the area. It also was poured into tanker trucks that were responsible for keeping the dust down on the road.

Today, near the path of the springbox are a number of deep, straight grooves etched into the side of the canyon. Some of these are more than ten feet wide, twenty feet deep, and are long enough to appear on aerial photographs. Because of their lack of consistent orientation, they have been the subject of many discussions over the years as to their purpose. Thanks to Bob Lincoln, Jr., the mystery of the grooves has been solved. The Monterey Bay Redwood Company had installed donkey engines at the top of Santa Rosalia Ridge. Because of the steep terrain, the company found it was easier to simply drag logs to the top of the ridge and then skid them down to the confluence of Hinckley Creek and the East Branch of Soquel Creek. The abrasion of hundreds of logs being dragged over relatively soft earth led to the initial grooves in the hillside, which then became worse over the years from erosion from winter rains.

One last curiosity also remains today near the bottom of Badger Springs: the Harris Grove. This stand of old-growth redwood trees was allowed to remain intact by James Harris, who held the company's annual picnic at the grove starting in the mid-1930s. It was workers who named it after their general manager. Harris liked the grove so much that he ensured it would never be cut, and so it still survives to this day. Of the rest of Badger Camp, very little survives. The springbox collapsed many decades ago and all three of the cabins are gone. The only remnant is a small, abandoned weather station with its fallen rain-gauge tower surrounded by a rotting fence. This is located between Hihn's Mill Road and the East Branch of Soquel Creek, across from the start of the Sawmill Trail in the Soquel Demonstration State Forest.[115]

The Monterey Bay Redwood Company in financial peril

By the end of 1931, the Monterey Bay Redwood Company was experiencing substantial financial problems. It was unable to pay more than interest to the Valencia–Hihn Company throughout the year and remained in debt to them $140,000. Around 48 million board feet of lumber had been produced by the company by this point, far below the predicted output.

The company was run locally by James Harris, general manager; Fred Ingerson, sales manager; John Dahlgren, logging boss; Gus Simerly, mill superintendent; Tom Reilly, planing mill supervisor; Al Bowman, machine shop supervisor; Ralph Hughes, steam engineer; and Lyle Hughes, oil, greaser, and woodfeeder. Despite the economic situation, the mill itself remained a well-run operation thanks to Harris, who was well-liked by workers and retained employee loyalty.

The lack of repayment to Valencia–Hihn was posing a problem for Frederick Day Hihn, though. On October 1, 1931, Hihn wrote to the company's stockholders:

> *At all times during the past year, we have been in close touch with the Monterey Bay Redwood Company's General Manager James A. Harris Jr. and his superintendent. Either one, or both have accompanied us on examinations of the tract and assisted us very courteously in every way possible in giving information regarding the operations of the company.*
>
> **Sawmill, Planing Mill, and Dry Kiln**
> *These facilities are kept up and are apparently in good condi-*

tion. Very little refuse is allowed to accumulate and the fire protection is adequate. On account of the low condition of the waters of the Soquel Creek and adjacent springs and the extremely high content of minerals in these waters, difficulty is being experienced in being able to keep sufficient steam in the boilers to efficiently run the large mill. Every known method of remedying such trouble is being tried, but with very little success. Inasmuch as the mill has been run only one half the time, that being sufficient to supply the demand for lumber, the water problem has not been as serious as it would have been under normal conditions.

The lack of water in the East Branch of Soquel Creek and from the nearby springs, plus their high content of minerals was solved by bringing water in pipes down from Spignet Gulch which fed directly the boilers in the sawmill.

Lumber in Lumberyard
As of the above date the stock in the yard totalled approximately 3,200,000 board feet.

Road
A good road has been constructed from the sawmill to Camp Badger, about 2 1/2 miles, and also about 1/2 mile up into Amaya Gulch.

Logging
The logging is clean and very little timber is broken or wasted considering the nature of the ground which is quite steep in places.

The logs are snaked down on high line with donkey engines to the road, where they are loaded on large trailers and hauled to the millpond by caterpillar tractors.

At the time the haul is approximately 2 1/2 miles.

As of the above date there is approximately 1,500,000 board feet of logs down but not yet logged out of the woods. These logs are being brought in as fast as possible and before the arrival of the heavy rains. No timber has been cut recently.

Method of Delivery

Motor trucks are used for delivery of the lumber to all areas in this district.

Without doubt the railroad grade will not be used for a railroad for purposes of hauling lumber as it would not now prove economical to do so.

Markets for Lumber

The present economic condition in combination with the many lumber substitutes has placed quite a hardship upon the lumber manufacturers of the country.

A few facts taken from the Economic Survey Report No. 28, Research Department, California State Chamber of Commerce may prove of interest. This report shows that 13 California mills produced in 1930 a quantity of lumber 13.9 percent less than the year before and that orders for 1930 were 22.9 percent less than 1929.

The number of employees in California sawmills and logging camps in December 1930 was 28.4 percent less than in the same month in 1929.

Out of a total of 68 cities in the State of California, the building permits issued were 25 percent less in 1930 than they were in 1929.

Recent California reports indicate that the first eight months of 1931, with regard to wood manufacturers, they are approximately 20 percent lower than the corresponding period of 1930.

It can readily be seen that the lumber mills have been and are now facing a serious situation with regard to the disposal of their products.

Upon half time operating basis, the volume would appear to be too small to enable any mills to operate at a profit.

Lumber production totals versus the A. W. Elam Report

The A.W. Elam Company's cruise figures as per their cruise maps and reports dated July 15, 1916, apparently show that there is more timber on the tract than can actually be cut therefrom.

> *The amount of timber actually cut from the 1,705 acres as shown on the report is approximately as follows:*
>
> | | |
> |---|---|
> | *Elam Report yield...* | *59,967,000 board feet* |
> | *Mill Cut...* | *48,040,000 board feet* |
> | *In Millpond...* | *300,000 board feet* |
> | *Cut but not yet logged...* | *1,500,000 board feet* |
>
> *This figure of Mill Cut, In Millpond, and Cut but not yet logged totaling some 49,840,000 board feet is approximately 10,127,000 board feet, or 16.9 percent, less than is shown for the cruise area on the Elam map for the above areas. If this percentage holds true for the remainder of the tract, as shown.*
>
> | | |
> |---|---|
> | *Elam cruise figures...* | *113,781,000 board feet* |
> | *Less 16.9 percent...* | *19,218,000 board feet* |
> | *[TOTAL]* | *94,563,000 board feet* |
>
> *Of course, some of these figures are averages only and are estimated, but they are very close to the correct figures, but in view of the fact that the actual cut from Spignet Gulch was lower than the Elam cruise figures by about the same percentage, it is logical to assume that the estimate of the Elam cruise is high.*

The accuracy of a timber yield cruise depends on several factors, including the quality of the men performing the cruise, the percentage of the timber cruised, and the judgment used by the fellers in the forest. The fellers need to consider the remoteness of the timber and prepare the ground properly to test the quality of the tree. And when the tree falls, they need to see if it remains whole or breaks apart. They also need to calculate how much of a tree's sapwood will remain in any given log, a statistic that changed greatly between time periods and companies. Historically, almost all of the sapwood would be removed from a log, leading to a loss of up to twenty-five percent of a tree's usable wood. By the 1910s, old-growth redwood had become more precious and processes had improved such that much more sapwood was retained.

On October 27, Hihn made another report to the stockholders of the Valencia–Hihn Company:

The enclosed exhibits must give you a very comprehensive idea of the condition of the Monterey Bay Redwood Company.

As you will note, their cut for the past year has been comparatively small owing to lack of market and price. Therefore, our security has not been greatly depreciated.

Last summer, a Mr. Humphries from Denver, representing some of the largest stockholders, was here and had an interview with the writer. He asked us to waive both principal payments this year and the one falling due next spring. After much discussion and explanations, I told him I would recommend our waiving the principal payments this year but as far as next year spring was concerned, we would have to take it up at that time. This was all dependent upon their paying the interest in full.

Mr. Patterson and the writer have gone over this ground and can vouch for the accuracy of the information given us by the Redwood Company.

I have talked the situation over with several lumber men and also with Mr. J. E. Garner. They are all of the opinion that we should give all the help to the company we can.

As we are getting six and a half percent interest on the deferred balance and our security is staying essentially the same, I feel that we should grant their plea. As far as the payment that is due next April, we will have to take that up at that time. It is sure that we do not want to take over the property which might happen if we demanded full payment at this time. What the future will bring forth, we are unable to say.

There is no doubt the Monterey Bay Redwood Company is operating the property as efficiently as possible under the circumstances. The main question is, if we closed down on them at this time, they might throw up their hands and turn over the property to us or it is possible they might dig up the $140,000 and pay us off in full. This is the question for us to decide.

If all the stockholders are not of the same opinion on what course to pursue, I feel we should hold a meeting and make some decision.

Yours very truly, Frederick Day Hihn, President

Although the financial situation of the Monterey Bay Redwood Company remained precarious after 1931, how precarious is unknown. The records of the lumber company and the Valencia–Hihn Company for the years 1932 through 1942 have been lost. What does survive was held by Noel Patterson, who donated his collection of F. A. Hihn Company and Valencia–Hihn files to the University of California, Santa Cruz, shortly after the 1989 Loma Prieta Earthquake. The records ended up in the Map Room of the McHenry Library while waiting to be transferred to the Hihn–Younger Archives. I was fortunate to be in the library shortly after the records were delivered. During my search through them, I came across several handwritten records concerning mill outputs for the years 1934 through 1940.

In hindsight, it is possible that the mill was closed or running at a minimum capacity in 1932 and 1933, probably owing to the surplus of products sitting in the lumberyard. Bob Lincoln suggests that the mill was only partially operating. Assuming he is correct and based on available records, the mill produced the following approximate lumber totals in board feet during the period between May 15, 1926 and the end of 1935:

Year	Lumber produced in year	Lumber produced to date	Elam Report projection to date
1926	8,000,000	8,000,000	9,638,554
1927	8,000,000	16,000,000	19,277,108
1928	8,000,000	24,000,000	28,915,662
1929	8,000,000	32,000,000	38,554,216
1930	8,000,000	40,000,000	48,192,771
1931	8,040,000	48,040,000	57,879,518
1932	2,000,000	50,040,000	60,289,156
1933	2,000,000	52,040,000	62,698,795
1934	3,587,000	55,627,000	67,020,482
1935	4,115,000	59,742,000	71,978,313[116]

Timothy Hopkins settles his and the Loma Prieta Lumber Company's land in the Augmentation

On May 4, 1932, the Southern Pacific Railroad deeded, without charge, the right-of-way of the Loma Prieta Branch between Aptos Station and Tract 9 in the Augmentation to Timothy Hopkins. In total, the right-of-way included 2.1 miles of a 100-foot-wide grade through Rancho Aptos, the 60-foot-wide grade through Tracts 8 and 9 to the line's terminus near the confluence of Bridge Creek into Aptos Creek, and the grade between Molino Junction and the former mill. All of the surviving spurs and sidings were also included in the transfer. With the signing of this deed, Southern Pacific gave up ownership of all railroad property within the Augmentation except for the mainline track through Laurel. The next year, on August 15, Hopkins transferred the Rancho Aptos property to the Loma Prieta Lumber Company.

With the ownership of all of the properties within the Augmentation settled, Hopkins moved to consolidate his holdings. He contacted Wells Fargo Bank & Union Trust Company and entrusted them with 5,821.079 acres in Santa Cruz County. This included 570.7 acres in Eureka Canyon, namely the area around Buzzard Lagoon, and 1,150.949 acres within Tract 8 of the Augmentation. The remaining 4,099.43 acres was land held by Hopkins elsewhere in the county. Loma Prieta also placed its 4,985 acres—4,375 in Tract 9 and 610 in Tract 10—in a trust with Wells Fargo.

Hopkins and his wife, Mary, probably did this because Timothy's health was beginning to fail and the pool of Loma Prieta shareholders was rapidly shrinking. There was also the reality that the timber within the Aptos Creek watershed still had decades before it would be of a sufficient size for harvesting. The eucalyptus plan had failed, as well, and the Great Depression had led to the near-collapse of the lumber market. As a result, Hopkins and Loma Prieta were paying high property taxes for relatively valueless land.

During my research, I contacted Wells Fargo's corporate offices in San Francisco to confirm the precise date that the trust was formed. Strangely, they were unable to find a single reference to the company as a customer or client. Their records were either lost, misplaced, destroyed, or buried so deep in the vault that they were unwilling to look further. Woods Mattingley found in his interviews in the mid-1960s that Hopkins resigned as president of the Loma Prieta Lumber Company when the land was placed in a trust. In his place, Wells Fargo appointed Percy A. Wood, who was the head trust officer, in 1935. Harvey Bassett remained vice president and general manager, while Bert Stoodley stayed on as secretary.[117]

Partnership agreement between Charles Park, Horatio Ormsbee, and James and Veda Bias

In the aftermath of the stock market crash of 1929, Charles Park and Horatio Ormsbee found themselves with Allen Rispin's 2,500-acre Hinckley Gulch property and no interested buyers. After several years of searching for a buyer, the two men finally decided in April 1934 to bring on new partners instead. These individuals were James Belden Bias, Jr., and his wife, Veda.

Bias was a Santa Cruz native, born on June 24, 1890. For many years, he worked as a real estate broker for the Santa Cruz County Title Company, where much of the land he managed was former timberland. Bias likely joined Park and Ormsbee both in a personal and professional capacity, although a direct relationship between the Santa Cruz County Title Company and Hinckley Gulch has never been proven.

Shortly after the new partnership was formed, the group resumed preparing Hinckley Basin Unit No. 1 for sale. They had Lakewood Road (today's Hinckley Basin Fire Road) paved from Olive Springs Road to the subdivision. The water distribution system was improved and repairs were made to the flume. With these completed, the artificial lake was filled for the first time to capacity and the two water tanks were also filled. Cosmetic improvements were also made to the site such as planting shrubs and trees around the lake.

Once all was in order—probably in 1935 or 1936—lots were put up for sale. Several families bought property and built small summer cabins beside the lake. A few others built what can only be described as elegant shanties. The development and Hinckley Gulch attracted deer hunters, fishermen, and hikers.

Unfortunately for the partners, the subdivision never moved beyond this high point. By the early 1960s, only six to eight structures had been built and the development had begun to show its age. In the late 1950s, a pipe that carried water to the water tanks broke and was not repaired. Without this, the lake began to drain and the tanks were no longer maintained. The area had also attracted an unsavory crowd. The remoteness of Hinckley Gulch made it an ideal hiding place for wanted felons, jail escapees, junkies, and pot growers.

The venture was not a complete loss for the partners. Shortly after the partnership was finalized, they signed a contract with a man who wanted to harvest the tan oak bark in Hinckley Gulch. The initial contract gave him permission to harvest trees in roughly 300 acres of the gulch, of which he had to leave forty percent of the trees standing so that they could help repopulate the other sixty percent. The man was denied access to more acreage due to poor conduct while harvesting the initial 300 acres. Nonetheless, the income he provided to the partners helped them pay their taxes and maintain the property in and around the housing development.[118]

Bert Stoodley moves to the Aptos Forest

In the early 1930s, Bert Stoodley was given permission for his family to move onto Timothy Hopkins' or the Loma Prieta Lumber Company's land along Aptos Creek. He later explained: "in the 1930s, times were hard and jobs scarce. Allan [Bert's son] was out of school and was not working. In a little hidden gulch just off the upper line of the railroad, he had built a small cabin from old lumber that he had picked up." The cabin was located to the west of today's Loma Prieta Grade Trail, about 2,500 feet beyond Love Gulch. This gulch is crossed today with a small footbridge just beyond the trailhead on the Aptos Creek Fire Road near Molino Junction. Stoodley continues:

> *I do not recall that there was any water near and it was across the creek well away from the fire trail. In a better location, on the old village site, he had started another cabin. Underpinning and floor was completed but it was a long way from any available lumber.*
>
> *It was about this time that we decided to build a larg-*

er cabin. We began searching for the best location. A short distance above the sawmill and adjoining the fire trail road was a spot that seemed to us the best. It was about three feet higher than the road but mattock and shovel soon opened a way to drive a car in.

It was partially surrounded by redwoods and the water pipe from Spring Creek ran at the back of the lot at the foot of the hill.

Our first work was to patch leaks in the pipe. We began at the spring and followed it down to the mill, making repairs as we came. At that, the line was weak in spots and many times we were obliged to search for hidden leaks and make repairs so that we could have water.

I had spoken to the company President, Mr. Hopkins, about such a building and he was entirely willing to have us occupy a cabin there. He told me to use any material that we could find and even indicated that he might contribute a little but we never asked that.

Allan drew the plan and detailed the building.

The watchman, Clarence Srock had contrived a little one-man sawmill and picked up a few logs here and there. Any lumber that we could not find from the old buildings, we bought from him at a very moderate price. Picking up and transporting stuff to the cabin site was no inconsiderable job. If anywhere near the fire trail, we could load our find into the car trunk and haul it in. From old Dutch ovens we found brick for an outdoor fireplace. On one side was a barbecue and on the other the tall concave fireplace that served for the evening bonfires, both using the same chimney. We had many pleasant evenings in our half circle of chairs, facing the fire. If a cool wind began drawing up the gulch from the bay, we stretched a piece of canvas back of our seats, making all snug and warm. From the setting of the mill's boilers, we salvaged a lot of fire brick and with these paved a large section in front of the fireplace and around the barbecue. Many of the old cottages had some picket fence. We secured enough split pickets to build a fence along the south side of the lot. Against this, Ora

> [Bert's wife] *did much planting. From Schillings Camp a mile or so further down the gulch, a rose bush that had gone wild, this she planted at the corner of the cabin where it was soon thriving. Years later, she moved this bush to another cabin on Section 11 in San Mateo County. From this, she moved ferns to shady spots and some of these also went to Section 11.*
>
> *Our parking space behind the cabin could accommodate three cars. Our cabin room was limited but a wood-floored platform was built so that an umbrella tent could be set up. And counting the lounge in the living room, we could make up three, or even four beds.*
>
> *The road below was closed by a locked gate and for seven years [1939 to 1946] we enjoyed the seclusion and quiet of this cabin. Week-ends and holidays we had many invited visitors.*
>
> *About 1946, however, a bunch of Watsonville high school boys discovered our retreat, broke in and practically ruined everything inside, food supplies, furniture, and all. Figuring that from then on, we would never be secure from vandalism, we began looking for a suitable place elsewhere. It was following this that we bought the five acres in Section 11 in San Mateo County, from Cecil Gibson. We dismantled the cabin at Loma Prieta and loaded all useable lumber on a truck together with brick, several hundred feet of water pipe, and everything else we thought it likely we might be able to use.*
>
> *In the beginning, we knew that we had only squatter's rights, that the land might be sold at any time, but that was a chance we had to take. And anyway, there were no taxes for us to pay and we had comparatively little invested other than our work.*

The cabin must have been built after 1936, since the fire road did not exist before then. Its exact location can easily be found today. It is about 500 feet north of today's Trout Gulch Trailhead, between the fire road and Aptos Creek. The driveway is still easy to identify.

Stoodley lived on Aptos Creek for around twelve years. He said in his memoir that:

the main work in connection with the Loma Prieta Lumber Company was liquidating the company's assets. Old machinery and equipment were sold and several contracts for the harvesting of both the tan oak bark and the wood of the tree were entered into at times. I sold the old houses to farmers, mostly dismantled by them and hauled out for use on their ranches. Occasionally a man and wife would drive in, buy a cottage and both would work tearing it down. The wife would usually pull the nails then sort and pile the lumber ready for loading onto their truck.

He did much of this with the help of Srock. One of the more interesting documents that Bert left behind is a list of the buildings and facilities that were available for purchase along with the sale price. The following is the list just as Stoodley prepared it:

Location	Type of Structure	Qty	Selling Price
Upper Camp West Side	Cabin	1	$20.00
	House	1	$20.00
Upper Camp East Side	House	1	$30.00
	House	1	$30.00
	House	1	$30.00
	House (next to hill)	1	$15.00
	House (across ravine)	1	$40.00
	Engine shed	1	$5.00
Upper Camp West Side Above Bridge	Cabin (2) and Shed (1)	3	$20.00
	Sheds	3	$3.00
Upper Camp West Side Below Bridge	1st Engine Shed	1	$5.00
	2nd Engine Shed	1	$20.00
	Oil Tank Shed	1	$18.00
	Sand Dryer Shed	1	$7.00
	Store Group	1	$45.00
	Shed for Tractor Motor	1	$10.00
	Freight Warehouse	1	$15.00

	Iron Roof for Freight Warehouse	1	$13.00
	Lower Cookhouse	1	$75.00
	Cabins	5	$10.00
	Cabin	1	$5.00
East of Millpond	1st House	1	$20.00
	Cookhouse	1	$50.00
	2nd House	1	$30.00
	3rd House	1	$25.00
	Cabin at Dam	1	$20.00
East Side Below Mill	Office Building	1	$40.00
	Cabin North of Office	1	$8.00
	Blacksmith Shop	1	$10.00
	Part of Building at Molino Bridge	1	$5.00
	Hans Johnson Cabin	1	$10.00
	John Schilling Cabin	1	$12.00
	2" Plank on top of Long Tramway	1	$35.00
	Galvanized Water Trough in Mill	1	$5.00
	Round Iron Tanks, 1,850 Gallons	each	$45.00
	6x6 & 4x4 & Other Used Lumber in Small Lots		$20.00
	6x6 & 4x4 & Other Used Lumber 3,000' or more		$15.00
	Square Iron Tank about 3,300 gal		$60.00
	Drag Saw with one saw —cost $160.00)	1	$50.00
	Desk	1	$7.50

Stoodley had other duties as well: "My work, which did not take up all of my time, was general supervision of the properties, pay the taxes, make such sales of tan oak bark or fuel wood and take care of any small problems that might arise, and surprisingly, these problems were quite numerous." When not doing the company's chores, Stoodley lived life to the fullest. He explains in detail:

> *Loma Prieta had much to offer. There were the miles of fishing streams, poor fishing of course because they were not regularly stocked. There were the long walks on the fire trail, and another up the Trout Gulch road toward the Hill place. And by driving, there were the small lagoons on the Hinckley side of the ridge and White's Lagoon and the Dry Lagoon. And over the ridge was Buzzard Lagoon, which drained into Eureka Canyon. Near White's Lagoon was the long crack in the ground made of the 1906 earthquake. And the vertical drop on the side of the fault showing a face of about five feet. It was said that Dry Lagoon once had plenty of water but that a quake had opened up its bed so that it drained off. Part way up the switchback on the fire trail road was the trail down into the little glen in Spring Creek where our water supply originated. At the top of the incline was the little flat where the large donkey [engine] sat that lowered the cars down [where] the incline was anchored. Here also was the switchyard where several tracks had served the shop and storage shed.*

It was during these years that Stoodley wrote most of his memoirs, which serve as such an important source for this book.[119]

Timothy Hopkins dies

On January 1, 1936, following a prolonged illness, Timothy Hopkins died. The Associated Press wrote of him:

> *Timothy Hopkins, one of Stanford University's original trustees, died today at Stanford hospital at the age of 77 of lobar pneumonia.*
> *He was the son of Mark Hopkins, one of the "big four" who piled up vast fortunes in the old Central Pacific railroad when steel first spanned the continent.*
> *Born in Augusta, Maine, in 1859, he came to California as a youth. In 1883, only 24 years old, he was appointed treasurer of the Southern Pacific railroad.*

> He held directorships in the Wells Fargo company, Southern Pacific company, Pacific Telephone and Telegraph, Union Ice company and other large concerns.
> He was the oldest surviving member of the first Masonic lodge in San Francisco. His estate at Menlo Park has been one of California's show places.
> Survivors include the widow, Mrs. Mary Jane Hopkins, of San Francisco and a daughter, Lydia Hopkins.
> Funeral services will be held Friday in the Stanford Memorial church.

The *Santa Cruz Evening News* appended to the bottom of this obituary: "Timothy Hopkins was formerly a large owner of timber holdings in this county and still has landed property here."[120]

The Anglo–California National Bank sells stumpage rights to S. W. Allred concerning Tract 7 in the Augmentation

Near the beginning of 1936, the Anglo–California National Bank—the successor since 1932 of the Anglo–California Trust Company—sold stumpage rights to 752 acres within Tract 7 to S. W. Allred. As a part of the contract, Allred was allowed to build a small mill within the former Arden Forest housing development and cut timber according to a selective system established by the California State Forest Service. Over the next decade, Allred only harvested second-growth redwood trees from about 50 acres, and within this area, he left nearly half of the trees uncut.[121]

The Southern Pacific Railroad dismantles the Loma Prieta Branch and fire roads are graded through the Aptos Forest

In 1936, the Southern Pacific Railroad sent crews of mostly Mexican laborers into the Augmentation to remove the rails and ties of the former Loma Prieta Branch that were still useable. After everything was removed, the company sent in a road grader that leveled the gravel and ballast on the right-of-way. All of the railroad bridges were left standing. Bert Stoodley later explained: "The few [ties] they left were sold for firewood, or if they were in fair condition they ended up as a fence post."

This leveled grade soon became Aptos Creek Road and the southernmost section of the Aptos Creek Fire Road, from Soquel Drive in Aptos to the former village of Loma Prieta. In its earliest years, the road was

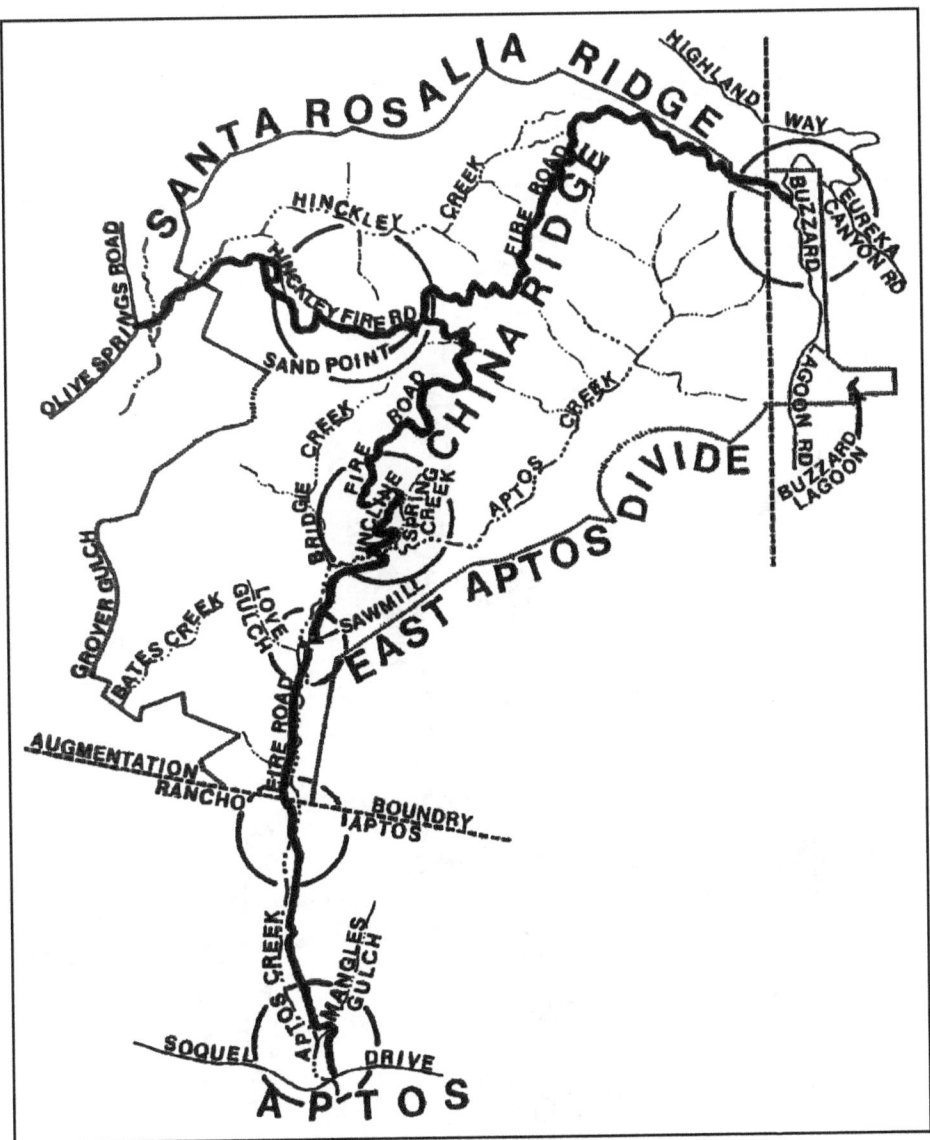

FIGURE 5.7 ROUTE OF THE APTOS CREEK FIRE ROAD

known alternatively as Hopkins Right-of-way, Hopkins Gulch Road, and Loma Prieta Railroad Right-of-way. Over the next few years, the Civilian Conservation Corps and the Works Progress Administration extended the fire road further, to the top of the former incline and along China Ridge and Santa Rosalia Ridge until reaching the boundary of the Augmentation at Buzzard Lagoon Road. The Department of Forestry and Fire Protection spent a considerable amount of money having these roads built. The project included replacing old bridges with fills wherever possible and installing a number of water tanks to supply water for fighting forest fires.

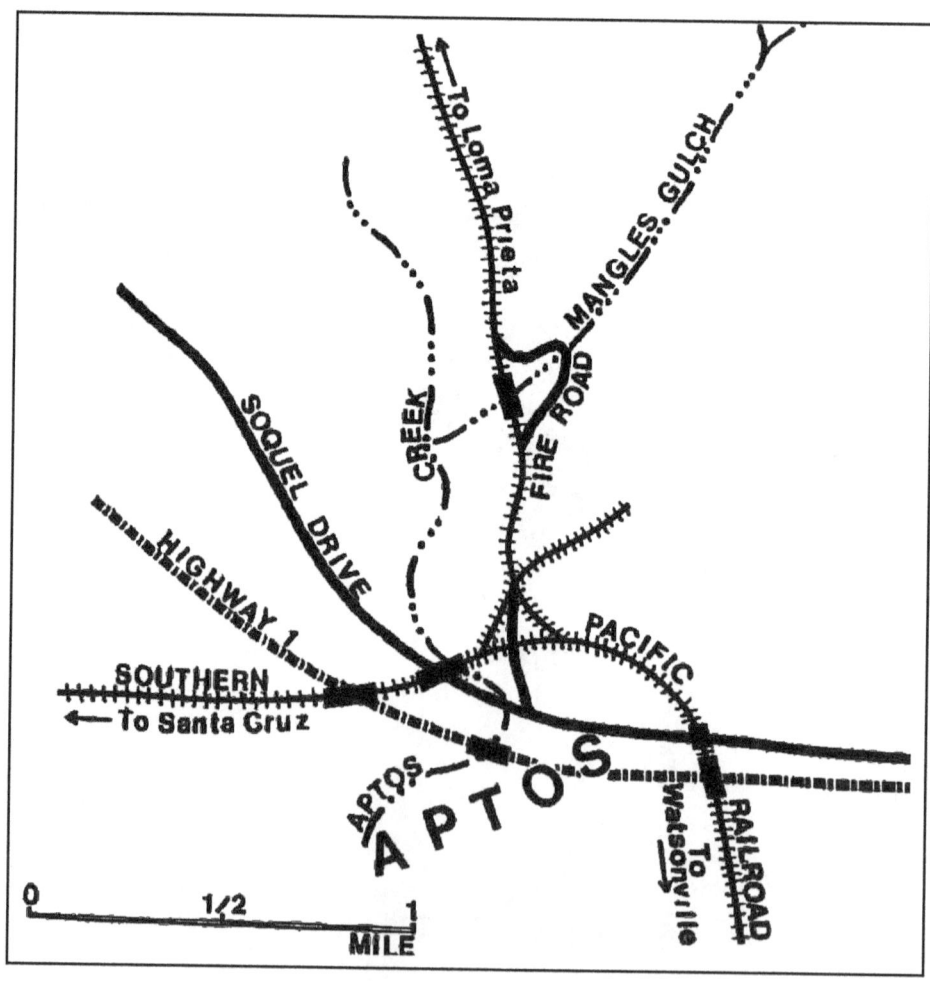

Figure 5.8 The southern end of Aptos Creek Road

The Feller's Last Felling 1936

Just south of the boundary of Rancho Aptos and the Augmentation, crews installed a new bridge across Aptos Creek. Bert Stoodley recalls: "Arrangements were made with the State to build a fire trail road about twelve miles long across the property, connecting Aptos with the Highland Way. The State built a heavy iron bridge across the Aptos a short distance below Long Gulch, which was said to have cost $40,000 which included taking out the long wooden bridge built after the railroad tracks were removed." This is the first crossing over Aptos Creek, which is still known as the Steel Bridge on park maps today.

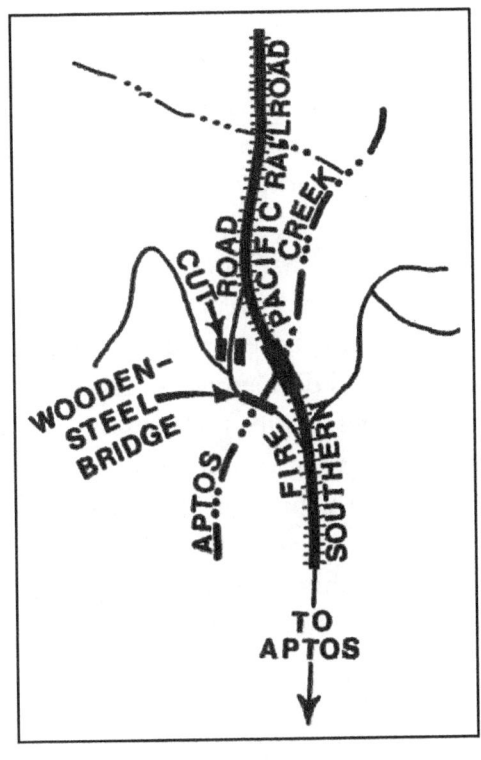

FIGURE 5.9 THE APTOS CREEK FIRE ROAD AT THE FIRST CROSSING OVER APTOS CREEK

North of the former Molino Station—now the Porter Family Picnic Area—crews installed another bridge capable of carrying vehicles across to the east bank of Aptos Creek. From the upper end of the bridge, the road passed the former mill building and continued north through the abandoned village of Loma Prieta. A half mile to the north of today's Trout Gulch Trailhead, crews reached the bottom of the former incline and the start of the curving bridge that had once brought Southern Pacific trains north to Monte Vista. The workers dismantled the bridge and built a smaller, shorter bridge for vehicles across Aptos Creek. From here, the fire road began its twisting journey up China Ridge's steep slope, paralleling for the most part the old Molino Timber Company's incline railroad. Today's graded road needs a mile and a half of twists and turns to reach the top of the incline's elevation of 1,000 feet.

Both the bridge at Molino Junction and the one at the bottom of the incline were washed away in a winter storm in early 1939, the same storm that convinced Clarence Srock to leave the forest and move to Soquel. After the storm, Forestry inspectors visited the Aptos Forest to survey the damage and decided not to replace the bridges. Instead, they sent in a grading crew to reroute the fire road directly through Aptos Creek. This created an extremely steep road at Molino Junction, so graders installed steel grates in the road to provide traction. Nevertheless, visitors often had to make multiple attempts up the grade in their cars before they could get enough momentum to reach the top.

Just around the next bend in the fire road after reaching the 1,000-foot elevation point on China Ridge, the road closely follows the route of the Molino Timber Company's railroad past Sand Point and on another 0.9 miles to Camp 2. From here, the two routes diverge, with the railroad to the west at a relatively even grade while the fire road begins a steep climb eastward toward the peak of Santa Rosalia Mountain.

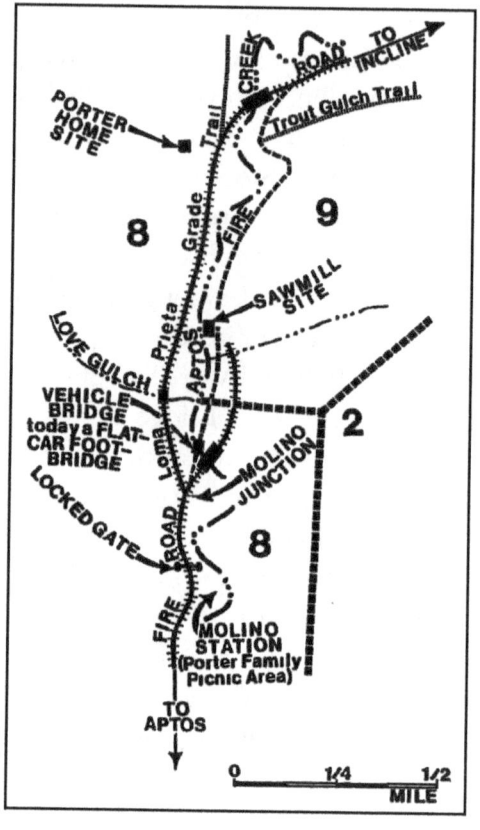

FIGURE 5.10 THE APTOS CREEK FIRE ROAD THROUGH THE FORMER LOMA PRIETA MILL SITE

At the same time the Aptos Creek Fire Road was being built and extended, the road between Olive Springs Road and Sand Point was widened and improved. From Olive Springs to Hinckley Basin Unit No. 1, this section had been improved and paved by Allen Rispin in 1927 and went by the name Lakewood Road at the time. Beyond that, the CCC and WPA installed a gravel road to Sand Point, after which that section of road became

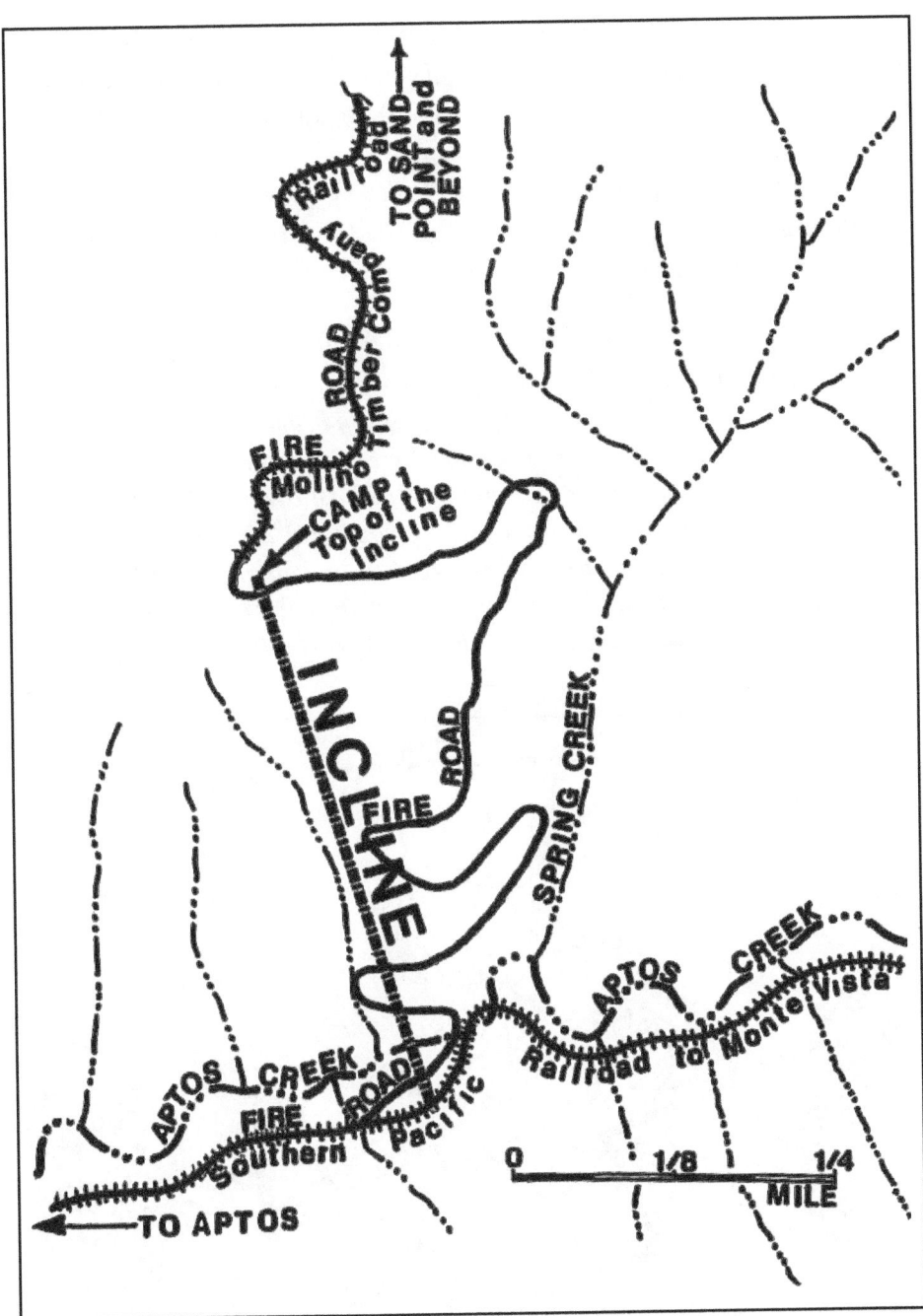

FIGURE 5.11 THE APTOS CREEK FIRE ROAD AT THE SITE OF THE INCLINE

known as the Hinckley Basin Fire Road. With the extension of the fire road to Sand Point by the late 1930s, fire services, Forestry staff, and property owners could access the Aptos Forest and Hinckley Gulch through multiple maintained roads.

Over the years, the Department of Forestry and Fire Protection made several improvements to the various fire roads in the Augmentation. Bob Lincoln, who worked near the Lakewood Drive bridge, recalls:

> *One day in 1948, the employees for the Monterey Bay Redwood Company working in the vicinity of Olive Springs Road to the south of Sugarloaf Mountain heard a loud explosion that seemed to come from the direction of the concrete and steel supported bridge that spanned the East Branch of Soquel Creek opposite Hinckley Creek. Upon their arrival at the bridge site, to their surprise it was gone. Obviously, it had been blown up, but by whom? There, inspecting their handy work were the culprits: the U. S. Army Corps of Engineering. It*

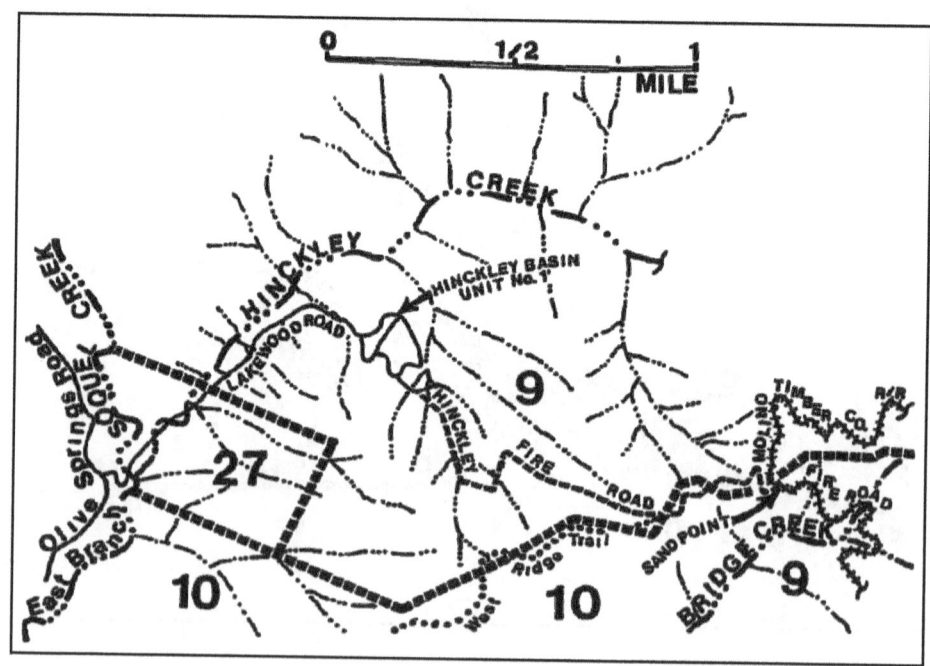

FIGURE 5.12 THE HINCKLEY FIRE ROAD TO SAND POINT

seems that they were in need of additional experience of blowing up a bridge then quickly replacing it. What with World War II over, there were few places that they could acquire the necessary practical experience. Immediately, the engineers began building a cement support along the Olive Springs Road side of the East Branch of Soquel Creek in order to support a new bridge that would be made completely of steel.

In the mid-1970s, the Youth Conservation Corps (YCC) were invited to build new trails and improve old ones. Part of this included erecting four new footbridges for visitors. Two of these were located just beyond the start of the Loma Prieta Grade Trail at Molino Junction: one crossed Love Gulch, while the other was located just beyond the Porter House Site across Porter Gulch on the subject trail. One of the other ones was built at the base of China Ridge, while the last—the so-called Schoolhouse Bridge—

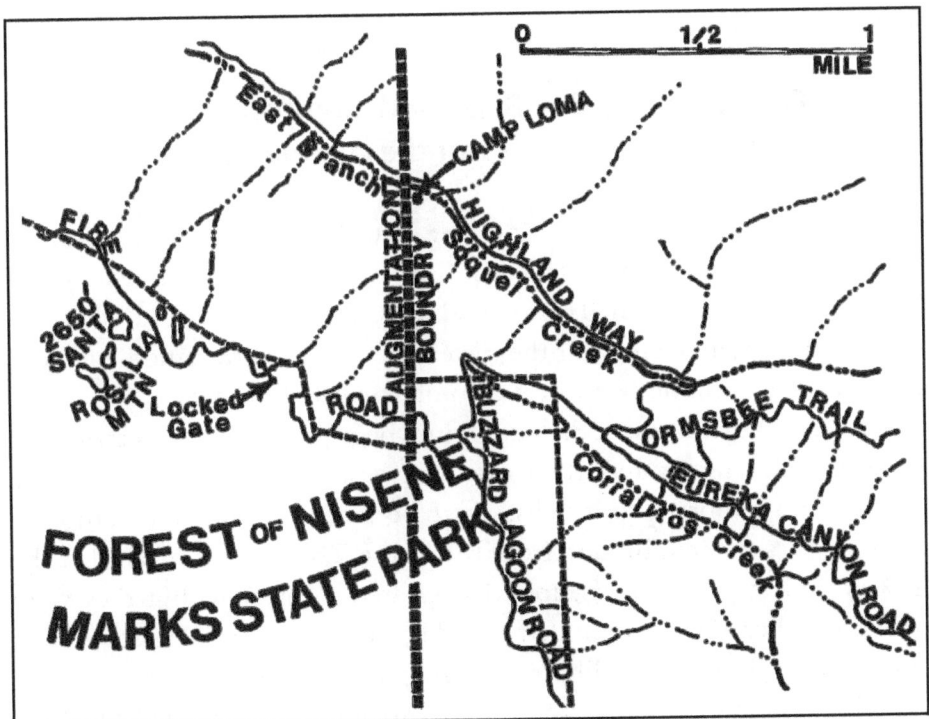

Figure 5.13 The northern end of the Aptos Creek Fire Road

connected the Porter House Site to the Schoolhouse Parking Area, where the former village of Loma Prieta was located.

For many years, vehicular access beyond the Schoolhouse Parking Area was restricted and a gate was installed. Following the storm of January 4, 1982, the gate was moved a mile downstream to the Porter Family Picnic Area. During that same storm, two of the footbridges were washed out: the Schoolhouse Bridge and the bridge at the base of China Ridge. Both were replaced: the former was moved slightly downstream, while the latter was rebuilt on the cement supports of the vehicular bridge that had been washed away in the winter of 1939. The rebuilt bridges were partially financed by federal government funds. In addition, since there was no longer a need for public vehicular access beyond the picnic area, an old railroad flatcar was installed across Aptos Creek at Molino Junction and the traction grates were removed. This makeshift pedestrian and bicycle bridge was funded by the Advocates for the Forest of Nisene Marks and the California Department of Parks and Recreation in Spring 1995.[122]

The Monterey Bay Redwood Company moves into Tracts 1 and 11 of the Augmentation

In early 1936, fellers for the Monterey Bay Redwood Company moved further up the East Branch of Soquel Creek toward the northern slopes of Santa Rosalia Mountain in Tract 11 and up Rattlesnake Gulch in Tract 1 of the Augmentation. Here, near the eastern boundary of the Augmentation, a little over 1.7 million board feet of timber awaited the axe.

Because the land east of Badger Springs began to ease from steep terrain to gentler, sloping ground, the roads were easier to maintain. This made them more appropriate for trucks, which became the dominant method of bringing logs to the millpond from the forest. This did not mean that the flatbed trailers pulled by tractors disappeared completely. But they were only used when the situation demanded it, such as to bring logs of greater length than the trucks could carry, logs from 32 to 40 feet in length.

The company itself was facing a dire fiscal situation by the late 1930s. The lumber market was depressed and most of the products produced at the Monterey Bay Redwood Company's mill sat unsold in its lumberyard. And the piles were growing annually. The Great Depression also led the company to hire fewer workers and cut less timber each year. The lack of revenue meant that most of the time, the company could still only make interest payments to the Valencia–Hihn Company. This slow output and down market allowed the standing timber in Tracts 1 and 11 to last years longer than it otherwise would have.[123]

Lawrence Cusack harvests timber at the headwaters of Aptos Creek

From the late 1920s until the mid-1940s, the Loma Prieta Lumber Company entered into many contracts for workers to perform various functions in the Aptos Forest. One of these was with Lawrence Cusack, who wanted to harvest tan oak bark in Tract 9 in the Augmentation. But what began as a small-scale operation expanded into a full-scale redwood logging operation, targeting old-growth trees left standing by Loma Prieta along

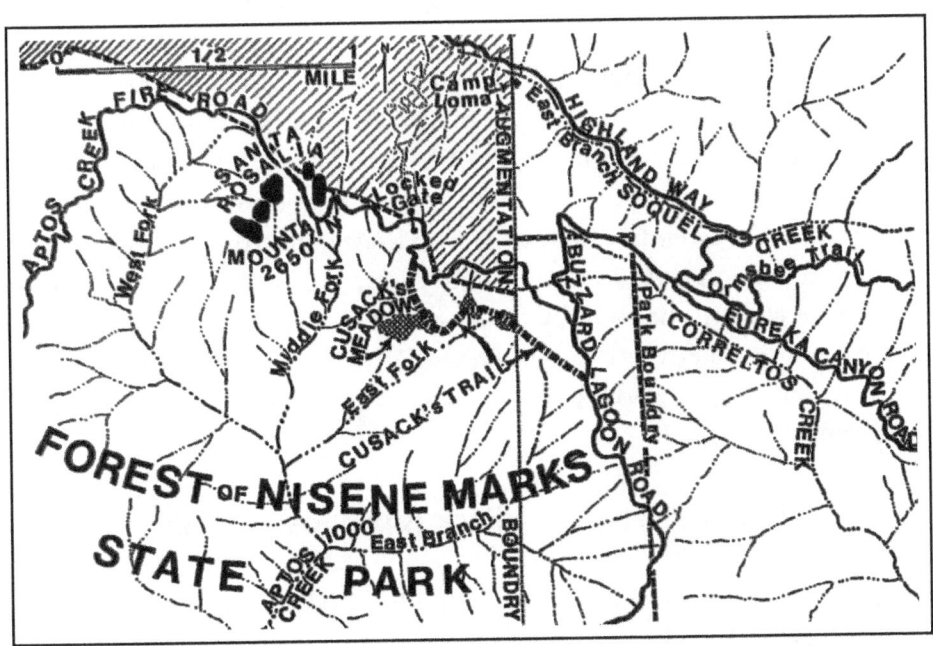

FIGURE 5.14 LOCATION OF CUSACK'S MEADOW NEAR BUZZARD LAGOON

Santa Rosalia Ridge at the far northern boundary of Tract 9. Cusack's operations, which began around 1936, focused specifically on the area that today is along the Aptos Creek Fire Road between Buzzard Lagoon Road and the locked gate.

The initial contract that Cusack made with Bert Stoodley, representing Loma Prieta, probably only allowed for the removal of the bark and the cutting down of a small number of hardwood trees to provide firewood. When precisely the scope of the operation was expanded is unclear. The redwood trees that Cusack harvested had been abandoned by Loma Prieta in the late 1890s due to the difficulty of getting the logs down to the railroad line far below.

Cusack built at least two mills at the headwaters of Aptos Creek's east fork. Access to the mills was from Buzzard Lagoon Road a short distance to the southwest. Cusack graded a gravel road from Buzzard Lagoon Road that extended through two meadows before reaching a third, larger meadow. On the first meadow, he built his mill. When the surrounding timber was harvested, he moved the mill to the third meadow. Cusack continued to run his mill into the 1940s, but when precisely the operation ended is unknown.

The road that Cusack graded is now called Cusacks Trail on The Forest of Nisene Marks State Park maps. The remote and poorly-maintained trail parallels the Aptos Creek Fire Road for a short distance from east of the locked gate to a point on Buzzard Lagoon Road just south of where the fire road ends. For anyone who braves this trail, they will eventually find Cusacks Meadow, the site of the second mill. A few remnants of the mill can still be found with a careful search. Nearby, evidence of Cusack's logging activity can be seen with little effort, mostly in the guise of overgrown logging roads and trails sloping down toward the middle fork of Aptos Creek.[124]

Loma Prieta State Park is proposed again

In January 1937, Horatio Ormsbee, James Bias, Jake Leonard of Hollister, and State Senator H. Ray Judah of Santa Cruz put forth a second proposal to turn a large part of the Santa Cruz Mountains between Soquel Creek and the Pajaro River into a state park. According to the *Sentinel–News*, the group had first joined forces in early 1929 with the support of the San Jose Chamber of Commerce and various local groups. They had hoped to turn approximately 60,000 acres over to the state, but in the intervening years, many lots had been sold for summer homes.

In an effort to head off more loss of land, the group submitted a plan to the state to initially purchase 19,000 acres, including the southern slopes of Loma Prieta and the western slopes of Mount Madonna. The park would include parts of the watersheds of Soquel, Corralitos, Uvas, Llagas, Almaden, and Los Gatos Creeks in Santa Cruz and Santa Clara Counties.

The *Sentinel* reported on February 11, 1937:

LOMA PRIETA PARK PROJECT
COMMENDABLE CIVIC PLAN

Will Do Much Toward Saving Local Forests

Plan Has Been Championed By Sentinel For Many Years

(By Paul E. Springer)
Many California newspapers are enthusiastically endorsing the grand new park proposed to be established with Loma Prieta mountain as its center, embracing a vast territory, the considerable proportion of which anciently was a great redwood forest. Coupled with the proposal is a plan to return the area to forest by replanting trees of the native variety which lumbering operations since 1870 almost entirely have destroyed.

The Sentinel can see in this great work consummation of a cherished plan initiated in its columns and in favor of which it never ceased to labor. The area, which the Hihn company long ago began to denude without thought of the future, is not fitted for agriculture nor for grazing, being extremely rough in contour, eroded into deep canyons between precipitous mountains, but does so well serve in supporting trees that even without the human assistance it should have had from the first felling, the forest has progressed quite appreciably toward its return.

The supreme advantage of taking this area into the park system is that with such action indiscriminate logging will cease, and under the direction of state officials trees will be removed for lumber purposes only when they have attained maturity and should be replaced. Unless parked, private ownership inevitably inflicts indiscriminate cutting with utter indifference to public weal.

Research directed to early Santa Cruz county history will furnish to the investigator astonishing facts concerning the abundance of water that existed while the tree covering was undisturbed. Streams of that day either have vanished or dwindled to mere rivulets. Trout and salmon no longer are to be taken along Aptos creek where the angling once was famous.

A corollating [sic] activity in connection with the establishment of the new park should be the erection of numerous small dams along the water courses to restrain the winter run-off with the paramount intention of preventing soil erosion, but with as nearly an important other aim—protection and propagation of fish which otherwise are killed or carried out to sea from lack of protection thus to be offered. The San Francisco News on February 8, 1937, carried a special article in which this plan was advocated for all the coast ranges and especially for the Santa Cruz mountains. Nor is this plan less vital to coastal populations in that it will double and treble the present potable water potentialities, now speedily growing so insufficient appreciable restriction is threatened to population increase there.

Another project, tying in with the formation of the new park, which The Sentinel has advocated, is the building of adequate boulevards to give access to the Loma Prieta country, and especially to the summit of the mountain itself, from which vantage point a series of unrivalled views not excelled anywhere else in the world is to be had. The mountain, it should be noted, bears at its summit cinders and other phenomena indicating very late volcanic action, probably as emphatical-

> ly as Mount Lassen. The boulevard proposed would be some alleviation of the lack Santa Cruz, dead-ended at the terminus of three indirect highways, long has suffered. In these motoring days municipalities which derive a main income from catering to tourists must have attractive, scenic drives to hold their guests more than over night.

In the end, the government was disinterested and declined the proposal in June. Ormsbee and Bias, though, were undiscouraged and continued to look for a means of creating a substantial state park in the region.[125]

More material is removed from the Splitstuff Area

In the two decades after the storm of September 1918, the Loma Prieta Lumber Company sent several crews to the headwaters of Bridge Creek to retrieve equipment and timber lost in the storm. By 1937, the Aptos Creek Fire Road had been extended to Sand Point so that it could connect with the Hinckley Basin Fire Road. This finally made it possible for trucks to directly access the abandoned Splitstuff Area. After several weeks of loading and hauling, crews had gathered almost all of the remaining piles of splitstuff and much of the cut timber. All that was left were larger logs, too heavy to transport, and worthless debris. Somewhere below the point, the ruined *Betsy Jane* also sat, still buried under piles of rubble.[126]

The Valencia–Hihn Company files articles of dissolution

After operating mostly as a holding company for twenty-two years, the Valencia–Hihn Company filed articles of dissolution on June 29, 1937. The actual dissolution was registered by the Santa Cruz County Clerk on January 7, 1941. With its dissolution, the last nominal remnant of the once-expansive property empire of Frederick Hihn vanished.[127]

The second High Bridge

In the winter of 1938, the high bridge over the East Branch of Soquel Creek just south of Amaya Gulch washed away during a rain storm. Because the bridge provided the only connection for its trucks between the mill and the areas that remained unlogged in Tract 1 of the Augmentation, the Monterey Bay Redwood Company promptly commissioned John Dalhgren to erect a replacement structure. The new bridge, which closely resembled the style of its predecessor, survived for the next thirty-two years.[128]

The Anglo–California National Bank grants stumpage rights in Tract 7 of the Augmentation

In 1938, the Anglo–California National Bank granted the same unnamed man who had harvested tan oak bark for Charles Park, Horatio Ormsbee, and James Bias in Hinckley Gulch the right to harvest tan oak bark from trees within the Arden Forest in Tract 7 in the Augmentation. This man had lost his contract to operate within Hinckley Gulch probably in 1937 due to poor performance. In the aftermath of this, he must have sought out similar properties where he could operate. He worked in the Arden Forest for two summers before the Anglo–California National Bank also cancelled his contract due to poor performance.[129]

The Coast Counties Gas & Electric Company obtains a right-of-way across Tract 8 in the Augmentation

On August 31, 1938, Wells Fargo Bank & Union Trust Company granted a right-of-way to the Coast Counties Gas & Electric Company across Tract 8 in the Augmentation. Coast Counties was also granted a 20-foot-wide right-of-way for a single line of poles with wires, plus the right of ingress and egress to reach the poles and wires. Furthermore, the company was given a 10-foot-wide right-of-way for pipelines over an agreed-upon route.

The overhead electrical line included in this agreement passed over the boundary of Rancho Aptos and the Augmentation just to the south of Long Gulch, where West Ridge Trail begins on the Aptos Creek Fire Road. From there, the line turns sharply to the northwest for a short distance before heading west out of Tract 8 and into Tract 7, just to the south of the Anglo–California National Bank's property.[130]

Land transfer from the Anglo–California National Bank to James Bias concerning Tract 7 in the Augmentation

On December 10, 1941, the Anglo–California National Bank sold the 752 acres that they held in trust within Tract 7 of the Augmentation to James and Veda Bias for about $30,000.[131]

The last year of the Monterey Bay Redwood Company

After a decade of a down lumber market and terrible economic conditions, the Monterey Bay Redwood Company began its recovery in 1941. Conscription in preparation for World War II saw a substantial drop in unemployment, while increased industrialization meant more orders for timber products. The company was finally able to hire a full crew for the first time since the 1920s and put them to use immediately.

The Japanese attack on Pearl Harbor on December 7, 1941 poured gasoline into the engines of lumber production and the year 1942 should have been one of the company's best. Early in the year, the United States Government purchased all of the timber products that had been sitting in the lumberyard for years. This should have been a windfall for the company, but the government set the prices for the products, undercutting the company's revenue. High-grade lumber had to be sold at the low-grade, pre-war price of $35 per thousand board feet. Ironically, this meant that the lower grade lumber could be sold at a higher price, sometimes netting up to $85 per thousand board feet. Regardless of the circumstances, this rapid sale of stock finally allowed the Monterey Bay Redwood Company to repay all of its debts to the the trustees of the former Valencia–Hihn Company.

Meanwhile, fellers were entering one of the last untapped sources of old-growth redwoods in the Augmentation: the so-called Crazy Forest. The Monterey Bay Redwood Company had already been harvesting timber from parts of the forest since around 1936, when crews moved east from Amaya Gulch and Badger Springs. The forest, created by tectonic forces unleashed during the 1906 San Francisco Earthquake, most likely spanned both sides of the East Branch of Soquel Creek, although most witnesses said the heart of this strange forest was within Tract 11 of the Augmentation, between the creek and Santa Rosalia Mountain.

The *Sentinel* reported on August 3, 1941:

> *Crazy Forest, freak of the 1906 earthquake, is going to be removed, it was learned here yesterday from officials of the Monterey Bay Redwood company.*
>
> *Lumber company crews, working up Soquel creek, have cut around it and removed a small corner of the 50-acre plot of crooked redwood trees at the head of Soquel creek.*
>
> *Soon they will begin removal of the best trees from the most peculiar and one of the most beautiful virgin groves of redwood in the coast region. Those who wish to see the Crazy Forest, which can be viewed from Highland way, are advised to make the trip this summer, as its removal by the loggers is scheduled for sometime during the next year.*
>
> *"The best view of the grove can be had from the Highland way, looking down onto the forest," James A. Harris III of the Monterey Bay Redwood company said yesterday. "Our crews will not destroy the forest, but will take from it the trees which will make timber. There are many dead and twisted trees in the grove which cannot be used for lumber. These will remain, but of course the view of the forest before we cut into it will be more interesting."*

Of Hihn Forest

> *The forest, in a remote region of the Santa Cruz mountains at the uppermost headwaters of Soquel creek and on the eastern slope of Santa Rosalia mountain, occupies a 50-acre portion of the vast Hihn forest, one of the last of the Santa Cruz mountain redwood timber stands to survive the logger's ax.*
>
> *Thirty-five years ago a logging outfit on the upper Aptos started to harvest its timber.*
>
> *The earthquake of April, 1906, rumbled down the San Andreas fault with its cruel devastation, striking at the heart of the forest.*

Giant redwoods were tossed like jackstraws. A log jam buried the creek. A lake was formed by the earthquake dam. On the other side of the ridge a great slide buried the mill, killing nine men, and left deep scars still evident on the steep slopes.

Crazy Forest Is Born

In the wake of the temblors of devastation was Crazy Forest.

Trees 200 feet high leaned against one another for support. They were bent and twisted into grotesque shapes. Others were prone, with their roots still clinging to the earth. Shoots grew from these great fallen trunks, and became trees in their own right.

This Crazy Forest was discovered when the wreckage of Highland way was cleared.

The quake had opened new crevices in the rock and earth. Springs gushed with new energy, bowers of fern sprang up, moss filled the ravines. Wild flowers, berries and other shrubs filled the glades. Birds came there by the hundreds and it became a home for small game including deer, which seemed not to notice the trick nature had played on the magnificent forest.

Never Exploited

It was never exploited because of its isolation. The only road to it was frequently impassable. It was left untouched except for an occasional woodchopper taking a shingle belt or a bundle of stakes from a fallen giant on the fringes of the Crazy Forest, or a geologist in search of earthquake data.

Now sightseers are warned that the Crazy Forest is going to lose all its good trees, and those who do not view the spectacle this summer will never see it in its most awesome form.

Following the harvesting of the Crazy Forest in the summer of 1942, the Monterey Bay Redwood Company shut down its mill at Olive Springs permanently. It did so on the one-year anniversary of the bombing of Pearl Harbor: December 7, 1942. The start of the war had made finding workers difficult, and the remoteness of the operation so far up Soquel Creek cut into profits. There was also only enough uncut timber to support the mill for a few more years, which was insufficient to keep the company comfortably afloat.

The Monterey Bay Redwood Company's mill operated for seventeen years. The redwood lumber output figures for 1936 to 1940, below, were provided by Noel Patterson, while the final two years' figures are estimates since the original records have been lost:

Year	Lumber produced in year	Lumber produced to date	Elam Report projection to date
1936	5,683,000	64,425,000	78,825,301
1937	5,608,000	71,033,000	85,581,927
1938	4,985,000	76,018,000	91,587,952
1939	5,203,000	81,221,000	97,856,626
1940	4,594,000	85,815,000	103,391,566
1941	6,000,000	91,815,000	110,620,482
1942	6,000,000	97,815,000	117,849,398

These figures assume that output increased in the final two years because of increased demand by the government and more readily available labor, as attested to by Bob Lincoln.

Patterson recorded that, in addition to the quantities of redwood lumber noted above, a total of 1,887,000 board feet of fir was cut between 1934 and 1940, with the majority cut in the first four years of that span.

With the closure of the mill, the High Bridge over the East Branch of Soquel Creek near Amaya Gulch fell into disrepair and the route to the bridge was frequently closed due to landslides. These made vehicular use of the bridge impossible, but locals continued to use it to cross the gulch by foot or horse. By the 1960s, Sulphur Springs had become a popular destination for motorcyclists who would use the bridge to access their retreat in the redwoods.[132]

The Loma Prieta Lumber Company's mill on Aptos Creek is destroyed in a fire

Three years after flooding along Aptos Creek forced Clarence Srock to abandon his post as watchman of the former Loma Prieta Lumber Company's mill, disaster struck the deteriorating complex. Sometime during the summer of 1942, several youths entered the facility and set it alight. No firefighters came to extinguish the flames—it simply burned itself out. Afterwards, all that was left of the mill were several large beams that once supported the floor of the building. These were soon covered in thick overgrowth and attempts to expose the beams have always proven fruitless.[133]

Large-scale logging ends in the Augmentation

With the closure of the Monterey Bay Redwood Company's mill on Soquel Creek on December 7, 1942, the last large-scale logging operation within the Augmentation came to an end. Nearly two-thirds of the Augmentation's 32,702 acres—22,529 acres in total—were logged by four groups since its boundaries were finalized by the United States Surveyor's Office on June 4, 1859. These concerns were Grover & Company, the Loma Prieta Lumber Company, the Hihn family's companies (the Aptos Milling Company, the F. A. Hihn Company, and the Valencia–Hihn Company), and the Monterey Bay Redwood Company. Although each company would have performed its own cruises through the timberland prior to harvesting timber, only the report of the A. W. Elam Company, which cruised Tracts 1, 6, 10, 11, and 25, survives.

Using the Elam report, flawed as it may have been regarding the quality of the timber within the Augmentation, it is possible to gather some rough estimates regarding the Augmentation as a whole. The report estimated that within the 4,488 acres sold by the Valencia–Hihn Company to the Monterey Bay Redwood Company, there was approximately 166 million board feet of useable redwood. Because logging practices had changed dramatically from the 1860s to the 1940s, this is a relatively high estimate and a more realistic average would probably be up to

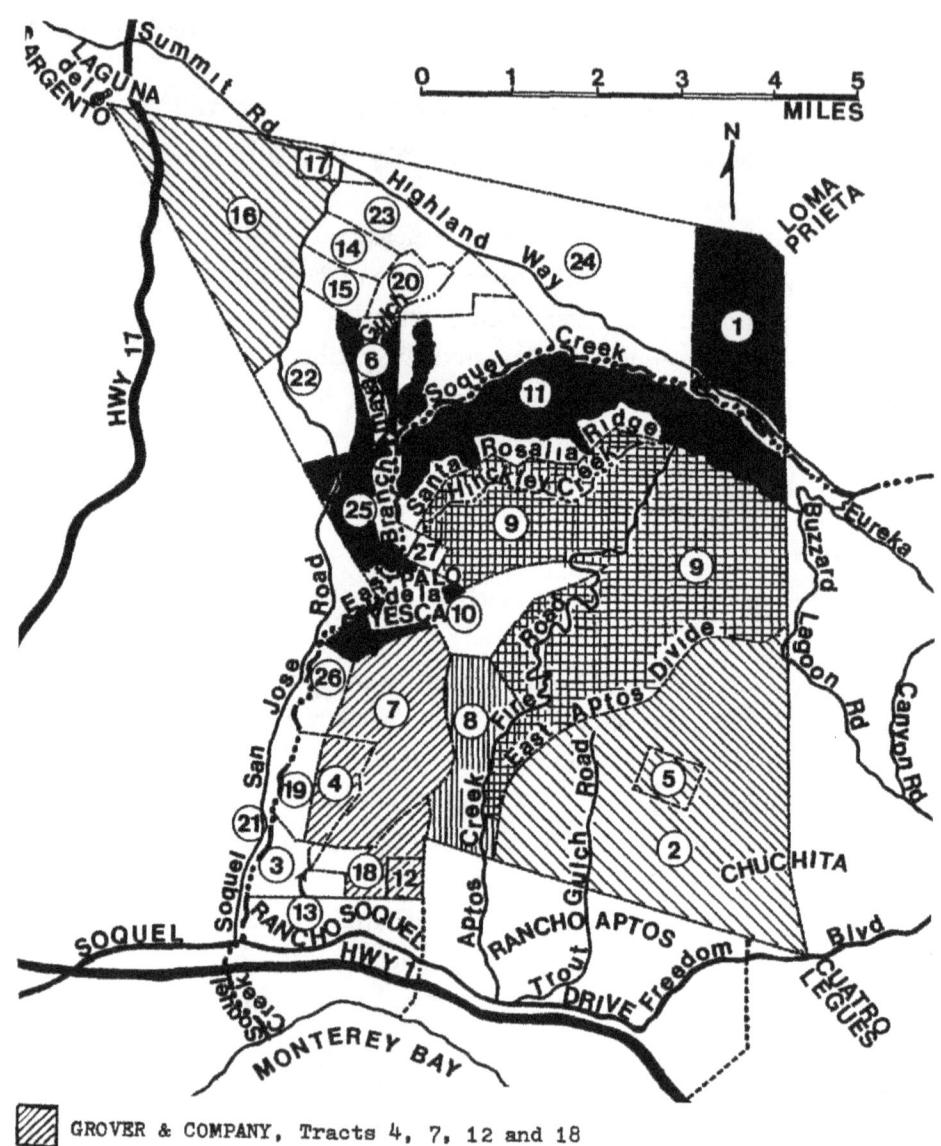

FIGURE 5.15 AREAS OF LARGE-SCALE LOGGING IN THE AUGMENTATION

twenty percent less output over the entire period. This was primarily because earlier lumber companies disposed of a lot of usable wood in order to remove sapwood from the finished lumber. From these figures, the Monterey Bay Redwood Company cut about 36,000 board feet of timber per acre, which was cut into about 30,000 board feet of rough lumber. Extrapolated across the entire area of the Augmentation harvested by these companies, around 811,044,000 board feet of timber was cut and from this the equivalent of 675,870,000 board feet of timber products were produced between 1865 and 1942.[134]

Chapter 6

~

From Exploitation to Preservation

Mark Paddock is hired by James Harris to remove the remaining timber in Tracts I and II in the Augmentation

After the Monterey Bay Lumber Company wrapped up operations in the Augmentation, James Harris looked for other ways to continue logging the headwaters of the East Branch of Soquel Creek. He allowed several former employees to remain on the property and he provided to them whatever equipment they needed to run small-scale operations. These were men that, due to age or health, had not been called up for service in World War II. The most prominent of these men was Mark Paddock, whom Bob Lincoln recalled was a "kind of character."

Paddock, who took the role of site boss, was joined by two local men, Arnold Fidel, a long-time resident of the Stetson Road area in the upper Amaya Creek watershed, and Al Young, the owner of the A. L. Young Machinery & Equipment Company in San José. They also had the help of Fred Ingerson, former sales manager for the Monterey Bay Redwood Company.

Paddock and Ingerson used the machinery left by the recently-shuttered Grendemann box and lumber mill, which had operated near the top of Amaya Gulch above Comstock Mill Road since the early 1930s. They moved this to a clearing downstream from Sulphur Springs. The mill's main equipment was a small, gasoline-powered 'groundhog' facility that could cut at best two truckloads of logs per day. The trees that fed the mill were cut with gasoline-powered reciprocating saws or dragsaws, forerunner to today's chainsaw. These were then dragged by a Caterpillar tractor to the mill. Remains of the mill lie along the north side of Hihn's Mill Road about two-thirds of the distance from Badger Springs to Sulphur Springs.

Lincoln, who worked at a lathe facility at Olive Springs in the years that Paddock ran his mill, remembers that the average production of the mill was around 6,000 to 8,000 board feet of lumber daily. But on its best day, it could produce up to 10,000 board feet. The entire operation was very low budget, paying the Monterey Bay Redwood Company $5 for each thousand board feet of finished lumber cut, or $30 to $40 per day.

As an example of the shoestring nature of Paddock's mill, his staff car was a 1927 Pierce Arrow limousine that he used to haul the loggers and millers into the forest. One day, a wildcat kitten was found by a logger and locked in the car during the day prior to be taken home as a potential pet. The wildcat lived up to its name, completely destroying the interior upholstery, already in somewhat disheveled condition from carrying around muddy, sawdust-covered lumbermen and oil-stained mechanics.

In the early years, Paddock mostly logged within the vicinity of the mill site, reaching no further than Sulphur Springs and extending from the East Branch of Soquel Creek up to the top of Santa Rosalia Ridge. Around 1946, he moved further west, along the route where the truck road exited the basin and headed to the former Olive Springs mill. Here, the Monterey Bay Redwood Company had left behind many large first growth redwoods for one reason or another. Paddock concentrated his efforts in this narrow gulch for several years, logging it by truck. He then moved to the boundary of Tract 11, beyond the High Bridge.

In order to get the logs to the mill, Paddock first slid the logs down the steep side of Soquel Creek's canyon before allowing them to drop by gravity to the creek over a hundred feet below. He would then pull them up to the truck road along the creek's west side. Once on the road, they were dragged behind a tractor and across the High Bridge. Getting logs from the vicinity of the bridge to the mill several miles away, through rugged and steep terrain, was a task none of Paddock's employees liked to do.

By 1948, Paddock was dissatisfied with the operation. Not enough logs were making it to the mill. One day, he decided to show the tractor operator how the task should be done. With a load of logs attached to the rear cable, more than normal, he backed the tractor down the hillside, released the logs farther down than usual, and then began to winch the tractor back up the hill to the clearing at the top. Before he reached level ground, however, he noticed that the tracks of the tractor were turning forward while he was heading backwards. He managed to jump clear just before the tractor went over the side into the creek. Because the tractor belonged to the Monterey Bay Redwood Company, Paddock had to pay Harris $4,000 for the damage. He then sent crews down to the creek, had them disassemble the tractor, and took the parts to the truck road south of the High Bridge, where the tractor was reassembled. This adventure ended Paddock's profit stream from the logging venture and he gave up on the operation.[135]

The Soquel Water System Company is sold by the Coast Counties Gas & Electric Company to the Monterey Bay Redwood Company

In May 1942, Coast Counties Gas & Electric Company purchased the Soquel Water System Company from the receivers for the Foshay Utility Corporation, which was a former subsidiary of the W. B. Foshay Company. The latter company was an early casualty of the stock market crash and had gone bankrupt on November 1, 1929. The utility company, though, survived for several more years, albeit as an independent firm. At the time, the company owned several water companies in Santa Cruz County, including in the San Lorenzo Valley, on the North Coast, and in Soquel and Capitola. The Soquel system provided water to around 600 customers.

Coast Counties did not retain the water system for long. The *Sentinel-News* reported on October 17, 1943:

> *The Soquel-Capitola water distribution system has been*

sold by the Coast Counties Gas and Electric company to the Monterey Bay Redwood company for $40,000.

Application for approval for the transfer has been filed with the state railroad commission.

Acquisition of the Soquel–Capitola system, with its reservoir on the banks of Bates creek just above Soquel, rounds out the area in which the water supply systems are now owned by the Monterey Bay Redwood company, incorporated originally as a sawmill operation.

The company, of which James A. Harris, Jr, is president and George W. Cooper is vice president, now owns but has not taken over operation of the Monterey Bay Water company, which supplies Aptos, Opal Cliffs, the Monterey Bay Country club property, Rio del Mar and Zayante.

It operates but does not own the La Selva water property.[136]

Horatio Ormsbee once again proposes a state park in the Augmentation

Following the rejection of the Loma Prieta State Park proposal made by Charles Park, Horatio Ormsbee, Jake Leonard, and H. Ray Judah in 1937, Ormsbee set to work revising the plan. On December 26, 1945, he submitted a new proposal to Reed Hayes. This park would only encompass 10,000 acres. Hayes liked the plan but requested changes before he would submit it to the state government for consideration.

On March 26, 1946, Ormsbee submitted his revised proposal. The new park would include:

- 752 acres in Tract 7, known as the Arden Forest, owned by James and Vera Bias
- 2,500 acres in Tract 9 encompassing Hinckley Gulch, owned jointly by Park, Ormsbee, and James and Veda Bias
- 6,718 acres that he called the Loma Prieta Lands, comprising 4,345 acres in Tract 9 and 610 acres in Tract 10 owned by the Loma Prieta Lumber Company, and 1,167 acres in Tract 8 and 571 acres in Eureka Canyon, including Buzzard Lagoon, owned by the Hopkins Estate. It also included 25 acres in Rancho Aptos for the fire road. At the time,

From Exploitation to Preservation 1946

these lands were held by Wells Fargo Bank & Union Trust Company.

His report concludes with the following statements:
- This forest is particularly suited for public use, such as a Park, Recreation Forest, or a Memorial Forest. It is located in a metropolitan area and is accessible all the year round to a large population within reasonable traveling distance.
- It is the furthest south extremity of the famous redwood forest of the Pacific Coast, equaled nowhere in the world. It should be preserved intact rather than broken up and operated for timber.
- Some surplus timber could be removed and sold and so improve the forest, under competent forest management, but to allow it to be cut clean would be a bad thing indeed.
- It is well served with roads, and at Lone Tree Prairie and also Buzzards Lagoon, there are suitable lays of ground for air fields. Probably the Buzzard Lagoon field is the best. It is the largest and has been under cultivation and is easily identified from the air. It has roads and water.
- The forest itself is an impressive thing and each year it will improve. The forest is young and growing and is going forward, not backward.
- The lands slope toward the sea at Monterey Bay and there are many fine marine views to be had from the upper levels. It is restful, impressive, and beautiful. It should be preserved for the public.

Lone Tree Prairie is not the same as Lone Tree Flat. Rather, it is today's Sheep Camp Meadow a quarter mile further north along the Aptos Creek Fire Road. The meadow is easily identified by a large water tank that had been installed in the late 1930s to help fight forest fires. It is located along the north side of the meadow and is nearly hidden from sight by trees. Strangely, the tank was never filled with water. Several years after it was put in place, a group of workers went to inspect the tank. When they opened one of its valves, the contents that poured out melted the boots of one of the workers. They quickly sealed the tank up and declared it unfit for purpose. It was abandoned and has been rotting away ever since.

Just like in 1937, Ormsbee's proposal was rejected by the state government in early 1947. This time, they made it clear that there was no possibility of the plan moving forward. Ormsbee gave up on his dream and left the idea of a state park to a future generation.[137]

Oil drilling begins in the Augmentation

In 1861, a group of lumbermen accidently came across oil seeping out of the ground in what today is called Moody Gulch. The gulch's creek runs into Los Gatos Creek just above Lexington Reservoir. The gulch can be easily identified because it runs along the north side of Redwood Estates. This discovery was the beginning of California's oil industry. In 1865, the newly-formed Santa Clara Petroleum Company began drilling in the gulch with a steam drilling rig reaching the 470-foot level, from which little oil was produced. This small well was the first commercially operated oil well in the state. Even though the well and several others remained in operation into the twentieth century, they never produced enough oil to call the activity in the gulch a bonanza.

Over the years, many indications have been found that there is oil at different locations throughout the Santa Cruz Mountains. After the discovery of the oil seepage in Moody Gulch and much searching, it was concluded that the oil territory extended from the vicinity of the gulch southeasterly to the headwaters of Los Gatos Creek and then down the southernmost slopes of the Santa Cruz Mountains at Sargent south of Gilroy. Traces of oil were found near Hotel de Redwoods (at the junction of today's Redwood Lodge Road and Soquel San Jose Road) and on the farm of M. G. Norton near Skyland. In 1865, two oil promoters, Theodore G. McLearan and Henry Palmer, leased 2,500 acres of land from Lyman John Burrell. They agreed to pay Burrell an initial $10 and, if they hit oil, they would give him 1/120th share of all oil found during the life of the six-year lease. Although a well was begun on Burrell's property, oil never appeared and the well was abandoned.

At the advent of the twentieth century, Frederick Hihn along with a number of others believed that there was oil to be found in the Augmentation. Truth of this can be found in many deeds and agreements that Hihn and other Soquel Creek property owners registered. The first known prospecting for black gold by a major oil company within the Augmentation was conducted by the Union Oil Company of California.

On August 4, 1948, Union Oil entered into a lease agreement for an unspecified number of acres with Wells Fargo Bank & Union Trust Company, on land owned by the Loma Prieta Lumber Company and the Hopkins Estate. The contract was signed by Loma Prieta's new president and the bank's head trust officer, Percy Wood. The company was given one year to start drilling, with the possibility of a one-year extension if drilling proved a success and another year extension if several criteria were met.

On April 21, 1949, an amendment was added to the lease by Wells Fargo that Union Oil's search for oil covered a total area of 4,955 acres. That meant that the company was given access to all of Loma Prieta's Tract 9 and 10 lands in the Aptos Forest. The first two wells were drilled on August 17. They were located on the Aptos Creek Fire Road between the top of the incline and Sand Point just to the south of White's Lagoon Trail. They are identified today by two large slabs of cement that have become nearly, if not totally, covered after years of road grading.

During the period that the company was drilling for oil at the two locations, it was actively exploring other potential sites. It concentrated its major effort within the vicinity of White's Lagoon. In order to enter the area with its trucks, the company improved today's White's Lagoon Trail, turning it into an access road. It also built several roads that branched off from the fire road and the latter trail. Several of these branching roads extended across the headwaters of Spring Creek and ended on today's Big Slide Trail just before it begins its steep descent to Aptos Creek. Along several of these roads, most of which are difficult to identify today due to the vegetation, there are the remains of small exploratory wells. Below White's Lagoon, there is a cabin that several men lived in while they were prospecting. Because the two wells on the fire road blocked the road to the cabin, a parallel road was built just to the east within Spring Creek's gully. This bypass road begins just to the north of the top of the incline (before the cement platform that remains on the fire road) and is easily followed until it reaches the top of Spring Creek.

The two oil wells did not operate for long, probably shutting down in early October 1949. There was just not a sufficient quantity of oil to make them profitable. Wells Fargo gave Union Oil until November 15 to drill a new well or it would forfeit its contract. The company failed to meet its obligations, but rather than give up on the attempt, Union Oil asked the bank to reduce its acreage to 3,238.5 acres to reduce its financial burden. The company was paying about $1.00 per acre annually as a part of the agreement. Wells Fargo granted the reduction but only gave the company until August 4, 1950 to make its third bore. Union Oil failed to identify a site in time and forfeited its option.[138]

The Coast Counties Gas & Electric Company negotiates easements in Tracts 7 and 8 in the Augmentation

Because of the increased demand for electricity in the Santa Cruz Mountains, Coast Counties Gas & Electric needed more electrical lines in the Augmentation. On January 23, 1950, James Bias granted an easement through Tract 7 of the Augmentation for a single line of poles and wire. In addition, the electric company was given the right to ingress and egress in order to reach the poles and wires for maintenance purposes.

Two weeks later, on February 7, Wells Fargo Bank & Union Trust Company gave Coast Counties permission to relocate its powerlines north to the vicinity of the former Loma Prieta mill site just above Molino Junction in Tract 8. These lines still pass through The Forest of Nisene Marks State Park, crossing Aptos Creek and the Loma Prieta Grade Trail south of the mill site and then continuing west up Love Gulch to West Ridge Trail and over the top of the hill into Grover Gulch. This new alignment required Coast Counties to renegotiate with Bias regarding the right-of-way. The new route was agreed to on March 14.[139]

A steel bridge for Aptos Creek

Although the venture would ultimately fail, the Union Oil Company needed to get its trucks up to the top of China Ridge, which meant that they needed to be able to cross Aptos Creek several times. At the same time, the Forest Service also needed to maintain the fire roads and its trucks were becoming larger. The narrow, rickety wood bridge on the Aptos Creek Fire Road just south of the Augmentation's boundary with Rancho Aptos was no longer fit for purpose.

Rather than build a new bridge, the Forest Service decided to save money by disassembling the steel bridge that the U. S. Army Corps of Engineering had built across the East Branch of Soquel Creek at Olive Springs. It was disassembled by the Forest Service and installed at its new location in 1950. Today, the steel bridge across Aptos Creek is probably the best-known landmark along the entire Aptos Creek Fire Road.

On Olive Springs Road, the bridge was not replaced. Residents of Hinckley Basin Unit No. 1 were forced to drive through Soquel Creek in order to visit their summer homes, something that was sometimes impossible due to bad weather. It was another factor leading to the subdivision's eventual abandonment. The only evidence that a bridge once crossed the creek at Olive Springs is a single surviving concrete abutment located on the west bank of the creek.

Land transfer from James and Veda Bias to the Marks family concerning Tracts 7 and 9 in the Augmentation

Horatio Ormsbee and James Bias had long held a dream of turning the former Loma Prieta Lumber Company property in the Augmentation into a state park. After the state rejected their proposal in June 1947, they began seeking potential champions who could lead the movement into the next decade.

Meanwhile, the Union Oil Company had left the Augmentation and it was once more ripe for exploitation by an interested party. All along the California coast, oil speculators were looking for the elusive resource. Noble Johnson of Ventura led the charge and convinced several others to join him. One such gentleman was Herman Marks, who quickly drew his siblings, Agnes and Andrew, into his plans. Their family fortune—combined with a love of the wilderness and its natural beauty that supposedly was instilled in them by their mother, Nissen—inspired Ormsbee and Bias to reach out to the family in late 1950.

Nissen Andreasen Bonde was born in Schleswig-Holstein, Denmark on

April 12, 1859 to Andreas Pedersen Bonde and Catherine Maria Nisdatter Roos. When and why Bonde moved to the United States is unknown, but on August 14, 1879, she married Benjamin J. Marks in Tucson, Arizona. Marks was born in Prussia (now Germany), where he had learned five languages and worked as a teacher. His family hoped that he would become a minister, but Marks wanted to be a doctor. In the end, he turned to farming. The Marks settled in the Huachuca Mountains in Arizona. After problems with a local Apache tribe, they relocated to Charleston, Arizona, where their first child, Alice Margaret Marks, was born in 1880. Further troubles with the Apache, as well as threats from the Clanton family and fights in Tombstone, prompted the Marks to move to California. They first settled in Jamesburg near San Diego, at the time a small fishing village, before shifting north to Tassajara and then Salinas. During this period, Agnes K. (b. 1883), Herman Henry (b. 1885), and Andrew Peterson (b. 1889) were born to the Marks. In Salinas, the family initially settled on Rancho Toro, south of the city, where Benjamin died in 1893.

Widowed at only 33 with four children and a heavily-mortgaged ranch, Nissen fought hard to secure her property and turn a profit. Young Andrew may have been instrumental in the family's change of fortune. In the early 1900s, he developed a feed for animals that became very popular across the region. With the proceeds from this product, the family was able to repay its debts and buy the property outright. It also allowed them to buy other properties and make speculative investments. By the 1910s, the family had moved to Alisal, east of Salinas, although they retained their old Toro estate as well.

Nissen herself became less involved as her children took over the farm and became independently wealthy. With her inborn love of the wilderness and its natural beauty, she would take long walks in the untouched fields and woods of the areas near her home in Salinas. She also reveled in visiting parks and forests and entertaining children. The death of her eldest daughter Alice in 1942 was likely a heavy blow for her but she remained with her surviving children as they began their speculative journey into the forest that would one day bear her name.

Over the years, Nissen's name saw many different spellings. The earliest in Danish records was Nissen, while conflicting marriage records call her Nasena or Nacena. Census and other United States Government records alternatively call her Neseme, Nesime, Nicene, Nissine, and other variants. But her children always spelled her name Nesine, and that is what appears on her headstone and in her obituary. Nonetheless, when the time came to name the state park in the Augmentation, Herman, Agnes, and Andrew chose Nisene since they considered it the easiest variant to pronounce and spell.

Although the Marks family had never lived in Santa Cruz County, they were aware of the area and its potential. In 1920, Andrew Marks married Alzoe Katherine Leibbrandt, a granddaughter of John Jacob Leibbrandt who had founded the Leibbrandt Bath House at the Santa Cruz Main Beach in 1872. It seems likely that Andrew and Alzoe with their three children visited their Santa Cruz relatives on occasion, which allowed them to remain aware of the conditions there.

How precisely Ormsbee and Bias first came into contact with the Marks family is unknown. The most likely candidates are Bias himself or J. Don Thompson, both of whom were real estate brokers. Thompson was the broker for the Marks family in Monterey County who handled their land transactions before they became involved in Santa Cruz County. After the Marks became interested in purchasing land in the county, Thompson joined in a partnership with Bias. Bias, meanwhile, was based out of Santa Cruz and may have known Andrew Marks or had a chance encounter with Herman. Because of the role Thompson played in the formation of The Forest of Nisene Marks State Park, a bench was named in his honor near the West Ridge Trail Camp.

Initially, Herman Marks' obsession with finding oil was not apparent to Ormsbee and Bias. Herman convinced the men that his main interest was in the land itself and that their goals for the property were aligned. To his credit, Herman and his siblings held a strong belief in preserving wilderness areas, but this was countered by Herman's ambition to explore, discover, and profit from oil.

On January 10, 1951, Don Thompson convinced James and Veda Bias to sell their land in Tract 7 in the Augmentation, encompassing 752 acres, to the Marks siblings for $30,080. This gave the Marks possession of all the land directly north of today's Land of Medicine Buddha property, including the failed Arden Forest residential subdivision. The only portion of Tract 7 not sold was 11.997 acres purchased by H. M. Howard in the early 1900s, which in 1951 was held by the Western Title Insurance Company in trust for the family.

Six months later, on June 13, Thompson on behalf of the Marks family negotiated the purchase of 2,500 acres of Tract 9 in the Augmentation encompassing the whole of Hinckley Gulch. Unlike the previous sale, this land transfer proved more contentious. Ormsbee and Bias insisted on adding a clause to the deed that made it illegal to cut or destroy the remaining standing timber, or destroy any new growth except for the clearing of rights-of-way for roads, within Hinckley Gulch. Herman strongly objected to the insertion of this clause and refused to agree to this condition until the day the deed was signed.

With the signing of this deed, the Marks family owned a total of 3,252 acres within the Augmentation. Now they could set their sights on the lands they had placed the highest priority on: those held in trust by Wells Fargo Bank & Union Trust Company on behalf of the Hopkins Estate and the Loma Prieta Lumber Company. This included Tract 8 and some land in Eureka Canyon, the remainder of Tract 9, and 610 acres on the eastern side of Tract 10. Bias inquired about the properties on March 26, 1952 on behalf of Thompson and the Marks family, but was told that the land could not be sold at the time. The company's agent admitted that the value of the land had not been assessed nor had its trustees authorized its sale.[140]

Lease agreement between the Monterey Bay Redwood Company and Victor Maddock concerning Tract 25 in the Augmentation

Since early 1929, the Monterey Bay Redwood Company had leased the land around Sugarloaf Mountain within Tract 25 of the Augmentation to Santa Cruz County in order to operate a quarry. Whether the county performed the operations itself or they were subcontracted is unknown. These operations continued intermittently until May 1, 1953, when a new lease agreement was signed between the lumber company and Victor W. Maddock. Soon after, Maddock incorporated the Olive Springs Quarry Company, which

From Exploitation to Preservation 1953

still operates on the northeastern side of Sugarloaf Mountain. Over the years, additional land has been added and it now encompasses some 283 acres. Since operations began in 1929, almost the entire eastern half of the mountain has been taken away by truck.

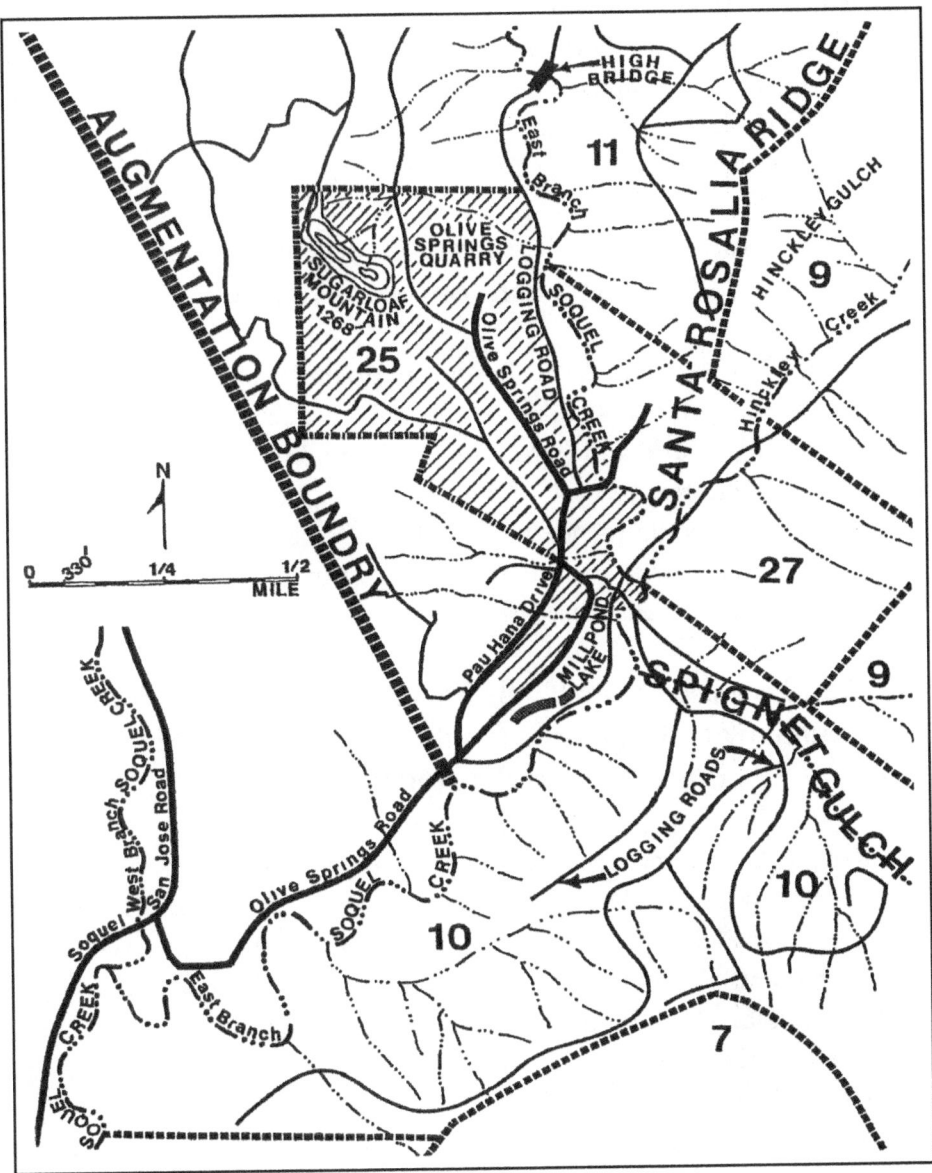

Figure 6.1 Olive Springs Quarry on Tract 25 in the Augmentation

On February 19, 1957, William Hellier founded the Soquel Asphalt Products Company. A former mining engineer, Hellier was a Soquel native who had served as the United States Government's director of public works in Guam. His company briefly worked with Maddock to sell commercial-grade rock and asphalt mined from the quarry to businesses and individuals. All mention of the company in newspapers vanishes after 1958 and Hellier moved to Chicago in 1964. It seems likely that he sold the business to Maddock prior to his departure, after which it operated as the retail wing of the Olive Springs Quarry Company.[141]

State Water Resources Board proposes building a dam on Aptos Creek

In August 1953, the State Water Resources Board issued "Bulletin No. 5" in which it proposed that a 176-foot-high dam be erected one mile north of Aptos on Aptos Creek. This structure would create a reservoir capable of storing 4,100-acre-feet of water. For comparison, Lexington Reservoir on Los Gatos Creek contains nearly 20,000 acre-feet. The construction cost of the dam and reservoir infrastructure was estimated at $1,406,000, with an annual cost of $58,200 thereafter.[142]

Land transfer from Wells Fargo Bank & Union Trust Company to the Marks family concerning land in and adjacent to the Augmentation

On March 6, 1953, almost a year to the day that Wells Fargo Bank & Union Trust Company told the Marks family that it had insufficient information or permission to sell the Loma Prieta Lumber Company and Hopkins Estate's land within and adjacent to the Augmentation, Don Thompson gave the bank a check for $16,000 signed by Herman Marks. Along with the check, Marks made an offer of $256,000 for the properties.

A week later, on March 12, the bank arranged for the properties to be appraised, a process that would take about a month. The deadline for the appraisal was extended twice before a cruiser submitted his report around April 15. As a result, Marks gave the bank until April 28 to make a decision regarding the sale of the property. Ultimately, Wells Fargo failed to make a decision by the deadline. When April 28 arrived, the bank returned the deposit check stating that there were questions concerning the properties that required further investigation. The bank pledged to contact Marks if the questions could be adequately resolved and the properties sold.

On October 16, the bank contacted Thompson to inform him that the properties should be available for sale by the middle of November. However, the bank did not follow up. This prompted Thompson to write to Wells Fargo on December 31 asking for an update. Apparently, the response was favorable, although it was likely given over the phone since no record of the communication survives. On March 10, 1954, Thompson mailed a deposit check for $25,000 to the bank with Marks' conditional offer to buy the properties, valid for ten days. The bank followed up on March 18 by requesting a credit check of the three Marks siblings.

Thompson provided the following letter to the bank on March 23, listing the credit history and references of his clients:

> *To: Percy A. Wood, Head Loan Officer and President of the Loma Prieta Lumber Company*
>
> *From: J. Don Thompson*
>
> *Subject: Credit References for Nisene Marks, Herman Henry, Andrew P. and Agnes K. Marks*
>
> *This family consists of the mother, who is very aged, two brothers, Herman and Andrew, and a sister Agnes.*
> *Their mailing address is P.O. Box 1251, Salinas, California. They have lived in Monterey County for many years and through diligence and good management, they have acquired considerable properties. They have fine homes near Salinas, land on the Monterey Peninsula, the Arden and Hinckley forests in Santa Cruz County, farm land near Salinas and Greenfield, as well as other properties. The*

> Greenfield ranch is one of the best in the area and good crops of grain, beans and row crops are produced.
>
> There are many good references, but I suggest Mr. William Fossat, Salinas Bank of America, and Mr. E. J. Drussel, manager of the Salinas Title Guarantee Company, 22 W. Gabilan Street, Salinas, who has handled most of their real estate transactions.
>
> I have handled considerable properties for these people and have found them to be strictly honest in all transactions, even when it meant a loss to them.
>
> Also, they are one of the few, who believe in conserving our natural resources and as such <u>they have no idea of destroying any timber land</u>. If they are able to purchase this property, it will give them a large tract of timber land which they will be able to use as a recreational and conservation area, which in years to come will be one of the few in the area.
>
> As I told you when I talked to you in San Francisco, this offer is higher than the appraisal was but they are willing to pay the higher price. As in all transactions, they will offer a good price but will not dicker. As to the mineral rights, they will not give any of this away, but possibly would while they owe anything on the property. Regarding this, I give you my word that they have no idea of using any of the minerals, even if they knew there were any there.
>
> As to the purchasers, you will find them to be good credit risk having had five figure unsecured bank loans in the past.
>
> Sincerely, J. Don Thompson

While the bank contacted references and finalized its part of the agreement, Thompson and James Bias, as the Marks family's real estate brokers, made a private agreement on April 1 to split the commission of the sale between them. Whatever the final amount, the agreement stipulated that Thompson would receive $1,000 more than Bias.

Despite the letter, references, and general agreement to sell, Wells Fargo was still noncommittal. Much of the negotiations must have occurred over the phone, but by May 6, it became clear that the point of contention re-

From Exploitation to Preservation 1954

lated to mineral rights within the properties. Several of the Loma Prieta Lumber Company's board members wished to retain a half interest in the mineral rights of the properties for a period of fifteen years, after which all rights would transfer to the Marks family. In a tense exchange that day, Thompson reluctantly conceded the rights with the Marks family's permis-

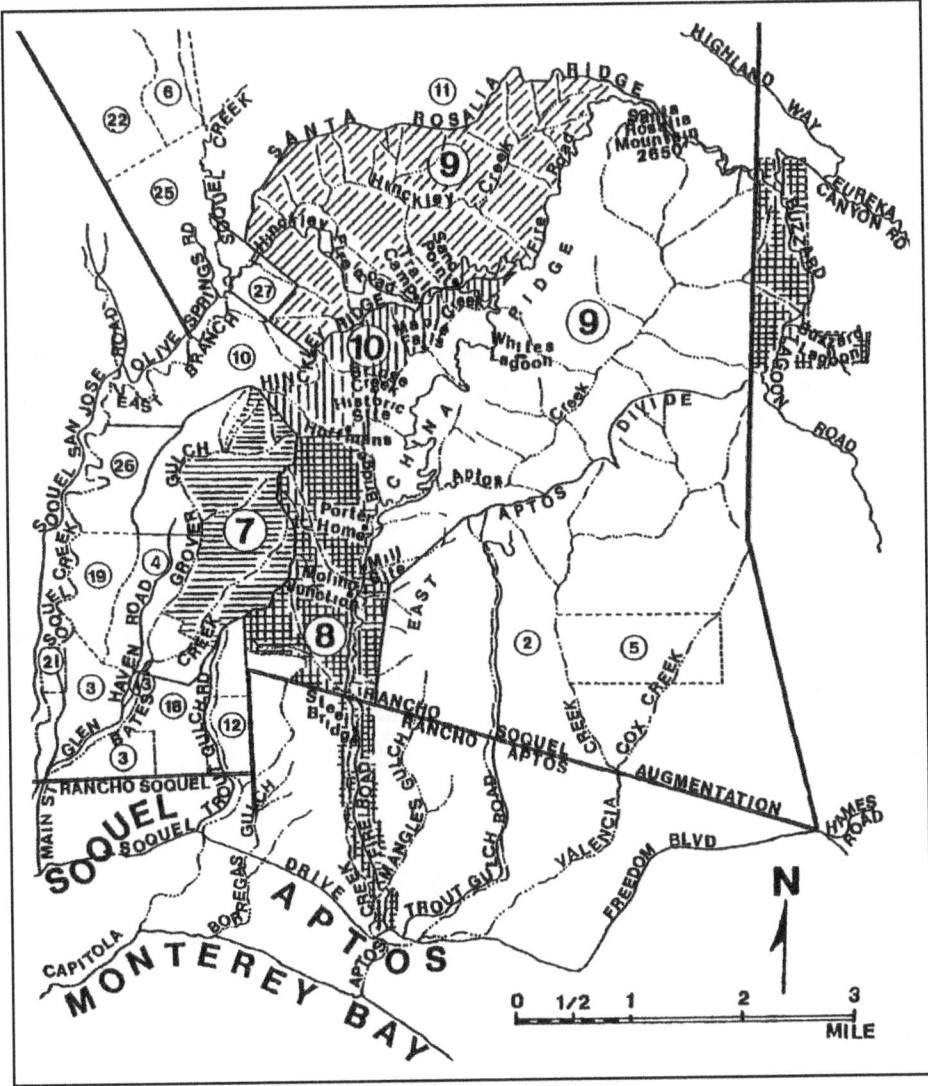

FIGURE 6.2 PROPERTY IN AND AROUND THE AUGMENTATION PURCHASED BY THE MARKS FAMILY

sion. The next day, the bank requested a thirteen-day extension in order to communicate with the lumber company's shareholders.

Finally, over two years after the initial offer had been made, the transaction was completed. On June 24, Herman Marks and Thompson met Percy Woods and other bank officials in San Francisco to finalize the sale. Through the sale, 5,941 acres of land were sold by the Loma Prieta Lumber Company and the Hopkins Estate to Agnes, Herman, and Andrew Marks for $256,000. After the agreement was signed, Herman made his first payment of $50,000 to the bank. The remainder would be paid in installments of $20,600 annually for ten years at an interest rate of 4.5 percent.

The deed of sale included several clauses. First, the Marks family agreed that the Loma Prieta Lumber Company retained a one-half interest in the mineral rights of Tract 9 for a period of fifteen years. Furthermore, all of the new owners except Andrew's wife, Alzoe, retained a one-half interest in all oil, gas, and other hydrocarbon compounds extracted from the properties, as well as the right of ingress and egress at all times for the purpose of exploring or mining for the period of fifteen years. Lastly, Alzoe affirmed that her husband was the sole owner of his portion of the property and she declaimed any and all interest in and to the property.

After the completion of this transaction, the total land owned by the Marks family in the Augmentation was 9,374 acres, comprising part of Tract 7 (752 acres), Tract 8 (1,167 acres), Tract 9 (6,845 acres), and Tract 10 east of Hinckley Ridge (610 acres). With the addition of 571 acres around Buzzard Lagoon and the 25 acres in Rancho Aptos of the entry road, the Marks owned 9,970 acres in the hills above Aptos.[143]

Letter to the California Redwood Association from Don Thompson

On July 19, 1954, Don Thompson wrote to the California Redwood Association requesting information regarding "tree farming and timber conservation in the California redwoods." In his letter, Thompson stated:

> *A client of mine has purchased some 9,500 acres of old timber land that contains second growth redwood, hardwoods and*

some scattered virgin trees. These people are truly conservation minded and they want to perpetuate their holding. By correct forest practices enough timber could be cut to pay expenses and the timber growth increased in value.[144]

Stumpage rights granted by the Monterey Bay Redwood Company to Al Young

Before the summer of 1955 began, the former partner of Mark Paddock, Al Young, was granted stumpage rights to all of the remaining standing timber within the Monterey Bay Redwood Company's land in the Augmentation. In the agreement made with James Harris, Young agreed to pay $8.00 per thousand board feet for fir and $10.00 for redwood.

During the six-month period after the agreement was in effect, Young removed fir and redwood trees from the top of the ridge between Amaya and Hester Creeks, as well as along Hester Creek and on the south side of the East Branch of Soquel Creek at the far eastern end of Tract 11 near Camp Loma. Young was not permitted to cut old-growth timber around Sulphur Springs or in the vicinity of the Harris Grove at Badger Springs. He also was not allowed to cut any timber from Tract 1, which still had around 300,000 board feet of unharvested redwood, nor from the area directly north of the High Bridge.

At the end of the season, Young and Harris concluded that there was still around $40,000 worth of standing redwood and fir timber—or 3 to 4 million board feet—on the Monterey Bay Redwood Company's land. They also estimated that there were about 50,000 cords of oak and madrone, and possibly twice that number, which at the time was valued at $1.00 per cord.[145]

Nesine Marks dies

At the age of 96, Nesine Marks died at her home in the Toro area of Salinas on July 19, 1955. The *Salinas Californian*, in addition to mentioning her three surviving children, noted that Nesine was survived by three grandchildren—Lloyd M., Andrew Jr., and Avalon Brugger—and four great-grandchildren. It added that she outlived her two siblings, Peter Bonde and Mrs. H. H. Hollenstein. She was buried in the Garden of Memories in Salinas.[146]

Another disastrous storm strikes the Augmentation

Rain fell unrelenting for several days and nights before December 23, 1955. At about nine o'clock in the evening, the San Lorenzo River in Santa Cruz reached a depth of eleven feet, which meant it had reached flood stage. The river rose three more feet by morning and one-third of the city was underwater. On December 24, the river reached its highest recorded depth of 22 feet and it doubled its width through the city.

In the mountains, road conditions were dangerous and many communities were cut off. In Soquel at the bridge that carried Soquel Drive across Soquel Creek, driftwood from upstream created a jam of logs, houses, and cottages. It created a twisting pile of destruction that began to destabilize the bridge itself.

By the time the storm had run its course, the damage was so catastrophic that assistance was called in from the United States Army base at Fort Ord in Monterey. Rescuers focused on the populated areas, but the backcountry was isolated for many days. When crews finally reached the former Monterey Bay Redwood Company mill at Olive Springs, they found several roads washed out, bridges damaged, and blocked culverts undermining roads. It would take years for the damage to be fully repaired and some areas of the Augmentation still show signs of damage from the storm of 1955.[147]

Stumpage rights granted by the Monterey Bay Redwood Company to Mr. Olsen

In spring 1956, James Harris, as representative of the Monterey Bay Redwood Company, was approached by a Mr. Olsen, who requested permission to log the remaining 300,000 board feet of standing timber in Tract 1 in the Augmentation. Harris agreed and Olsen spent the summer cutting down the remaining trees within Rattlesnake Gulch. The next year, he received permission to continue cutting the trees left by Al Young on the south side of the East Branch of Soquel Creek in the vicinity of Camp Loma. The redwood trees cut here were the last vestiges of the Crazy Forest.[148]

Appraisal of the Monterey Bay Redwood Company's land is completed

In late 1955, at the request of the city manager of Santa Cruz, Robert N. Klein, and under an agreement with the Santa Cruz City Council, Noel Patterson and J. T. Nittler made an appraisal of the land owned by the Monterey Bay Redwood Company. This was completed on December 1, 1955 and submitted on February 9, 1956. The reason for this appraisal is fairly clear: the City of Santa Cruz was running out of sources of drinking water. The earlier proposal to build a dam on Aptos Creek and later proposals to build dams elsewhere on Soquel Creek and on Newell Creek were all related to this investigation.

The two appraisers estimated that the value of the remaining saleable old-growth redwood and fir was from $10,000 to $30,000, and that there were large areas in the middle of the property either side of Sulphur Springs that contained ground suitable for the development of mountain homes and recreational areas.

Concerning the property's water sources—Ashbury Creek (today Fern Creek), Laguna Creek (today Ashbury Creek), and Rattlesnake Creek—they supply water year-round that can be utilized for numerous purposes. The report noted that even after a dry late spring and summer, Rattlesnake Creek contained a fine flow of water into the autumn. This would be important if the East Branch of Soquel Creek were to be impounded to create a year-round water supply.

The report concluded that the estimated value of the property was $270,000 or $60 per acre, while the 4.25 miles of the Hihn Railroad Grade between the south end of the tract and the Southern Pacific Railroad's station in Capitola was worth $6,749, or $321 per acre. The railway grade, especially, could be useful for building a pipeline to Santa Cruz if a reservoir were to be made in the property.

In the end, the Monterey Bay Redwood Company's land was not chosen for a reservoir. Instead, in 1960, Newell Creek was impounded and a 170-acre reservoir created, now known as Loch Lomond, capable of holding up to 1.2-million-acre-feet of water.[149]

The Marks family begins searching for oil in the Augmentation

It seems that at some early date, Herman Marks entered into a lease agreement with the Western Gulch Oil Company concerning oil exploration, probably on the family's properties in Monterey County. On December 27, 1956, an amendment was added to the lease in which Marks allowed the oil company to search for oil on his land in Santa Cruz County. The amendment mentioned specific areas of exploration, including just to the south of Spanish Ranch within the vicinity of Summit Road and Highland Way, and along Soquel Creek north of its mouth at various locations.

Test drilling began along Aptos Creek in early 1957. Soon, at the Marks family's expense, a large derrick was erected on the creek. Nowhere in Don Thompson's papers is the location of the well mentioned, but according to a letter, it was located between Molino and the Porter House Site along today's Loma Prieta Grade Trail. This makes the most likely location for the well just south of the mill site on a small shelf between Aptos Creek and the Aptos Creek Fire Road.[150]

Arnold Svendsgaard offers to buy Tract I in the Augmentation from the Monterey Bay Redwood Company

On March 16, 1957, Arnold Svendsgaard made an offer to buy the Monterey Bay Redwood Company's 5,350 acres in the Augmentation for $500,000. Noel Patterson and the company's real estate broker, Carl H. Blake, were placed in charge of negotiations. Svendsgaard was vice president and treasurer of the Pacific American Distribution Company, headquartered in Oakland. It had offices and representatives throughout the Far East, in New Zealand and Australia, South America, Switzerland, and Germany. However, when Svendsgaard made his offer, he represented neither his company nor himself, but rather a foundation headquartered on the East

Coast, for which he was a trustee.

Within weeks of receiving the offer, Patterson was made another offer, this time from Hannes Schroll, who also agreed to pay $500,000. Little is known about Schroll other than that he lived in Palo Alto, owned a large ranch in Panoche Valley in San Benito County, and was part owner of the Sugar Bowl ski resort in the Sierra Nevada. While Svendsgaard's reason for wanting to purchase the tract has not been discovered in Patterson's files, Schroll's reason is known from his earliest contact: he wanted the land for residential, industrial, and recreational purposes.

Realizing that he had competition, Svendsgaard signed a deposit receipt on August 21 in which he agreed to pay the offered amount. Included in the receipt was the need for improvements that included right-of-way and easements, mineral rights above and below the ground, water and timber rights, and the land occupied by the Olive Springs Quarry Company. After signing the receipt, Svendsgaard then signed a promissory note for $5,000 that was due in 60 days (on October 21). He agreed to pay the remaining balance of $495,000 as follows:

$45,000: November 20, 1957
$50,000: December 20, 1957
$100,000: February 20, 1958
$150,000: May 20, 1958
$150,000: to be paid one year from the date that escrow closes

Patterson accepted Svendsgaard's offer, but the latter promptly failed to make his first two scheduled payments. On December 12, the California Pacific Title & Trust Company sent a letter to Svendsgaard in which it demanded that he pay a total of $50,000: $5,000 to cover the note signed that was due on October 21 and $45,000 for the amount due on November 20. The company threatened to take all appropriate action to collect the money.

Schroll took advantage of Svendsgaard's failure to pay to maneuver to purchase the property. He, his attorney, a real estate broker, and representatives of the Monterey Bay Redwood Company exchanged several telephone calls in the late months of 1957. On December 22, Patterson submitted maps of the company's land to Coldwell Banker & Company of Palo Alto, which undoubtedly was associated with Schroll. Accompanying the maps was a breakdown of the property's value after subtracting from the asking price a total of $50,000 for Tract 1's Rattlesnake Gulch and $110,000 for the quarry property that was leased to the Olive Springs Quarry Company.

Svendsgaard had not yet given up, though. On January 3, 1958, a meeting was held in the offices of the Pacific American Distribution Company in Oakland between Svendsgaard, Patterson, and Blake. The meeting was followed three days later by a letter from Svendsgaard to Patterson where the former apologized for the delay in not meeting the dates agreed for payment. The reason for the failure was due to difficulties he was having in obtaining the necessary funds from the Philippines. While he stated that pesos had been deposited in the bank, he claimed that it could take up to a year to convert that amount into dollars. He added that several additional methods of securing the money from other sources had been looked into, but they had all been found to be unacceptable due to unattractive demands and conditions.

A year later, after Svendsgaard had failed to secure financing, Patterson decided to accept Schroll's offer. On January 6, 1959, Patterson sent a letter to A. E. Jones, Schroll's attorney, explaining what should be included in the Option to Buy agreement. It explained that the agreement needs to include a method of payment for amounts owed following the signing of a Deed of Trust, and whether these payments will be made monthly, quarterly, or semi-annually. This letter is the first solid proof of Schroll's intention to buy the company's land in the Augmentation.[151]

The Marks family's loans are refinanced

On December 3, 1958, Wells Fargo Bank & Union Trust Company accepted the Marks family's request to postpone their loan payment. The next payment of $20,600 was due on June 24, 1959, but Don Thompson, the Marks' attorney, had it pushed back seven months to January 24, 1960. On February 7, 1959, Thompson submitted several additional requests. First, he asked if all future annual payments could be scheduled for January 1, beginning with the amount owed in 1960. Second, he asked for the 6 percent interest rate to be reduced to 5.5 percent to keep it in line with the family's other, similar investments. And third, he wanted the amount owed for 1960 reduced slightly to reflect this requested change in interest.

Thompson and the Marks requested these changes for several reasons. Crop prices in the late 1950s were low, meaning that the family's farmland in Monterey County was not turning as strong of a profit compared to earlier years. Herman Marks was also spending a lot of time and money drilling for oil in the Augmentation, and he had yet to find a profitable bore. In addition to these problems, the family owed a substantial inheritance tax following the death of Nesine and had taken out a loan from an insurance company to pay the amount. As they were seeking with Wells Fargo, the family had to postpone payment of their loans from Bank of America in Monterey County, too. They hoped that by rescheduling their loan payments and matching interest rates, they would be on better footing for repayment moving forward from January 1960.

Wells Fargo was not entirely in favor of the requested changes. They agreed to lower the amount owed, but they would not budge on the interest rate. The original interest rate for the property had been 4.5 percent, but because the Marks had missed several payments over the previous few years, the rate was increased to 6 percent as a penalty and the bank was not confident in the family's ability to make scheduled payments in the future.[152]

Option to Buy agreement between the Monterey Bay Redwood Company and Hannes Schroll concerning land in the Augmentation

On April 28, 1959, Hannes Schroll was granted an exclusive right and option to purchase the 5,118 acres in the Augmentation held by the Monterey Bay Redwood Company in exchange for a $2,500 deposit, which he submitted to James Harris on behalf of the company. The option was for six months with an expiration date of midnight on October 28. The purchase price, which did not include the quarry on Sugarloaf Mountain within Tract 25, amounted to $500,000, payable as follows at a five percent annual interest rate:

- $197,500 at the time that the Deed of Trust is signed
- $300,000 to be paid in six installments of $50,000 plus interest beginning January 1, 1960 and continuing through 1963

During the term of the option, Schroll had the right to enter the property to locate property lines, conduct engineering work, and reconstruct roads, all at his own expense. If Schroll needed more time to finalize the purchase, the option could be extended until December 1 if the following conditions were met:

- An immediate payment of a $5,000 deposit
- An acceptance that all improvements to the property valued more than $5,000 would be to the benefit of the Monterey Bay Redwood Company without compensation to Schroll if the Deed of Trust was not signed
- That Schroll could not cut or remove any timber except that necessary for road construction, and that no minerals, leaf mold, or timber could be removed from the property during the term of the option

After several months of delays, on September 24, Schroll was finally able to take action on the property and commissioned his field representative, Carl Nelson, to accompany Noel Patterson on a tour of the property. On the tour, Nelson made several important observations:

- The road through the property was drivable from one end to the other.
- Culverts had not been installed in all places where one was needed.
- The clearing of brush and debris in the vicinity of Badger Springs and on to the eastern boundary of the property (to today's Camp Loma on Highland Way) in order to prepare the area for eventual home and recreation development was nearly completed.
- The study to develop a water source on Rattlesnake Gulch's creek in Tract 1 north of Highland Way was completed. The system was planned to provide a gravity supply to the area between Badger Springs and the eastern boundary of the property, which was being cleared of brush and debris.
- There was discussion concerning building an access route from Soquel San Jose Road to north of Sugarloaf Mountain to reach the

western slope of Amaya Gulch.
- A study to erect a dam in Amaya Gulch near the High Bridge capable of impounding 4,000-acre-feet of water was completed.
- That over $5,000 in work had been performed clearing and repairing roads and that an extension of the Option to Buy was needed in order to prepare the roads for winter.
- That the Amaya Gulch section should be released to Schroll as soon as $200,000 was paid so that the dam could be constructed and the area developed in coordination with other interested parties. Nelson hoped to enter into lease agreements with other parties in order to cover the expense of constructing homes, building boating infrastructure, and erecting other recreational facilities. These plans had not been discussed or included in the Option to Buy agreement, but Nelson hoped both parties would look favorably on them.

A week later, on September 30, Schroll requested an extension of his Option to Buy under advice from Nelson. The extension, which was to February 1, 1960, was because Nelson was concerned that several miles of road were still subpar and that more culverts were needed to be installed before the start of winter.[153]

Nature Conservancy is given permission to operate in California

On July 18, 1957, the Nature Conservancy, a Washington, D.C.-based non-profit organization, applied for a Certificate of Qualification to operate within California. Its request was approved on December 7, 1959.

The organization was formed to:

- Preserve or aid in the preservation of all types of wild nature, including natural areas, features, objects, flora and fauna, and biotic communities.
- Establish nature reserves or other protected areas to be used for scientific, educational, and aesthetic purposes.
- Promote the conservation and proper use of our natural resources.

- Engage in or promote the study of plant and animal communities and of other phases of ecology, natural history, and conservation.
- Promote education in the fields of nature preservation and conservation.
- Cooperate with other organizations having similar or related objectives.

Several members of the organization would later prove instrumental in organizing The Forest of Nisene Marks State Park, including Donald Graeme Kelley, the organization's Western Regional Director; George L. Collins, the organization's president; and H. Putman "Put" Livermore, an attorney for Chickering & Gregory Law Firm, which handled the Marks family's relationship with the organization.[154]

Hannes Schroll applies for water rights to the East Branch of Soquel Creek

Hannes Schroll filed an appropriation with the State Water Rights Board in Sacramento on February 11, 1960 in order to draw up to 1,800-acre-feet of water from the East Branch of Soquel Creek for recreational and possibly industrial uses.

On March 13, an article appeared in the *Sentinel* concerning Schroll's potential purchase of the lands along the East Branch of Soquel Creek:

> *The 5,000 acres Monterey Bay Redwood company may be purchased and turned into a large year-round recreation center and homesites, it was learned last night.*
>
> *Hannes Schroll of Palo Alto, part-owner of Sugar Bowl ski resort, announced that he plans to buy the logged-off timber property for an estimated $500,000. James Harris III, company secretary, confirmed that Schroll has an option on the property.*
>
> *He reported that the latest extension of the option has been made to June.*
>
> *The vast property is located four miles beyond Soquel and runs from Olive Springs to Loma Prieta, covering the*

> *northern slope of the east branch of the Soquel watershed. Approximately 500 acres at the top of Loma Prieta is in Santa Clara county.*
>
> *Harris reported that full scale operation of the timberland ceased in 1942.*
>
> *Schroll explained that he plans to erect a dam and have a lake. He has not made definite plans on the facilities for the park.*
>
> *"I am wide open for ideas," Schroll stated. "I have not made up my mind."*
>
> *The Sugar Bowl owner expects the deal to be consummated "very soon."*
>
> *An application to the state water rights board for taking water from Soquel creek has been made out by Schroll. He is seeking 10.5 cubic feet per second and [1,]800 acre feet per year from the Soquel Creek, tributary to Monterey Bay. The estimated cost is $265,000.*
>
> *Lewis Nelson, chairman of the board of supervisors and representative of the Soquel district, said as a "routine" matter the directors (supervisors) of the county flood control and water conservation district will enter a protest.*
>
> *Schroll's plan for construction of a dam will not affect the proposed mid-county water district, he stated.*

On May 27, Noel Patterson wrote to L. K. Hill of the State Water Rights Board in Sacramento that it had come to the attention of the Monterey Bay Redwood Company's management that there were a number of water appropriations filed concerning the main Soquel Creek below the confluence of its East and West branches. Also, he heard that there were filings that had been made on a portion of the East Branch of Soquel Creek.

Patterson asked if it was possible to obtain a list of the persons granted rights to Soquel Creek water in order that the lumber company's management could properly plan the usage of the creek on its own land. On June 3, the water board sent a complete list of all of the applicants who had been granted or had applied to draw water from the creek and its branches. Three of the thirteen applications were noted as incomplete.

The California Water Commission had applied on September 24, 1958 to draw each year 6,800-acre-feet of water from Soquel Creek from below the confluence of the East and West branches, and 7,250-acre-feet from the latter branch above the confluence. The water was intended for irrigation, domestic, municipal, industrial, and recreational uses, while the 1,800-acre-feet requested by Schroll was planned for irrigation and recreational uses. It was likely because the State Water Rights Board rejected Schroll's proposed usage application that he withdrew his Option to Buy around August 1960.

As an afterthought to Schroll's inquiry about water rights, Patterson sent a letter to the State Water Rights Board on September 15 asking: "since [Schroll] is not the owner of the land that the water is to be withdrawn from and does not have an option any longer to purchase the land, could he still qualify as a user of the water?... Since his application has not been considered by your office and he is out of the picture in so far as his purchase of the land is concerned, what can be done to eliminate him as an applicant?" On September 23, the State Water Rights Board answered Patterson's inquiry, stating that, unless there is a reason to the contrary, any water rights action initiated by Schroll is personal and does not belong to the owner where use of the water is made, upon forfeiture, abandonment, or expiration of the option. On the other hand, if Schroll lost his option and is not granted access to the property, the board will not approve his application. The board instead will request that Schroll either cancel his application or assign it to the present owner of the property, if the owner wishes to continue with the application. Furthermore, the board assured Patterson that it would contact Schroll for his decision on the disposition of the application.[155]

Option to Buy agreement between the Monterey Bay Redwood Company and the Glenco Forest Products Company concerning land in the Augmentation

About midway through 1960, the Monterey Bay Redwood Company entertained another offer to purchase its property in the Augmentation. Headquartered in Sacramento, the Glenco Forest Products Company specialized in shooks (wood used in making boxes and barrels), lumber, cut stock, Pres-To-Logs, and sheet board. It was run by Curt F. Setzer and his two sons, Hardie Curt and Garner Cal. Although the Setzers were based in Sacramento, they owned a home in Santa Cruz.

While the preliminary Option to Buy agreement, dated August 15, 1960, closely resembled the two earlier agreements, it differed in two ways. First, the Monterey Bay Redwood Company management increased the asking price from $500,000 to $600,000. And second, the Hihn Railroad Grade was not included in the offer. The agreement would give Glenco the exclusive right and option to purchase the 5,000 acres for only one month—until September 15.

On October 13, the California Pacific Title & Trust Company received two deposit checks that totaled $25,000, a check from Curt Setzer for $12,500, and a second check for the same amount from Setzer's wife, Hazel. The deposits were made to secure all the land owned by the Monterey Bay Redwood Company, encompassing 5,118 acres, within Tract 1 (Rattlesnake Gulch), Tract 6 (Amaya Gulch), Tract 10 (Spignet Gulch), Tracts 11 and 25 (East Branch of Soquel Creek), and all interests, easements, and rights reserved in these properties. Despite being excluded from the Option to Buy, the Hihn Railroad Grade from the north side of Soquel Drive to the southern boundary of Tract 10 was also included in the transaction. The purchase was dependent on the widening of two roads through Kurt Roy's land from Olive Springs Road to Spignet Gulch to no less than 50 feet. At the time, the roads were 20 feet wide.

The price of the property was set at $505,000. Why the Monterey Bay Redwood changed its mind and reduced the price to just above Hannes Schroll's offer and included the railroad grade is unclear. A payment of $100,000, which included the $25,000 deposit, was due within two weeks of acceptance of the agreement. An additional payment of $100,000 was due on or before February 10, 1961. The remaining balance was to have a 5 percent annual interest rate and be paid in semi-annual installments of $30,500 plus interest beginning August 10, 1961 and subsequently occurring on February 10 and August 10 until the full amount was paid.

On October 28, the California Pacific Title & Trust Company received from Curt and Hazel Setzer a check totaling $75,000, which allowed the title company to sign a deposit receipt that signified that the Glenco Forest Products Company had met the first of several payments toward the purchase of the property.

The Setzers were quick to secure their newly acquired land rights. On November 11, Hardie Setzer wrote to attorney Eugene J. Adams in Santa Cruz requesting a release from the clause that restricted the cutting of timber until after the Deed of Trust was signed. Glenco wanted to undertake small-scale logging operations to salvage natural losses that were occurring throughout the tract. Setzer stated that, even though Glenco did not anticipate selling any part or parcel of the property at the time, it considered it wise to have a release clause added to the agreement that would allow for it. Setzer also requested that 1,000 acres of the property be released annually for sale.

On November 15, Adams sent Setzer's requests to the president of the Monterey Bay Redwood Company, James Harris, via Noel Patterson. The lumber company was in the process of dissolution and the liquidation of its assets was underway. Adams hoped that Glenco could benefit from this to accelerate its full purchase of the property, with its associated rights.

Three weeks later, on December 6, Setzer received a letter from Adams confirming the Monterey Bay Redwood Company's intent to revoke the timber-cutting clause from its deed. The letter clarified that all timber cutting would be in accordance with applicable forest practice rules and that no cutting would be allowed in the Badger Springs area (the 20 acres that included the Harris Grove), or within the grove of weeping redwoods in the vicinity of Sulphur Springs.

Regarding the request to sell up to 1,000 acres of land annually, the Monterey Bay Redwood Company rejected the proposal, noting the difficulty in subdividing the properties with their complex watersheds, topographies, access rights, and easements. Instead, the company agreed to consider each proposed land sale on an individual basis regardless of the size of the land under negotiation.[156]

From Exploitation to Preservation   1960 – 1961

The Monterey Bay Redwood Company liquidates its assets

On December 20, 1960, the Monterey Bay Redwood Company liquidated all of its remaining assets. All but 10 of the company's 4,969 shares were held by the Harris family. In reality, the company had ceased operating shortly after the start of World War II, when all the lumber in the yard was sold to the United States military. Most of the accessible old-growth redwood on its land had been cut and it would still be many years before the second-growth redwood would be ready to harvest. Beginning in 1946, most of the company's investors pulled out. Thus, in the end, the Monterey Bay Redwood Company was a Harris family operation with Noel Patterson handling finances and administration, when necessary.[157]

Western Title Insurance Company is contacted concerning H. M. Howard's Tract 7 in the Augmentation

On January 5, 1961, Don Thompson contacted the Western Title Insurance Company and offered to pay $7,000 and all associated costs for the 11.997 acres in Tract 7 in the Augmentation that the company held in trust for the deceased H. M. Howard. This property sat just to the north of the former Arden Forest subdivision.[158]

Land transfer from the Monterey Bay Redwood Company to the Glenco Forest Products Company regarding land in the Augmentation

Sometime before 1961, the Monterey Bay Redwood Company sold to an undetermined person around 144 acres along the eastern side of Tract 11 in the Augmentation between the top of Santa Rosalia Ridge and the East Branch of Soquel Creek. After the sale, the new owner built a small sawmill that served local residents into the mid-1980s.

On February 1, 1961, James Harris signed the deed that passed title to some 5,000 acres in the Augmentation that had been owned by the Monterey Bay Redwood Company to the Glenco Forest Products Company. When

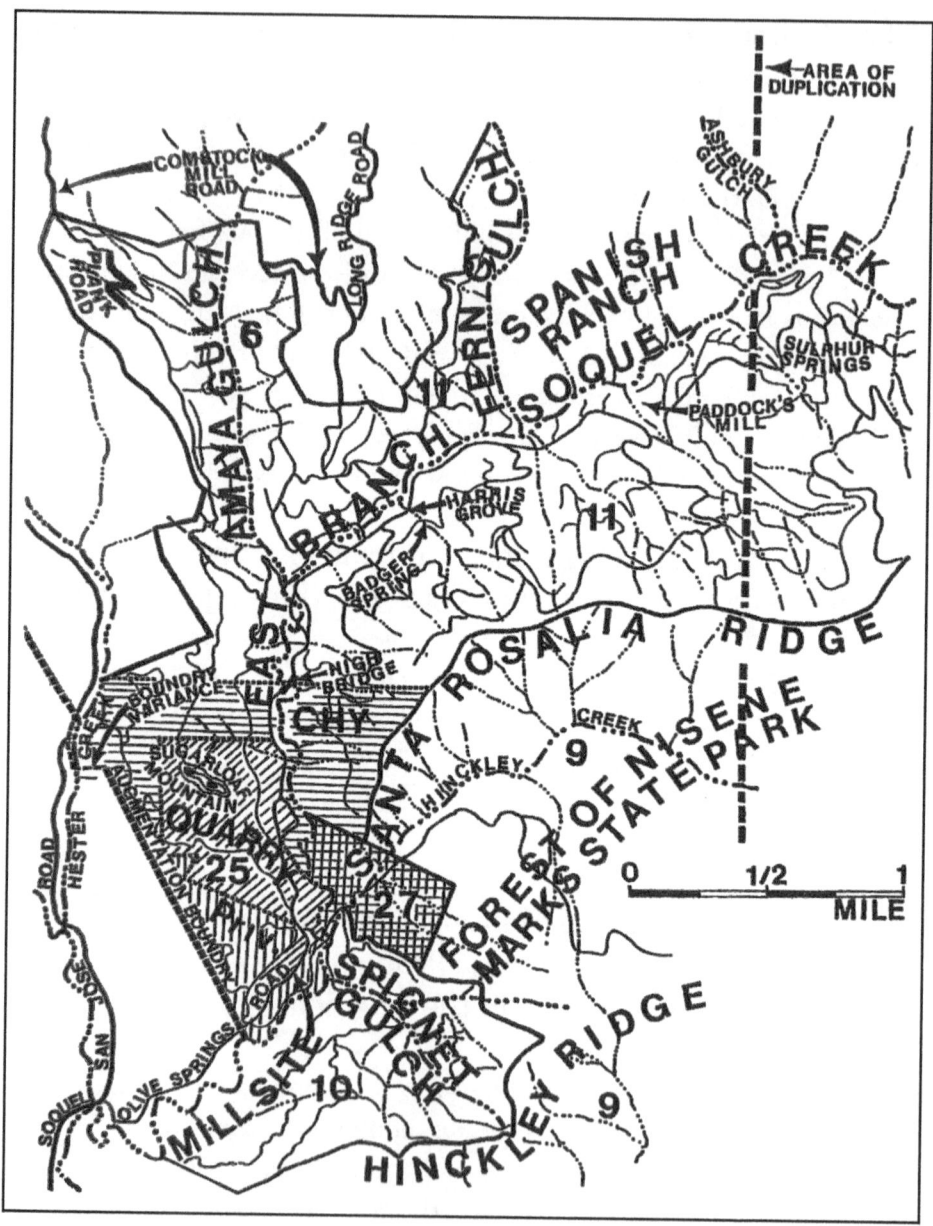

the deed was signed, a payment of $100,000 was passed to Harris, bringing the total amount due down to the agreed $305,000.

Not included in the 5,990 acres that the Monterey Bay Redwood Company purchased from Valencia–Hihn in 1925 were 283 acres in Tract

From Exploitation to Preservation — 1961

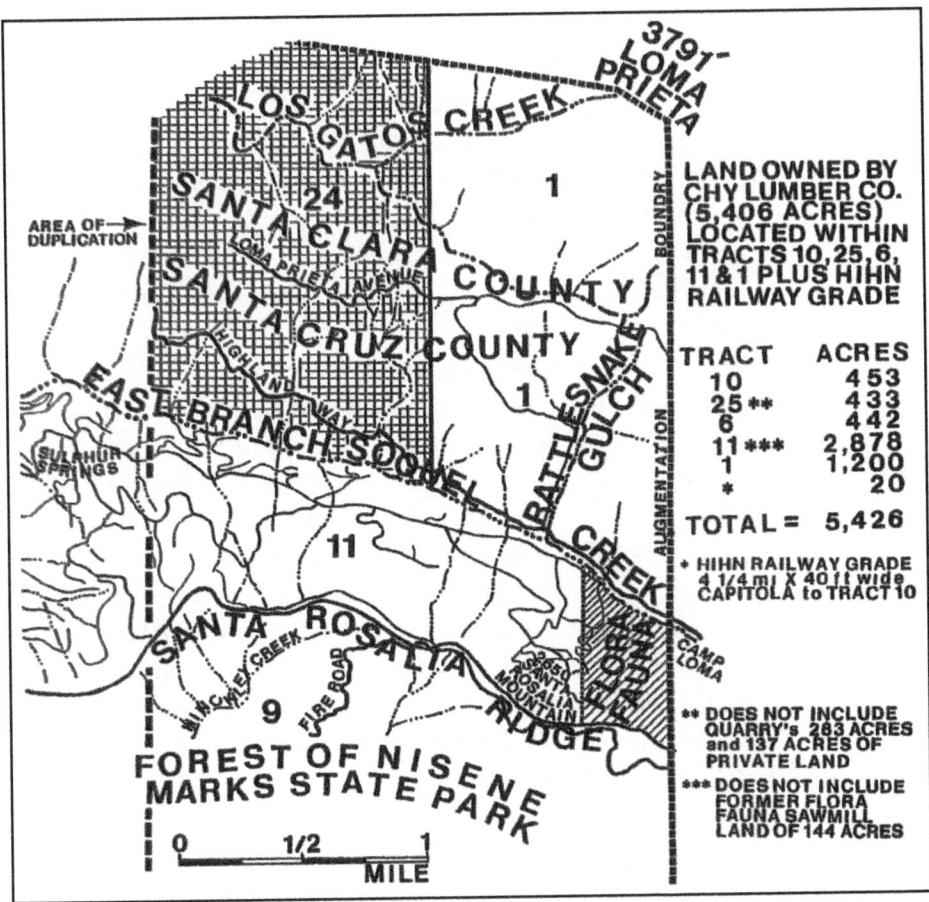

FIGURES 6.3-4 PROPERTY PURCHASED WITHIN THE AUGMENTATION FROM THE MONTEREY BAY REDWOOD COMPANY BY THE GLENCO FOREST PRODUCTS COMPANY

25 leased to the Olive Springs Quarry Company on May 1, 1953, and 137 acres that were later added to the 144 acres in Tract 11 owned by the mysterious pre-1961 buyer. This means that Glenco obtained 5,406 acres in the Augmentation, as well as 20 acres from the Hihn Railroad Grade, which was within the former Rancho Soquel.[159]

Horatio Ormsbee dies

On April 5, 1961, Horatio Ormsbee died at his home in Santa Cruz.

The *Sentinel* reported:

> Horatio N. Ormsbee, 77, a native of Michigan and a resident of Capitola for more than 55 years, died yesterday in a local nursing home after a short illness. He was a retired forest engineer and had been associated with the California division of forestry for many years. Deeply interested in forestry and water conservation, he was the first chairman of the Santa Cruz county water committee.
>
> He was graduated from Phillips Exeter academy in New Hampshire and his parents, long time Vermont residents, had come by way of Wisconsin and Minnesota to Michigan where he was raised.
>
> His wife, Mable Chase Ormsbee, whom he married in Greenville, Mich., in 1908, preceded him in death in 1954. His only son, Lieut. Sidney C. Ormsbee, was killed in action in Messina, Italy, in 1943, when he was 27 years old. The Sid Ormsbee lookout on Pinion mountain in Monterey county was named in his honor.
>
> Ormsbee was greatly interested in family history and took much pride in family portraits which were painted by Benjamin Franklin Mason, noted Vermont artist. Among these is a painting of his grandfather, Samuel Belknap, which is dated 1828.
>
> He is survived by a niece, Mrs. Mary O. Free of Bakersfield; three cousins in New Canaan, Conn., and other nieces and nephews.

Ormsbee had been instrumental in surveying and cruising the lands of the F. A. Hihn Company in the Augmentation in 1916. He also oversaw the construction of the Monterey Bay Redwood Company's mill on Soquel Creek in the mid-1920s and facilitated the eventual acquisition of Tract 10 by Allen Rispin in 1927. In 1929 and 1937, he was one of the principal advocates for the creation of Loma Prieta State Park, the earliest known attempts to create a large nature preserve in the Santa Cruz Mountains between Soquel Creek and the Pajaro River.[160]

Marks family offers to sell land in the Augmentation for a state park

As their debts accumulated and their hunt for oil in both Santa Cruz and Monterey Counties proved fruitless, the Marks family began considering ways they could repay their debt while retaining some of their potentially oil-rich land. Their solution was to try and sell their land in Santa Cruz County to the California Department of Parks & Recreation for the creation of a state park.

On September 9, 1961, Herman Marks wrote to Charles DeTurk, the chief of the Beaches & Parks division. He offered to sell the Arden Forest (Tract 7), Hinckley Gulch and the Aptos Forest (Tract 9), as well as 610 acres in Tract 10, to the state for the proposed park. He set the price for the Arden Forest at $410,000, while he pledged to gift the remainder to the state so long as it remained in a primitive state.

Marks later met with Charles Mehlert, the planner for Beaches & Parks. During their meeting, Mehlert convinced Marks to allow camping within Tract 8 and around Buzzard Lagoon, two properties that were not originally included in his offer. Marks confirmed the changes to his offer in a letter to DeTurk dated October 11.[161]

James Harris Jr. dies

Less than a year after the Monterey Bay Redwood Company was dissolved and its properties sold to Glenco, James Harris, Jr., died on October 14, 1961. His later life proved somewhat tragic. He spent seventeen years through the Great Depression trying hard to make a profit from his lumber company, and then he spent another eighteen years trying to sell the property for a profit. Yet when the property was finally sold, he had no time to reap the fruits of his labor.

The *Sentinel* reported after his death:

> *James Armstrong Harris Jr., owner of the Monterey Bay Water company for the past 17 years, died yesterday evening at a local hospital after a lengthy illness. He was 74.*

A longtime resident of Santa Cruz, Harris came to Santa Cruz in 1925 as organizer and president of the Monterey Bay Redwood company. He was well known throughout the area.

Harris was born on October 31, 1886 in Cleveland, Ohio. He was the son of James A. Harris and Mabel Almira White. He is survived by his widow, Margaret Dodge Harris, and three children, James A. Harris III and Francis M. Harris of Santa Cruz, and Mrs. Arthur D. Magee of Buffalo, New York. He is also survived by seven grandchildren.

Harris was a charter member of the Pogonip Polo club, St. Francis and Santa Cruz Yacht clubs, a member of the Elks lodge, former commander of Santa Cruz American Legion Post 64, and former commander of the 13th district of the American Legion.[162]

Parks & Recreation Department rejects Marks family's offer of land for a state park

On October 17, 1961, Herman Marks received a letter from Charles DeTurk thanking him for his generous offer. However, despite his own desire to obtain the property, he was forced to decline the offer of land since the department was not in a position to make acquisitions outside of its current schedule. He hoped that a bond measure going to vote in November 1962 would allow for more funds to be allocated to land acquisitions and development programs. DeTurk concluded by promising Marks that his department would study the property and consider it for future acquisition.[163]

Chapter 7

~

Marked for Posterity

Nature Conservancy accepts Marks family's plan for a state park in the Augmentation

After the Department of Parks & Recreation rejected his proposal for a state park in the hills above Aptos and Soquel, Herman Marks, via Don Thompson, contacted the Nature Conservancy and presented a new plan. A meeting was held after which members of the Conservancy took a tour of the property. It appears that the members liked what they saw.

On October 28, 1961 in Washington, D.C., the board of governors of the Conservancy met. President George L. Collins and Doris F. Leonard, an officer in the National and Regional program of the group, proposed a resolution to create a park from the Marks family's property. They resolved:

> *WHEREAS, the Board of Governors has been informed through members of the Nature Conservancy living in California that the Marks family properties of some 9,700 acres in Santa Cruz County are, through the generosity of the*

family, available for a public park at a small fraction of their commercial value, and

WHEREAS, these properties are an outstanding example of the natural conditions rapidly being overwhelmed by the growth of population in the San Francisco area, therefore...

BE IT RESOLVED that the Board of Governors in principle favors establishing a State Park on the Marks tract and desires to record its appreciation of the public spirit manifested by the members of the Marks family (Resolution No. 156-61).

On December 7, John H. Knight, the Deputy Director for the California Department of Parks & Recreation, wrote to Marks thanking him for his family's gift of 1,000 acres in the Black Mountain area near Salinas. This area did not become part of the State Park system; instead, it became part of Toro County Park.

Regarding the offer of land in the Augmentation, Knight wrote:

Concerning your Santa Cruz County proposal, we find ourselves in a particularly awkward position. While it is a wonderful offer of an outstanding area, because it is not offered as a gift, our acceptance would require an expenditure of State funds, funds which at the moment we do not have and that can only be obtained through budgetary processes. We are also faced with another problem that Santa Cruz County is on record as opposing the removing of additional lands from the tax rolls for park purposes. In order to obtain funds no matter how slight the amount in proportion to the value to be received, we must supply the controlling agency with operating costs, development costs, public benefits to be derived, and many other facts which can only be arrived at through land use and development studies.

The preceding are in progress and we are hopeful that funds will be made available through the use of bond money. This proposal is currently being examined by an Interim Committee and will be subject to the deliberation of the Legislature during the coming session.

At the same time, George Collins was in San Francisco organizing a field trip into the land owned by the Marks family in Santa Cruz County. The tour happened on December 14 and included members of both the Park & Recreation Department and the Nature Conservancy. Collins and Leonard summarized their findings in a letter to Walter S. Boardman, executive director of the Conservancy, and Donald Graeme Kelley, Western Regional Director, dated December 19:

> *On December 14, 1961 the following people met at Aptos to discuss the proposed State Park: Herman Marks, of Salinas, J. Don Thompson, of Salinas, the personal representative of Herman Marks, Charles Mehlert, of Monterey, Recreation Planner for the State Division of Beaches and Parks, Mrs. Richard M. Leonard and George L. Collins, of San Francisco, Conservation Associates, John R. McDaniel, of Carmel, Chairman of the Nature Conservancy, Monterey Bay Chapter, Richard Swan and Ned Graves, of Carmel, members of the Monterey Bay Chapter of the Nature Conservancy.*
>
> *The group toured the land under discussion for several hours, observing its resources and its potential utilization as a park. It is impossible for a qualified parkman to see this area and to think of it in relation to the California Public Outdoor Recreation Plan and the San Francisco Bay–Monterey Bay expanding populations, without becoming enthusiastic over its park qualities; and appreciative of the deep sense of obligation Mr. Marks shows toward his fellow man in his determination to place the area in the public hands to be preserved forever as a cultural heritage.*
>
> *Mr. John R. McDaniel, acting in his capacity as Chairman of the Nature Conservancy, Monterey Bay Chapter, is the person whose understanding and initiative, together with the help of his associates in the Nature Conservancy, brought Herman Marks initially into the State Park proposal, together with Mr. Mehlert and other officials of the State Division of Beaches and Parks. Thus, the Nature Conservancy has a strong local supporting role in the proposal. This has brought the three members of Conservation Associates into the effort,*

as Mrs. Leonard and Mr. Collins are active officers in the National and Regional programs of the Nature Conservancy. All three members of Conservation Associates are in constant touch with the State Park and Recreation authorities on a variety of affairs. Mrs. Varian is deeply involved in the work of completing the Castle Rock and Big Basin projects, located only a few miles from the Marks project area.

On the day after the tour, Mr. Collins talked to Mr. John Knight, Deputy Director of the Department of Parks & Recreation in Sacramento, about the Marks State Park proposal. This was the latest in a series of discussions in person and over the telephone, with Director Charles DeTurk, Deputy Director John Knight, and others, which Leonard and Collins have had concerning the proposal. Mr. Knight reported that no money is available now for acquisition of the Marks land. He has explored all of the possibilities, he believes. The State Department of Finance offers no encouragement as to immediate availability of funds. A suggestion was made to Mr. Knight that if the State could find even a few thousand dollars with which to begin acquisition of the Arden Forest, as a token of intention, that might serve as a sufficient State commitment to this particular park proposal to establish interest and confidence in the proposal on the part of private sources of funds which could be induced to option the land, or even to buy it outright from Mr. Marks, then hold it until the State can pay for it.

Mr. Knight explained that even if the State could find some money for this purpose, they could not spend it without Legislative approval. He said the State, through his Department, can take options for lands for parks provided they involve no cost to the State. In other words, if private funds could be raised with which to pay Mr. Marks for an option, then Mr. Marks could give such option to the State and the State then would be as nearly as possible committed to follow through with the proposal. But the State could never pay back the cost of the option, as such. As State land acquisition money becomes available (through legislative appropriation, *a bond issue, or in any manner carrying legislative approval) the land can be bought, of course.*

Mr. Knight explained a growing awareness among legislators and other State officials for the need to take advantage of special opportunities, such as we have in this case, that may be lost if not acted upon promptly. He reported a talk he had on the 15th of December with Department of Finance authorities. This was immediately following the call made to him by Leonard and Collins. The forthcoming session of the Legislature beginning next month will be a budget session. The Department of Parks & Recreation has to have its budget ready very soon.

Since a budget session is not allowed to run beyond mid-March, Mr. Knight's Department will know by sometime in April or May whether a bond issue in aid of land acquisition for parks is authorized for submission to vote of the people in November, and what general or appropriated money they are going to have for the ensuing two years, and can begin negotiating expenditures. Actual cash is not available for payment until July 1. Mr. Knight is a man of long experience, well and very favorably known to many of us for his knowledge and good judgment.

Meanwhile action needs to be taken. The State must be reminded constantly of the importance of official authorization of the Marks property as a State Park project, so that funds when available can be invested by the State in all phases of the undertaking.

Following the tour of the Marks property on the 14th of December, Mr. Richard M. Leonard, leading conservationist, who has had a great deal of experience with land matters in his various legal capacities, was asked to review and advise in the State Park proposal. Although Mr. Leonard at this writing has not seen the property, he is wholly in accord with the State Park proposal on the basis of reports he had had, and urges quick action to guard against loss of the property to other purposes in view of the possibility of sudden changes in the Marks family situation. He believes this to be an un-

usually challenging opportunity for any organization willing to take the initiative and the lead in this proposal, remembering that the State cannot guarantee to do anything that will cost money until authority and means are provided by the Legislature. He states, looking at the matter realistically, that because time is so much of the essence, it would be best to consider the possibility of an intermediary acquiring and holding the property (possibly for several years because there is no assurance that the State can act promptly).

It is Mr. Leonard's thoughts that ideally one organization should carry the entire enterprise, rather than to spread the responsibility between several conservation groups, or foundations, or others. Thus, if it is determined for example that a loan of half a million dollars or less should be obtained by some public spirited group in aid of the proposal, that agency should also expect to raise money in future years to meet interest payments, taxes, and any other costs pending payment for the property by the State. Others could be expected to assist the one selected to be chiefly responsible, of course, but banking and other principal business he believes best be conducted through the one agency. This could be the Nature Conservancy, one of the foundations, or any other qualified tax-exempt organization.

Mr. Leonard has indicated, based upon his constant business relationships with financial groups, that in his opinion if land values are as great as indicated, no great difficulty would be encountered in obtaining a loan in an amount sufficient to pay off Mr. Marks and hold the land until it can be put into the hands of the State.

As far back as 1945, sixteen years ago, the land alone, some 9,752 acres, was appraised at $526,000, or $54 per acre. The timber at that time was valued at $344,600. These totals were arrived at by Horatio N. Ormsbee. Mr. Marks told the group on the 14th of December that he has an offer of more than $3,000,000 for the whole property, land and timber. This figures at about $300 per acre. Mr. Marks and Mr. Don Thompson commented at that time that some of the land is valued today at from $400 to $600 per acre, depending upon specific location. There can be no question as to the adequacy of the property's value as collateral for a loan. The market value appears to be far in excess of the $410,000 Mr. Marks has to have for it (as is fully recognized).

Mr. Leonard in discussing possible courses of actions, suggests consideration of a two-year renewable loan to the Nature Conservancy on the basis of paying interest only (nothing on principal) during that time unless, of course, the State should be in a position to allocate the money for acquisition during that period, in which case the whole obligation could be retired. Again thinking realistically, however, it is only common sense to plan on having to hold the property privately for several years as there is no assurance of quick action on the part of the State, however desirous the State authorities may be of having the Marks area for a State Park.

Mr. Leonard observes that for such a public purpose as is contemplated in this case a financing agency might be able to justify a waiver on payment of principal during a two year period, and that the loan might be renewed on the same basis. Interest would run to some $20,000 per year on a loan large enough to handle the transaction. In addition, there would be taxes and possibly other recurring costs, so that annual carrying charges might well be on the order of $30,000. The longer the loan period the higher the ultimate cost to the State, because the intermediary should recover all outlay in order to be in strong financial position to handle similar public-benefit opportunities in the future. Mr. Leonard and Mr. Collins will explore the question further with Mr. Leonard and some of the financial authorities in San Francisco.

The following procedure is suggested...

Select an intermediary, possibly the Nature Conservancy, willing to be responsible for a loan in an amount sufficient to buy the property, and carry it until the decision on the proposed bond issue is made by the Legislature and the voters, or money is appropriated from general funds, or some other source of funds is found. Presumably the decisions on *these matters as far as the State is concerned will be made by the Legislature during the next three months, as the Budget Session ends in March.*

Support the State Department of Parks & Recreation in the plea before the Legislature for furtherance of the proposed bond issue in aid of Parks and Recreation in California. Leonard and Collins already are working diligently on this matter, as individuals, together with other local conservationists.

Signed by George L. Collins and Doris F. Leonard.[164]

Letter from Don Thompson to Senator Frederick Farr

On February 2, 1962, Don Thompson, on behalf of the Marks family, wrote a letter to Frederick Farr, state senator for the 25th District in Monterey County, calling to his attention the item in the governor's budget for the acquisition of the 9,700 acres in the Augmentation for use as a state park. Thompson wrote:

> *This property is owned by the Marks family of Salinas and they have turned down an offer of 4,000,000 for the land. They are offering timber land to the State for a park and all they are asking is about $450,000 for the Arden Forest land with the balance of the land to be given to the State as a gift.*
>
> *Also, as you probably know, these people are now in the process of giving their Carmel Highland property as an addition to the Point Lobos State Reserve and 20 acres to the Saint Johns College.*

Curiously, Thompson gave Farr an amount of $4,000,000 as the value of the land, while Marks had told the group in December that the amount was only $3,000,000. Thompson concluded his letter by asking the senator to support the appropriation of funds for the acquisition of the land in the budget bill, to be approved the following week.

Farr answered Don Thompson's letter on March 20, stating that: "there is no item in this year's budget to purchase the Marks family property, and that he has been advised by the Division of Parks & Recreation that there are no funds presently available for the project." The senator concluded by recommending that the Nature Conservancy buy the property and hold it until the state has the necessary funding. The letter ends with the following: "I am most interested in this project, and I shall give it my whole-hearted support."[165]

Don Thompson meets with Put Livermore

In early March 1962, Don Thompson discussed the matter of the Marks' property in the Augmentation with Put Livermore, an attorney from Chickering & Gregory who was assigned to work on the sale on behalf of the Nature Conservancy. On March 4, Thompson sent Livermore a preliminary report concerning the sale of the Arden Forest (Tract 7) property. Until this report was received, the Conservancy was unable to begin the transaction.[166]

Nature Conservancy submits an Option Agreement to purchase Tract 7 in the Augmentation

On March 14, 1962, Edward F. Dolder, chief of Beaches and Parks for the Parks & Recreation Department, reiterated in a letter to Don Thompson that it was unfortunate that the state could not move more rapidly toward accepting the generous offer made by the Marks family. He also stated that California did not have the funds at the time and it would take several months to clear up all the red tape in order to accept the gift of the land of the former Loma Prieta Lumber Company and Hopkins Estate. Consequently, he recommended that, in addition to selling the Arden Forest to the Nature Conservancy, the remainder of the property be gift deeded to the Conservancy with the understanding that the state would acquire all of it as soon as the red tape was cleared and funds appropriated for its protection. The state would continue to work with the Conservancy toward eventual acquisition of the Arden Forest, on which rested the deed of trust.

In an effort to move the matter along, Put Livermore sent to Thompson and Herman Marks a proposed Option Agreement for the purchase of the Arden Forest by the Nature Conservancy on March 16. The agreement included a clause that put a six-month time limit on the purchase, which Livermore said he would try to reduce.

A week later, on March 24, Thompson replied to Livermore with a revised copy of the agreement, which now included the sale of the entire 9,700 acres to the Nature Conservancy. The Marks family insisted on retaining mineral and oil rights for the property since Herman still had a few locations where he wanted to drill a test bore. Thompson promised that "this should be for a short time only." He added that, "as the Aptos Road is the only way to the railroad for pipelines, this will have to be reserved." Furthermore, "concerning the Hinckley Gulch and Aptos areas, both are to be kept in their natural state, while the Arden Forest and the two Timothy Hopkins areas are to be limited to campsites and minimum developments."

The Conservancy sent a check for $500 on March 30 to secure the Option to Purchase. The check included the first written reference to the proposed park's name: The Forest of Nesine Marks.

The matter of oil and mineral rights would not be resolved easily. The Conservancy did not like the idea of oil pipes possibly following the route of the access road. In a series of letters exchanged between April 9 and 12, it proposed that any pipelines should exit the Augmentation via the shortest and most direct route once the locations for the test bores were determined.[167]

Letter from Diane Cooley to Don Thompson concerning Tract 8 in the Augmentation

On April 9, 1962, Don Thompson received a letter from Diane Cooley concerning 42/100s of an acre of land in Tract 8 of the Augmentation that Timothy Hopkins had deeded to her great grandparents, John and Fanny Porter, in 1894. This was not the first contact between Cooley and Thompson. The first was in October 1961 when Thompson sent a letter to Cooley, who lived in Connecticut at the time, offering to purchase her property. In her reply, Cooley revealed that she was unaware of the property and, "since I am no longer in the Monterey Bay area and have no current knowledge of property values there, I would be interested in your estimated evaluation of the property you mention. I shall look forward to your response so that we may continue a more informed discussion of this matter."

This property was the Porter House in the former Compound area of the village of Loma Prieta. Throughout the 1890s, Warren Porter and his family had lived there during the lumber season. Although the Porters were supposed to return the land to Timothy Hopkins once logging ended on Aptos Creek, they had not done so and Hopkins never tried to take it from them. It had remained in the Porter family's possession for over seventy years. However, with the impending transfer of Tract 8 to the state as part of the Marks family's gift, it was necessary to settle unresolved land claims such as that of the Porters.

On April 18, Thompson sent his reply to Cooley. He summarized recent events in the Augmentation and estimated that the value of her land within the Augmentation was probably around $500. After bringing the Nature Conservancy into the conversation in May, Thompson and Cooley agreed to a higher price on May 28, raising the value of the land to $1,500.[168]

Letter to Don Thompson from Wells Fargo Bank & Union Trust Company concerning oil and mineral rights in the Augmentation

Shortly after the Nature Conservancy agreed to purchase the Arden Forest, Don Thompson wrote to Wells Fargo Bank & Union Trust Company offering to purchase on behalf of the Marks family the bank's claims to mineral and oil rights within the Augmentation. In a letter dated April 6, 1962, he offered to pay $5.50 per acre to purchase the rights contingent upon receipt of payment from the Conservancy.

On April 24, the bank replied that they had obtained approval to sell the rights that the trustees of the Loma Prieta Lumber Company and the Hopkins Estate held within the Augmentation. Their clients agreed to the recommended price, which amounted to a total cost of $35,200. However, the bank did not feel that the transaction should be contingent on the sale of the land to the Conservancy. They preferred to enter into a regular escrow with a time limit of not more than 90 days.

The next day, Thompson submitted a personal check for $3,520 to the bank on behalf of the Marks family. Herman Marks promised in a letter to pay the remaining balance within 90 days and stated that he had opened an escrow account with the Western Title Guarantee Company of Salinas.[169]

California State Park Commission votes to use bond money to purchase the Marks family's land in the Augmentation

In San Leandro on May 17, 1962, the State Park Commission voted in favor of acquiring the Marks family's land in the Augmentation for use as a state park by using bond money. With the passage of this resolution, the eventual incorporation of the property into the state park system was assured.

Earl P. Hanson, deputy chief of the Division of Beaches and Parks, notified the Nature Conservancy on May 28 of the successful vote. He wrote: "I wish to thank you for the extremely effective contribution of time, effort and effective action by your organization in assuring that this fine property will be available to the State of California as a unit of the state's park system."

Four days later, on June 1, the Conservancy passed a resolution:

> *RESOLUTION: APTOS FOREST PROJECT*
> *It was moved by Commissioner Harriam that the following resolution be adopted:*
> <u>WHEREAS</u>, *Miss Agnes Marks, and Messrs. Herman Marks and Andrew Marks have offered properties in the County of Santa Cruz totaling some 9,750 acres to be acquired for park purposes as a memorial to their mother, Mrs. Nesine Marks, at an extremely generous price; and*
> <u>WHEREAS</u>, *The staff of the Division of Beaches and Parks has worked with Mr. Herman Marks, has examined the property and finds it extremely suitable for park purposes; and*
> <u>WHEREAS</u>, *The Nature Conservancy became interested through Conservation Associates and has acquired this property in order to assure its availability when State funds can be appropriated for its purchase;*
> <u>NOW, THEREFORE, BE IT RESOLVED</u> *that the California State Park Commission approves in principle the*

concept of the Aptos Forest Project, and
BE IT FURTHER RESOLVED that the appreciation of the Park Commission be expressed to the Marks family, Conservation Associates and to Nature Conservancy for their generosity in offering and assuring that this outstanding project become a portion of the State Park System.
Seconded by Commissioner Stern and approved[170]

Letter from the Parks & Recreation Department to the Nature Conservancy concerning the Marks family's refusal to identify potential oil drilling sites

On July 17, 1962, Edward Dolder of the Beaches and Parks unit of the Department of Parks & Recreation wrote to Put Livermore to express his concern that the Conservancy and the state might not be seeing eye-to-eye regarding the Marks' property in the Augmentation. He wrote:

the law is quite clear in the manner in which minerals may be reserved from the lands that are acquired by the state for park purposes. While minerals may be reserved to the grantor and exploited, they must be extracted from beneath the surface of the ground since drilling or removing minerals by other means may not be done from the surface. Up to this point, I believe, all are informed as it is well understood that drill sites are being selected.

The real problem that all may not be fully informed upon is that the state cannot own these drill sites in fee. They will have to be held by the owner or Nature Conservancy since the state may not accept title. Therefore, in our opinion it is paramount that these sites be determined so no surveys may be made and legal descriptions established. The drill sites, in whatever number there are, may be recorded as exceptions together with easements thereto. The easements, however, may be reservations with the state owning the underlying fee. You can understand why it would be difficult to prepare the necessary maps required and establish a legal description for deed purposes without the identity of these sites since there would be no way to describe the exceptions.

Time is passing rapidly and insofar as the state is concerned in order to prepare maps and descriptions which would be acceptable to us from the Nature Conservancy, it would appear that the first order would have to be the establishment of these sites.[171]

Letter from the Western Title Insurance Company to Don Thompson concerning Tract 7 in the Augmentation

On July 23, 1962, the Western Title Insurance Company, which held the 11.997 acres in Tract 7 for the late H. M. Howard in trust, notified Don Thompson that it had received the necessary authorization from the family to sell the land at the agreed price of $7,000.[172]

Rights transfer from Wells Fargo Bank & Union Trust Company to the Marks family regarding oil and mineral rights in the Augmentation

On July 24, 1962, the deed was signed by Wells Fargo Bank & Union Trust Company management in which title to its oil and mineral rights within the Augmentation was sold to the Marks family. The total number of acres of rights that changed ownership in this deed was about 6,526.[173]

Deed of Trust between the Marks family and the Nature Conservancy concerning land in the Augmentation

After several years of hard work, the day that Herman, Andrew, and Agnes Marks had been waiting for finally arrived on August 3, 1962. Following behind-the-scenes negotiations with several parties and a substantial loan from Wells Fargo, the Nature Conservancy obtained control of the Marks family's 9,803 acres within the Augmentation, encompassing the Arden Forest (Tract 7), Bridge Creek (Tract 10), Hinckley Gulch and the Aptos Forest (Tracts 8 and 9), the west side of Buzzard Lagoon, and the right-of-way through Rancho Aptos. The Marks family retained oil and mineral rights for the time being.

Included in the deed of trust were clauses that established campsites on Aptos Creek between the southern boundary of the Augmentation and the Porter House (along the Loma Prieta Grade Trail north of the old sawmill site). These would be used as one of the arguments against building the dam on Aptos Creek since this land would be inundated according to the plan. The Marks also agreed that the total acreage that would be devoted to oil exploration drilling would not exceed 50 acres across an area spanning a few hundred acres, although these drilling sites had still not been decided upon.

Shortly after the deed was signed, Don Thompson gave the following speech at an unspecified event:

> *This must be saved for the generations yet to come, so that they will know that we have known, and there's so little time to do it. These words, spoken a decade ago by a kindly man, named Herman Marks, in whom was installed a great love of nature, were the seeds of an idea developed from a dream to full accomplishment.*
>
> *Agnes, Herman and Andrew Marks, brothers and sister, were brought up from early childhood with a great reverence for nature. Their life story, commencing with their father and mother, is one that may only be heard in America. As in many American families their parents came to America as immigrants and lived through the years when history was being made in the states of California and Arizona. After living in several areas, the family settled near Salinas, California, where they established the family home. The deed to this first family home is now known as Toro Park. At the age of 34, the mother was left a widow with four small children and a mortgage on the farm which seemed impossible to pay off in those days of hardship when eggs were selling for 25 cents for three dozen and butter at 10 cents a pound. But by hard work and thrift, the family grew up to see the debt load paid off. Before she passed away, at age of 96, she had the satisfac-*

tion of knowing that her three remaining children had built up earthly possessions which would ensure them of comfort in their later years, but most of all, a love of God and all his creations of nature.

The attempt to realize the ambition of the Marks family, in saving a beautiful area in Santa Cruz County, required sacrifices in money and doing without many things, but it was worth it. This magnificent area of 9,700 acres is a typical coast range mountain land, heavily forested with redwoods, fir, oak and many other trees. Much of it is rugged and steep, broken by canyons of live streams with many flat meadows and benches of level land and easy slopes.

The Marks family had many tempting offers of tremendous profits from lumber and development people who saw the potential value of the property, but even when money was scarce, the Marks looked forward to the day when they could realize their dreams.

As they were all in their seventies, they decided, about a year ago, that the time had come for them to culminate their work. The State of California Department of Natural Resources was contacted and a study made by park officials who all agreed, emphatically, that the state must have this area because of its superlative scenery, its scientific and recreational potential and its location near the burgeoning metropolitan areas which are devouring the natural landscape at an unbelievable rate. After detailed research, it was concluded that the state would take over. There was one hurdle, which at the time deemed insurmountable. The Marks still owed money on the property and the state would not have funds to pay the debt until after the November elections, and only then if the voters decided in favor of a $5-million bond issue to aid in land acquisition for State Park development. About this time, after meeting with many conservation-minded people, the problem was solved.

As may always be found in America, even in the hurry and scurry to get ahead in the world, there are people yet be found who will take time out to work for a worthy cause. Such a group was found in the Nature Conservancy, a non-profit membership organization, dedicated to the preservation, in the natural state, of biologically or geologically significant example of the American landscape. They are supported by members with dues and contributions and individuals with gifts and bequests of money and land and, lastly, through foundations with grants from funds at their disposal. With headquarters in Washington D.C., and a branch office in Berkeley, California, it operates across the United States with official representation in many states and sixteen state chapters.

The Nature Conservancy has now secured an option on the Marks property and will borrow the funds to pay off the deed of trust, with the lands thus held until such time as the State of California may repay the Conservancy, and acquire another addition to its outstanding park and beach recreation system. It is stipulated that the greater part of the 9,700 acres will be kept as a primitive area with no access except hiking trails and fire protective roads. Two areas on the outer boundaries will be devoted to public campsites and administration and protection centers. Thus, in the future, there will be present, for untold generations, a great natural area from which may be viewed the Pacific Ocean and the majesty of nature.

Thus, the dreams and ambitions of the pioneer family will soon be realized. The great park, to be known as "The Forest of Nisene Marks," ensuring that nature in all her beauty will be preserved for millions yet to be born.

This unassuming family will continue with their daily chores, Herman, taking care of business details and developing rare plants; Andrew, supervising the operation of a large ranch and studying natural resources; and Agnes, doing the household chores and keeping the books.

Certainly the mother, Nisene, looking down upon her children may well be proud of them.

In closing, here are the words of Herman Marks: "We want no thanks—we are repaying God for his generosity to us. All we ask from the world is that they love, protect and enjoy nature."[174]

Diane Cooley rejects offer to sell her property in Tract 8 in the Augmentation

On August 31, 1962, Don Thompson wrote to Diane Cooley regarding the Porter family's property in Tract 8 of the Augmentation. In the letter, he informed Cooley that her land was now surrounded by Nature Conservancy property and that it was to be turned into a state park. Furthermore, he informed her that a section had already been allocated as a picnic area named in memory of Warren Porter's wife, Mary Easton. In her reply, Cooley was disinterested in selling the property despite living in Connecticut and never having seen it. Thompson and Herman Marks decided to leave the matter to the state when it acquired the surrounding land from the Conservancy.[175]

Don Kelley writes about The Forest of Nisene Marks

On September 12, 1962, Don Kelley of the Nature Conservancy wrote an unpublished newspaper article on the topic of The Forest of Nisene Marks:

> *Because a 14-year-old Danish girl came to California in 1873 with an innate love of nature, the Golden State will soon have a major addition to its chain of parks. The ninety years between the arrival of the girl named Nisine and the soon-to-be-realized dedication of the 9,750-acre "Forest of Nisine Marks" have witnessed a familiar pattern of land use and abuse. But in this mountainous part of southern Santa Cruz County about two hours drive from San Francisco, thanks to Nisine's three living children and the love of unspoiled land she gave them, the pattern has been broken. For Herman, Andrew, and Agnes Marks, now all around the 80-year point in their pioneering life on Monterey Bay, have refused to sell the land their mother cherished to developers for sums ranging upwards to four million dollars. Instead, they have offered it to the State and people of California, through The Nature Conservancy, for just $410,000, which is principally to cover certain outstanding obligations on the land itself. (The Marks family's generous spirit is further ex-*

emplified by their outright gift, not long ago, of 120 acres for an addition to the celebrated Point Lobos State Park which has been called one of the world's most beautiful meetings of land and water. The family had been offered $300,000 for this property).

Much California history is woven into the story of the Marks' Santa Cruz County tract, which includes the Aptos Forest, far-flung across the ridges north of Aptos and Soquel, east of the old San Jose Road. In 1769 the Portola expedition camped in this vicinity—the year before Monterey was founded. Father Juan Crespi's diary mentions unfamiliar trees that dominated a magnificent flora new to the world; we recognize these as the redwoods, Douglas firs, oaks, madrones, California laurel, and others so characteristic of the Coast Ranges in these latitudes. Parts of the Aptos Forest were logged in the following century, after the grant of the old Soquel Rancho in 1844 to Martina Castro. But by the time Nisine Marks' children had begun to acquire parcels of the Rancho's rugged, stream-cut uplands, the forest had sprung back in all its virginal beauty, and this their mother had known.

She had married a teacher, Benjamin Marks. In 1893 he died and she was left not only with their young children but with heavy indebtedness on their Monterey ranch property. She lived until 1956. In her 97th and last year, she could look back to those hard struggling times when she and her children were building security and ultimate substantial success on their start with a few chickens. But her most deeply satisfying recollections must have been those of the long walks in the woods and hills which were the recreation she and the children shared, and of their growth in appreciation of nature. The land had demanded much of them in backbreaking toil, but along with some material wealth it gave back to them the richer rewards of being in tune with trees and wild things and clear running water and sparkling skies.

With the help of an astute Salinas realtor, J. Don Thompson, Herman, Andrew, and their sister Agnes Marks began during their mother's closing years to make real their dream of "The Forest of Nisine Marks" which would be a wilderness park for all to enjoy. At the same time, the California Division of Beaches and Parks was roughing in the same area on its master plan for ultimate State acquisition. Dream and plan were in essential harmony. As might be expected, however, it would take much time and the thought and effort of many people to put the new park on the California map. The Marks family wealth was moderate. The Aptos and Hinckley and Timothy Hopkins and smaller parcels could not be consolidated into one ownership, for dedication to one idealistic purpose, without resort to mortgage financing. Their other land and business enterprises were not enough to carry the burden of a magnificent free gift to the State, in accord with the ideal. They could, and did, hold on and refuse to sell at fantastic prices offered by the land-hungry developers, while their own offer to the Division of Beaches and Parks had to wait on the availability of State funds. But added to the threat of eventual foreclosure was another, one of even graver import to the park dream. If one of the Marks trio should die, the survivors would face an inheritance and estate contingency which could wreck the whole plan.

This was the situation when the Western Regional Office of The Nature Conservancy came into the picture, through the Division and Conservation Associates on the one hand, and through the Marks' friend, Mr. John R. McDaniel of Carmel, on the other. As chairman of The Nature Conservancy Monterey Bay Chapter, John McDaniel knew that the Conservancy was primarily concerned with natural areas for their scientific value. He knew also, however, that there was precedent in at least two other states, New York and Virginia, for The Nature Conservancy cooperation with state park departments in the acquisition of park lands. Discussions with California officials—Director Charles DeTurk and Deputy Director John R. Knight of the Parks and Recreation Department, Edward Dolder, Chief of the Division of Beaches and Parks, Robert Hatch, Harry Dean,

Charles Mehlert, and others concerned with land acquisition, regional management, and planning, brought out the State's commitment to the ideal, here, that nearly three-fourths of the Aptos Forest land should remain wilderness, with areas at both ends totaling some 2,500 acres to be given to overnight camping and day use. These two areas would be connected by foot and horse trails only (existing primitive roads will provide access for firefighting equipment).

The Marks family dream is now well on the way to realization. With a purchase option and Deeds of Trust signed by Herman, Andrew, and Agnes Marks, the Western Regional Office of The Nature Conservancy is now negotiating a half million-dollar loan from the Head Office of the Wells Fargo Bank in San Francisco, through the good offices of The Nature Conservancy Western Region legal counsel, Mr. H. P. Livermore of the San Francisco firm, Chickering & Gregory. Six public-spirited Californians have agreed to sign the Conservancy's note for this unprecedented loan: Mr. William M. Roth, Mr. Walter A. Starr, Mr. Osgood Hooker, Mr. and Mrs. Richard M. Leonard, and Mr. H. P. Livermore.

When the Forest of Nisine Marks has been dedicated as a California State Park, it will owe its existence to an abundant Nature; to a devoted, idealistic, and generous family; to a conscientious realtor; to earnest and farseeing public officials working in the public interest and trust; to a small but effective Chapter of The Nature Conservancy; to the high-minded guarantors of a venturesome financial undertaking—to a team, in short, which set out to win a portion of our natural heritage away from the engulfing tide of "development."

While keeping its sights on the primary goal of preserving natural areas for their long-range value to humanity through scientific study, The Nature Conservancy has in securing this fine and large tract of land for immediate public use demonstrated its effectiveness as a private organization serving the pressing open-space needs of our own time. We recognize this as an equally essential role for The Nature Conservancy. D.G.K.[176]

The Nature Conservancy demands that the Marks family identify oil drill sites in The Forest of Nisene Marks

On October 10, 1962, George Collins wrote to Don Thompson regarding his recent ascendancy to the presidency of the Nature Conservancy. Near the end of his letter, Collins commented on a trip that he had made four days earlier on October 6 to the newly-acquired property to observe the oil exploration rig being operated by the Western Oil Company. He expressed how shocked he was to see the rig at the old Loma Prieta Lumber Company's mill site, even though he concluded that there was a minimum of damage to the landscape considering the size of the operation.

The next month, on November 6, Collins wrote to Charles DeTurk of the Department of Parks and Recreation to summarize a meeting he had had the previous day with Thompson and Doris Leonard. Leonard and Collins both concluded that the Marks family needed to show on an official map of the proposed park a line which would include all of the areas that might conceivably be involved in oil exploration and extraction. They did not want the drilling operation scattered throughout the forest, but rather restricted to an area of relatively small extent along the most favorable line geologically for exploration purposes. They reminded Thompson that Herman Marks had agreed to this in the deed to the Conservancy. If a line could be defined, then the Conservancy could move forward with its goal of transferring the property to the state.

Yet another month passed before Edward Dolder gave his thoughts on the matter to Thompson on December 6. In a letter, Dolder explained that the area for oil extraction must be defined for the land transfer to move forward since the state could not purchase land that retains private privileges. Thus, once the oil extraction areas were defined, the state could buy the rest of the property from the Conservancy leaving the oil extraction areas for a future acquisition once the Marks wrapped up operations there. The matter was pressing because the state had the funds to buy the land and the Conservancy wanted to transfer it as soon as possible to divest itself of the high-interest loans it had used to acquire the property.

Meanwhile, also on December 6, Don Kelley, Western Regional Director of the Nature Conservancy, submitted his report on a tour through the

Forest of Nisene Marks. The purpose of the tour was to examine road and timber trespass at Buzzard Lagoon, discuss the mineral rights situation, and resolve fringe property acquisitions. In attendance were Marks, Thompson, Jess Chaffee, Harry Dean, Charles Mehlert, Durrell Knoefler, John McDaniel, and Kelley himself. Kelley reported:

> *After meeting at the Aptos Hotel, the party drove through the Marks Forest, passing the oil exploration and drilling site—the rig and pipe lines to Aptos Creek and the pump, all have been removed with a large pile of dead trees and slash covering the ground at the edge....*
>
> *With the admitted failure of the first large-scale and costly drilling on the site, the Marks family appear committed to further extensive exploration in the hope of recouping and ultimate gain. They are deeply involved with certain oil speculators, Noble Johnson of Ventura, and others. Herman Marks said that exploration has stopped for the winter and could not continue until "sometime next year." He would not say when, and would not set any time limit. He said that they "must not" be bound by the 50-acre limitation, but that in order to gain their objective, for the ultimate profit of all concerned, and he made pointed reference to ultimate monetary gain for the Nature Conservancy—they must be free to exploit the entire property with the exception of the Arden Forest (Tract 7).*
>
> *Herman Marks presented the following proposition: That the Nature Conservancy at once sell the Arden Forest to the State and thereby become free of its financial obligation, and that at the same time the Nature Conservancy deed back the rest of the property to the Marks family, enabling them to proceed at will with their oil exploration which they will ultimately make a gift to the state.*

Marks argued at great length to convince the state and Conservancy representatives of the merits of his proposal. He argued that the original proposition to the state had been the sale of the Arden Forest and gift of the remainder, and that the Conservancy had played its part and had no further obligation, moral or financial, to anyone. That the ultimate fulfillment of the whole park undertaking would speed up because the oil exploration might take a very long time; meanwhile, the Division of Beaches and Parks would have the Arden Forest now and the Marks' promise of the rest in time to come. He kept repeating that, in effect, this proposed handling was now the only workable course for the family, and that it must be done this way.

In reply, Kelley said that the Conservancy had committed itself to a certain course of action, that it was morally as well as financially obligated to the loan guarantors and could not contemplate a change of course without the full consent of all parties, including the state. Kelley reminded Marks that what the family now owned was certain specified mineral rights, that the Conservancy on its part must now move with all due dispatch from its present position to the fulfillment to its commitment of turning the entire property, in whole, over to the state.

Kelley then proposed to Marks that, since he insisted on immediate clarification and resolution of the whole situation, the first step, to be taken as soon as possible, was for the Marks family to state their situation, their views and arguments, and their specific proposal clearly in a letter. It appeared that this suggestion was not altogether agreeable to Marks, but he said he would write the letter, but only after necessary consultation with his collaborators. Kelley re-emphasized the need for haste and promised that the letter would be given the promptest attention by both the state and the Conservancy. He then emphasized that the Conservancy must work in concert with the Beaches and Parks unit and that the oil sites must be clearly delimited to enable the transaction with the state to proceed.

On December 13, a meeting was held between Collins, Leonard, Mehlert, and Dean. Collins stated that, within the meaning of the deed, the Conservancy could not undertake any major amendment which would involve acquiring and selling to the state mineral rights in one or more of the parcels named. He stated further that the Conservancy agreed to the sale of the entire property to the state at the earliest time, reserving to the Marks the Hinckley Basin Natural Area for oil exploration purposes. This was with the understanding that eventually oil exploration and drilling sites would be located and total no more than 50 acres, thereby freeing up the remainder of the Hinckley Basin for transfer to the state. Collins also wanted to subtract from the 50 acres the area already under oil exploration at the old mill site on Aptos Creek.

Three days later, on December 15, Marks wrote two letters to Kelley stating his present situation and his views regarding oil rights within The Forest of Nisene Marks. In the first letter, he gave his public position on the matter, while in the second he discussed his personal views.

Marks began the first letter by presenting the position and opinion of the family. That:

> *(1) The Nature Conservancy deed the Arden Forest to the State. The State pay the Conservancy the agreed purchase price, plus accrued interest and incidental expenditures (included is the 11.997 acres on Bates Creek in Grover Gulch that is to be deeded to the State and the first installment of taxes that we paid on the 10th of December, 1962).*
>
> *The Nature Conservancy pay all involved indebtedness to the Wells Fargo Bank.*
>
> *(2) The Nature Conservancy deed to us (Agnes, myself and Andrew) the Aptos, Hinckley and Timothy Hopkins Estate.*
>
> *(3) We three deed all oil and mineral rights in the Arden Forest, Aptos, and Timothy Hopkins Estate to the Nature Conservancy.*
>
> *The value of these oil and mineral rights at $11.00 per acre will be around $79,000.*
>
> *The Nature Conservancy, arranging with the State, is to use this to help the State acquire the land by Buzzard Lagoon, along the Buzzard Lagoon Road, and to the Highland Way.*
>
> *(4) We three deed the Hinckley, Aptos, and Timothy Hopkins Estate to the State. Also the oil and mineral rights on the Hinckley (these have a valuation of $27,500).*
>
> *(5) The State gives us an oil and mineral lease on the Hinckley for 10 1/3% (ten and one third per cent) of the net profit (current drilling and attendant costs not to be considered as net).*
>
> *We have all necessary rights attendant on such lease, and we to use all possible caution in exercising them.*
>
> *Sincerely, Herman Henry Marks*

> MEMO: In regard to No. 1, we request a clause prohibiting horseback riding in the Arden Forest and the 11.997 acres on Bates Creek (to be inserted in the deed to the State).

In his second letter, Marks wrote:

> And now I write a personal response to you.
> The geologist and Andrew have given us their considered opinion.
> We are of the opinion that the few horse riders should not be permitted to ruin the trails and terrain for the majority so will you see that a prohibiting clause is inserted in your deed to the State for the Arden Forest, and also for the eleven acres on Bates Creek?
> I had a short talk on the 11th of December with Harry Dean about all this; a few minor points we have thought of since.
> If acceptable to all, it should take only a short while to finish as there is no surveying, the land and oil and mineral rights belonging to the State, and the Hinckley survey lines seem acceptable.
> The oil and mineral rights we turn over to you, will, I think, give you all and our State Park a leverage to get the money you will need for the Buzzard Lagoon area, along the Buzzard Lagoon Road and to the Highland Way, from the State.
> If possible of acquisition, I can agree that the land of "the Apple Tree," by Buzzard Lagoon, would be wonderful to have in the park.
> The Buzzard Lagoon Road has been timbered, so it seems the evidence is at hand that all of us have no time beyond next spring to get our job done in that area.
> The time that has passed since we met over there has given us all a clearer view of what should be done, but it has been at a cost of over $1,000 to the State, the cost of interest and taxes. Perhaps for the best, and yet I think we all would have liked to have had more park land for it.
> The title company will, I think, release any necessary document to Don Thompson for our signatures and notarizing.

With high faith in this combined effort, and our best wishes to all of you for a happy and healthy Christmas and New Year, I am...

Sincerely, Herman Henry Marks

The land of "the Apple Tree" was roughly 800 acres located to the north of the 571 acres outside the Augmentation near Buzzard Lagoon. Today, it is the area from the junction of Highland Way and Eureka Canyon Road along the east side of Buzzard Lagoon Road. In 1962, the area was still under development and both the Nature Conservancy and the state wanted to purchase it before logging began. Neither succeeded, though, and the land was subsequently logged and turned into a residential subdivision.

It took the Nature Conservancy only twenty-five days to answer Marks' letter on January 9, 1963. George Collins wrote:

As you are aware, the Nature Conservancy and those who have backed that organization in acquiring your property, for the State have wanted to complete the Forest of Nesine Marks transaction with the State at the earliest possible time. One of our reasons for the desire is to establish our record for efficient workmanship so that we will show up well when we seek new and additional projects. However, with the delay arising from the exercise of the oil and mineral rights, and our growing awareness of the difficulties in moving the project forward as long as those rights confront us, we are not carrying forward as we had hoped. Nevertheless, the Nature Conservancy and others have been able to assist the State effectively in holding that property off the market for the time being, and we are all hoping as you are that the means will be found to acquire it for State Park purposes. While there is much to be done at least we are not asleep at the switch.

Now, as to the various steps you outline in your suggested plan of action as per your letter of December 15 to Don Kelley.

(1) In answer to this position of yours: To have the Nature Conservancy deed the Arden Forest to the State, this presupposes, as we understand it, that the State would pay for the Arden

Forest alone the entire amount due the Nature Conservancy on account of the whole acreage of 9,750 acres, including taxes, interest, and any other operations and overhead costs. It would be understood, we assume, that the amount paid by the State would be enough to cover all of the land costs for the entire project area, but technically with step (1) only the Arden Forest would go to the State. The State would not have the oil and mineral rights to the Arden Forest, and, technically, would be paying around $450,000, more or less, for but a small portion of the entire project. I would not want to be the one to try to convince the Department of Finance in Sacramento that step (1) should be adopted.

(2) In step (2), you propose that the Nature Conservancy deed back to you (the Marks family) the Aptos, Hinckley, and Timothy Hopkins properties. In other words, all of the total project area except the Arden Forest under your proposition (2) would be deeded back to the Marks family. I have to say that your backers upon whom we depended to guarantee the bank loan would not approve of such a move, nor would the Nature Conservancy, because their interests would be placed in financial jeopardy.

The various steps you outline are so interrelated that unless step (1) is acceptable it appears that the others would lose point. We, all of us, worked out and executed an arrangement between the Marks family, the State and the Nature Conservancy, which we here feel is good and should stand.

(3) This proposal, as we understand it, is to acquire a down payment on the Buzzard Lagoon property. The State and everyone involved agrees that the ultimate park boundary should include some of the land bordering the present area in the Buzzard Lagoon vicinity. Charles Mehlert and Harry Dean calculate that about 800 acres is needed there. Don Thompson, with whom we spoke over the phone to on December 28, is going to try to ascertain about what that land would cost. It appears to us at this time that anything realized from the sale of oil and mineral rights, as you suggest, would not go very far toward acquiring that land. Also, we

feel that the Nature Conservancy would be saddled with a pretty expensive undertaking which we would find it impossible to justify in view of our stringent limitations financially. We have as much as we can do now and should not get in any deeper. As President of the Nature Conservancy I would not want to be responsible for involving the organization in any land acquisition venture based upon speculative interest such as I feel would be the case if we tried to get the State to buy the oil and mineral rights.

(4) Next we come to your proposal (4). Following your reasoning in your paragraph (3) the Nature Conservancy would already have accepted the oil and mineral rights in the Arden Forest, Aptos and Timothy Hopkins properties and would have sold them to the State and used the money for a start on acquisition in the Buzzard Lagoon vicinity. Thus, the Nature Conservancy would be left with an obligation to acquire 800 acres in the Buzzard Lagoon vicinity, with nothing to buy in with unless we could go back for another bank loan.

(5) Finally, under step (5) you would in consideration of all of the previous steps, be given an oil and mineral lease on the Hinckley property in consideration of 10 1/3% of the net profit recoverable from any oil or other minerals extracted therefrom.

It is our thought, concerning your paragraph (5), that if you would be willing to confine the 50 acres total of oil and mineral surface exploration sites to a portion of the Hinckley Basin Area, of 2,500 acres approximately, and give up oil and mineral rights on the rest of the 9,750 acres, which we understood from your letters you agree to in principle, I believe we could move forward positively with the State. We haven't been able to do so because of the uncertainties to us in your exercise of the oil and mineral rights. This is brought out in Edward Dolder's letter of December 6, 1962, and in many other communications.

We do not know that the State could legally assume any ownership in the Hinckley Basin Natural Area as long as there remained in private hands the rights to explore for oil and minerals, therefore might not be in a position to grant any

> *leases, and we would to make certain on this point because otherwise the Nature Conservancy might find itself holding that 2,500 acres and paying taxes on it indefinitely for the benefit of private oil and mineral interests who would still be in a position to come and go as they pleased in that zone. However, if the State can take title to all or the major part of the Forest of Nisene Marks from the Nature Conservancy, knowing that the oil and mineral exploration activities, with their drill rigs, roads, pipelines, and other installations will be confined to that one zone of 2,500 acres, or less if possible, we ought to be able to move ahead. There would be plenty of justification meanwhile with the Arden Forest, Timothy Hopkins and Aptos properties for full scale planning and administration, holding the Hinckley Basin in reserve pending cessation of the oil and mineral exploration activities.*

The letter concludes by referring the prohibition on horseback riding in the Arden Forest to the state, and acknowledging Marks' comments regarding the acquisition of the 11.997 acres in Tract 7.

With this and earlier letters, Marks realized that if he wanted to ensure continued access to drilling sites for the Western Gulf Oil Company in The Forest of Nisene Marks, he needed to identify the locations for drill sites as soon as possible. On February 7, Andrew Marks finally submitted his report to his brother. He identified 80 acres in Hinckley Gulch that correspond remarkably well to the original Hinckley Basin Unit No. 1 subdivision laid out by Allen Rispin in 1927. The drill sites all sat along the 800-foot elevation line adjacent to the Hinckley Fire Road.[177]

Land transfer from H. M. Howard property to the Western Title Insurance Company and the Nature Conservancy concerning Tract 7 in the Augmentation

On March 22, 1963, the Nature Conservancy paid the Western Title Insurance Company $7,000 for the 11.997 acres along the north side of the Arden Forest held in trust for H. M. Howard. Both the Nature Conservancy and the state agreed with Herman Marks that this purchase was necessary for the success of the Arden Forest development. This proved to be the last purchase made within the Augmentation for inclusion in The Forest of Nisene Marks. An additional 407 acres were later added to the state park on January 1, 2004 to increase the width of the Aptos Creek Fire Road, but this land came from the former Rancho Aptos.

It is ironic that the Arden Forest, Hinckley Gulch, and the Buzzard Lagoon area were the most highly-sought parts of what became The Forest of Nisene Marks State Park, yet today they are used far less than the Aptos Forest and Bridge Creek areas. None of the three areas was ever substantially developed and they, for the most part, sit outside the park's trail network. Indeed, Hinckley Gulch has no trails or fire roads through it at all and is only visited by the most inquisitive or daring hikers.[178]

Frederick Farr writes legislation authorizing the right of the state to buy for the purpose of a state park property with existing private oil and mineral interests

On April 23, 1963, a meeting was held in Senator Frederick Farr's office in Sacramento between E. E. Powell, the Department of Parks and Recreation's Park Land Agent supervisor, and Harry L. Noland, an attorney representing the Marks family in their business with the Nature Conservancy and the state. Together, they prepared a draft bill that the senator planned to submit to the California State Senate. Farr made several comments on the bill and then submitted it to the Senate Committee on Governmental Efficiency on April 25:

> *The legislation sets forth certain authorities and controls under which the Director of the Department of Parks and Recreation shall accept and operate the property as a unit of the State Park System. I think you will agree that the whole situation has become somewhat complicated but the legislation is designed to provide certain authorities for the Director insofar as the Aptos Forest project is concerned and, more particularly, the Hinckley Basin area.*

The legislation in its presently proposed form permits the Director, with the consent of the Director of the Department of Finance, to accept by gift and by purchase all of the described lands as conveyed to the Nature Conservancy and limits his authority on granting of rights of way and other land use privileges.

The proposed legislation also provides that the Director may lease to the grantor (which we understand will now be the Marks family) all of the rights and privileges necessary for the purpose of exploring and extracting oil and gas. With this authority the Director will be in a position to lease under certain terms and conditions as he may prescribe which, of course, must be acceptable to the grantor; and, within this lease will be continued the time elements and all the detailed privileges.

Various types of easements will be necessary for roads, power lines, water, oil, etc., with a time limitation within which oil may be discovered in commercial quantities and if so discovered a time element will be established and conditions prescribed as to the manner of recovery. As to the prospects of the legislation passing, we, of course, can only hazard a guess; however, we are not aware of any opposition to a bill of this nature.

signed by Senator Frederick Farr

Two months later, on June 21, Senate Bill No. 1418 was passed by the Senate, having already been approved by the Assembly on June 17. It modified Section 5006.2 of the Public Resources Code, the relevant part in relation to The Forest of Nisene Marks stating:

Because of the uniqueness of the proposed park and the very generous gifts of the grantor in establishing this large state park to be preserved for posterity and not withstanding restrictions hereinabove enumerated the Director of Parks and Recreation, with the consent of the Director of Finance, may within the Hinckley Basin Unit, some 2,500 acres, more or less... lease to the grantor his heirs and assigns the right to explore for, extract, and remove oil and gas and hydrocar-

bons including the right to disturb the surface under such terms and conditions as he may prescribe. He may with the consent of the Director of Finance issue permits for access to any drill site as may be selected including easement for power, telephone, water, and ~~oil~~ pipe lines which are to be used exclusively by lessee in his exploration and extraction for oil, gas, and hydrocarbons and by the State as suits their needs for park purposes.

The bill was signed by the governor shortly afterwards, paving the way for the state to finally purchase The Forest of Nisene Marks regardless of the Marks family's oil and mineral interests.[179]

Land transfer from the Nature Conservancy and the Marks family to the State of California concerning land in the Augmentation

On June 25, 1965, the Nature Conservancy passed title to Tract 7 in the Augmentation, encompassing the Arden Forest and the former Howard land, to the State of California. While the precise amount of money transacted for the 764 acres is not known, a letter from November 5, 1963, provides clues. In it, Wells Fargo Bank & Union Trust Company reported to the Western Title Company that the principal balance of the Nature Conservancy's loan was $569,494.92. The letter also stated that there was a total of $93.94 due each day that the payment was delayed after November 6, 1963. Thus, by adding to the principal the daily additional cost until June 25, 1965, the total amount comes to $625,671.04. However, it seems likely that at least some of this debt was repaid by the Nature Conservancy or assumed by it upon the sale of the land to the state.

Immediately after this was signed, Agnes, Herman, and Andrew Marks made a gift deed to the state of Tracts 8 and 9, and their portion of Tract 10, as well as their property at Buzzard Lagoon and the right-of-way to the Augmentation through Rancho Aptos. The gift deed transferred 9,051 acres to the State of California, which, when added to the Arden Forest, encompassed a total area of 9,815 acres for use as a state park.

The property occupied twenty-eight percent of Martina Castro's original Shoquel Augmentation, confirmed to her by the United States government on June 4, 1859.

The transfer of the property from the Nature Conservancy and the Marks family to the state was not without restrictions. The Marks had ensured that certain conditions for use were included in the deeds. These differed from tract to tract:

Tract 7 (Arden Forest)

In the Arden Forest, the state is allowed to build camping and associated facilities as long as the facilities are in keeping with the area's natural surroundings. There are few restrictions concerning the facilities in this section of the park.

Tract 8 (Lower Bridge Creek)

The state is allowed to build camping facilities, hiking trails, and conduct camping-associated activities such as nature studies, but they must be in keeping with the area's natural surroundings.

The core of this tract may be viewed from two trails: from the Loma Prieta Grade Trail from its beginning on the fire road at Molino Junction over a distance heading north of some 2.3 miles until Hoffman's Historic Site is reached, which marks the boundary with Tract 10; and from the first two miles of the West Ridge Trail until it reaches the ridge, which marks the boundary of Tract 7.

Buzzard Lagoon and the Aptos Creek Fire Road

The Buzzard Lagoon area and the area adjacent to Aptos Creek and the Aptos Creek Fire Road shall be held in their natural state. Any facilities built for public convenience, such as trails, water drinking and sanitary facilities shall be in keeping with the natural surroundings.

Tracts 9 and 10 (Aptos Forest)

The Aptos Forest, made up of Tract 9's Aptos Creek Canyon and the Bridge Creek side of Tract 10, shall be held in their natural state. Any facilities built for public convenience, such as trails, water drinking and sanitary facilities shall be in keeping with the natural surroundings. Group and family hike-in campsites are allowed on parcels A, B, and C, as shown on the Parcel Map for the Aptos Forest, as long as they conform to their natural surroundings.

This area forms the heart of the state park and includes nearly everything east of Aptos Creek, Bridge Creek, and the Aptos Creek Fire Road. As such, all trails and roads on the east bank of Aptos Creek, including the switchback to the ridge, the Aptos Creek Trail to the Loma Prieta Epicenter sign and beyond, the White's Lagoon Trail, and the Big Slide Trail are within Tract 9. The headwaters of Aptos Creek beyond Five Finger Falls remain in a state of nature with no trails or other modes of access. Along China Ridge, everything on both sides of the Aptos Creek Fire Road beyond Sand Point is within Tract 9. On Bridge Creek, a hike to Maple Falls beyond Hoffman's Historic Site passes into Tract 10, which otherwise has no formal trails.

To this day, the Parks and Recreation Department either does not know or does not want to know where the parcels designated for hike-in campsites are located.

Hinckley Basin

There shall be no violation of the oil and gas lease entered into between the state and the Marks family. The lease is for a period of 49 years, but if enough commercial oil or gas is not found and produced within eight years, the lease ends.

The use of Hinckley Basin, called special portions, shall be limited to camping, nature study, hiking, and associated activities, and if any of these activities are conducted or structures built, they shall be in keeping with the natural surroundings. If camping facilities are built, they shall be kept at the 800-foot elevation on the Hinckley Basin Fire Road where the proposed oil drilling sites are to be located.

Today, the Hinckley Fire Road is the only formalized right-of-way through a part of Hinckley Basin. The rest of the basin remains in a state of nature with no trails or other modes of access. No campsites were ever built within the confines of the basin.

Additional Grant and Gift Deeds Restrictions

In addition to the tacit agreement that the state, through its Division of Beaches and Parks, would preserve, protect, and hold the former Marks family's properties in trust for all time, the deeds to the state provide as a condition subsequent that the property must be held in its natural state. Upon the breach of this condition, the grantors or their assigns may declare the forfeiture of that portion of the property affected by the breach, and all right, title, and interest of the state therein shall immediately vest in the grantors or in their assigns.

Other restrictions included:

- Horseback riding is restricted throughout the property.
- The Aptos Creek Fire Road and the Hinckley Basin Fire Road shall be barred from public use except in an emergency or to access a private property, as negotiated by the state. Vehicular tours authorized and conducted by park staff may be given but no private vehicular tours are allowed.
- The public may have vehicular access under park control on the existing road from the eastern boundary of the Buzzard Lagoon parcel, westerly along the ridge for a distance of approximately 3,000 feet, to a point where the road crosses the 2,500-foot contour near the headwaters of Hinckley Creek.
- The Marks family reserves a non-exclusive twenty-foot-wide ingress and egress for pipelines and utilities through Tracts 8 and 9 and the right-of-way through Rancho Aptos for the purpose of extracting oil and natural gas from Hinckley Basin. The locations of these easements are to be mutually agreed upon between the state and the family. The easements are to be located both as to terrain and ground conditions so that erosion will be at a minimum and so that trees shall not be cut or destroyed unnecessarily.

An eight-year time limit was put in place for the Marks family to prove the commercial viability of oil and gas collected from within the park.[180]

Land transfer from Diane Cooley to the State of California concerning Tract 8 in the Augmentation

Shortly after the Marks family transferred their property to the state, government officials reached out to Diane Cooley to inquire about her small, 1,170-square-foot parcel within Tract 8. The former Porter House, which occupied the property, was in desperate need of repair and was no longer safe to enter. After a short negotiation, Cooley agreed to donate the property to the state in exchange for establishing a picnic area in her family's memory. Thus, the Porter Family Picnic Area, located at the former site of Schillings' Camp and Molino Station, was designated according to her wishes. The picnic area now marks the end of the Aptos Creek Fire Road for vehicular traffic.[181]

Woods Mattingley proposes a railroad along the former Bridge Creek spur

Around November 1965, Woods Mattingley put forward a plan to purchase a narrow-gauge Shay locomotive and rolling stock in order to run a tourist railroad along the former Loma Prieta Branch from Aptos to Big Tree Gulch. By January 1966, the scope of this plan was narrowed to a two-mile-long railroad between the site of the village of Loma Prieta, where the state park's parking lot was initially to be located, through Hoffman's Historic Site to Big Tree Gulch. Along with restoring the right-of-way and bridges, Mattingley hoped to restore several of the dilapidated buildings that still stood along the route, repurposing one for a camping supply store and another for a museum. Likely due to a lack of funding and resistance from the Marks family and the Division of Beaches and Parks, nothing ever came of the proposal.[182]

The Monterey Bay Redwood Company's mill and millpond is demolished

In the December 26, 1965 issue of the *Sentinel*, Margaret Koch reported:

Old Mill Only A Memory

Last traces of one of Santa Cruz county's most colorful lumber mills disappeared the other day

The Monterey Bay Redwood company has been non-existent since 1946. But a picturesque remnant of its busy heyday remained at the Millpond angling club just recently: a portion of the old mill building and the pond itself where the great redwood logs once floated.

Now this end of the pond, which extended beneath the old mill building, has been filled with earth. A new clubhouse and fish cleaning center is to be built on the site. It overlooks the larger part of the pond which remains, stocked with fat trout for eager anglers.

The angling club was formerly owned and operated by Kurt Roy. He and his wife still live in a cottage on the grounds but the club is now the property of Mr. and Mrs. Louis Keller.

The Kellers, natives of Seattle where he worked for Boeing aircraft for 15 years, decided to leave what they call the busy rat race for suburbia.

"The rats were winning," Keller added with a grin.

They discovered the Millpond quite by accident, during a summer visit to Keller's brother's cabin in the area.

"This is just what we want: peace, quiet, a chance to be ourselves and enjoy life."

The millpond, once part of the extensive Monterey Bay Redwood company, once echoed to the shouts of loggers and the splash of virgin redwood logs coming down Soquel creek.

The company, organized in 1924 by James A. Harris Jr. and David Mills, comprised about 6000 acres including much of the Soquel Augmentacion Rancho Mexican Grant. It took in 500 acres in Santa Clara county plus the top of Loma Prieta. It also included the Olive Springs Quarry.

The property was purchased by Harris and Mills in 1925 from the Valencia-Hihn Lumber company with Noel Patterson handling the transaction.

Just above Amaya Creek there is a spot called Badger

Camp where the original trees were left standing for their beauty, according to James Harris III. To the cleared field there, F. A. Hihn used to come by buggy to take sulfur spring baths, he noted.

Hihn had owned the mill machinery which had been used in the Hihn mill at Laurel, before being purchased by Mills and Harris.

When the mill started operations in 1926, the area adjacent to the millpond was logged with steam donkeys. About 1926 they started hauling logs down to it via trailers pulled by tractors. Then with the advent of more powerful trucks, they started trucking logs down to the mill, according to Harris.

"When the stock market crashed in 1929 we couldn't GIVE lumber away," he recalled.

The mill "racked along" during the '30s and in the '40s sold out all lumber on hand for the defense effort. In 1942-43 the company sold all its stock and a group of former employees banded together to install a small circular mill to cut out all remaining timber.

"It was finished completely about 1945-46," Harris said.

All equipment was sold and in 1961 the acreage was sold to Glencoe Forest products of Sacramento—with Patterson again handling the transaction.

The building at the millpond was just a small part of the original mill which spread out over several acres of the flat up above the pond.

Harris noted that it included a planing mill, dry kiln and storage yard, blacksmith shop and office as well as the mill buildings. For years A. L. (Gus) Simerly was mill superintendent. John Dahlgren was logging boss, Tom Reilly was planing mill superintendent and Al C. Bowman was master mechanic.[183]

State Senate introduces bill to build a dam on Aptos Creek

After fourteen years of intermediate discussion and over two years of debate between the state legislature and the Department of Parks and Recreation, on June 1, 1967, the California State Senate introduced Senate Bill No. 1072 with the express purpose of building a dam across Aptos Creek and inundating a large portion of The Forest of Nisene Marks State Park.

Unsurprisingly, the Nature Conservancy, the Sierra Club, and the Audubon Society strongly opposed the bill and the precedent it would set. The Nature Conservancy argued that the reservoir would eliminate a proposed camping area included as a requirement in the original gift deed of the land for the park. Ironically, that same camping area has never been built and there seems to be no intention of doing so in the future.

On the opposite side of the debate, the Santa Cruz County Department of Public Works and the County Board of Supervisors championed the project and paid for advertising in local newspapers. Nonetheless, the bill was defeated on June 26. The Senate's legal counsel stated that it would be unconstitutional to build the dam since it violated restrictions put in place by the Marks family. In response, those wishing to build the dam pledged to pass new legislation allowing eminent domain law to be applied in such cases. However, no reservoir was ever built in the park nor has such a law been passed by the state.[184]

The Big Creek Lumber Company

From the time that the deed was signed passing the Monterey Bay Redwood Company's property to the Glenco Forest Products Company in 1961, Glenco's main activity within the Augmentation was the small-scale logging of second-growth redwood trees and remnant old-growth redwoods. By 1967, however, the company felt that enough of the second-growth trees had matured to justify expanding timber harvesting operations. As a part of this, the company incorporated the CHY Lumber Company as a subsidiary retail front. The name was a reference to Curt Setzer's three children: Cal, Hardie, and Yvonne. To harvest and process the timber, Glenco contracted out to the Big Creek Lumber Company of Swanton.

Big Creek Lumber traces its beginning to the period immediately after World War II when Frank McCrary, who had just been discharged from the military, his sons Frank "Lud" and Homer T. "Bud," and his brother-in-law Homer Trumbo set up a small portable mill in the hills above their home in Swanton. When they incorporated on June 29, 1948, they named their small operation Big Creek Timber Company, planning to keep the company strictly within the family. Their main areas of focus were Mill and Scott Creeks. But as the demand for lumber increased, they decided to build a planing mill on Highway 1 north of Davenport.

Their success attracted the attention of Theodore Hoover, who owned much of Waddell Creek. The Waddell Creek basin had been harvested in the 1860s and 1870s until shortly after its namesake, William Waddell, was killed by a grizzly bear in 1875. Since that time, much of the forest had grown back. In the early 1950s, Hoover granted Big Creek Timber stumpage rights on his land. It was an opportunity that almost overnight propelled the small company into the county's largest logging operation. With this vast new acreage, Big Creek Timber constructed a new, larger mill on Waddell Creek's West Fork.

After the mill felt the full wrath of the December 1955 storm, the company decided to move the mill to a safer location: next to its planing mill on the marine terrace south of Waddell Creek. On April 5, 1960, the company reincorporated as Big Creek Lumber Company. The family-owned company rapidly expanded, logging along Waddell Creek's West Fork until the area was purchased by the state and incorporated into Big Basin Redwoods State Park. Today, the company continues its successful logging activities using a controlled management program that is designed to both protect and foster increased productivity within its forestland, land that extends north of Davenport into San Mateo Country.

After receiving the contract from Glenco, Big Creek set up a small base of operations near Sulphur Springs, where the north side of Santa Rosalia Ridge begins to transition into a more gentle-sloping landscape. It is here that the company began logging both the remaining old-growth and second-growth redwoods, as well as Douglas fir trees. After the trees were on the ground, stripped of their branches and bark, and cut into manageable lengths, they were loaded onto trucks and taken to the mill in Davenport. Hardwood trees were also cut and sold to the public as fuel wood.

In its first year, Big Creek Lumber harvested a total of 375,000 board feet of lumber from the Augmentation, of which 137,000 was old growth, 73,000 second growth, and 165,000 fir. In the second year, the company removed another 625,000 board feet of timber: 147,000 old growth, 227,000 second growth, and 251,000 fir. Together, this meant that Big Creek harvested approximately one million board feet of lumber in its first two years of operation along the East Branch of Soquel Creek. Over the next nine years, an additional 3 million board feet of various types of timber were removed from Glenco's land. While the majority of activity was around Sulphur Springs and Badger Springs, smaller operations also harvested the timber of Spignet Gulch (the western part of Tract 10).[185]

The High Bridge burns down

Although the High Bridge over Amaya Gulch had long ceased to support automobile traffic, both because of landslides on either side and more generally because of the age of the bridge, it still remained intact. A motorcycle club used Sulphur Springs as its base and the bridge was one of only two access ways into the property. Unfortunately, the bridge burned down in 1970 under suspicious circumstances. Some at the time claimed that stoned hippies burned the bridge, but the more likely culprit was a former motorcycle club member.

Charley Duncan recounted that a local youth had been banished from the club because of his disturbing habits of collecting rattlesnakes, his pyromania, and his reliance on his girlfriend's Honda 50. Feeling ridiculed, he set fire to the main entry bridge to the club in an attempt to block the club's members from accessing the property. The bridge was destroyed and not replaced—the members of the Sulphur Springs motorcycle club found other ways to reach their hangout.

Bert Stoodley dies

Following the lease of the former Loma Prieta Lumber Company's lands to the Union Oil Company in 1948, Bert Stoodley entered a twenty-four-year retirement where he finished writing his memoirs and enjoyed life as a grandfather and great-grandfather. When he died in Santa Cruz on October 31, 1970 at the age of 97, he was survived by his wife, Ora, son, Allan, three grandsons, and two great-grandsons.[186]

Agnes and Andrew Marks die

On April 4, 1976, the oldest of Nesine Marks' surviving children, Agnes, died at her Toro Park home at the age of 93. According to the *Salinas Californian*, Agnes had been born in Watsonville and lived there for six years before moving to Salinas around 1889. She had never married and left no children.

A month later, on May 13, her youngest brother, Andrew, died at the age of 87. He was born at Toro Park shortly after his family relocated there and served during World War I. Afterwards, he ran a ranch for many years in Greenfield before returning to his family in Salinas. His wife, Alzoe Leibbrandt, had died in 1956 and both of their sons, Andrew Jr. and Lloyd M., had also predeceased their father. The couple's daughter, Avalon Barbara Marks, had married Marvin Clarence Kryger in 1952. Among his siblings, Andrew was the only to leave descendants—at the time of his death he had eleven grandchildren and one great-granddaughter.[187]

Land transfer from the CHY Lumber Company to the Pelican Timber Company concerning land in the Augmentation

After several months of negotiation, on June 15, 1979, the CHY Lumber Company's owner Curt Setzer sold around 83 percent of the company's land within the Augmentation, as well as the Hihn Railroad Grade and property in the San Lorenzo Valley, to the Pelican Timber Company for $8,250,000. Pelican prioritized road repair and then selective second-growth redwood harvesting within its new property. The first area it focused on was Badger Springs from the East Branch of Soquel Creek to the top of Santa Rosalia Ridge. Pelican also harvested a small amount of timber in Amaya Gulch. Any hardwood that Pelican found was sold to the Pacific Firewood Company of Aptos, owned by Tim Taylor. Pacific Firewood set up a large wooden chute at Sulphur Springs that allowed firewood to be loaded onto trucks. This has since been removed by State Forest staff.

Not long after Pelican began harvesting, it turned its focus to the final old-growth redwood trees still standing within its property. The largest group of these was located on the western slope of Santa Rosalia

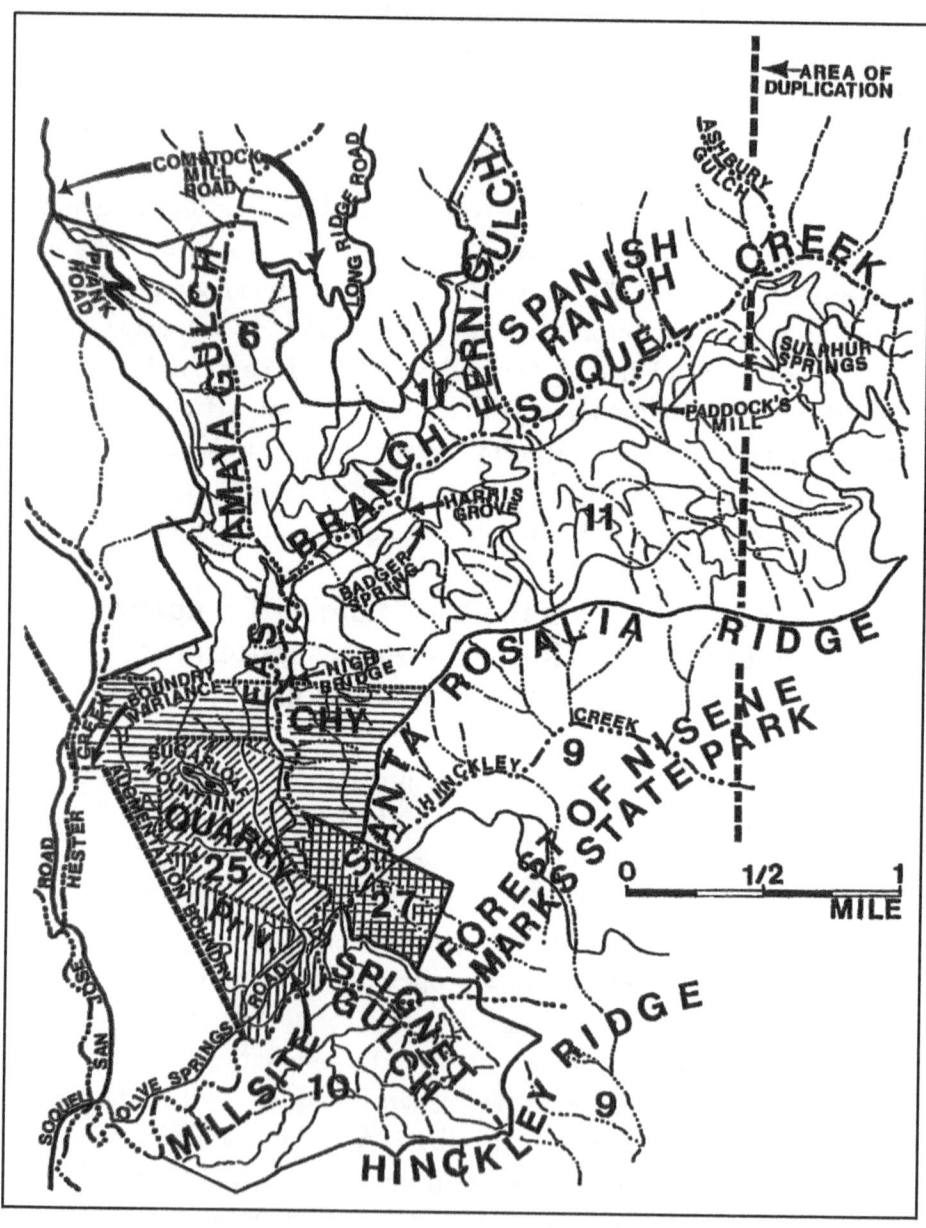

FIGURES 7.1-2 PROPERTY PURCHASED WITHIN THE AUGMENTATION FROM THE CHY LUMBER COMPANY BY THE PELICAN TIMBER COMPANY

Ridge between Amaya Gulch and the site of the High Bridge. Because the boundary between The Forest of Nisene Marks State Park and Pelican's land was poorly defined in places, several of the state park's old-growth trees were accidentally cut and removed by Pelican at this time. Meanwhile,

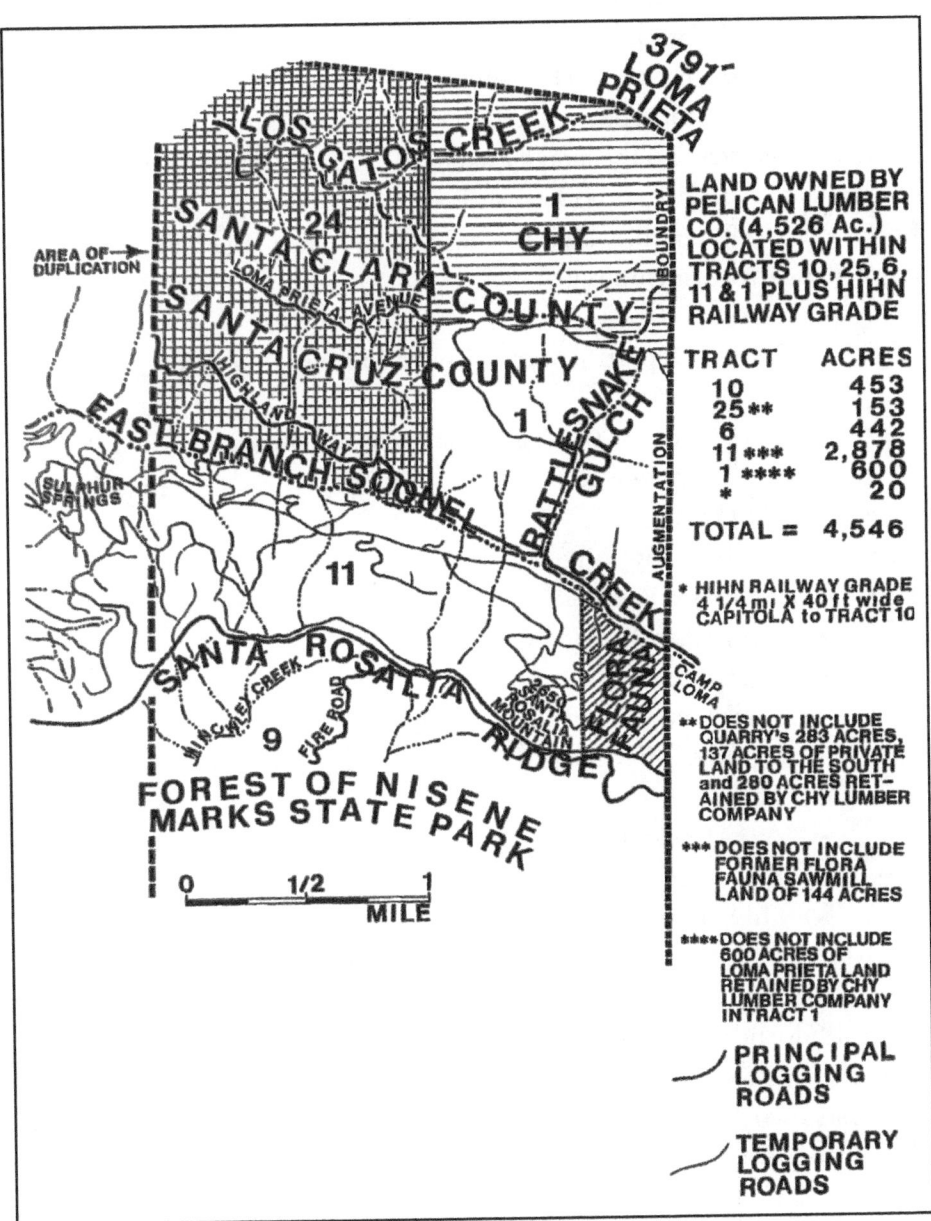

Pelican found itself in a dilemma. No lumber mill on the Central Coast was able to process the larger logs of the old-growth redwood trees cut in the Augmentation. After an extensive search, a facility that could manage the logs was found in Mendocino County. However, to reach the mill, all of Pelican's trucks had to run at night to comply with traffic rules over the Golden Gate Bridge.

The 17 acres that the CHY Lumber Company retained from the sale was being used by third parties at the time of the sale and providing a steady income. This included the land leased to the Olive Springs Quarry in Tract 25 and the northeastern corner of Tract 1 from Loma Prieta Avenue to Loma Prieta Mountain, which was leased to various companies and government agencies, including:

- California Department of Forestry and Fire Protection for a lookout station
- Standard Radio & Television Company (Channel 11 KNTV)
- Pacific Telephone & Telegraph Company
- Tel-Rad Inc.
- Pacific Telescription Systems
- Pacific Gas & Electric Company, which subleased land to:
    - Sungarden Packing Company
    - Southwest Airways Company
    - Lockheed Aircraft Corporation
    - Farmers Mercantile Company
    - Frank Quement Inc.
    - A. L. Castel Inc.
    - Bell & Griffen
    - Hildebrand & Young Trucking Inc.
    - U. S. Department of Justice & Immigration Service

In 1961, these 9.128 acres brought the CHY an annual rent of $6,330. The company also kept some land in Tract 25, which it hoped to use to establish its own quarry, and a small section near Camp Loma on Highland Way within Tract 11.

Herman Marks dies

On June 23, 1982, Herman Marks died at the ripe old age of 97 at his home in Toro Park, the last of Nesine Marks' children. He never married and left no children. In their short century in California, Herman and his siblings had either sold or gifted the entirety of The Forest of Nisene Marks State Park in Santa Cruz County, 150 acres in Point Lobos State Natural Reserve, 1,200 acres in Toro County Park in Monterey County, land for the Church of the Good Shepherd in Corral De Tierra, and 20 acres to Saint John's College of Annapolis, Maryland. The family's legacy lives on in the name of the state park and Marks Canyon in Toro County Park.[188]

Storm heavily damages The Forest of Nisene Marks State Park

On January 4, 1982, one of Santa Cruz County's most disastrous storms struck. Damage was widespread across the county, but Soquel and Aptos Creeks were especially impacted due to their lengths and origins high up in the Santa Cruz Mountains. Additional storms in February and March caused most of the county's state parks to be closed for months, including The Forest of Nisene Marks, the access road for which was completely washed out. Jerry Waggoner told the *Sentinel* in mid-April: "The extensive storm damage in Nisene Marks set the trails back 10 years... We've got a lot of slide and rerouting work to do. The park is now closed, but if we get enough volunteer help, we're hoping to reopen it—at least some sections."

In the aftermath of the storm, the Resource Protection Division of State Parks proposed classifying 8,270 acres of Nisene Marks as a wilderness area. This would mean that no vehicles, including ranger patrols and state forestry fire engines, would be allowed to continue along the Aptos Creek Fire Road beyond the former Loma Prieta mill site. The proposal divided park users and people concerned about preventing fires, maintaining power lines that pass through the park, deterring crime, and retrieving people injured within the park. In November, it was decided not to pursue a wilderness designation, but the fire road was cut back to the Porter

Family Picnic Area and vehicular access beyond that point was limited to state park and emergency vehicles.[189]

The Pelican Timber Company announces plan to harvest timber along Soquel Creek

By the mid-1980s, the people of the Soquel area were fed up with logging operations at the headwaters of Soquel Creek. Most of the Aptos Creek watershed had become a state park nearly twenty years earlier, and the floods caused by the storm of 1982 had been made substantially worse by the logging activity of the CHY Lumber Company and Pelican Timber Company along Soquel Creek. Thus, when Pelican announced in December 1983 its plan to harvest more than 3,000 acres of the Soquel Creek watershed, people finally took a stand against further commercial logging.

New state deregulation rules made it nearly impossible for the local government to block Pelican, but it could still delay the company until something could be done to potentially stop the harvesting operation. County officials planned to protest the move at the state level, while also contesting each of the permits Pelican had obtained thus far. Pelican clarified in mid-January that it also planned to subdivide the property after harvesting it to create up to 100 40-acre parcels for private homes, although the actual number would be less due to the terrain. The sudden announcement of this proposal did not change any minds, though, with county officials eager to restore the forest in order to protect the watershed and sources of drinking water. On January 24, the county's Board of Supervisors announced that it would pursue legal action against Pelican to stop both the logging venture and the residential subdivision plan.

On February 3, Gerard Partain, director of the Department of Forestry and Fire Protection, ruled that Pelican had permission to log the 911 acres that it had already received approval to harvest, as well as 445 acres along Amaya Creek. However, he deferred his decision regarding 775 acres around Sulphur Springs to the Board of Forestry and requested a special rule be created limiting the amount of annual timber harvesting within the Soquel watershed. The reason the Amaya Creek operation was approved, according to Partain, was because it "'will have an overall positive impact on Amaya Creek through the removal of logs deposited in the creek' in the last two severe winter storms." Locals and officials remained unconvinced by the ruling, and the Board of Supervisors unanimously decided on February 7 to take the matter to court. A restraining order against Pelican harvesting until the matter was settled was promptly approved at the end of the month. It proved unnecessary, however, since the lumber market was so poor that Pelican management decided not to harvest timber that year anyway.

Meantime, Pelican was the first to blink in the ongoing controversy. On March 7, the company withdrew its application to harvest the 775 acres that were the primary point of contention with residents. Two months later, at a meeting of the Capitola City Council on May 24, a new idea emerged that quickly gained ground: turn Pelican's property into a public park, either as an addendum to The Forest of Nisene Marks State Park or as its own entity. Pelican was not opposed to the idea, especially since the poor lumber market and endless legal fight were making its operation entirely unprofitable.

Around the beginning of September, Chop Keenan, president of Pelican, approached State Senator Henry Mello and Assemblyman Sam Farr and offered to sell the Soquel Creek property to the state. All of the local government agencies supported the acquisition, although each knew it would take several years to see the purchase completed. Keenan set the initial asking price for the 4,526 acres at $40,000, twice the amount he claimed the company had spent buying the property and operating on it. It was a steep cost, but local politicians saw the potential in acquiring the land, so they began the process of investigation and negotiation to see it realized.[190]

Land transfer from the Pelican Timber Company to the State of California concerning land in the Augmentation

Two years after the offer of the Pelican Timber Company's land along the East Branch of Soquel Creek was first made, the Department of Parks & Recreation decided to conduct an exploration of the property by vehicle and foot in early 1986. Fate would have it that a destructive El Niño storm struck the Central Coast on the night of February 15, 1986, the very day that the vehicular tour of the property was scheduled to begin. Vehicle access from

Highland Way and Olive Springs Road was impossible, forcing the Pelican employees, three State Park rangers, myself, and several others to explore the property entirely on foot. Our group postponed the exploration until February 26 and decided to focus on Spignet Gulch in Tract 10.

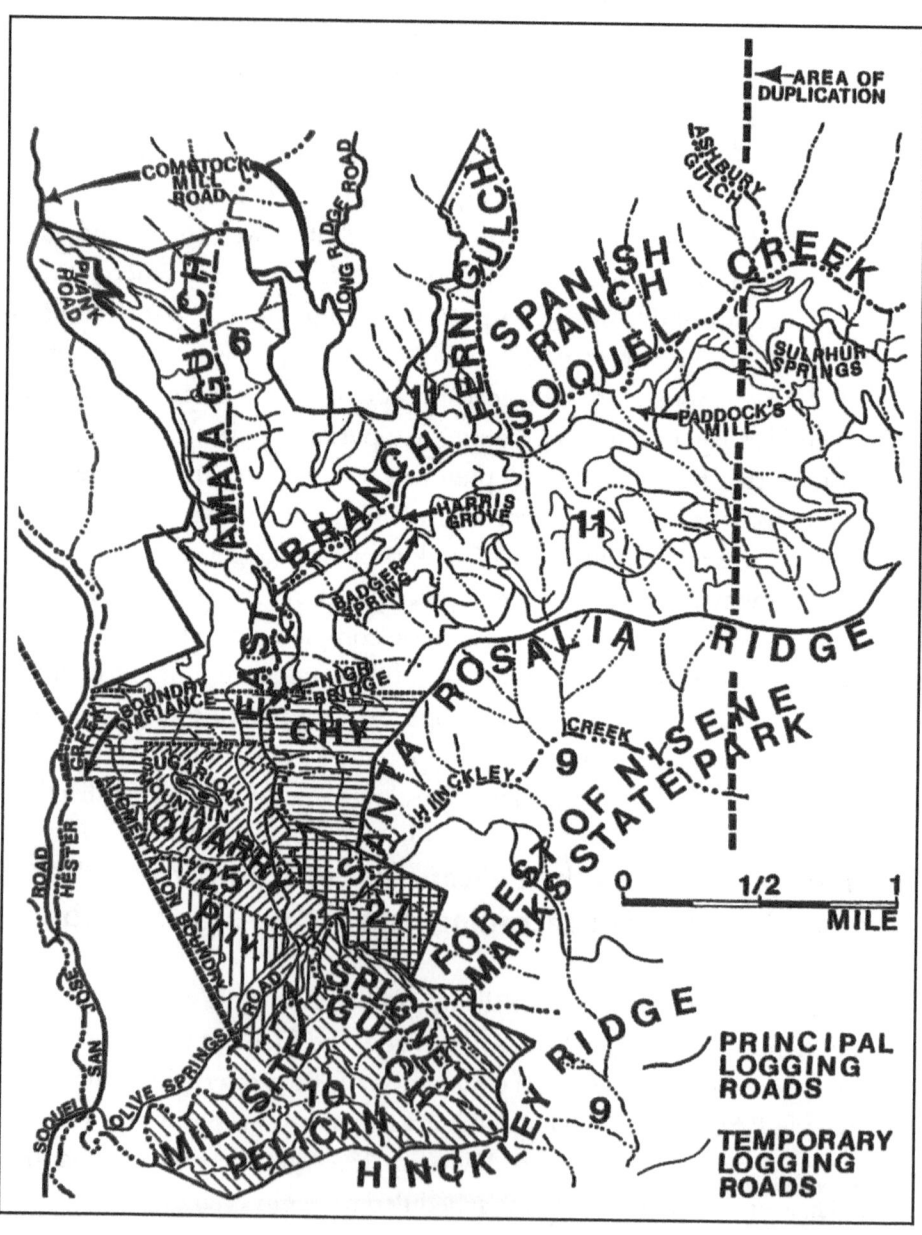

The first obstacle was crossing the East Branch of Soquel Creek and Hinckley Gulch. After a brief search, we found a safe crossing over both creeks. The three from Sacramento were very impressed with the gulch,

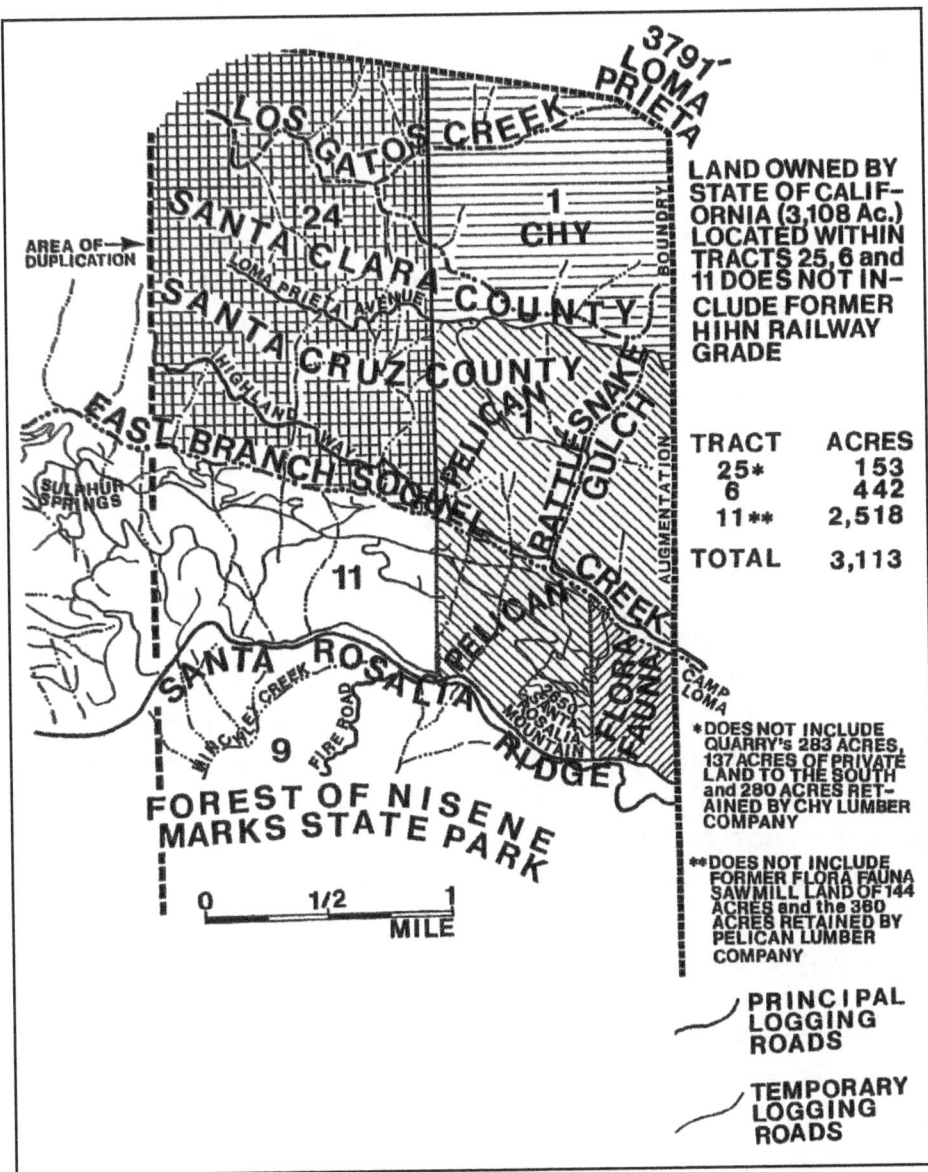

FIGURES 7.3-4 PROPERTY PURCHASED WITHIN THE AUGMENTATION FROM THE PELICAN TIMBER COMPANY BY THE STATE OF CALIFORNIA

especially with the discovery of Kenneth Keith Abbott's grave site (he died in July 1923 and was buried there by his parents) and with the size of the second-growth redwood trees at the gulch's lower end. Because this was their only exploration of the property, their report lacked insights into the benefits and attractions of the rest of the property.

A short while later, the Department of Parks and Recreation rejected Pelican's offer of the land. While the asking price was probably the main reason for the rejection, there were also several other reasons, such as:

- The state would not have control of the East Branch of Soquel Creek from its headwaters on Loma Prieta Mountain to the point where it enters the Augmentation at Camp Loma on Highland Way
- Management of the property would be difficult due to the property's remoteness and isolation
- Vehicular access, except via the Hinckley Creek Fire Road, would be across private property

In addition, Parks and Recreation was ignorant of the local history including the important role the area played in both Native American history and early American history.

In order to overcome the objections of the state concerning the asking price, Pelican began reducing the asking price until around 1988 it settled on half the original asking price, or $20,000,000. But even at this reduced price, the state considered it too high.

During this time, Charles "Chop" Keenan began lodging with the Department of Forestry and Fire Protection logging request reports in 500-acre plots throughout Pelican's land. He was hoping to be first in line to harvest the second-growth redwoods in the property if the state bought the land to use as a state forest. When news reached the public, locals along the Soquel San Jose Road made an outcry, fearing constant heavily-laden trucks using their road.

Meanwhile, California was on the brink of making a windfall from a banking scandal. For several years, Bank of America had been closing out unclaimed checking and savings accounts and pocketing the principal and interest from them without notifying the state. When the news finally broke in what began as a civil suit against the bank by a wronged account holder, the state stepped in and pressed criminal charges. The two parties settled when Bank of America agreed to repay all of the closed accounts and pay a matching fine for each into a fund that would be used to purchase land for the state. Most of this money went to buy forestland in Northern California, but $10,000,000 was earmarked for the Pelican Timber Company's property in Santa Cruz County.

When the state approached Pelican in early 1988 about purchasing the land for $10,000,000, Pelican agreed to sell only a portion of its property since the amount offered was only half of that requested. Pelican decided to retain Rattlesnake Gulch in Tract 1 (600 acres), 360 acres in Tract 11, and Spignet Gulch in Tract 10 (453 acres). That left the state with 3,113 acres, mostly between Soquel Creek and Santa Rosalia Ridge, and within Amaya Gulch. Specifically, the sale included 442 acres in Tract 6, 2,518 acres in Tract 11, and 153 acres at the northern end of Tract 25.

On April 13, 1988, Pelican transferred the 3,113 acres to the State of California and the Tehama Country Bank, which acted as co-trustee on behalf of the Controller's Environmental Trust fund. Prior to this, the California State Assembly had passed Assembly Bill No. 1965, which authorized the usage of funds to purchase the property. Following acquisition, the Nature Conservancy was appointed trust manager until it was decided which department would oversee the land: the Department of Parks & Recreation or the Department of Forestry and Fire Protection.[191]

The Loma Prieta Earthquake

On October 17, 1989, the massive Loma Prieta Earthquake struck the Central Coast with its epicenter located in the heart of The Forest of Nisene Marks State Park. While damage within the Augmentation was minimal, the quake caused several changes along Hinckley Creek and in the vicinity of Sulphur Springs. The San Andreas Fault crosses through the north side of the Augmentation, while the Zayante Fault traverses the southern portion. These caused many landslides and large cracks to form. Several cold sulfurous springs once more began to flow and hydrogen sulfide gas once more began to issue out of long-clogged holes.

The epicenter of the quake was located within the boundaries of The Forest of Nisene Marks and became a popular tourist magnet afterwards. The *San Francisco Examiner*, in a highly-circulated article, explained in its Christmas Eve issue:

HIKERS FLOCK TO EPICENTER OF THE QUAKE
By John Flinn of the Examiner Staff

FOREST OF NISENE MARKS STATE PARK, Santa Cruz County – At the epicenter of the Oct. 17 earthquake, huge redwood trees lie on the ground, snapped like toothpicks, and the smell of freshly cracked timber still hangs in the air.

A 62-year-old grandmother visiting from Burlington, Iowa, pauses at a sign marking the site and shudders as she stares up at a hillside stripped bare by a massive landslide.

"That's enough to convince me," says Pat Wagner. "I've never been in an earthquake – and I never want to be."

Wagner and her family had spent Tuesday afternoon walking the 3-mile trail to the epicenter, trekking through dense redwood forests, hopping rocks across rushing streams and scrambling over downed trees.

They weren't alone. Two months after the 7.1-magnitude quake, the hike along Aptos Creek in this formerly obscure park has become one of the hottest attractions in the entire state park system.

Last weekend more than 1,000 people made the pilgrimage, their vehicles overflowing a trail head parking lot designed to hold perhaps 30 cars. Rangers are scrambling to print more trail maps and keep up with the flood of calls.

Even on Tuesday—normally a pretty slow time for a state park—the parking lot was full and the trail packed with hikers, scientists and the just-plain curious, eager to tell friends they had stood at ground zero of the Loma Prieta quake.

"It's an exciting place to be," said park Superintendent Bud Getty. "This was the major quake of people's lifetimes, and it really captures your imagination to walk out to the *epicenter. You can really see the power of the earth."...*

It didn't take long for the U.S. Geological Survey to pinpoint the epicenter of the Oct. 17 quake 10 miles southeast of Santa Cruz in Forest of Nisene Marks State Park—specifically in Aptos Canyon, about 7 ½ miles upstream from where Aptos Creek drains into Monterey Bay.

But it wasn't until Ranger Jerry Waggoner erected a sign there that the location became known to the general public. Rangers say the spot was calculated according to latitude and longitude, and that the precise epicenter is probably a few yards uphill from the sign.

Plus, the actual hypocenter—the underground spot where the ground actually moved—is 11.5 miles beneath the earth's surface. Waggoner's sign marks the closest you can get to it without digging a very deep hole.

The region owes its helter-skelter topography to the fact that the San Andreas, Zayante and Corralitos faults beneath the park have scrunched up the coastal hills like a rug, forming a bewildering maze of twisting gorges and ridges.

The walk to the epicenter takes about an hour, and the second half isn't exactly a cakewalk.

From the trail head at the Porter Family Picnic Area, the route follows a gently graded dirt fire road through a dense forest of redwood, Douglas fir and tan oak, past an old mill site and open glens. Alert hikers sometimes catch glimpses of black-tailed deer and raccoons.

After 1 ½ miles, the route turns right off the road onto the narrow Aptos Creek Trail, which follows the jumbled landscape up and down hillsides, in and out of narrow, fern-lined side canyons and across the creek twice for 1 ½ miles before arriving at the epicenter.

Rangers late in the week removed several downed trees that had become an awkward hurdle for some hikers.

Some visitors expect to find 500-foot-feep fissures at the site, and a few kids are disappointed not to see dinosaurs emerging from a newly opened channel to the center of the earth.

But the site of 4-foot-diameter redwood trees snapped

off at the ground and the 150-foot wide landslide above the epicenter sign are enough to make most visitors quiver at the frightening power of an angry Mother Nature.

"Can you imagine what it took to rip these trees out?" asked Julie Dawson of Milpitas. "And can you imagine the sound it made? Snap, crackle and pop!"

She added: "I can see why this has become a tourist attraction. I stayed away from San Francisco because I didn't want to be a rubble necker. I wouldn't want that in my neighborhood. But there's no one to bother out here."

Everywhere is evidence of how nature continues to manhandle the landscape. Just beyond the epicenter, the Aptos Creek Trail is closed because of danger from new landslides. Rangers expect some of the hillsides to let loose shortly after the next big rainstorm.

Farther back in the park, the now-closed Big Slide Trail traverses an 80-acre landslide kicked loose by the 1906 quake. And on the west side of the forest, in Hinckley Canyon, the recent quake triggered a new slide at the site where a massive landslide buried seven lumberjacks and an unknown number of Chinese laborers in 1906.

At the epicenter, three generations of Wagners surveyed the devastation. Pat's son, David, lifted up his own son to have their picture snapped next to the sign.

"We could have gone roller skating," he said, "but old dad wanted to tell his poker buddies he was at the center."[192]

The Soquel Demonstration State Forest is established

After over two years of indecision, the state finally celebrated on July 13, 1990 the creation of the Soquel Demonstration State Forest on the land in the Augmentation deeded to the state by the Pelican Timber Company. It was the eighth state forest—the first added to the system since 1949—and remains the fifth largest state forest in California.

As with all other state forests, the Soquel Demonstration State Forest was placed under the management of the Board of Forestry and Fire Protection, part of the California Department of Forestry and Fire Protection (CAL FIRE). Unlike state forests in other states and national forests, all nine of California's state forests are called a "demonstration forest" because it wants them to be experimental in nature. Government-protected forests in general provide recreational and educational opportunities, as well as protecting and conserving their wildlife, soil, fisheries, and watersheds. But demonstration forests have the added goal of demonstrating how proper forest management practices can promote sustainable timber harvesting. California's other eight demonstration state forests are:

- Jackson State Forest in Mendocino County
- Latour State Forest in Shasta County
- Mountain Home State Forest in Tulare County
- Boggs Mountain State Forest in Lake County
- NF Mokelumne State Forest in Amador County
- Las Posadas State Forest in Napa County
- Mount Zion State Forest in Amador County
- Ellen Pickett State Forest in Trinity County

The board set several goals for the Soquel Demonstration State Forest. It wished to trial sustained-yield forest management practices on five percent of the property, thereby allowing commercial logging to continue. Linked with this, it wanted to use the logging venture for educational purposes by showing visitors how proper timber management, forestry practices, and recreational uses are interrelated and compatible with one another. Furthermore, the state hoped to use the property to educate the public on the management of redwood forest ecosystems by broadening knowledge that could lead to improved attitudes toward natural resources and forestry in general. Ultimately, the state wanted the knowledge gained from these activities to help change the negative image associated with forest management practices.

The first General Forest Management Plan was approved by the board in 1998 following years of discussion and consultation. A provisional cruise of the property in 1991 had estimated that the forest had a total volume of over 77 million board feet of redwood and fir trees. This was twice the amount of timber in the forest compared to 1978, and it was approaching the amount still present when the A. W. Elam Company had cruised the property following Frederick Hihn's death in 1916. A second cruise by the board in 2006 revealed that the volume had increased substantially to 117 million board feet, suggesting a remarkable regeneration of the forest since largescale logging had ended. A 1993 growth and yield survey had calculated that the forest regrew at a rate of roughly three percent, or 2.6 million board feet of timber, per year.

With the results of these cruises and reports finalized and the Forest Plan approved, small-scale experimental logging commenced. Indeed, in 1995, the Longridge Timber Harvesting Plan was enacted, which tested single-tree selection harvesting across 50 acres. Crawler tractors, rubber-tired skidders, and horses were used to harvest around 550,000 board feet over the year. Ten Douglas fir trees were also limbed to create homes for cavity-nesting birds. By 2001, all but one of the trees was in use and local bird diversity had increased.

In 1998, the Amaya Timber Harvesting Plan was put in place across 138 acres. In addition to the techniques trialed in 1995, highwires were used to move felled trees. Around 1.5 million board feet of timber were harvested. More importantly, selective harvesting was used to create areas along Amaya Creek where old-growth habitats could re-form, with a long-term goal of restoring water quality for fish.

From 2011 through 2015, a third timber harvesting plan called Rim was enacted in an area of 158 acres west of Sulphur Springs. This operation only used tractors and rubber-tired skidders and resulted in 1.6 million board feet of timber being harvested. In the latter year, a timber harvesting plan also focused on 201 acres in Fern Gulch used tractors, skidders, horses, and highlines to move logs. This operation produced 2.2 million board feet of timber.

After nearly twenty years of successful experimental harvesting and nearly 6 million board feet of timber cut, the board began revising its Forest Plan in 2014. It hoped, through sustainable methods, to increase annual output from the anticipated 800,000 board feet in 2015 to 1.6 million by 2020. The first program under this new scheme, the Comstock Timber Harvesting Plan, covered the west side of Amaya Creek across 228 acres, resulting in 2.1 million board feet of timber. In 2016, implementation of

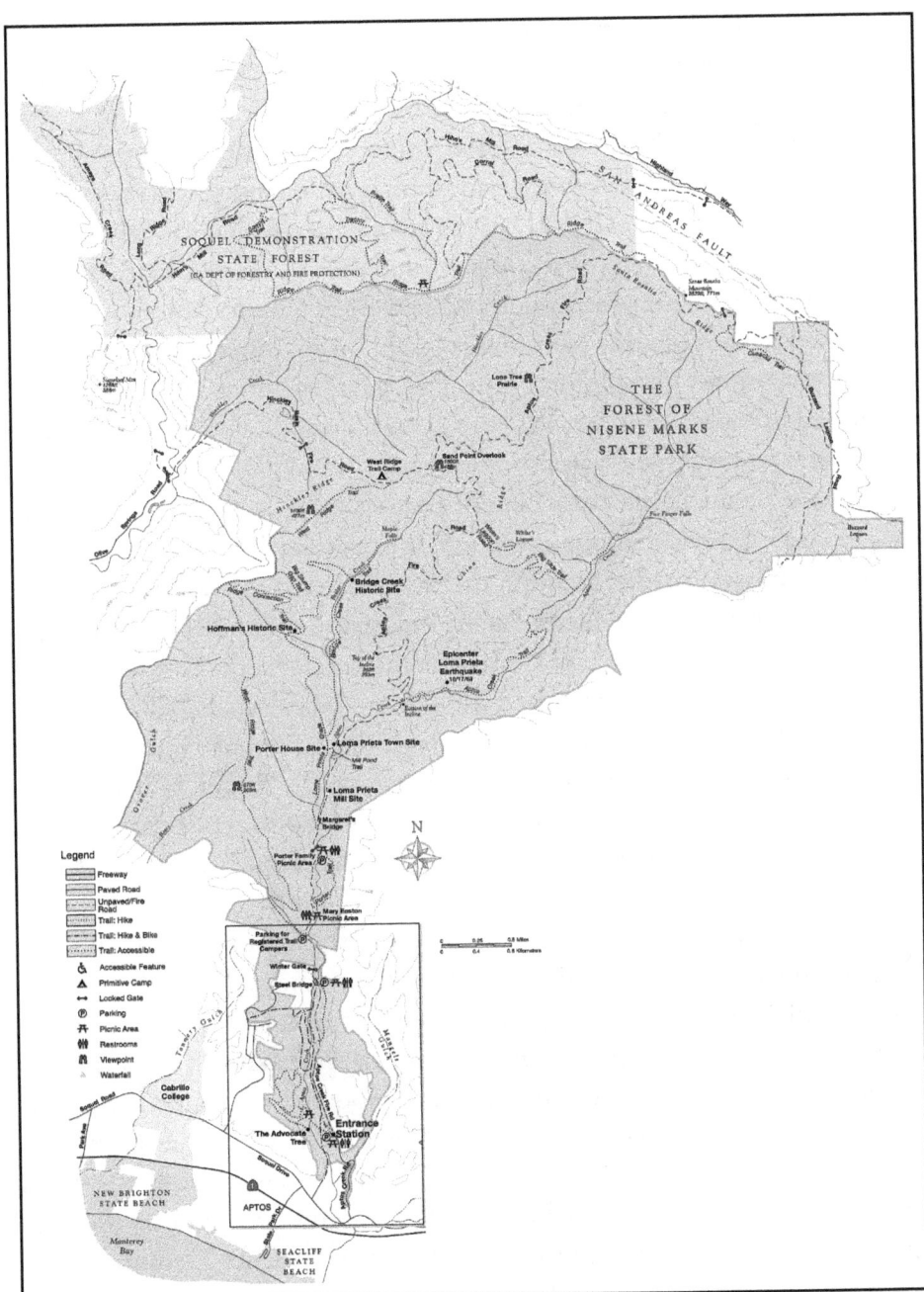

FIGURE 7.5 THE SOQUEL DEMONSTRATION STATE FOREST AND THE FOREST OF NISENE MARKS STATE PARK IN 2018 (COURTESY CALIFORNIA STATE PARKS)

the Meridian Timber Harvesting Plan began with a focus on 220 acres on the northern slopes of Santa Rosalia Ridge. This operation concluded in 2019 after harvesting 1.6 million board feet.

Increased fire risks caused by drier winters and hotter summers meant that operations within the forest had to be handled more cautiously. This was exacerbated by the COVID-19 pandemic beginning in 2020, which greatly shortened the harvesting season, and the CZU Lightning Complex fires in August of that year, which reduced air quality to dangerous levels and pulled resources away from the Soquel Forest. Together, these caused the board to miss its 2020 harvesting targets. In June 2022, the board submitted its notice of intent to set aside a new area for experimental harvesting in the vicinity of Sulphur Springs.

The timber cut in the forest has not gone to waste. In the 25 years following the start of the Longridge operation, the majority was sold to Big Creek Lumber Company. Smaller amounts of timber have gone to Redwood Empire Sawmill of Cloverdale and Sierra Pacific Industries, with mills located across the West Coast. Meanwhile, the timber cut in the Soquel Forest has provided CAL FIRE with a net profit of $3.5 million as of the end of 2020.

Since 1858, the area that comprises today's Soquel Demonstration State Forest has been logged almost continuously. Roger Hinckley and John Shelby were the first to cut timber on the land to repay their debt to Augustus Noble, from whom they purchased the property. They sold it to Richard Savage in 1859, who attempted to mill lumber but was unable to turn a profit due to legal restrictions caused by the Shoquel Augmentation Partitioning Suit. Frederick Hihn then bought or otherwise acquired Tracts 1, 6, 11, and 25 by 1868. Over the subsequent decades, Hihn, the F. A. Hihn Company, and the Valencia–Hihn Company harvested much of the timber along the headwaters of the East Branch of Soquel Creek. Further operations by the Monterey Bay Redwood Company, CHY Lumber Company, and Pelican Timber Company continued the process into the 1980s. With the land now under the care of CAL FIRE, it can be hoped that the days of extensive deforestation are over and that the Soquel Demonstration State Forest, like its neighbor The Forest of Nisene Marks State Park, can become a healthy, vibrant redwood wilderness once again.[193]

Afterword
by Jeff Thomson

Tucked away in the coastal mountains of central Santa Cruz County is one of the hidden treasures of the California state park system, The Forest of Nisene Marks. Covered in second-growth redwood trees, the park's 10,000 acres are a labyrinth of cool creek canyons and steep mountain ridges that seem to run helter-skelter in all directions. Over 40 miles of fire roads and trails lace the park making it a haven for runners, mountain bike enthusiasts, and equestrians.

The park's topography is partially the result of earthquakes which have gradually raised the mountains over millions of years. The San Andreas fault skirts the northern boundary while the Zayante fault slices diagonally through the center of the park. The epicenter of the 1989 Loma Prieta earthquake, which registered 6.9 on the Richter scale, is located on the Aptos Creek Trail about five miles from the park entrance.

While earthquakes raise the mountains, stream erosion slowly grinds them down. Starting near Santa Rosalia Ridge at the park's upper boundary, Aptos and Hinckley Creeks cut through the mountains on their path to the sea. Aptos Creek rises to the surface at an elevation of 2,500 feet then

Afterword

sets course through the center of the park where it joins another perennial stream, Bridge Creek. From its headwaters, Hinckley Creek drops 2,200 feet in only 4.5 miles on a twisting path before joining Soquel Creek along the park's western edge.

The forest is made up of three vegetation communities that vary with the elevation. In the cool, moist canyons at the lower elevations, the redwood forest including the creekside riparian community dominates. It gives way to the mixed evergreen forest which in turn gives way at the upper elevations (above 1,800 feet) to bristling chaparral along the hot, exposed ridges.

The coast redwood (*Sequoia sempervirens*) is the dominant tree in The Forest of Nisene Marks. It is the world's tallest tree and also one of the most ancient. Genetically it dates back millions of years to the time of the dinosaurs. Because of dramatic changes in climate and geology, these "living fossils," which once covered much of the North American continent, have retreated to a 500-mile-long strip of land from southwest Oregon in the north to the Santa Lucia Mountains near Carmel, California, in the south. Their zone of growth is also narrow, only about 30 miles wide, and corresponds with the coastal fog belt.

Prior to 1880, the redwood trees that grew on what is now state park property were majestic old-growth specimens, perhaps up to 1,500 years of age. Then the loggers came. When they left 40 years later, the land was charred, creeks ran muddy, and only a small number of the ancient giants remained. However, today 20%-30% more redwood trees are growing in the park than before the logging era—testimony to the redwood's prolific power of regeneration.

Almost 100 years after the end of the logging frenzy, the forest is still in a state of recovery and regeneration. The over-arching interpretive theme that this park offers is one of optimism and hope. Despite being brutally assaulted, the landscape can regenerate itself. One lesson offered here is that humans have the ability to change their relationship with the land from one of exploitation to one of management and stewardship.

The "disappearing" history of The Forest of Nisene Marks State Park

At first glance, The Forest of Nisene Marks may appear to be a primeval forest untouched by civilization. In reality, this area was a beehive of activity during an intensive 40-year logging frenzy (1883-1923). The estimated 140 million board feet of lumber that were removed from the forest, would, if loaded onto railroad flatcars, stretch a distance of almost 39 miles!

By 1923, the lumber companies had pretty much exhausted the supply of old-growth redwoods. They sold off what equipment buildings they could and abandoned the rest. Over the years, much of what they left behind has been obscured by a tangle of bushes and vines, buried under landslides, or washed away by violent winter storms. In short, most of the evidence of the logging era has disappeared. However, the alert visitor can still find clues that stir the imagination and provide a window into this colorful chapter in Santa Cruz County history.

Since many of today's hiking trails follow the old railroad grades, you may still see wooden crossties, metal spikes, and the occasional rusting rail. Wire cables used to pull the logs are also scattered about. Other clues to the park's history can be found in some of the creek beds in the form of wooden train trestle timbers. At some of the old logging campsites, dilapidated cabins and housing foundations are still evident. Also, places where the loggers lived are sometimes marked by non-native plants such as ivy and periwinkle. In the upper regions of the park, stacks of cut wood can still be found along with downed trees that were never removed.

The Storm of January 1982

It had been raining since New Year's Day. A few days later, a large Alaskan storm front moved in and stalled over the Santa Cruz Mountains. It was joined by another mass of wet air coming from the south making for a storm that slammed into Santa Cruz County on January 4. Before it was over, an estimated fifteen inches of rain fell in the upper reaches of the park. Rain fell so hard that the rain gauges filled and spilled over

Afterword

before they could be read, so we will never know how much rain fell during those three days.

Aptos Creek became a snarling, raging brown monster, tearing out creek banks and pulling entire trees with roots intact into the stream. Many of those trees and logs eventually formed massive log jams downstream.

One measure of the flood in Aptos Canyon was the number of historic monuments that were carried away. Railroad trestle footings that had stood above Aptos Creek since they were built in the 1880s disappeared, as did old logging structures all along the area's streams.

If the structures that were carried away were any measure, this was probably the largest such event in the past century. Bridge Creek rose over 15 feet, tearing out old buildings and leaving mud marks high on the tree trunks. Footbridges were swept away, and when the water receded, the steeper canyon walls up in the Aptos Creek canyon were scoured clean of vegetation.

After the storm, the park was closed for almost a year. It took several years to repair and replace the trails that had been lost. The Aptos Creek trail was the most heavily damaged, and was not back into good repair until 1986.

The Trails

The park's trails mirror the landscape and range from easy to strenuous, although most fit into the moderate range with some steep grades mixed with level stretches. Some trails lead to historic sites tracing railroad grades built well over 100 years ago. Others wind through lush creek canyons or up to viewpoints along the mountain ridges. Here's a sampling:

> **Aptos Creek Road/Aptos Creek Fire Road**: This dirt road travels through the heart of the park and provides access to most of the trails. Sections of this road follow old railroad grades built between 1883 and 1912. It is also possible to reach the Soquel Demonstration State Forest trail system which connects with the fire road 9.4 miles north of the Porter Family Picnic Area.

Aptos Creek Trail: This trail crosses the Zayante Fault and passes the epicenter of the 1989 earthquake as it winds through flood-ravaged Aptos Creek Canyon.

Aptos Rancho Trail: This trail is on property that was once part of the Aptos Rancho land grant awarded to Rafael Castro by the Mexican government in 1833. Along this route, you will travel through open sunny areas and the cool, shady Aptos Creek Canyon.

Bridge Creek Trail: This trail follows sections of the old 30-inch narrow-gauge railroad line (built in 1917) up the creek canyon to the Bridge Creek Historic Site.

Loma Prieta Grade Trail: The first section of this popular trail leads to the Porter House Site by tracing the railroad grade built in 1883. The Loma Prieta Grade Trail continues past the connection with the Bridge Creek Trail and up to Hoffman's Historic Site, which was once the best-preserved logging camp in the park.

Mill Pond Trail: This short trail connects the fire road with the Loma Prieta Grade Trail. It crosses Aptos Creek on a bridge through an area once occupied by the Loma Prieta millpond.

Old Growth Loop Trail: The Old Growth Loop Trail travels through an area which many people consider the most beautiful area in the park. Along this trail you will see magnificent old-growth redwoods, attractive fern-covered canyon walls along Aptos Creek, and a "crazy forest" of unusual redwoods called the Twisted Grove.

The Forest of Nisene Marks offers you the opportunity to explore a slice of Santa Cruz County history and experience miles of trails in a se-

Afterword

rene, natural setting just minutes from the rush of civilization. First-time visitors are often surprised to find this island of seclusion and serenity so close to the urban canyons of the San Francisco Bay Area. Even Santa Cruz County residents are often startled by the abrupt transition from the noise and traffic of nearby Aptos and the peace and solitude found only a mile up the park's main access road.

A Personal Note

I met Ron Powell in the early 1990s when I was beginning work on my guidebook, *Explore the Forest of Nisene Marks State Park*. This led to a years-long tutorial about the Soquel Rancho, Aptos Rancho, and Soquel Augmentation Mexican land grants. He kindly allowed me unlimited access to his voluminous historical research and photo collection and for that, I will always be grateful. Unfortunately, I was only able to include a small summary of the park's history in a general-purpose guidebook, so I am very pleased that Derek Whaley and Zayante Publishing have brought Ron's work to everyone in this fine trilogy. I hope it will motivate many of you to come and explore The Forest of Nisene Marks State Park.

To learn more about what's going on in the park today and to view historic photos visit www.nisenemarks.org.

For more stories of life
in the Santa Cruz Mountains
of the Central Coast of California,
check out the full range of local
history books available from

www.ZayantePublishing.com

NOTES

1. Aptos Library, miscellaneous articles and records; Michael Bergazzi, oral history interview, conducted by Woods Mattingley (Santa Cruz, CA, 1966); Vince Carbone, oral history interview (January 17, 1956); Brian Dervin Dillon, *Archaeological and Historical Survey of the Soquel Demonstration State Forest, Santa Cruz County, California* (Sacramento, CA: Department of Forestry and Fire Protection, 1992); Bernard Woods Mattingley, personal files (1965); Ralph Mattison, oral history interview, conducted by Woods Mattingley (Santa Cruz, CA, 1966); Bud Pasha and John B. Wikkerink, oral history interview, conducted by Woods Mattingley (Santa Cruz, CA, 1966); Irene Williams Stewart, oral history interview, conducted by Woods Mattingley (Santa Cruz, CA, 1966); Albretto Stoodley, oral history interview, conducted by Woods Mattingley and J. Don Thompson (date unknown); Albretto Stoodley, personal papers, Sandy Lydon collection; Harvey West, oral history interview, conducted by Woods Mattingley (Santa Cruz, CA, 1966); U. S. Geological Survey, California: Loma Prieta Quadrangle. 7.5 Minute Series (Topographic) (Washington, DC: Department of the Interior, 1955; reprinted, 1968).

2. *Evening Sentinel*, 01/16/1900, 3:1; ibid, 02/23/1900, 3:2; ibid, 07/11/1900, 3:3; *Surf*, 02/21/1900, 1:2.

3. *Evening Sentinel*, 05/09/1901, 2:5; ibid, 08/21/1902, 3:4; ibid, 08/20/1903, 3:4; ibid, 09/06/1904, 1:5; Houghton v. Loma Prieta Lumber Company (152 Cal. 500); *Sentinel*, 06/09/1900, 3:1; ibid, 04/13/1901, 2:5; Southern Pacific, Coast Division Time Table No. 17 (April 9, 1899); *Surf*, 02/04/1901, 1:2; ibid, 04/13/1901, 1:2; ibid, 06/11/1901, 1:1-3; ibid, 06/12/1901, 3:5; ibid, 06/15/1901, 4:4. See also Ronald G. Powell, *The Tragedy of Martina Castro: Part One of the History of Rancho Soquel Augmentation* (Santa Cruz, CA: Zayante Publishing, 2020), 473-475.

4. *Evening Sentinel*, 10/30/1900, 4:1; F. A. Hihn Company, corporate records (Santa Cruz, CA: University of California, Santa Cruz, McHenry Library Map Room); *Sentinel*, 12/08/1900, 3:3; ibid, 09/03/1902, 3:2; *Surf*, 10/29/1900, 4:1; U. S. Geological Survey, California: Laurel Quadrangle. 7.5 Minute Series (Topographic) (Washington, DC: Department of the Interior, 1955; reprinted, 1968). See also Stanley D. Stevens, "Laurel – F. A. Hihn's Company

Notes

Town," in *Redwood Logging and Conservation in the Santa Cruz Mountains—A Split History* (Santa Cruz History Journal 7) (Santa Cruz: Museum of Art & History, 2014), 84-99.

5   *Evening Sentinel*, 12/06/1900, 3:2; ibid, 03/12/1901, 3:5; *San Francisco Call*, 09/22/1901, 1:24; *Sentinel*, 03/10/1901, 3:1; ibid, 09/21/1901, 3:1, 2; Stoodley, oral history; *Surf*, 03/27/1901, 4:1; ibid, 04/13/1901, 1:1; ibid, 04/19/1901, 4:2.

6   Stoodley, oral history.

7   James Miller Guinn, *History of the State of California and Biographical Record of Santa Cruz, San Benito, Monterey and San Luis Obispo Counties* (Chicago: Chapman Publishing, 1903), 696-697.

8   *Evening Sentinel*, 08/27/1901, 3:1; F. A. Hihn Company; Southern Pacific Company, "List of Officers, Agencies & Stations," 1902; ibid, Coast Division Employee Time Table No. 79 (October 24, 1909).

9   Stoodley, oral history.

10 Stoodley, oral history.

11 *Aptos Times*, October 1995; *Evening Sentinel*, 10/18/1902, 3:2; Stoodley, oral history; ibid, personal papers.

12 F. A. Hihn Company; *Sentinel*, 08/24/1902, 3:1; ibid, 09/03/1902, 3:2; ibid, 09/04/1902, 3:1.

13 Stoodley, oral history.

14 *Evening Sentinel*, 04/04/1903, 3:1; ibid, 07/21/1903, 3:1; F. A. Hihn Company; *Sentinel*, 07/22/1903, 3:2.

15 *Surf*, 07/30/1903, 1:3.

16 *Evening Sentinel*, 09/01/1903, 3:2; ibid, 09/09/1903, 3:1; F. A. Hihn Company; Ronald G. Powell, *The Reign of the Lumber Barons: Part Two of the History of Rancho Soquel Augmentation* (Santa Cruz, CA: Zayante Publishing, 2021), 393-404; *Sentinel*, 09/19/1903, 3:2; ibid, 09/23/1903, 3:2; Stoodley, oral history; *Surf*, 09/17/1903, 6:5.

17 *Surf*, 09/28/1903, 5:3. See also Powell, *Tragedy of Martina Castro*.

18 Sanborn Map Publishing Company, "Santa Cruz, California" (New York: Sanborn Map Publishing Company, 1905), Map 23; *Surf*, 03/07/1904, 8:5.

19 Santa Cruz County Records Office, miscellaneous records.

20 D. D. Emery, A. S. Seayrs, and C. B. Lewis, Plat of Proposed Road from Laurel to the East Branch Soquel Creek (July–August 1905); F. A. Hihn Company.

21 *Surf*, 08/16/1904, 5:1.

22 Santa Cruz County Records Office.

23 Santa Cruz County Records Office.
24 F. A. Hihn Company.
25 Donald Thomas Clark, *Santa Cruz County Place Names: A Geographical Dictionary*, second edition (Santa Cruz, CA: Kestrel Press, 2008), 225; *Surf*, 06/17/1905, 4:5.
26 Emery, Seayrs, and Lewis; F. A. Hihn Company.
27 *Surf*, 12/01/1905, 5:4.
28 *Evening Sentinel*, 03/26/1906, 2:4; ibid, 01/24/1906, 7:5; Stoodley, oral history; *Surf*, 01/19/1906, 1:3-4; ibid, 01/20/1906, 3:4; ibid, 01/22/1906, 1:3.
29 Rick Hamman, *California Central Coast Railways*, second edition (Santa Cruz, CA: Otter B Books, 2002), 134-141; Stephen Michael Payne, *A Howling Wilderness: A History of the Summit Road Area of the Santa Cruz Mountains 1850–1906* (Santa Cruz, CA: Loma Prieta Publishing, 1978), 141-142; *Surf*, 04/18/1906, 1:1, 2:1, 2:2-3; ibid, 04/19/1906, 1:3; ibid, 04/21/1906, 6:3; ibid, 10/20/1906, 1:1-4; Caroline Swanson, "Villa Del Monte: A Historical Review 1850–1976" (Dec 1986); John V. Young, *Hot Type & Pony Wire: My Life As a California Reporter from Prohibition to Pearl Harbor* (Santa Cruz, CA: Western Tanager Press, 1980), 94-100; ibid, "The Crazy Forest," *American Forests* 47:11 (Nov 1941), 511.
30 Stoodley, oral history; *Surf*, 04/30/1906, 1:4.
31 *Surf*, 05/08/1906, 7:4.
32 Earl LaPorte, oral history interview, conducted by Woods Mattingley (Santa Cruz, CA, 1966); *Mountain Echo*, 05/12/1906; Stewart; Stoodley, personal papers.
33 F. A. Hihn Company.
34 Payne, 95.
35 *Surf*, 01/09/1907, 3:2.
36 *Surf*, 01/14/1907, 1:5-6.
37 F. A. Hihn Company; *Mountain Echo*, February & May 1907; Stoodley, oral history.
38 F. A. Hihn Company; Santa Cruz County Records Office.
39 Southern Pacific Company, unspecified corporate records.
40 Hamman, 203. For more information on the financial crisis, see Robert F. Bruner and Sean D. Carr, *The Panic of 1907: Lessons Learned from the Market's Perfect Storm* (Hoboken, NJ: John Wiley & Sons, 2009).
41 *Evening News*, 05/09/1908, 2:3; F. A. Hihn Company; *Sentinel*, 06/03/1908, 1:2; Stoodley, oral history.

Notes

42 *Surf,* 03/15/1908.
43 Stoodley, oral history.
44 *Surf,* 06/10/1908.
45 F. A. Hihn Company; Lloyd Bowman, Lands in the Soquel Augmentation Rancho, Santa Cruz and Santa Clara County (October 1929); ibid, Map of Subdivision No. 1 of the Arden Forest, being a Part of Partition of Tracts No. 4 and 7 of Rancho Soquel Augmentation (July 1908).
46 F. A. Hihn Company.
47 Stoodley, oral history.
48 *Surf,* 10/25/1909; ibid, 10/26/1909.
49 F. A. Hihn Company; Stoodley, oral history.
50 *Evening News,* 06/09/1910, 1:3; *Mountain Echo,* 09/10/1910; Stoodley, personal papers, 23-25.
51 Southern Pacific Company, records.
52 Southern Pacific Company, "List of Officers, Agencies & Stations," July 1911; Stoodley, personal papers, 27-33.
53 *Sentinel,* 03/23/1993, A12:6; Payne, 138.
54 Santa Cruz County Records Office; *Sentinel,* 08/27/1911, 4:4.
55 F. A. Hihn Company; Stoodley, oral history.
56 Santa Cruz County Records Office.
57 F. A. Hihn Company; Stoodley, personal papers, 36-38.
58 F. A. Hihn Company; Stoodley, oral history.
59 Stoodley, personal papers, 35.
60 *Evening News,* 08/23/1913, 1:3-4.
61 F. A. Hihn Company.
62 Bernard Klink, oral history interview, conducted by Woods Mattingley (Santa Cruz, CA, 1966); Stoodley, personal papers, 36-38.
63 *Evening News,* 05/18/1914, 5:4; ibid, 05/25/1914, 3:3; ibid, 05/16/1914, 4:3 and 5:4 Stewart; Stoodley, oral history.
64 Stoodley, oral history.
65 Stoodley, oral history.
66 Stoodley, oral history.
67 Stoodley, oral history.
68 Noel Patterson, personal papers (Santa Cruz, CA: University of California); Santa Cruz County Records Office.

Notes

69   F. A. Hihn Company; Horatio N. Ormsbee, multiple appraisals of the Arden Forest, Hinckley Basin, and Loma Prieta Lumber Company's lands (1945–1946); Patterson.
70   Santa Cruz County Records Office.
71   Stoodley, oral history.
72   Southern Pacific Company, Right of Way and Track Map for the Loma Prieta Branch, Aptos to Loma Prieta (June 30, 1916).
73   Horatio N. Ormsbee, Reported submitted…on the Redwood Timber Owned by Valencia–Hihn Company (San Francisco, CA: A. W. Elam Company, July 15, 1916); Patterson.
74   Stoodley, oral history; Patterson.
75   F. A. Hihn Company; Patterson.
76   Santa Cruz County Records Office.
77   Stoodley, oral history; ibid, personal papers, 34.
78   Stoodley, oral history.
79   Patterson.
80   Patterson.
81   *Evening News*, 08/06/1917, 4:3-4; Loma Prieta Lumber Company, Map of Bridge Creek Tract being a part of Tract 10 of the Soquel Augmentation Rancho (July 1917); Patterson; Santa Cruz County Records Office.
82   Stoodley, oral history.
83   Patterson; Southern Pacific Company, "List of Officers, Agencies & Stations," 1918–1928; ibid, unspecified corporate records.
84   Patterson.
85   *Surf*, 01/17/1918; Stoodley, oral history.
86   Stoodley, oral history; ibid, personal papers.
87   Carolyn Swift, "Swiftcurrents," *The Mid County Post*, 06/28/1994, 07/11/1994, and 08/05/1996.
88   Nils Bergman, personal conversations; Wayne Dennis, personal conversations; Larry Green, personal conversations; Rick Hamman, personal correspondence; Doug Richter, personal conversations; *Surf*, 09/14/1918; Stoodley, oral history; ibid, personal papers.
89   Patterson.
90   *Evening News*, 12/31/1918, 8:1-2; Patterson.
91   Paul Johnston, oral history interview, conducted by Woods Mattingley (Santa Cruz, CA, 1966); Stoodley, oral history.
92   *Evening News*, 04/21/1919, 1:3-4.

Notes

93 Clark, 281; Santa Cruz County Records Office; *Evening News*, 07/30/1919, 1.
94 *Dayton Daily News*, 03/29/1920, 3:3; *Evening News*, 11/29/1920, 2:2.
95 Stoodley, oral history.
96 *Cabrillo Times & Green Sheet*, 11/27/1970; Teck B. Cathey, oral history interview, conducted by Woods Mattingley (Santa Cruz, CA, 1966); Stoodley, oral history.
97 *Cabrillo Times & Green Sheet*, 11/27/1970; Cathey; John Starbird Sandoval, *Mt. Eden: Cradle of the Salt Industry in California* (Hayward, CA: Mt. Eden Historical Publishers, 1988), 171; Santa Cruz County Records Office; Stoodley, oral history.
98 Mike Musal, personal papers; Patterson.
99 Southern Pacific Company, unspecified corporate records; Stoodley, oral history.
100 James A. Harris, Jr., oral history interview (about 1956); Patterson; *Santa Cruz News*, 06/09/1925; ibid, 11/10/1925; *Sentinel*, 04/01/1951, 8:6-7.
101 Southern Pacific Company, unspecified corporate records.
102 Harris; Patterson; *Santa Cruz News*, 04/03/1926.
103 Arnold M. Baldwin, Survey of Hinckley Creek Road as Now Built and Travelled Across Lands of Elizabeth J. Corcoran in Tract 27 of the Augmentation, June–July 1929; Santa Cruz County Records Office.
104 Harris; Monterey Bay Redwood Company, Map showing truck roads in Tracts 1, 6, 10, 11 and 25; Patterson.
105 Santa Cruz County Records Office.
106 Stoodley, oral history.
107 Interstate Commerce Commission, Finance Docket No. 6615; Southern Pacific Company, "List of Officers, Agencies & Stations," 1928; ibid, unspecified corporate records.
108 Santa Cruz County Records Office.
109 Patterson.
110 Cathey; Edward Porter Pfingst, oral history interview, conducted by Woods Mattingley (Santa Cruz, CA, 1966); *Surf*, 12/31/1918.
111 Robert Lincoln, Jr., personal correspondence.
112 *Evening News*, 05/24/1929, 10:1.
113 Harris; Patterson.
114 *San Jose Mercury-News*, February 1966; *Sentinel*, 02/20/1966, 7; Clarence Srock, oral history interview, conducted by Woods Mattingley (Santa Cruz, CA, 1966).

Notes

115 Harris; Patterson.
116 Harris; Industrial Appraisal Company, Map of Monterey Bay Redwood Company's Layout of Mill and Yard (March 1933); Patterson.
117 Santa Cruz County Records Office; Southern Pacific Company, unspecified corporate records; Stoodley, oral history.
118 James Belden Bias, Jr., oral history interview (January 24, 1956).
119 Stoodley, oral history; ibid, personal papers.
120 *Evening News*, 01/01/1936, 2:2.
121 Patterson; Santa Cruz County Records Office.
122 Lincoln; *Sentinel*, 04/26/1995, A3:4-6; Stoodley, oral history.
123 Patterson.
124 Stoodley, personal papers.
125 Bias, oral history; *Sentinel*, 02/11/1937, 7:5; ibid, 07/06/1947, np.
126 Stoodley, personal papers.
127 Patterson; Santa Cruz County Records Office.
128 Patterson.
129 Bias.
130 Santa Cruz County Records Office.
131 Santa Cruz County Records Office.
132 Patterson; *Sentinel*, 08/03/1941, 8.
133 Stoodley, personal papers.
134 F. A. Hihn Company; Ormsbee, multiple appraisals; Patterson; Stoodley, personal papers. See also Powell, *Reign of the Lumber Barons*.
135 Harris; Al Young, oral history interview (about 1956).
136 *Evening News*, 12/24/1930, 1:8; *Sentinel*, 10/17/1943, 1:1-2.
137 *Sentinel*, 07/06/1947.
138 J. Don Thompson, personal papers.
139 Bias, oral history.
140 Bias, oral history; John Ferninade, Jr., "Who Was Nisene Marks?" *Aptos Times*, 07/1995; Dorothy H. Vera, *Californian*, unknown date 1963; Thompson.
141 *Sentinel*, 05/15/1957, 1:6-7.
142 State Water Resources Board, "Bulletin No. 5: Santa Cruz–Monterey Counties Investigation" (Sacramento: State Water Resources Board, 1953), 226-227.
143 Thompson.

Notes

144 Thompson.

145 Harris; Young, oral history.

146 *Californian*, 07/20/1955, 2:5-6.

147 *Sentinel*, 12/23/1955, 1, 12

148 Harris.

149 J. T. Nittles and Noel Patterson, Map showing Railway Grade known as Hihn Railroad Grade, owned by Monterey Bay Redwood Company, Santa Cruz, California, from Old Santa Cruz Watsonville Highway to Southerly Boundary of Timber Tract, accompanying Appraised Report to City of Santa Cruz (December 1, 1955); Patterson, personal papers.

150 Thompson.

151 Patterson.

152 Thompson.

153 Patterson.

154 Thompson.

155 Patterson; *Sentinel*, 03/13/1960, 1:7.

156 Patterson.

157 Patterson.

158 Thompson.

159 Harris; Patterson; Santa Cruz County Records Office.

160 *Sentinel*, 04/06/1961, 1:1.

161 Thompson.

162 *Sentinel*, 10/15/1961, 1:6.

163 Thompson.

164 Thompson.

165 Thompson.

166 Thompson.

167 Thompson.

168 Thompson.

169 Thompson.

170 Thompson.

171 Thompson.

172 Thompson.

173 Thompson.

174 Thompson.

175 Thompson.

176 Thompson.

177 Thompson.

178 Thompson.

179 "Senate Bill No. 1418," Senate Bills, Original and Amended, Number 1371-1631 (Sacramento: California State Printing Office, 1963); Thompson.

180 Thompson.

181 Thompson.

182 *Western Railroader* 28:11 (November 1965), News Supplement 2; *Pacific Rail News* 53 (January 1966), 15.

183 *Sentinel*, 12/26/1965, 8.

184 Letter from County of Santa Cruz Department of Public Works to the Nature Conservancy, dated 11/16/1965; Letter from County of Santa Cruz Department of Public Works to the Santa Cruz County Board of Supervisors, dated 6/26/1967; California Legislature–Senate, Senate Bill No. 1332, Senate Bills, Original and Amended, 1965 Regular Session: Numbers 1200-1370 (Sacramento: California State Printing Office, 1965); ibid, Senate Bill No. 1072, Senate Bills, 1967 Regular Session: Numbers 1026-1160 (Sacramento: California State Printing Office, 1967); *Sentinel*, 06/28/1967, 9:1-2; Thompson.

185 *Santa Cruz Express*, 06/18/1981.

186 *Sentinel*, 11/02/1970, 20:7, 8.

187 *Californian*, 04/06/1976, 2:1; ibid, 05/14/1976, 2:3.

188 *Californian*, 06/24/1982, 12:1.

189 *Sentinel*, 04/11/1982, 28:4; ibid, 10/17/1982, A3:3-7; ibid, 11/07/1982, A16:4-5.

190 *Sentinel*, 01/08/1984, 1:A5-6, A14:2-3; ibid, 01/11/1984, A2:3-5; ibid, 01/17/1984, A3:2-4; ibid, 01/18/1984, A3:4-6; ibid, 01/24/1984, A1:3-6; ibid, 02/05/1984, A1:1-4, A5:1-3; ibid, 02/08/1984, 1:5-6; ibid, 03/01/1984, A1:1-4; ibid, 03/07/1984, A1:5-6; ibid, 05/25/1984, A4:1-2; ibid, 09/17/1984, A2:3-4; ibid, 10/24/1984, A3:1-4.

191 Dillon; *Sentinel*, 03/09/1988, A3:4-6; ibid, 06/12/1988, A19:5-6.

192 *San Francisco Examiner*, 12/24/1989, 1:3, 13:1-2.

193 California Department of Forestry and Fire Protection, "Demonstration State Forests," https://www.fire.ca.gov/programs/resource-management/resource-protection-improvement/demonstration-state-forests; ibid, "Improving Soquel Demonstration State Forest Access" (Soquel, CA, November 1, 2017); ibid, "Soquel Demonstration State Forest—2020 Annual Report,"

Notes

prepared by Angela Bernheisel (Soquel, CA, September 23, 2021); ibid, "Soquel Demonstration State Forest—General Forest Management Plan" (Soquel, CA, November 5, 2014); Thomas Sutfin Kerr, "The History of Timber Harvesting in the Soquel Demonstration State Forest," in *Redwood Logging and Conservation in the Santa Cruz Mountains—A Split History* (Santa Cruz History Journal 7) (Santa Cruz: Museum of Art & History, 2014), 186-188; *Sentinel*, 7/13/1990, 2:4-5. See also Powell, *Tragedy of Martina Castro* and *Reign of the Lumber Barons*.

Select Bibliography

Newspaper articles are cited in full within the endnotes and not included in the list below. The following newspapers have had their titles simplified: *Santa Cruz Evening News* (*Evening News*), *Santa Cruz Evening Sentinel* (*Evening Sentinel*), *Santa Cruz Sentinel* (*Sentinel*), and *Santa Cruz Surf* (*Surf*).

Aptos Library. Miscellaneous articles and records.
Baldwin, Arnold M. Survey of Hinckley Creek Road as Now Built and Travelled Across Lands of Elizabeth J. Corcoran in Tract 27 of the Augmentation. June–July 1929.
Beal, Richard A. *Highway 17: The Road to Santa Cruz*. Second edition. Aptos, CA: Pacific Group, 1991.
Bergazzi, Michael. Oral history interview. Conducted by Woods Mattingley. Santa Cruz, CA, 1966.
Bergman, Nils. Personal conversations. 1980s.
Bias, James Belden, Jr. Oral history interview. January 24, 1956.
Bowman, Lloyd. Lands in the Soquel Augmentation Rancho, Santa Cruz and Santa Clara County. October 1929.
---. Map of Subdivision No. 1 of the Arden Forest, being a Part of Partition of Tracts No. 4 and 7 of Rancho Soquel Augmentation. July 1908.
California Department of Forestry and Fire Protection. "Demonstration State Forests." https://www.fire.ca.gov/programs/resource-management/resource-protection-improvement/demonstration-state-forests.
---. "Improving Soquel Demonstration State Forest Access." Soquel, CA, November 1, 2017.

Bibliography

---. "Soquel Demonstration State Forest—2020 Annual Report." Prepared by Angela Bernheisel. Soquel, CA, September 23, 2021.

---. "Soquel Demonstration State Forest—General Forest Management Plan." Soquel, CA, November 5, 2014. https://www.fire.ca.gov/media/kqgjj2xl/2014_sdsf_gfmp_ada.pdf.

California Legislature–Senate. Senate Bill No. 1418. Senate Bills, Original and Amended, Number 1371-1631. Sacramento: California State Printing Office, 1963.

---. Senate Bill No. 1332. Senate Bills, Original and Amended, 1965 Regular Session: Numbers 1200-1370. Sacramento: California State Printing Office, 1965.

---. Senate Bill No. 1072. Senate Bills, 1967 Regular Session: Numbers 1026-1160. Sacramento: California State Printing Office, 1967.

Carbone, Vince. Oral history interview. January 17, 1956.

Cathey, Teck B. Oral history interview. Conducted by Woods Mattingley. Santa Cruz, CA, 1966.

Clark, Donald Thomas. *Santa Cruz County Place Names: A Geographical Dictionary*. Second edition. Santa Cruz, CA: Kestrel Press, 2008.

County of Santa Cruz, California. Assessor's Map No. 40:10. Santa Cruz, CA: County Assessor's Office, 1951.

---. Assessor's Map Nos. 98:10, 14, 16. Santa Cruz, CA: County Assessor's Office, 1953.

---. Assessor's Map Nos. 99:10, 14, 17-23. Santa Cruz, CA: County Assessor's Office, 1953.

---. Assessor's Map Nos. 104:2, 7-8. Santa Cruz, CA: County Assessor's Office, 1954.

---. Assessor's Map No. 106:2. Santa Cruz, CA: County Assessor's Office, 1954.

Dennis, Wayne. Personal conversations. Early 1980s.

Devereaux, Kent. Unpublished manuscript.

Dillon, Brian Dervin. *Archaeological and Historical Survey of the Soquel Demonstration State Forest, Santa Cruz County, California*. Sacramento, CA: Department of Forestry and Fire Protection, 1992.

Emery, D. D., A. S. Seayrs, and C. B. Lewis. Plat of Proposed Road from Laurel to the East Branch Soquel Creek. July–August 1905.

Bibliography

F. A. Hihn Company, corporate records. Santa Cruz, CA: University of California, Santa Cruz, McHenry Library Map Room.
Green, Larry. Personal conversations. 1980s.
Guinn, James Miller. *History of the State of California and Biographical Record of Santa Cruz, San Benito, Monterey and San Luis Obispo Counties.* Chicago: Chapman Publishing, 1903.
Hamman, Rick. *California Central Coast Railways.* Second edition. Santa Cruz, CA: Otter B Books, 2002.
---. Personal correspondence. 1980s.
Harris, James A., Jr. Oral history interview. About 1956.
Herrmann, A. T. Map of a Survey of Part of the Lines of Tract 8 of the Partition of the Rancho Soquel Augmentation. May 1896.
Houghton v. Loma Prieta Lumber Company (152 Cal. 500).
Industrial Appraisal Company. Map of Monterey Bay Redwood Company's Layout of Mill and Yard. March 1933.
Interstate Commerce Commission. Finance Docket No. 6615.
Jensen, Billie J., and Reece C. *A Trip Through Time and the Santa Cruz Mountains.* San José, CA: Ghastly Gallimaufry, 1998.
Johnston, Paul. Oral history interview. Conducted by Woods Mattingley. Santa Cruz, CA, 1966.
Kerr, Thomas Sutfin. "The History of Timber Harvesting in the Soquel Demonstration State Forest." In *Redwood Logging and Conservation in the Santa Cruz Mountains—A Split History,* Santa Cruz History Journal 7, 176-189. Santa Cruz: Museum of Art & History, 2014.
Klink, Bernard. Oral history interview. Conducted by Woods Mattingley. Santa Cruz, CA, 1966.
Koch, Margaret. *Santa Cruz County: Parade of the Past.* Santa Cruz, CA: Western Tanager Press, 1973.
La Porte, Earl. Oral history interview. Conducted by Woods Mattingley. Santa Cruz, CA, 1966.
Letter from County of Santa Cruz Department of Public Works to the Nature Conservancy. Dated 11/16/1965.
Letter from County of Santa Cruz Department of Public Works to the Santa Cruz County Board of Supervisors. Dated 06/26/1967.
Lincoln, Robert, Jr. Personal correspondence.

Bibliography

Loma Prieta Lumber Company. Map of Bridge Creek being a part of Tract 10 of the Soquel Augmentation Rancho. July 1917.
Marks Family. Personal files. Sandy Lydon collection.
Mattingley, Bernard Woods. Personal files. 1965.
Mattison, Ralph. Oral history interview. Conducted by Woods Mattingley. Santa Cruz, CA, 1966.
Monterey Bay Redwood Company. Map showing truck roads in Tracts 1, 6, 10, 11 and 25.
Musal, Mike. Personal papers.
Nittles, J. T., and Noel Patterson. Map showing Railway Grade known as Hihn Railroad Grade, owned by Monterey Bay Redwood Company, Santa Cruz, California, from Old Santa Cruz Watsonville Highway to Southerly Boundary of Timber Tract, accompanying Appraised Report to City of Santa Cruz. December 1, 1955.
Ormsbee, Horatio N. Multiple appraisals of the Arden Forest, Hinckley Basin, and Loma Prieta Lumber Company's lands. 1945–1946.
---. Reported submitted…on the Redwood Timber Owned by Valencia-Hihn Company. San Francisco, CA: A. W. Elam Company, July 15, 1916.
Pasha, Bud, and John B. Wikkerink. Oral history interview. Conducted by Woods Mattingley. Santa Cruz, CA, 1966.
Patterson, Noel. Personal papers. Santa Cruz, CA: University of California.
Payne, Stephen Michael. *A Howling Wilderness: A History of the Summit Road Area of the Santa Cruz Mountains 1850–1906*. Santa Cruz, CA: Loma Prieta Publishing, 1978.
Pfingst, Edward Porter. Oral history interview. Conducted by Woods Mattingley. Santa Cruz, CA, 1966.
Powell, Ronald G. *The Reign of the Lumber Barons: Part Two of the History of Rancho Soquel Augmentation*. Santa Cruz, CA: Zayante Publishing, 2021.
---. *The Tragedy of Martina Castro: Part One of the History of Rancho Soquel Augmentation*. Santa Cruz, CA: Zayante Publishing, 2020.
Punnett Brothers. Unnamed map. 1906.
Richter, Doug. Personal conversations. 1980s.

Bibliography

Sanborn Map Publishing Company. "Santa Cruz, California." New York: Sanborn Map Publishing Company, 1905.

Sandoval, John Starbird. *Mt. Eden: Cradle of the Salt Industry in California*. Hayward, CA: Mt. Eden Historical Publishers, 1988.

Santa Cruz County Records Office. Miscellaneous records.

Southern Pacific Company. Coast Division Employee Time Table No. 17 (April 9, 1899).

---. Coast Division Employee Time Table No. 79 (October 24, 1909).

---. "List of Officers, Agencies & Stations." 1902, 1911, 1918–1928.

---. Right of Way and Track Map for the Loma Prieta Branch, Aptos to Loma Prieta. June 30, 1916.

---. Unspecified corporate records.

Srock, Clarence. Oral history interview. Conducted by Woods Mattingley. Santa Cruz, CA, 1966.

State Water Resources Board. "Bulletin No. 5: Santa Cruz–Monterey Counties Investigation." Sacramento: State Water Resources Board, 1953.

Stevens, Stanley D. "Laurel – F. A. Hihn's Company Town." In *Redwood Logging and Conservation in the Santa Cruz Mountains—A Split History*, Santa Cruz History Journal 7, 84-99. Santa Cruz: Museum of Art & History, 2014.

Stewart, Irene Williams. Oral history interview. Conducted by Woods Mattingley. Santa Cruz, CA, 1966.

Stoodley, Albretto. "The Loma Prieta Lumber Company and Santa Cruz in the Early Twentieth Century." Oral history interview. Conducted by Elizabeth Spedding Calciano. Santa Cruz: University of California, Santa Cruz, McHenry Library, 1964. https://escholarship.org/uc/item/8pq1n4qt

---. Oral history interview. Conducted by Woods Mattingley and J. Don Thompson. Date unknown.

---. Personal papers. Sandy Lydon collection.

Swanson, Caroline, "Villa Del Monte: A Historical Review 1850–1976." 12/1986.

Thompson, J. Don. Personal papers.

U. S. Geological Survey. California: Capitola Map. Washington, DC: Department of the Interior, 1914.

Bibliography

---. California: Laurel Quadrangle. 7.5 Minute Series (Topographic). Washington, DC: Department of the Interior, 1955; reprinted, 1968.

---. California: Loma Prieta Quadrangle. 7.5 Minute Series (Topographic). Washington, DC: Department of the Interior, 1955; reprinted, 1968.

---. California: Los Gatos Quadrangle. 7.5 Minute Series (Topographic). Washington, DC: Department of the Interior, 1953; reprinted, 1968, 1973, and 1980.

---. California: Rancho Soquel and Shoquel Augmentation Map. Washington, DC: Department of the Interior, 1915–1916.

---. California: Santa Cruz Quadrangle. 5x11 Minute Series (Topographic). Washington, DC: Department of the Interior, 1955; reprinted, 1968 and 1981.

---. California: Soquel Quadrangle. 7.5 Minute Series (Topographic). Washington, DC: Department of the Interior, 1954; reprinted, 1968 and 1980.

---. California: Watsonville Quadrangle. 7.5 Minute Series (Topographic). Washington, DC: Department of the Interior, 1955; reprinted, 1968 and 1980.

West, Harvey. Oral history interview. Conducted by Woods Mattingley. Santa Cruz, CA, 1966.

Young, Al. Oral history interview. About 1956.

Young, John V. "The Crazy Forest," *American Forests* 47:11 (Nov 1941).

---. *Ghost Towns of the Santa Cruz Mountains*. Expanded edition. Santa Cruz, CA: Western Tanager Press, 1984.

---. *Hot Type & Pony Wire: My Life as a California Reporter from Prohibition to Pearl Harbor*. Santa Cruz, CA: Western Tanager Press, 1980.

INDEX

Advocates for the Forest of Nisene Marks, 268, 390
Allred, S. W., 260
Amaya Gulch, 69-70, 231-232, 244-246, 247, 274, 275, 283-284, 301, 309, 360-361, 364-367, 370-371, 375, 380
Anglo–California Trust Co., 99, 104, 260, 274-275
A. P. Hammond Lumber Co., 104-105, 106-107, 109, 168
Aptos, ix, 16, 159, 168, 175, 218, 241, 300, 323, 325, 365, 390
Aptos Creek, x, 4, 29, 65-69, 73, 84, 114, 119, 124, 128, 141, 145, 196, 236, 242-243, 270, 272, 290-291, 296, 303, 304, 337, 345, 356-357, 361-362, 369, 376-377, 385-386, 388-389
Aptos Creek Fire Road, 3, 9, 11, 15, 84, 122, 128, 129, 131, 136-137, 150, 197, 215, 254, 260-268, 270, 273, 274, 287, 289, 290-291, 353, 356-359, 388
Aptos Creek mill (Loma Prieta Lumber Co.), 15, 24, 25, 26, 37, 81-83, 87-91, 105, 110, 113, 124, 148-150, 167, 174-175, 179, 180-182, 187-188, 190, 201, 203, 206, 213, 217, 219, 279, 347
Arden Forest, 4, 95-102, 260, 274, 286, 294, 297, 319, 326, 330-333, 336, 345-351, 356
Aptos Hotel, 345
Aptos Milling Co., 194, 279
Arbor Villa, 64
Augmentation, *see* Shoquel Augmentation
A. W. Elam Co., 157, 159-167, 212, 218, 248-249, 251, 278, 279
Awaswas-speaking peoples, 7-10
Badger Springs, 232, 245-246, 268, 275, 301, 308, 314, 364, 365
Baldwin, Arnold, 117, 119, 136
Bassett, A. C., 24, 76-77, 93, 113, 114, 145-147
Bassett Gulch, 11, 15
Bassett, Harvey, 146, 190, 199, 214, 218, 229, 242, 253
Betsy Jane (F. A. Hihn Co.), 134-136, 186, 190, 192-198, 273
Betsy Jane (Santa Cruz Railroad), 195
Bias, James and Veda, 253-254, 270-275, 286, 290, 291-294, 298

Index

Big Basin, 76, 326, 363
Big Creek Lumber Co., 362-364, 382
Big Tree Gulch, 82-83, 90, 179, 198-199, 200-207, 210, 212-214, 359
Bishop, James, 241-242
Black Tuesday, 240
Blodgett, Orrin, 152, 155, 167
Bridge Creek, x, 10, 15, 37, 83, 90, 97, 113, 116, 122, 124-125, 129-136, 163, 165, 166-167, 175, 179-180, 182-196, 200-207, 212-214, 219, 252, 273, 336, 353, 356-357, 359, 386, 388, 389
Burrell, 70, 79, 288
Buzzard Lagoon, 73, 252, 259, 269, 286-287, 300, 319, 336, 347-351, 353, 355, 356, 358
California Department of Forestry and Fire Protection (CAL FIRE), 3, 8, 262, 266, 368, 370, 375, 378
California Department of Parks and Recreation, 268, 319, 323-324, 327, 330, 335, 344, 353, 361, 371, 374, 375
California Fruit Growers' Assoc., 182, 226
California Redwood Association, 300-301
California Pacific Title & Trust Co., 229-231, 232-234, 305, 313-314
California Redwood Park, *see* Big Basin
Camp 1 (Molino Timber Co.), 119-123, 193, 201
Camp 2 (Molino Timber Co.), 136-141, 144-145, 150, 152, 182
Camp 3 (Molino Timber Co.), 150-152, 158-159, 170-174
Camp 4 (Loma Prieta Lumber Co.), 182-188, 193, 205, 212
Camp 5 (Loma Prieta Lumber Co.), 200-207, 212-214
Camp Loma, 70, 71, 301, 303, 308, 368, 374
Capitola, 33, 47, 49, 143, 159-160, 162, 169, 191, 208-210, 224, 229, 232, 240, 285-286, 371
Capitola Heights, 191, 210
Capitola–Hihn Co., 105, 169
Capitola Investment Co., 99
Capitola Park Co., 43-44, 66, 95-104
Castro, Martina, x, 341, 356
Chase, Oscar, 76, 110-111, 145, 148, 159, 211
Cathey, Teck B., 174, 214, 217-218, 219, 236
China Ridge, 3, 8, 9, 12-13, 26, 69, 84, 90-91, 114-116, 120, 122, 124, 125, 136-139, 172-173, 179, 186, 188, 193, 201, 217, 262-264, 267-268, 290, 357
CHY Lumber Co., 362-364, 365-368, 370
Coast Counties Gas & Electric Co., 274, 285-286, 290
Collins, George L., 310, 323, 325-330, 344-352
Commodore Hotel, 168
Comstock brothers, 47
Cooley, Diane, 332-333, 340, 359

Index

Cope, Katherine C. (*née* Hihn), 155, 169, 200, 208-210
Cowden, A. F., 148, 211
Cusack, Lawrence, 269-270
Daubenbiss, Fred, 111-112, 211
DeTurk, Charles, 319, 320, 326, 342, 344
Dougherty Extension Railroad, 79, 86
earthquake (1906 San Francisco), 57-71, 73, 78, 81-82, 84, 97, 104, 141-142, 159, 175, 259, 275-277
earthquake (1989 Loma Prieta), ix, 6, 13, 375-378, 385, 389
eucalyptus nursery, 92-94, 110, 252
F. A. Hihn Co., 14-15, 16, 21-24, 28, 29-30, 33-34, 35-37, 39, 41, 42, 44, 45-47, 54, 61, 78, 81, 82-83, 86, 87, 94-95, 97, 104-105, 106-107, 109-110, 116, 124-125, 129-136, 143, 169, 175-177, 199, 224-226
Fairview Park, 168
Farr, Frederick, 330-331, 353-355
Forest of Nisene Marks State Park, The, xi, 3-13, 193, 194, 270, 290, 293, 310, 336-339, 340-358, 361-362, 369-370, 371, 375-378, 381, 385-390
Forgues, J. W., 41, 43-44
Gage, Stephen T., 77, 145
George's Picnic Area, 180
Glenco Forest Products Co., 312-314, 315-317, 362-364
Gold Gulch, 14, 28, 87, 106, 134, 143, 168, 196

Great Depression, 240-241, 252, 269, 319
Grover & Co., xi, 29, 41, 95, 97-102, 148, 279
Haire, George, 180
Hall, Theresa (*née* Hihn), 155, 168
Hammer, Charles, 152, 155, 167
Harris Grove, 245-246, 314
Harris, James A., Jr., 224, 226, 228, 231, 241, 245-246, 283-286, 301, 302-303, 307, 314, 315-316, 319-320, 360
Harris, James A. III, 276, 310-311, 320, 361
Heins, Ralph, 152, 155, 167
Hellier, William, 296
Henderson, Katherine, *see* Cope, Katherine C.
Hester Creek, 301
Hester Creek School, 79
High Bridge, 231, 244, 273-274, 278, 284-285, 364, 367
Highland, 59, 63, 68, 79
Hihn, August C., 155, 168-169, 199-200
Hihn, Frederick A., x, 64, 82-83, 97-98, 104-105, 141-143, 167-169, 177, 194, 203-204, 207-208, 288-289, 361
Hihn, Frederick D. C., 168-169, 200, 218, 249-250
Hihn, Frederick Otto, 155, 168, 200
Hihn, Grace (*née* Cooper), 200
Hihn–Hammond Lumber Co., 106-107, 109, 168

Index

Hihn, Harriet, 168
Hihn Investment & Building Co., 10
Hihn, Jack E., 156
Hihn, Louis W., 156, 168
Hihn, Minnie (*née* Chace), 168
Hihn Railroad Grade, 99, 102, 303, 313, 317, 365
Hihn's Sulphur Springs, 9, 20, 37, 223, 278, 284, 301, 303, 314, 363-364, 365, 370, 375, 380, 382
Hihn, Teresa A., 156, 168-169
Hihn, Therese (*née* Paggen), 155, 167, 177, 200, 207-208
Hihn Water Co., 105, 169
Hinckley (Creek, Gulch, and Ridge), x, 3-13, 45, 47-54, 67, 127, 131, 135, 136-141, 144-145, 150-152, 158, 167, 170-173, 180, 188-191, 193, 212, 215-217, 229-231, 232-234, 241, 253-254, 266-267, 274, 286, 294, 297, 300, 319, 332, 336, 342, 346-352, 353, 354-355, 357-258, 375, 378, 385-386
Hinckley Basin Unit No. 1, 13, 215-217, 232-234, 253, 264, 291, 352-354, 357
Hinckley Creek mill (Loma Prieta Lumber Co.), 15-21, 24-27, 30-32, 34-35, 37, 41, 42-43, 48-49, 52-54, 58-62, 71-77, 79, 81-82, 87-89, 105, 110, 113
Hoffman's Camp, *see* Camp 5
Hopkins Estate, 286, 289, 294, 296, 300, 331, 333, 347,

Hopkins, Timothy (*né* Nolan), 15-16, 27-28, 35, 76-77, 82-84, 97, 110, 113, 114, 124, 135, 145-147, 148-149, 159, 167, 170, 172, 174-177, 179, 182, 193, 201, 214, 219, 252-253, 255, 259-260, 333
Hotel Capitola, 209
Hotel de Redwoods, 59, 61-63, 288
Hotel Miltonmont, 63
Howard, H. M., 95, 294, 315, 336, 352-353, 355
Huber, John, 236-238
Jansen, A. S., 152, 157, 199
Jap Camp, *see* Camp 2
Japanese, 137-138, 275
Judah, H. Ray, 270
Kelley, Donald Graeme, 310, 325, 340-343, 344-347
Land of Medicine Buddha, 293
Laurel, ix-x, 14-15, 21-24, 29-30, 33-34, 35-36, 41, 42, 44, 45-47, 54, 61, 78, 81, 86, 87, 97, 109-110, 124, 134-135, 143, 182, 196, 224-226, 252, 361
Leonard, Doris F., 323, 325-330, 344, 346
Leonard, Jake, 270
Lincoln, Robert, Jr., 238, 245, 251, 266-267, 278, 283-284
Lindsay, H. N., 200, 218
Loma Prieta (mill and village), 217, 236-237, 243, 254-259, 261, 263, 311
Loma Prieta (mountain), 69, 221, 223, 271, 333

Index

Loma Prieta (train station), 83, 115, 135, 235
Loma Prieta Branch, x, 11, 15, 27-29, 84-86, 97, 113-114, 118-120, 122, 159, 169-170, 175, 180-182, 186-187, 205, 210-211, 213, 219, 228, 234-235, 241, 252, 260, 359
Loma Prieta Lumber Co., 7, 15-21, 24-27, 29, 31-33, 34-35, 39, 41, 47-54, 58-61, 65, 71-77, 79-83, 86-94, 105, 109-110, 139, 145-150, 167, 177, 179-180, 182-188, 191-194, 198-199, 200-207, 214-218, 229-231, 235, 252, 257-259, 269-270, 273, 279, 289, 297-299, 331, 333
Loma Prieta No. 1 (locomotive), *see* Molino Shay
Loma Prieta No. 2 (locomotive), 186, 190-191, 192, 201, 207, 211, 213-214, 242-243
Loma Prieta State Park proposal, 238-240, 270-273, 286-288
Maddock, Victor W., 294, 296
Maple Falls, 124, 135, 179, 182, 186, 188, 196, 197, 357
Marks family, 291-294, 296-300, 304, 306-307, 319, 320, 323-352, 353-358, 365, 369
Mattingley, Woods, 206-207, 359
Matty, Louis, 36
McKiernan, Frank, 62-63
Meyer, Ernst Emil, 62
Mill Creek, 80-81, 109-110, 113, 114, 136

Mills, David W., 218-219, 221, 224, 228-229, 231, 360-361
Molino (train station), 130, 119, 137, 159, 173, 190, 219, 235, 263, 359
Molino Junction, 29, 175, 196, 205, 243, 252, 254, 264, 267, 268, 290, 356
Molino mill (Pacific Improvement Co.), 28
Molino Shay, 117-123, 144-145, 158, 186, 190-191, 192, 193, 201, 207, 211, 213-214, 217-218
Molino Timber Co., xiii, 4-5, 7, 12, 110-113, 114-123, 124-130, 136-141, 144-145, 148, 150-152, 158-159, 167, 170-174, 179-180, 182, 188-191, 192-193, 201, 211, 217, 218
Monte Vista, 67-68, 73, 84, 263
Monterey Bay Redwood Co., 221-229, 231-232, 235-236, 238, 241, 244-251, 268-269, 274, 275-278, 279-281, 284-286, 294-296, 301, 302-306, 307-309, 310-317, 359-361
Morrell, Hiram, 63
Mt. Eden, 218
Native Americans, *see* Awaswas-speaking peoples
Nature Conservancy, 309-310, 323-332, 333-356, 362, 375
Notley Barrel & Box Factory, 148-149
Ohlone, *see* Awaswas-speaking peoples

Index

Olive, Elizabeth, 123-124, 125
Olive, George, 16-17, 38-40, 44-45, 50-52, 123-124
Olive, James, 125
Olive Springs Quarry Co., 17, 40, 294-296, 305-306, 316-317, 360, 368
Olive Springs Resort, 16-18, 20-21, 27, 38-41, 44-45, 48-52, 91-92, 125, 179, 215, 224, 284, 291, 302
Oliver Salt Co., 218
Opal (train station), 16, 26-27, 35, 47, 59, 82, 87, 105, 110, 111-113, 135
Ormsbee, Horatio N., 157, 159, 218, 224, 229-231, 234, 241, 253-254, 270-273, 274, 286-288, 291-294, 317-318
Pacific Firewood Co., 365
Paddock, Mark, 283-285, 301
Panic of 1907, 86
Park, Charles T., 229, 234, 241, 253-254, 274
Patterson, Noel, 224, 250-251, 278, 303-306, 308, 311-312, 315, 360-361
Pelican Timber Co., 365-368, 370-375, 378
Peoples Savings Bank of Santa Cruz, 214-218, 234
Pfingst, Edward P., 236
Porter Family Picnic Area, 28, 263, 268, 359, 369-370, 377, 388
Porter House Site, 114, 182, 196, 201-202, 213, 218, 267-268, 304, 332-333, 337, 340, 359, 389
Porter, John T., 29, 77, 332,

Porter, Warren R., 29, 77, 114, 145, 236, 333
Rambo mill, 78, 80, 81
Rancho Rincon, 168
Rancho Soquel, 152, 317, 341
Rancho Soquel Augmentation, *see* Shoquel Augmentation
Rancho Zayante, 168
Ready (train station), 180-182
Ready, Ruth, 155, 169, 175-177, 180-182, 219
Redington, C. H., 77, 145
Riebanack, F. H., 230, 234
Rispin, Henry Allen, 13, 191, 208-210, 232-234, 241, 253, 264, 318, 352
Rossi, Joseph J., 119
Rossi, Sena, 119, 121
San Francisco Mountain, *see* Sugarloaf Mountain
Sanborn, E. J., 77, 114, 145
Sanborn, Helen A., 77, 114, 145
Sand Point, 9, 89, 116, 120-121, 125-130, 132, 134, 136-137, 150, 188, 190, 192-198, 264, 266, 273, 289
Santa Cruz, Capitola, and Watsonville Railway, 35
Santa Cruz Water Co., 105, 169
Santa Rosalia (Mountain and Ridge), 3-13, 26, 41, 44, 75, 139-140, 150-151, 188, 245, 262, 264, 268, 270, 276, 284, 315, 363, 365-368, 375, 382, 385
Schillings' Camp, 27-29, 118-119, 130, 256, 359

Index

Schroll, Hannes, 305-306, 307-309, 310-312
Setzer family, 313-314, 362, 365
Severance, Fred, 76, 111, 145, 211
Severance, J. S., 77
Shasta Hotel, 168
Shoquel Augmentation, ix-xiv, 12, 13, 15, 23, 27-28, 33, 36-38, 64, 95-98, 109, 110, 111, 113, 114, 125, 138, 152, 157-166, 177, 180, 182, 200, 203, 212-215, 218, 223, 239, 252-253, 260-268, 274, 275, 279-281, 286-290, 291, 293-294, 296, 299, 300, 302, 304, 307, 315-317, 319, 323, 332, 334, 336-337, 353, 355-358, 360, 363, 365-368, 371-375, 375-378
Shoquel Augmentation Partitioning Suit, 17, 41, 382
Smith, William, 41, 91-92
Soquel, 17, 20-21, 26, 27, 33, 53, 232, 243, 264, 302
Soquel Asphalt Products Co., 296
Soquel Creek (East Branch), ix-x, 4, 6, 8-9, 10, 15-18, 24-25, 40, 41, 42, 44-47, 48-52, 64, 69-71, 73, 91-92, 94-95, 179, 215, 223, 228-229, 230, 231-232, 238, 244-246, 247, 266-267, 268-269, 273-274, 275-278, 283-285, 291, 301, 303, 310-312, 313, 315, 364, 365, 370-375, 382
Soquel Creek (West Branch), 14, 21, 78

Soquel Demonstration State Forest, xi, 3, 8, 47, 70, 139, 246, 378-382
Soquel Paper Mill, 27
Soquel San Jose Road, 16-18, 42, 47, 63, 79, 98, 135, 244, 288, 308, 374
Soquel Water System, 105, 169, 208-210, 285-286
Southern Pacific, x, 11, 14, 15-16, 30, 37, 54, 61, 62, 70, 78, 81, 83, 84-86, 87, 89, 97, 102, 109-110, 113-114, 118-119, 130, 135, 146, 159, 169-170, 175, 180, 182, 186-187, 207, 217, 219, 228, 229, 234-235, 252-253, 263
Spignet Gulch, 39, 82, 124, 135, 164, 178-179, 226-227, 228, 244, 247, 249, 313, 364, 372, 375
Splitstuff Area, 130-136, 179, 186, 188-198, 201, 205, 219, 273
Spring Creek, 29, 84-86, 89, 91, 105, 113, 114-115, 255, 259, 289
Srock, Clarence, 241-244, 255, 257, 264
Stanard, Walter F., 121
Stoodley, Bert, 4-5, 33, 35, 50, 59-61, 69, 74, 76, 110-112, 114-123, 125, 126-130, 135, 137, 138, 141, 144-145, 148-150, 159, 170, 173-175, 187, 190-191, 211, 212-213, 214, 229-231, 253, 254-259, 260-261, 263, 264
Sugarloaf Mountain, 40-41, 135, 238, 244, 266, 294-296, 307-309
Svendsgaard, Arnold, 304-306

Index

Terrace Grove Hotel, 63-64
Thompson, J. Don, 293-294, 296, 297-301, 306-307, 315, 323, 328-329, 330-334, 336, 337-339, 340, 341, 344-345, 350
Tre Monte Hotel, 64
Trout Gulch, 175-177, 180-182
Union Oil Co., 289-291
Valencia Creek, x, 28, 37, 87, 143, 194, 196
Valencia–Hihn Co., 152, 156-157, 159-167, 177-179, 180-182, 198-200, 215, 218-219, 221-223, 235-236, 239, 241, 246, 249-251, 269, 273, 275, 279-280, 360
Watsonville, 16, 36, 47, 61, 94, 106-107, 112, 149, 162, 168, 200, 235, 240, 256
Watsonville Mill & Lumber Co., 235

Wells Fargo Bank & Union Trust Co., 252-253, 260, 274, 286-287, 289-290, 294, 296-298, 306-307, 333-334, 336, 343, 347, 355
Western Gulch Oil Co., 304
White Motor Car Co., 218, 229
White's Lagoon, 68, 69, 73, 120, 129, 259, 289
Williams, Alfred L., 29, 58, 60, 76, 110-111, 147-148, 211
Wood, Percy A., 259, 289, 297
Woodwardia Hotel, 123
Wrights, 36, 54, 61, 64, 70, 87
Young, Al, 283, 301
Younger, Agnes (*née* Hihn), 155, 168-169, 200, 207-208, 218
Zayante Fault, 375, 377, 385, 389

Ronald Gabriel Powell was an electrical engineer and local researcher from Los Altos, California. He received his engineering degree from Cogswell Polytechnic Institute in San Francisco in 1953. For most of his career, he worked at Lockheed's Missile Systems division, Rytheon, and GTE Sylvania. He retired in the late 1970s and started exploring and photographing The Forest of Nisene Marks. Around 1990, he began writing his long history of Rancho Soquel Augmentation and later donated his research to the McHenry Library at the University of California, Santa Cruz. Powell died on September 11, 2010 at the age of 79.

Derek R. Whaley is a historian, librarian, and former resident of Felton, California. He earned a doctorate in history from the University of Canterbury in 2018. He began researching Santa Cruz County history in 2011 and continues to do so from overseas. He has worked at the Santa Cruz Beach Boardwalk and The Tech Museum of Innovation, volunteered at the San Lorenzo Valley Museum and Santa Cruz Museum of Art & History, and is well-known for his Santa Cruz Trains book series and website. He currently lives in Aotearoa New Zealand.

Jeff Thomson is the author of a guidebook titled *Explore the Forest of Nisene Marks State Park*. He is also on the Board of Directors of the Advocates for the Forest of Nisene Marks, a non-profit volunteer organization founded by local community members to support the park. The Advocates are a partner with California State Parks in driving fundraising and implementing capital improvements and special projects in the park. You can learn more about the Advocates by visiting their web site at www.nisenemarks.org.

www.ingramcontent.com/pod-product-compliance
Lightning Source LLC
Chambersburg PA
CBHW021139160426
43194CB00007B/625